Japanese Economic Development

Japanese Economic Development offers a wide-ranging account of Japan's economic development between 1600 and 2000, taking into account economic, cultural, social and political theories about why Japan emerged as the first truly wealthy country in Asia in the modern age. The author presents three distinct approaches to understanding how and why Japan made the transition from a relatively low-income country mainly focused on agriculture to a high-income nation centred on manufacturing and services.

Penned by an expert in Japanese economic history and economic development, the book explores all theories in depth and includes arguments rooted in culture and social norms, arguments couched in political terms, and arguments both technical and non-technical developed by economists. The book makes a case for "over determination" in economic behavior. Because individual, firm level and governmental behavior is simultaneously determined by the interaction of markets, norms, and structures, change over time is rarely if ever limited to the economy operating in isolation from social norms and structures. A virtue of the treatment in this book is that it covers a period spanning 400 years, devoting considerable attention to the Tokugawa era antedating Japan's industrialization. It consists of twelve chapters that can be used in a variety of social science and history courses devoted to Japan, including courses aimed mainly at the post-1945 period.

In offering an eclectic account of Japan's economic development, this book will appeal to students in a broad group of disciplines including economics, political science, sociology, geography, and history. It can also be usefully employed, more specifically, as a reading in economic history and economic development courses, especially those dealing with non-Western countries.

Carl Mosk is Professor of Economics at the University of Victoria, Canada. He specializes in economic history, population economics and Asian economies, especially the Japanese economy. He is the author of a number of books on the demographic and economic history of Japan and is author of the Routledge book, *Trade and Migration in the Modern World* (2005).

Japanese Economic Development

Markets, norms, structures

Carl Mosk

Routledge
Taylor & Francis Group

LONDON AND NEW YORK

First published 2008
by Routledge
2 Park Square, Milton Park, Abingdon, Oxon OX14 4RN

Simultaneously published in the USA and Canada
by Routledge
270 Madison Ave, New York, NY 10016

*Routledge is an imprint of the Taylor & Francis Group,
an Informa business*

© 2008 Carl Mosk

Typeset in Times New Roman by
Newgen Imaging Systems (P) Ltd, Chennai, India
Printed and bound in Great Britain by
Antony Rowe Ltd, Chippenham, Wiltshire

British Library Cataloguing in Publication Data
A catalogue record for this book is available from the British Library

Library of Congress Cataloging in Publication Data
Mosk, Carl.
    Japanese economic development: markets, norms, structures/Carl Mosk.
      p. cm.
    Includes bibliographical references and index.
      1. Japan – Economic conditions. 2. Japan – Economic policy. I. Title

    HC462.M6363 2007
    330.9552–dc22   2007020798

ISBN13: 978–0–415–77159–7 (hbk)
ISBN13: 978–0–415–77158–0 (pbk)
ISBN13: 978–0–203–93587–3 (ebk)

For Donna

Contents

Figures

Tables

To the instructor

In writing this book I have aimed at meeting the needs of a variety of audiences. While I have not written a monograph, I do hope that scholars concerned with economic development, economic history and/or the Japanese economy may find the work of some interest. This said I must emphasize that my principal goal was to produce a textbook that can be employed by instructors in a wide range of university, perhaps even high school, courses.

To be specific, I have in mind courses listed in economics department curricula that deal with economic development, economic history, and the economics of the Asian region; in the curricula of sociology, geography, anthropology and political science departments courses focused on Japan; and in the curricula of departments of history or Asian Studies courses focusing on early modern and modern Japan.

To accommodate these diverse student audiences I have designed the book so that the instructor can either emphasize or de-emphasize the formal economic models discussed in the Appendix to Chapter 1 ("Economic Models"). It is my belief – indeed my experience – that many students who have not been exposed to formal economic models can master the basic intuition, the simple logic, underlying these models provided they are discussed as stories, tales, or fables.

Still some instructors may elect to avoid assigning the Appendix to Chapter 1 as required reading, simply recommending that the student peruse the section if he or she finds it interesting and helpful. While I do believe that all students would benefit from studying this Appendix, I am realistic. I realize that some instructors may well feel that they cannot adequately answer questions concerning the material contained in it, thereby eschewing it. I feel that this is a viable strategy. I feel that a student can work his or her way through the volume and come away with a useful account of Japanese economic development without reading the Appendix to Chapter 1.

For students in economics who are accustomed to mathematical and graphical presentations of economic concepts, the need to assign the Appendix to Chapter 1 depends upon the particular student audience involved. It is my suspicion that upper division students in economics departments will already be familiar with the content of the Appendix. If this is true for a particular instructor's course, perhaps the students should be encouraged to skim the material quickly to make sure they are acquainted with it.

I have written the book in chronological fashion, beginning with the Tokugawa period (Chapter 2) then moving forward to the period 1870–1945 (Chapters 3–6). I devote Part III of the volume to the period between the end of World War II and the mid-1970s (Chapters 7–9), following this account with a relatively brief account of the post-miracle growth economy (Chapters 10–12) that emphasizes the impact of the institutions key to Japan's economic development over the 1868–1975 period upon Japan's post-1975 economic performance.

In structuring the book along these lines, I feel I have written a text that can be used in courses primarily concerned with pre-1940 Japan, courses that will be mainly concerned with Chapters 2–6; and a text that can be used in courses focused upon post-World War II Japanese, Asian or general economic development. I feel that this chronological approach well suits the diverse student audiences that I hope will find this volume helpful in their studies.

In writing for students in history, sociology, political science, anthropology, geography, history and Asian studies, I am well aware that my reading can hardly match that of instructors who specialize in these fields. I am by training and academic appointment an economist toiling in the field of economics, interacting with colleagues who proudly declare themselves members of the Econ tribe.

When you spend enough time within a tribe it is difficult to appreciate how a member of another tribe may evaluate the arcane rituals and language of discourse of your own tribe. Still I have done my best to capture what I think is the essence of what historians, political scientists, anthropologists and sociologists have to say upon Japanese economic development. Perhaps I have failed to adequately do justice to the views prevalent in these other academic tribes to which I do not belong. If so, I trust the instructor can set the record straight for his or her students with the lectures, perhaps encouraging the students to critique my account from the viewpoints of other authors discussed during the semester or semesters of the courses employing this text. I am a firm believer in providing the students in my courses with alternative viewpoints. I hope the instructor will make use of this book in the same spirit, one that embraces alternative theories, one that recognizes the possibility of over-determination in human behavior, one that emphasizes critical understanding of complex reality.

Finally a word about the Romanization of Japanese used throughout this volume. Japanese names appear in the order common amongst Japanese, family names preceding given names. Macrons are used sparingly, eschewed in a number of contexts. Emphasis is on accessibility as it should be in a text aimed at a wide-ranging audience.

To the student

Mastering critical thinking is one of the most important, potentially the most important, by-products of study at an institution of higher learning. Probing myths, appreciating how scholars armed with different viewpoints steeped in different bodies of evidence can reach different conclusions, understanding the crucial role of scholarly debate, is part and parcel of critical learning. One of the goals of this text is to encourage you to visualize the key features of Japanese economic development through a variety of intellectual lenses.

To take this stance is not to deny that facts, hard data, exist. There are facts, give and take errors in measurement and calibration. Still, generating data involves interpretation; more crucially, understanding data encourages viewing it through interpretative prisms. Appreciating the give and take between interpretative viewpoints and underlying reality is central to the approach taken in this text. Emphasizing diversity of interpretation of complex reality is a credo of this volume.

Because I have crafted this volume with a variety of intellectual disciplines and viewpoints in mind, I suspect that some of you may be better grounded in mathematics and statistics – in reading charts, in working through algebraic equations, in taking in the meaning of tables bristling with numbers – than others. I have written this book for a wide range of courses dealing with Japan's modern economic and social development. I know that some of you appreciate formal argumentation more than others.

Those of you comfortable with the level of mathematics assumed in reading the Appendix to Chapter 1 and the Appendix to the book ("Japanese Economic Development, 1886–2000: A Statistical Portrait") are encouraged to read this material early in your perusal of the volume. To those who are less confident of their analytical skills, let me say "do not despair." Economic models and their statistical analysis boil down to story telling employing numbers and mathematical symbols. Focus upon the stories, thinking of graphs and equations as a convenient – a concise – format for telling the stories.

At the end of each chapter I list the key terms or concepts encountered there in. Please use these lists to test yourselves on your mastery of the contents of the chapter, perhaps picking a term or concept that intrigues you for a term paper.

Finally a word about the Romanization of Japanese used throughout this volume. Japanese names appear in the order common amongst Japanese, family names preceding given names. Macrons are used sparingly, eschewed in a number of contexts. Emphasis is on accessibility as it should be in a text aimed at a wide-ranging audience.

Acknowledgements

My accumulated debt to those who have taught me, to scholars who have critiqued my published research and conference presentations, is far too extensive and wide-ranging for me to give a full account in these pages. Still I feel comfortable listing some of the individuals whose views have made the greatest impression on my intellectual development.

Among American scholars senior to me, I believe five individuals have particularly impacted my understanding of Japan's economic development: Albert Craig, historian; Chalmers Johnson, political scientist and student of Japan's industrial policy; Hugh Patrick, economist, expert on Japan's financial system, and a key actor in keeping the Japan Economic Seminar afloat; Henry Rosovsky, economist and quantitatively oriented economic historian; and Thomas Smith, historian, expert on Tokugawa and post-Tokugawa Japan.

Amongst North Americans contemporary to me I wish to single out Marie Anchordoguy, J. Mark Ramseyer, and David Weinstein whose writings have shaped my thinking, whether I agree or disagree with their conclusions.

Amongst Japanese academics who have sponsored my stays in Japan, pointing me to the literature on Japan's economic development published in Japanese and assisting me in locating data sets rich in quantitative information about Japan's economy past and present, the following names stand out: Koike Kazuo, Nakata Yoshi-fumi, Minami Ryōshin, Odaka Konosuke, Ohkawa Kazushi, Osamu Saito, Umemura Mataji, and Yasuba Yasukichi.

Throughout the early 2000s my knowledge of Japan's contemporary economy has been enriched through internet-based interchange in forums. In particular, I have found NBR's Japan Forum (Econ) especially useful. Among the contributors to this forum I have found particularly informative are Arthur Alexander, John Campbell, Gregory Clark, Earl Kinmonth, Richard Katz, Robyn Lim, William Stonehill and Michael Smitka. While I believe the terms "globalization" and "information age" are much overused, like so many others I have found internet-based interchange a convenient way to keep abreast of recent developments involving the Japanese economy. In this arena I am particularly indebted to NBR's Japan Forum.

At Routledge, I am particularly indebted to Robert Langham who encouraged me to take this project on. I am grateful to Rob for guiding me with a steady hand through the lengthy process of manuscript development.

Finally I wish to express my greatest debt to my wife Donna for bringing me immense joy and warm wonderful companionship. Without her in my life I know that this book would never have seen the light of day.

Carl Mosk, Victoria, 2007

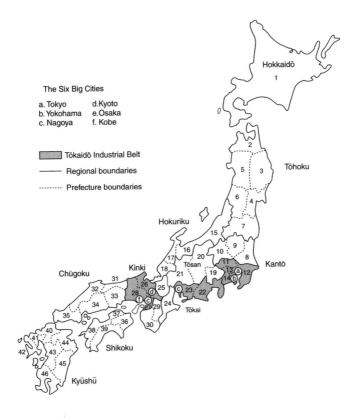

The Six Big Cities

a. Tokyo	d. Kyoto
b. Yokohama	e. Osaka
c. Nagoya	f. Kobe

▨ Tōkaidō Industrial Belt

—— Regional boundaries

------ Prefecture boundaries

Regions and Prefectures

HOKKAIDŌ
1 Hokkaido

TŌHOKU
2 Aomori
3 Iwate
4 Miyagi
5 Akita
6 Yamagata
7 Fukushima

KANTŌ
8 Ibaraki
9 Tochigi
10 Gumma
11 Saitama
12 Chiba
13 Tokyo
14 Kanagawa

HOKURIKU
15 Niigata
16 Toyama
17 Ishikawa
18 Fukui

TŌSAN
19 Yamanashi
20 Nagano
21 Gifu

TŌKAI
22 Shizuoka
23 Aichi
24 Mie

KINKI
25 Shiga
26 Kyoto
27 Osaka
28 Hyogo
29 Nara
30 Wakayama

CHŪGOKU
31 Tottori
32 Shimane
33 Okayama
34 Hiroshima
35 Yamaguchi

SHIKOKU
36 Tokushima
37 Kagawa
38 Ehime
39 Kochi

KYŪSHŪ
40 Fukuoka
41 Saga
42 Nagasaki
43 Kumamoto
44 Oita
45 Miyazaki
46 Kagoshima

Map The prefectures and regions of Japan, the Tōkaidō industrial belt, and the six big cities.

Note: Smaller islands and the sourthern prefecture Okinawa (the forth-seventh prefecture are not shown on the map.

Part I
Introduction

1   Markers, norms, constraints

Prologue

The corpse of a samurai is discovered in a grove, his breast pierced by the stroke of a sword. Blood from the wound soils the bamboo-blades but the sword is nowhere to be found. A rope at the foot of a nearby cedar suggests that the samurai had been bound before being killed.

An investigation ensues. A Buddhist priest testifies that he saw the man accompanying a woman – his wife the priest learns later – who was riding on a horse. A robber infamous throughout the region is taken into custody. He confesses that he forced himself on the samurai's wife, then killed the samurai in a sword fight, urged on to battle by the violated woman declaring that she could not endure to live if two men survived to tell of her shame. The wife confesses as well. She says that her husband's expression of contempt for her once she was violated by the thief brought her such grief that she attempted a double suicide, stabbing her husband who silently begged her to dispatch him, failing to kill herself. Finally a medium relates the story as told by the deceased samurai. In his account he died a suicide, the act of desperation brought on by the horror of hearing his wife encourage the thief to kill him.

The story is one of the great classics of Japanese literature, "In the Grove" by Akutagawa Ryunosuke.[1] At its heart is a brutal acknowledgement that we never really know the full truth about an event. Rather we operate with interpretation. In the Akutagawa story each person gives an account that reflects his or her sense of pride, or his or her sense of guilt. Facts do matter (certain outcomes need to be fitted into any account, namely the death of the samurai by a sword wound) but so does the inner life of the interpreter. We need to acknowledge that interpretation can be multifaceted, the facts called upon to buttress it shifting from account to account.

I would like the reader of this volume to approach the study of Japanese economic development with an appreciation of how and why interpretation varies. In particular I want the reader to approach the question of why growth in Japanese per capita income took the form that it did in Figure 1.1 with an open mind. I want the reader to understand how different social sciences might arrive at radically divergent accounts explaining the fact of long-run growth in the standard of living in Japan.

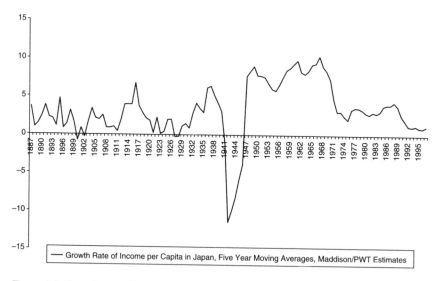

Figure 1.1 Growth rate of income per capita in Japan (based on Maddison and Penn World Table figures), five year moving average.

From a philosophical or methodological point of view, this text operates with an assumption that over-determination takes place in economic, social and political affairs. The over-determination concept assumes social norms and values, political and legal constraints, and the way markets operate mutually reinforce one another.

Why are Japanese automobiles built to high standards, generally requiring few repairs over the first ten years of their use? Is it because there is a Japanese law requiring rigorous vehicle inspection after a few years? Or is it because of the production methods instituted in Japanese manufacturing establishments, the way quality control operates on the shop floor? Or is it because Japanese consumers are fussy and demanding? The over-determination argument acknowledges a multiplicity of possibilities, stressing interaction. For instance, if Japanese consumers were bitterly opposed to the regulations, they could voice their opposition in the political arena, promoting an aggressive consumer advocacy campaign by forming and funding an organization devoted to doing away with the testing. Because the Japanese consumer is quality conscious, he or she typically supports – grumbling about it but doing precious little to get rid of – regulation as a mechanism for setting and maintaining quality standards. Knowing this, Japanese car and truck manufacture's organize their assembly lines and components-producing divisions with a focus on generating high-quality vehicles conforming to mandated quality standards at minimum cost to their bottom lines.

What is the chicken? What is the egg? Each social science discipline offers a compelling account containing a kernel of truth. Despite this, each explanation is incomplete.

In the remainder of this chapter we will explore the basic elements of three approaches to understanding economic development in Japan: the market oriented approach; the approach that emphasizes norms, values and ideas; and the approach that highlights political and geographic constraints.

The student should keep in mind that the intertwining of advocacy and analysis is typical of social science. One rarely if ever meets an economist, a political scientist, or a sociologist who is completely disinterested in the implications of his or her research for public policy. An author's having an axe to grind is not a bad thing. A reader's failure to recognize that an axe is being ground is not a good thing. Always keep in mind that advocacy colors analysis, most notably in setting up "idealized benchmark scenarios" against which other so-called real world scenarios are judged and evaluated.

Markets

Any credible account of Japanese economic development must wrestle with purely economic arguments. In this section we shall consider the elements of the mainstream neo-classical theory taught in most North American, British and "modern economics" (*kindai keizai*) departments in Japan. The term "neo-classical" highlights the fact that the discipline grew out of the classical school of economics, a school that developed in England during the eighteenth and nineteenth centuries.

The initial elaboration of the classical British theory that price driven markets provide the most effective device for allocating resources, distributing income and generating growth is usually assigned to the critics of British mercantilism, especially to Adam Smith in his famous treatise *The Wealth of Nations* published in the 1770s and still considered today as the founding cornerstone of neo-classical economics.

Mercantilism involved the development of a set of policies designed to regulate domestic commercial activity and especially the foreign trade of a nation in the interests of maximizing the power, notably the military power, of the nation. To that end mercantilists advocated running a positive balance of payments in trade, exports exceeding imports, so that gold and other precious metals – being the basis for securing mercenaries and outfitting armed forces – would flow into the coffers of the state's central authorities. To that end mercantilists attempted to promote technological progress by subsidizing economic activities viewed as simultaneously augmenting the military and economic prowess of the state.

The critics of mercantilism rejected this view of the world. They argued that the wealth of a nation would be far greater if markets were left as unregulated as was practically feasible than if they were shaped by the state. They maintained that allowing prices established in markets through the buying and selling of goods and labor services, each buyer or seller pursuing their narrow self interest, each buyer or seller anonymously attempting to maximize their individual wealth through these exchanges in response to the prices that they observed in the markets to shape behavior, was a far more effective mechanism for maximizing national wealth than was mercantilist regulation.

Central to the advocacy of the critics of mercantilism was the freeing up of labor markets. Many British defenders of market principles were vocal advocates for the abolition of slavery and serfdom, the dismantling of the vestiges of feudal labor exchange and onerous guild rules that created impediments to the freedom of workers to hire out their services at the highest wage offered by employers. In this sense the early classical school in England took up the natural law views of classical political liberalism (of John Locke for instance), grounding their arguments in a decided emphasis on individualism. Advocates of this position extolled the virtues of individual rights in both economy and polity. Relying upon the invisible hand of the market in which prices and profits refereed the system, allocating resources where they could be most judiciously utilized was optimal. Protecting free and unfettered voice in public affairs should be the foundation for the political infrastructure of a properly organized state.

The classical English school made the supply price of labor central to their analyses: Malthus built his theory of the iron law of wages (according to which the nature of fertility, especially marriage customs, and mortality shape the long-run supply price for labor driving the level to a so-called culturally determined subsistence wage), Mill and other classical writers of the nineteenth century adhering to a wages-fund doctrine linking the supply price of labor to the prices at which goods exchanged in the market. This is known as the labor theory of value.

It should be kept in mind that the classical school in England developed during the industrial revolution that gradually but inexorably transformed the nature of employment in that nation. Workers shifted out of agriculture into manufacturing, flocking to the rapidly expanding industrial towns of the midlands, to Manchester, Sheffield, Leeds and Liverpool, famous for their steam machine driven textile mills, their iron and steel works, their mass production of household goods (the industrial revolution is discussed in Chapter 2).

Manchester school doctrine emerged in early nineteenth-century England as a concomitant of industrialization. It advocated free trade in goods, especially foodstuffs, arguing that imports would cut down the price of domestic grains, meats and vegetables, the cost of which was crucial to determining the real purchasing power of domestic manufacturing wages. Associated with the name of David Ricardo, the political drive to secure free trade set the stage for the abolition of mercantilist policies like the Navigation Acts, the repeal of the Corn Laws that restricted imports of grains, and the negotiation of a most favored nation trade agreement between England and France. All of this occurred between 1800 and 1860, ushering in a regime of free trade and free mobility of labor, forging a model of capitalism that the rest of the world had to take seriously.

It is important to keep in mind that alternative economic doctrines other than classical British economics flourished in the nineteenth century, often justifying policies diametrically opposed to those associated with free trade. For instance in Germany, the historical school predominated, emphasis being placed on the stages economies went through in moving from pre-monetary exchange to monetized market exchange. In both Germany and the United States theories of infant industry protectionism were elaborated. These theories noted that free trade in all goods might consign a country to remaining pre-industrial, its domestic manufacturers being unable to compete against the most efficient producers in an advanced industrial power like England. Protecting domestic manufactures in certain key sectors behind high tariff walls, promoting national infrastructure development (e.g. canals, roads and natural waterway improvements during the eighteenth century, the railroads during the nineteenth century), were enticing vehicles for building up domestic industry. In Germany Frederick List stepped forth into the public eye as a critic of free trade; in the United States, Alexander Hamilton preached the virtues of a national system of manufactures, rejecting the views that became central to the English classical school in the nineteenth century.

The protectionism advocated by List and Hamilton is best characterized by the term "economic nationalism." Economic nationalism shares some ideas with mercantilism. It is aimed at promoting specific industries, by protecting them from foreign competitors through tariffs and quotas, or through direct subsidies (e.g. tax breaks, direct payments from government). By restricting imports protectionism tends to diminish the magnitude of any positive gap between imports and exports that might develop through international trade. However, there are important differences between mercantilism and economic nationalism. Protectionism is not necessarily aimed at enhancing the economic and political prowess of nation states. It might have that aim but it might not. Nor is one of its priorities necessarily the generation of a trade surplus, exports exceeding imports as it is under mercantilism. Generating a trade surplus might be a goal of government officials pursuing a strategy of economic nationalism. But it might not be.

From a purely theoretical viewpoint the chief weakness of the classical English school was its preoccupation with supply, namely the labor theory of value, the idea that commodities exchanged at prices determined solely by the cost of labor embodied in them. Counterexamples were well known to economists – gold and other precious metals are usually cited in this context – and on the continent theorists did elaborate frameworks taking into account both demand and supply. In England rejection of the supply driven approach and the embracing of a full blown demand and supply analysis that explained how prices were shaped both by the demand for them as well as by their supply (hence by the costs of producing them that was the main focus of the classical school) is most prominently associated with the name of Alfred Marshall whose *Principles of Economics* became a classic textbook for the field, going into manifold editions and shaping the views of economists throughout the English speaking world. The Marshallian "scissors" of supply and demand operating independently of one another became one of the great cornerstones of neo-classical, as opposed to classical, theory. In the Marshallian world the equilibrium price for a market is the price that just exactly equates supply and demand, the price that just clears the market.

Building a theoretical foundation for the Marshallian scissors became a preoccupation of many economists during the period between World War I and World War II. A rigorous theory of consumer preferences, and a mathematical framework for analyzing production on the supply side with production functions (like the Cobb-Douglas production function discussed in the Appendix to this chapter), advanced the neo-classical paradigm whose basic concepts were laid out in the *Principles of Economics*. Ironically, all of this research took place when unemployment rates soared in many of the industrial countries, in England during the 1920s, in the United States during the 1930s in the aftermath of the 1929 stock market collapse.

If markets were operating as Marshall suggested they did, why was there sustained unemployment? For unemployment to exist, the demand for labor must fall short of the supply of labor. In this case one would expect the cost of a unit of labor to fall, until supply and demand equalized at the lower wage that clears the market. It was this problem, perplexing to the advocates of Marshallian neo-classicism, that encouraged some mainstream economists – most notably John Maynard Keynes in his famed *General Theory of Employment, Interest and Money* published in the mid-1930s – to reject a theory of employment founded on the "scissors" logic of individual commodity markets, substituting for it a theory rooted in the notion of aggregate economy-wide demand.

To be sure Keynes developed his ideas of effective aggregate demand around advocacy. Arguing that unemployment was rising because capitalists were becoming increasingly gloomy and pessimistic about future demand for their products, therefore cutting back on their investment levels, Keynes felt that government spending had to take up the slack dragging down aggregate demand. At the same time that he rationalized the policies he favored by elaborating a theory that he believed was general, he also brought into the fold of economic theory national income accounting, a statistical discipline devoted to estimating the annual flow of goods and services within an economy.

In the aftermath of World War II, American economists in particular developed a neo-classical "synthesis" that wedded Keynesian aggregate demand analysis to the Marshallian "scissors" principles. The resulting synthesis can only be described as an intellectual alliance of convenience, economists realizing that market clearing principles are not consistent with the idea that sustained unemployment can arise in a market oriented economy, the demand for labor falling short of the supply of labor. For this reason some economists have developed theories of the second best, rooted in analyses about how and why friction develops in the real world, generating employment and booms and busts as outcomes. We shall consider a group of these theories in the text that follows. The point to keep in mind is that there are differences of opinion among mainstream economists concerning the importance of friction as a general concept, and of the various possible types of friction.

Some economists cling to the view that markets basically work well, that it is government interference that causes them to go awry. Others believe that there are fundamental economic principles undermining market clearing, at least for certain markets, thus offering a rationale for Keynesian type approaches and Keynesian type policies, including the aggressive use of fiscal policy to correct sustained bouts of unemployment potentially destabilizing liberal capitalism itself.

Having completed this brief overview of the evolution of neo-classical doctrine, let us turn to a discussion of a select group of economic models, treating them as stories. This discussion is meant to ease the student gradually – especially the student who has not been exposed to any formal economic analysis, the student who is not especially comfortable with graphs – into an understanding of the basic principles of mainstream economics. Slightly more formal presentations of these principles, including some graphs designed to illustrate the logic of particular arguments, appear in the Appendix to this chapter.

The student should attempt to master the basic logic of the various economic models, going back and forth between their description in the main text of this chapter and their corresponding elaboration in the Appendix, thinking about the models as formalized tales, stories, ultimately not really very dissimilar from the short stories of writers like Akutagawa who always has a point to make, a pointed message to deliver. To drive home the story-like aspects of the theories, I will distill a small set of economic principles from the analyses.

The theory of market equilibrium in which a downward sloping demand schedule intersects an upward sloping supply schedule – price on the vertical axis and quantity supplied and demanded on the horizontal axis- is the workhorse model of mainstream neo-classical economics. The slopes of these lines are meant to capture the common sense notion that demand for a good or service falls off as its relative price rises; and willingness of producers to supply a good or service responds to the price that they can get selling it.

Graphs illustrating the equilibrium principle appear in the Appendix to this chapter as Figures 1.2 A and 1.2 B. Where the supply and demand curves intersect determines the equilibrium level of price and the equilibrium level of goods or services transacted in the market. This should be considered the benchmark model, the ideal type, against which more complex economic models, more elaborate economic arguments, are compared.

Note from Figure 1.2 A that an outward shift in demand for a good – demand increasing at all price levels perhaps because the good has been extremely fashionable, or because substitutes for it have risen in price relative to the good itself, or because the real incomes of consumers have risen – raises the equilibrium level of price and the equilibrium level of goods transacted. Suppose, for instance, within the personal computing market the demand for mobile laptop computers shifts out to the right because more and more business travelers are encouraged by their companies to stay connected to corporate headquarters while they are on the road. According to the basic logic of markets we would expect to see the relative price of laptops rise.

Pursuing this example further, let us see what happens in the market for desktop personal computers. These are substitutes for laptop computers, imperfect substitutes of course since taking a desktop on a trip is onerous, expensive and annoying. We would expect the demand for these to shift in to the left as the demand for laptops shifts out to the right, other things being equal. In the scenario we have just considered, we would expect the market adjustment to yield a rise in the relative price of laptops compared to desktop machines. For instance if laptops were initially twice as expensive as desktops, the impact of the market adjustment might be a situation where laptops were three times as expensive as desktops.

Now consider the impact of technological advances in the production of miniaturized chips and liquid crystal display screens generating a reduction in the costs incurred by producers of laptop computers. This state of affairs is captured in Figure 1.2 B in the Appendix. As a result of the advance, the supply of laptops shifts out to the right. The relative price of laptops falls.

Underlying this equilibrium analysis are two basic principles: arbitrage and the invisible hand.

The arbitrage principle says that equilibrium prices emerge in markets because any differences in price will be eliminated through the activity of market arbitrageurs who buy goods where they are cheap and sell them where they are dear. For instance suppose the price of a particular type of digital camera is cheaper in Osaka than it is in Tokyo, selling for the equivalent of $300 in the Osaka market and for $400 in the Tokyo market. Assume the cost of transporting the camera from Osaka to Tokyo is $10, including crating up a large box and shipping it by a nighttime running freight train. If this disparity persists for a while, we would expect an enterprising camera distributor in Tokyo to order cameras from Osaka, thereby driving down the price of cameras in Tokyo (more are supplied in Tokyo), and driving them up in Osaka (less are supplied in the Osaka marketplace). Eventually we would expect a single price – the only potential difference reflecting transport costs for shipping cameras from Osaka to Tokyo – to prevail in both markets.

The invisible hand principle refers to the idea that a market economy – as opposed to a centrally planned economy in which goods are produced in response to production quotas set forth by bureaucrats – is socially efficient because it operates through the anonymous force of supply and demand shifts spewing out price information to consumers and producers. Social efficiency here means that purchasers of goods and services can do as well as possible in allocating their income. And suppliers of products and services can maximize their profits, moving in and out of various lines of activity in response to changing opportunities to garner revenue net of costs stemming from shifts in the prices established for goods and services in markets. It should be emphasized that social efficiency occurs because everyone is acting rationally in the sense that they cannot do any better than they are already doing by changing the purchasing plans or their production decisions.

In a pure invisible hand world buyers are assumed to respond instantaneously to changes in the relative prices for goods and services, adjusting their purchases – substituting tuna for halibut when the price of tuna falls relative to halibut for instance – in such a way as to reach the highest level of welfare possible given the income that they enjoy, maximizing the real purchasing power of their economic resources.

In a pure invisible hand world producers, incurring no cost to refocusing their activities – computer manufacturers seamlessly switching from manufacturing desktops to laptops for instance – jump around in response to movements in the relative prices of products, forcing profit rates in all endeavors to a common level, competition squeezing out any excess profit opportunities. Barriers to entering exciting new endeavors and exiting from tired old lines of business do not exist in the benchmark model.

As should be apparent from this discussion, the benchmark case is highly idealized. It assumes perfect information about goods and services in the present. It assumes that sunk costs do not deter corporations from abandoning declining markets, and leaping into buoyant expanding markets. Before we consider a host of factors that economists take into account in modifying the benchmark model so that the resulting analysis corresponds more sensibly and closely to actual real world conditions, we need to say something about the prices for consumer durables like automobiles, refrigerators and houses and machines like lathes and dynamos.

The price of a consumer durable or a machine is typically hefty, far more than the price of a meal, or even the combined total of the cost of meals a household consumes over an entire year. Why are we willing to pay so much? The answer is that we do not consume a durable good the way we do the food we purchase in a supermarket. Typically we enjoy the benefits of owning and using the durable for an extended length of time, for years, perhaps decades. Thus it is the discounted present value of the benefits we expect to obtain from the durable that we should set equal to the purchase price, namely

$$\sum_{i=1}^{N} \frac{b_i}{(1+r)^i} = p \qquad (1.1)$$

where b_i are the flow of benefits expected from the purchase of the durable in the ith year, N is the number of years one expects to utilize the durable, r is the interest rate at which one would have to borrow funds to purchase the durable if one were securing it on credit (alternatively it is the interest rate that one forgoes by taking one's money out of bank account in order to secure the durable). If the discounted present value of the expected benefits falls short of the purchase price we should not buy the durable; if it is equal or exceeds the purchase price we should go ahead and buy it.

Likewise corporations make decisions about purchasing capital goods – trucks, factory buildings, electrical motors, stamping machines, hammers and screwdrivers – by comparing the cost of the purchase with the benefits they expect to secure from the purchase. If the price exceeds the expected present discounted value of the flow of benefits, management is making an economic mistake in going ahead with the purchase. If the price is less than or equal to the discounted present value of the expected benefits, an enterprise behaving rationally should acquire the equipment, build the building, secure the truck.

This is known as the cost/benefit principle. If the cost falls short of the discounted present value of the anticipated benefits, the project, the purchase, should be a go. Otherwise it is a mistake, at least from a strictly economic point of view.

It should be emphasized that benefits might include psychic rewards, enhanced social status, a feeling of being wealthy and powerful. Introducing this source of satisfaction from ownership of automobiles, televisions and microwave ovens is all fine and well – economists appeal to this logic all the time and we have probably all made decisions in which psychic rewards played a major role – but doing so makes rationalizing even the most stupid, ill conceived, economic decision possible. Just say that you are getting a warm glow from owning the durable, even if you are never using it!

To be frank, some critics of mainstream economics contend that most mainstream economic arguments contain a kind of "after the fact" rationalization, imparting a kind of self fulfilling circularity rendering them always true even in the face of evidence suggesting they are false.

That the benchmark arbitrage/invisible hand model is only an idealized framework for carrying out serious economic analysis is widely recognized in the profession. For this reason most economists subscribe to the theory of the second best, namely the view that perfect market outcomes are not possible, distortions occur, and policy makers should take these frictional elements into account in drawing implications from the models. The trick is bringing economic insights into the discussion of frictions impeding perfect market outcomes.

We shall consider seven sources of friction suggesting that simple supply/demand equilibrium stories about how prices are determined fail: information asymmetry; transactions costs; externalities; barriers to entry due to monopoly, oligopoly or organized cartels; the tragedy of the commons; crime and corruption; and moral hazard.

In the real world we have to work, we have to expend resources whether time or money, to acquire information. Suppose you are purchasing a home. You read the disclosure form signed by the sellers of the property. They claim that there are no defects in the structure. Can you believe them? One does not have to be suspicious by nature to doubt the validity of the claim. For this reason most real estate agents recommend a housing inspection by a licensed agent before completing an offer to purchase a home. The point is that the seller may know something about the property that the purchaser does not know and is unwilling to reveal lest the deal fall through. The information is asymmetrically distributed.

In the case of the used car market, it is well known that a good used vehicle sells for below its actual value, its reputation tarnished by the vehicles that are money pits that owners are trying to unload on an unsuspecting victim, the owners sick and tired of making repairs. In both the housing market and automobile market the principle is identical: it is information asymmetry.

Transactions costs refer to the costs involved in bargaining and haggling over wages, work conditions or the prices of goods and services. You can not run a business effectively if you have to engage in daily contract negotiations with every worker you employ from the janitor on up to managers. You need a regular employee pool that shows up every day prepared to do an assortment of tasks within their specified job assignment profiles, perhaps even take on chores that they have never before worked at. This is one reason why market approaches are rarely used by enterprises hiring workers, employers preferring a hierarchy approach in which the employee is paid a fixed wage only occasionally negotiated in exchange for carrying out a range of duties mandated by upper level management. Organizing a hierarchy is more cost effective than carrying out daily transacting in most employment situations, casual day labor markets being a prominent exception. Call this superiority of hierarchy over the market a major illustration of the transactions costs principle.

Externalities refer to benefits enjoyed by the public or producers or costs imposed on the public or producers spilling over from a particular activity. Pollution is an example of a negative or costly externality. If a chemical manufacturer disposes of its waste products in a stream, lake or bay it may well contaminate the water, sending out deadly toxic substances that are consumed by fish that are eaten by consumers who then become ill. If a steel plant burns coal as a byproduct of its manufacture of steel bar and plate, sending foul smelling black dust into the atmosphere that may cause lung diseases amongst the surrounding population it is creating a negative externality. If a bee keeper locates next to a flower producing farm it creates a positive externality for its neighbor, the bees pollinating the flowers. If a railroad company opens up a new station in a remote rural village it creates a positive externality for the villagers, who can now dispatch their rice, their raw silk, their pickles speedily at low cost to cities where they command far higher prices than they command in their isolated locality.

The point about externalities is that they cannot simply be handled through the force of supply and demand working through private markets. Regulation or government intervention is required to cope with their fallout. In the case of positive externalities like those generated by infrastructure – paved roads, deep water harbors, railroad lines, public schools, water purification plants, hydroelectric systems – there is a strong case for government subsidy or government regulation to ensure proper standards and consistency. In the case of negative externalities there is a strong case for government monitoring, setting acceptable and unacceptable cutoff levels for the externality, and for fining agents that violate the standards.

Barriers to entry most commonly arise when an enterprise's unit costs fall across a broad range of its production or when the unit costs for its marketing of its output are driven down as the scale of its production increases. Consider automobile production. Setting up a plant to produce three cars a month makes no sense if the plant is marketing cars for the mass market (it probably would not even make sense for a specialized automobile manufacturer delivering vehicles to a small coterie of extremely wealthy customers). Two much capital, too many skilled workers are required to make this an economically viable proposition. Setting up mass production means exploiting economies of scale. It also means exploiting learning by doing on the part of the employed labor force that gains skills as it repeats tasks over and over again.

Where steep fall off in production costs prevail within an industry it is extremely difficult for start up enterprises to break in. Already established firms can manufacture and market their products at lower cost than can a novice to the field. They can even collude temporarily – starting a price war, cutting their prices in tandem – to make it that much more challenging for the new entrant to survive for long.

Barriers to entry tend to appear in transportation, communications and utilities. Railroads, hydroelectric power suppliers, telephone companies or satellite telecommunications service providers are examples of firms that enjoy economies of scale that restrict competition. Not surprisingly, oligopoly – competition among the few – or even monopoly results in these cases. Markets in which there is competition amongst the few are known as concentrated markets.

In analyzing the way concentrated markets operate economists differentiate between three types of market concentration: monopoly in which there is a single seller for a commodity or a service – for instance the national militia within your country probably has a monopoly over certain types of legal violence – oligopoly, and monopolistic competition. Oligopoly refers to a situation where a small number of firms produce or process a homogeneous product, for instance coal, natural gas, unprocessed wheat, corn, soybeans and so forth. The product is not differentiated: coal is coal, gas is gas. Monopolistic competition refers to a situation where a small number of firms differentiate their product while competing with one another. For instance they may differentiate their product through brand name and advertising, usually employing design, unique taste or styling, or packaging to differentiate their peculiar version of the product from that offered by competitors. For instance Toyota cars are famed for their reliability and quality, Honda cars for their stylist racing car feel, BMWs for their driving performance and luxurious features, and so forth.

Where monopoly, oligopoly or monopolistic competition exists in markets, economists look for explanations in terms of scale economies, barriers to entry, and the way market power influences market choice.

Indeed, much economic analysis – applying sophisticated game theory in the case of oligopoly for instance – has gone into the study of industries where barriers to entry are overwhelming. It has been demonstrated that monopolies selling their output at a single set price tend to set this above the price that would prevail in a perfectly competitive situation with costless entry. At this price they produce an output that falls short of the output generated by competition with costless entry. Monopolists can move closer to, or even reach, the competitive level of output by segmenting the market, setting high and low prices for different subsections of the market in order to expand their scale of operation, in the extreme charging a different price for each consumer.

The point is that price determination in markets with a single, or a very small number of firms, does not usually follow the rules set down in the simple supply/demand equilibrium story. Strategic behavior – predatory pricing for example – is a problem commonly encountered in an industry characterized by oligopoly or monopoly. Stifling innovation by keeping out new startup competitors is another problem.

Citing the ills caused by strategic behavior and the snuffing out of innovation, many economists argue that there is a case for either regulating monopolies and oligopolies or alternatively using antitrust action to break them up. The principle of barriers to entry joins our other principles of market friction – information asymmetry, transactions costs, and externalities – that warns us off accepting blindly the invisible hand principle.

The tragedy of the commons refers to the possibility of resource depletion. Suppose a resource – fish in a lake or a particular zone of the ocean, oil in an oilfield, timber taken by cutting down forests – can be exhausted at least for a very long time, perhaps hundreds of years. If private actors are allowed to exploit these environments on their own without regulation by government or by a disinterested third party none of them have a selfish incentive to hold back on their level of activity so that exhaustion will not occur. What happens if the group of resource users cobbles together an agreement to slow down or temporarily cease use of the resource? Since each actor cannot completely trust his or her competitor, he or she must assume that someone else will take advantage of any moratorium that is arrived at. This is because each has a narrow short-run incentive to extract the maximum possible gain from the resource. Thus the forest may be decimated before forest rejuvenation can occur, leading perhaps to soil erosion and long-run destruction of the environment; the fish population may be wiped out; the oil reserves completely depleted before alternative sources of fuel are developed.

This is called the tragedy of the commons because it mimics the problems that arose in some open field agricultural settings on European manorial estates, the peasants and the lord of the manor jointly using a commons for grazing their sheep. The tragedy refers to the possibility that the commons is overgrazed, potentially leading to the starvation of sheep and humans alike.

In one sense the problem is that contemporary prices do not reflect long-run supply. If prices were set fully taking into account future outcomes, being discounted present values that reflect long-run scarcity of the resource of the sort envisioned by equation 1.1, exhaustion might not take place. As long as expectations about the future are unrealistic – for instance expecting forest to grow back faster than it actually can – prices for the resources might be too cheap, the unregulated market generating exhaustion of the resource. If prices are set high enough, demand for the resource will be less, and the market might yield an outcome appropriate for the long run.

Engaging in crime and corruption are two of the less attractive but nevertheless valid aspects of human activity undermining the simple logic of the invisible hand principle. The invisible hand principle assumes honest behavior. It assumes that people sell their labor services or the fruits of their efforts on the market if they are self employed, expending these earned resources upon food, clothing and housing, living within their budget constraints. Borrowing on credit is an option in the model since a borrower is still living within his/her long-run budget constraint, paying back the loan with future income flows (recall the logic of equation 1.1). Stealing from one another is not consistent with the simple invisible hand story since robbers do not live within their budget constraint, and those robbed may find themselves more constrained in terms of available resources than they expected based on their earning power.

The existence of a policing authority – private militia, protection by a powerful local warlord, or the military and police forces of a nation state monopolizing the use of force – and a judiciary typically operating with courts and the intent of protecting and the enforcing private property rights is usually considered a *sine qua non* for efficiently operating markets. This is sometimes known as the "night watch man" theory of the state, the state being responsible for maintaining law and order with its police and courts, providing security to ward off international aggression with its military, otherwise staying out of economic matters to the fullest extent possible. The government that governs least is the government that governs best.

What ensures that the courts will play by the rules, not favoring the interests of some parties over other parties, not falling into the hands of criminals and gangsters who through bribes and intimidation escape justice? The "night watch man" state can only operate effectively if corruption, especially corruption in government and the judicial system, is somehow boxed in, albeit not completely eliminated.

The doctrine of "neo-liberalism" popular in common law countries like the United States, Great Britain, and some of the nations of the British Commonwealth, is an ideology that has evolved out of the classical British liberalism of the eighteenth century. It argues that there is a social infrastructure – a set of political governance practices – that appears to be necessary for the emergence of efficient markets. This infrastructure includes:

1   the guarantee of civil liberties, and an independent media, the public able to voice its objections to corruption in high circles through free speech and a free press;
2   political accountability, politicians deriving their power from the public through regular cycles of referenda or elections;
3   a high-quality civil service that can operate independently of short-run political pressure;
4   a high level of regulatory quality, policies being developed that are market friendly, monitoring of bank activity and guarantee of shareholders rights in the event of bankruptcy being one important area of regulation;
5   the rule of law; and
6   control of corruption.

The influence of American thought in developing the doctrine of neo-liberalism is evident. Most of its principles were embedded in the Constitution of the United States written by the political founders of the United States of America during the late eighteenth century.

Let us use the term "the neo-liberal" principle to invoke the political and social management of crime and corruption.

In this context it should be noted that Ramseyer (1996) makes a strong case for the view that Japan – even though it is a civil code as opposed to common law country, hewing to the French and German traditions in which bureaucracy plays a greater role in regulating markets than do the courts through their decisions – has had most of the social infrastructure envisioned by the neo-liberal view since the late nineteenth century.

The final economic principle bolstering the argument that carefully crafted extra-market, political, constraints must be developed so that markets operate in an efficient manner, is the principle of moral hazard. Moral hazard refers to the fact that parties providing insurance to other parties may encourage profligate, irresponsible behavior on the part of the insured. Parents spoil children, being overprotective, failing to let them become independent adults responsible for their own actions. Governments spoil banks, using tax payers' funds to bail out financial institutions that have made bad loans, rashly throwing their depositors money at fantastical "pie in the sky" get rich schemes. This is one reason why insurance companies are reluctant to provide coverage that does not include a deductible, setting an extremely high price for deductible free premiums. The insurance company wants you to be a good driver, it wants you to take care of your home, fixing leaks, making sure rot does not set in, replacing your roof when necessary. Forcing you to bear part of the costs of repair in the event of a disaster – water damage, a fire – is one way to encourage you to be responsible.

In the remainder of this text we will illustrate each of these principles of economic friction. We will also explore some of them in more detail in the analytical Appendix to this chapter.

In addition to the various principles that we have just considered – involving information flow, transactions, externalities, barriers to entry, the tragedy of the commons, neo-liberalism, and moral hazard – economists have also concerned themselves with quantity adjustments at the aggregate level. As with the friction principles, quantity adjustment invokes the theory of the second best.

Economic models emphasizing quantity adjustment assume that price fluctuations are less important in the way economies adjust to exogenous shocks – to natural disasters like hurricanes or tidal waves or droughts, to collapsing international trade, to a dramatic collapse in the optimism of entrepreneurs about the wisdom of investment in plant and equipment for meeting future demand – than fluctuations in the quantity of production, fluctuations in the degree to which the labor force is employed.

The two models of quantity adjustment that we consider here – the input/output model and the Keynesian aggregate demand model – were initially developed during the period between World War I and World War II, the input/output model being elaborated by economists in the Soviet Union grappling with the problem of setting quotas for different industries in a centrally planned economy using the command and control methods characteristic of military organizations, the Keynesian model being elaborated to provide an escape from the unemployment gripping the United Kingdom after World War I and the United States after the collapse of the stock market in 1929. In the input/output model used by central planning regimes bureaucratic directives about quantity levels replace the signals that price imparts in an invisible hand world. In the aggregate demand model wages and prices are assumed rigid in the short run – perhaps because of monopoly and oligopoly, perhaps because wages are set at too high a level by consumer durable producing industries such as automobiles (see the Appendix to this chapter for the efficiency wage model that explains why this might occur in a world with information asymmetry) – quantities of output demanded falling in one or several key sectors of the economy generating a wave-like collapse, a ripple effect, throughout the remainder of the economy, as workers in the affected sector are thrown out of work, thereby cutting back on the purchase of goods and services in other sectors that in turn dispense with some of their employees.

The input/output example is most easily explained with a numerical example. Consider the following flow chart:

The basic flow table for a two sector economy without government

Selling sectors	Purchasing sectors and final demand components				
	A	**M**	**C**	**I**	**Total**
A	$25	$50	$200	$50	$325
	(5 bushels)	(10 bushels)	(40 bushels)	(10 bushels)	(65 bushels)
M	$100	$100	$400	$100	$700
	(5 tons)	(5 tons)	(20 tons)	(5 tons)	(35 tons)
Labor (wages)	$250	$350			
Investors (profits & interest)	$50	$100			

Where **A** stands for agriculture producing bushels of wheat, **M** stands for manufacturing producing tons of steel, **C** stands for the output that is delivered to the consumer, and **I** for the investment (capital) goods delivered to producers (farmers in the **A** sector, manufacturers in the **M** sector). Agriculture sells $25 to itself, farmers buying fertilizer for their orchards and vegetable gardens, grain to feed to their pigs and cows, from one another. Agriculture sells $50 of output to the manufacturing sector (for instance coal extracted from some of the farm land in this simple two sector example). In this simple flow chart the sum total of intermediate products (to be used as inputs into the final production of goods and services) sold by the **A** sector to itself and to the manufacturing **M** sector is $75. The remainder of its output – $250 – goes to final demand, to either consumers or investors. For manufacturing the sum total of its sales of intermediate products is $200. A total of $500 goes to final demand, consumers and investors.

It should be emphasized the final demand in the economy is equal to the income supplied. The final demand in this example is the sum of the value added generated by the agriculture and the manufacturing sectors – the sum of their revenue net of purchase of intermediate products that they employ to produce output going to final demand – namely $250 plus $500 which equals $750. If the total payments to labor and the owners of capital in this example are added – $250 plus $350 plus $50 plus $100 – the same figure is reached. Demand equals equal income generated.

Appreciating the interdependencies implicit in the input/output structure of an economy may help the student understand why a downturn in demand for the output of any one sector – say the consumer durables sector supplying refrigerators, televisions, computers and automobiles or the housing sector – might cascade throughout the economy, through declining demand for intermediate products, for glass, for steel, for electrical wiring, and so forth.

The Keynesian aggregate demand model offers a second useful tool for understanding how downturns in demand – say investment demand as investors become increasingly dispirited about their prospects for future sales, cutting back drastically on their purchase of plant and equipment – can spread throughout the economy. In this framework the key variables are fourfold: **C**, aggregate consumption demand; **I**, aggregate investment demand; **G**, government purchases of goods and services; and net exports **X** (equaling exports minus imports). Total aggregate demand $\mathbf{D_A}$ – equaling total income supplied – is the sum of the four demand components, namely $\mathbf{D_A} = \mathbf{C} + \mathbf{I} + \mathbf{G} + \mathbf{X}$.

With these aggregate demand variables we can break down the growth of an aggregate economy into the sum of the growth of its components, namely $\mathbf{\Delta D_A} = \mathbf{\Delta C} + \mathbf{\Delta I} + \mathbf{\Delta G} + \mathbf{\Delta X}$ where $\mathbf{\Delta C} = \mathbf{C_2} - \mathbf{C_1}$, consumption in a later year minus consumption in an earlier year, the other increments being defined in a similar fashion.

We can put these aggregate demand variables and their increments on a percentage basis, calculating the percentages of aggregate demand that flow from each of the four sources. For instance the percentage of aggregate demand due to consumption is **C** divided by $\mathbf{D_A}$, being put on a percentage basis, and so forth. We can also calculate the percentages of growth in aggregate demand attributable to growth in the various components, for instance as $\mathbf{\Delta C}$ divided by $\mathbf{\Delta D_A}$ and put on a percentage basis. This allows us to estimate which component of aggregate demand is playing a key role in causing aggregate demand to growth.

Estimates of the aggregate demand structure of the Japanese economy appear in the statistical Appendix to this volume, entitled "Japanese Economic Development, 1886–2000: A Statistical Portrait," specifically in Table A.6. The student should study this table now, also perusing the other tables provided there. Please note that Table A.3 gives another way of decomposing the aggregate structure of an economy other than input/output or aggregate demand structure, namely in terms of the percentages of the labor force and the percentages of output derived from each of the three main productive – not aggregate demand – sectors of the economy, primary, secondary and tertiary. The student should study this table now, noting that the relative labor productivity of a sector is the proportion of output generated by a sector divided by its proportion of the labor force. For instance for the period 1951–55, the relative productivity of the primary sector (agriculture, forestry and fishing) is 47.9, equaling 18.4 divided by 38.5, the ratio put on a percentage basis.

The Keynesian model – the so-called **IS/LM** version (**IS** standing for investment equals savings, **LM** for liquidity demanded equals liquidity supplied) – is laid out in the Appendix to this chapter. The discussion there may prove challenging to the student who finds graphs bewildering at best, annoying at worse. Please try to get through this material.

The key points can be summarized as follows:

1   if prices are fixed the aggregate demand for output that equals aggregate output supplied may not be at full employment;
2   in these circumstances, a government committed to reducing unemployment may employ stabilization policies to stimulate the economy, either fiscal policy (e.g. increases in government spending, or decreases in income taxes) being used to shift the **IS** curve, or monetary policy (expanding the money supply) used to shift the **LM** curve, or a combination thereof;
3   in the long run the assumption of fixed prices is unrealistic. If the labor market does not clear – supply exceeding demand – we would expect deflation to set in ultimately, wages dropping, drawing down production costs and hence prices. As prices fall the real value of the money supply (the nominal supply divided by the price level) increases, causing the **LM** curve to shift out even if the government does nothing.
4   Two special cases exist: the so-called classical case in which fiscal policy is useless, expansion of government spending causing interest rates to rise, perfectly crowding out investment demand; and the so-called liquidity trap case, monetary policy (and hence deflation) being useless.

Graphical illustration of the special cases appears in the portions of the Appendix to this chapter devoted to the aggregate demand model. The student is encouraged to study this material now.

It should be emphasized that analyzing an economy in terms of its aggregate demand structure, or developing stabilization policies based on governmental manipulation of the aggregate demand variables, requires coming up with an accounting scheme for estimating the national accounts of an economy. Accomplishing this is not a trivial task. The student should study the shaded passage on "national income accounting" to get a feel for the issues and pitfalls involved.

National Income Accounting

National income accounting attempts to measure the total annual value of all flows of goods and services produced and consumed within the confines of a national economy. In theory, estimating national output demanded and estimating national income supplied should yield the same figure. There is an inherent circularity in the estimation.

Summing consumption, investment, government expenditures and net exports yields a figure for total activity demanded by households, firms and governments operating within the economy, namely gross domestic expenditure (see Table A.6 in the Appendix).

Summing consumption, savings and taxes paid measures output, or equivalently income, broken down in terms of the uses to which income received by households and firms is put. Either the income fuels spending on food, clothing, housing or the like; or it goes to accumulation; or it ends up in the coffers of government as taxation.

Gross national product refers to the total incomes received by nationals of a country, incorporating income earned from investments abroad or income generated by nationals living in other countries and excluding income or output accruing to foreign investors or foreign nationals employed within a country. Gross domestic product refers to activity generated within the national boundaries of a country.

There are three practical methodological problems that government agencies must cope with in coming up with estimates of national or domestic output, or national or domestic income: scope, netness, and valuation. Scope refers to what goods and activities get counted. Are the estimates restricted to goods and services priced out in the market, namely transacted through a standard market method (e.g. sale of a good through a store that generates a sales receipt, purchase of a service that is properly invoiced for taxation purposes)? In many low income economies, for instance in Japan during the pre-1960 period, farm families produced rice and vegetables that they directly consumed in their houses, never selling or buying these products in a market. In the advanced industrial economies, many women work, putting their children in day cares or preschools. In this case the wages of the working mothers, and the wages of day care and preschool providers all get counted as part of national output or national income earned. But what happens when the mothers raise their children at home, eschewing careers, avoiding the use of daycare?

Netness refers to avoiding double counting. In principle estimates of national output are restricted to the final product, excluding the purchase and sale of products that are intermediate, used as inputs into higher stages of fabrication or assembly. For instance, it is undesirable to count the purchase of glass, rubber, steel and spark plugs by the Toyota Motor Company that are eventually incorporated into cars that it sells to consumers as part of final output. The estimate of the Toyota Motor Company's contribution to Japan's national output should be restricted to the value of its output net of purchases of intermediate purchases utilized as inputs in final automobile and truck assembly.

Valuation refers to pricing out the disparate goods and services spewed forth in a national economy. The most common way this is done is to price out goods and services in a nation's currency. Note that this makes comparison of changes over time in output or income levels within an economy tricky. Not all prices change at the same rate. Housing might become more expensive but computers cheaper. Adjusting for changes in *the overall price level that copes with different movements in relative prices involves choosing an index number.*

Consider a time series on inflation or deflation (see Table A.4 in the Appendix). To construct a price index, say an index based at 1955 and running to the year 2000, one can price out the cost of a fixed market basket of commodities at the relative prices of the base, early, year (e.g. pricing out each good or service at 1955 prices); or one can use the cost of the same fixed market basket of commodities and services at a late, final, year (e.g. working with the relative prices of a market basket of good and services in the year 2000). The price index generated using early relative price weights is not the same as the price index generated by using late relative price weights. Deflating nominal income or output by price indices in order to generate real series on income or output depends on how the price index deflator is computed. Thus there is always an element of arbitrariness in the construction of so-called real series of output or income.

Even more daunting is the task of making international comparisons of output or income. Official exchange rates are often used. Unfortunately official exchange rates depend upon trade flows and central bank policies regarding money supply management. Most goods and services that an economy generates are not traded (for Japan see the export and import percentages given in Panel A of Table A.6). Dissatisfaction with exchange rates has led to the estimation of purchasing power parity for currencies (i.e. by pricing out a fixed commodity basket in different national markets in order to estimate the actual purchasing power of the currencies in terms of a standardized target level of consumption). Attempts to use purchasing power parity adjustments to estimate long-run growth in real income per capita in so-called international dollars underlies the estimates of real income per head made by Maddison and reported in Table A.1 of the Appendix.

National income accounting blossomed in the twentieth century as the costs of computation and the capacity of governments to estimate economic activity improved. World War I gave a strong fillip to the exercise because most belligerent countries generated income estimates as a byproduct of collecting income taxes imposed to pay for the war. In the United States, the National Bureau of Economic Research (N.B.E.R.) was given the responsibility and the means for making estimates for Congress. In the United Kingdom John Maynard Keynes, pioneer of the aggregate demand model for national income determination, teamed up with Richard Stone to produce estimates for the United Kingdom. By the later 1940s, national income and output measures were being produced for a variety of advanced western economies, leading to the United Nations adopting a United Nations System of National Accounts (UNSNA) in 1953.

Aggravating difficulties of taking into account problems involving scope, netness and valuation is the fact that national agencies mandated to generate national income and output estimates change their procedures from time to time. During the postwar period the Japanese government has jettisoned systems that it once relied on, adopting newer methodologies. For instance perusal of the Statistical Yearbook for Japan for the year 2006 (see pp. 84–87) should convince the reader that Japan's system of national accounting has undergone significant change over the last four decades.

In sum, national income accounting is a method that rests on a variety of pragmatic methodological assumptions involving scope, netness and valuation. It does not measure welfare or happiness. It is restricted to market activity, ignoring the unpaid activities of family workers or the unreported income generated by criminals and others who barter and truck in the underground economy. Making comparison over time or between countries is difficult and to some extent rests on arbitrary assumptions. Still, used intelligently, the method yields important yardsticks about the economic performance of countries.

Let us summarize where we are so far. We have shown that the arbitrage/invisible hand model is a useful benchmark for doing economic analysis but that real world economic forces limit its universality. These include the various second best principles that we have laid out, those governing prices and those governing quantity adjustment. All of these principles – including input/output and aggregate demand in so far as they concern output and demand at a particular point in time – deal with the static equilibrium of an economy, not with its growth. In the remainder of the section on markets we shall consider two growth oriented models, the Swann-Solow model and the Schumpeterian model. Finally we will look at the openness issue, namely the principles regarding the influence of trade on economic performance.

The most widely utilized growth model of mainstream neo-classical economics is the Swann-Solow model. Key to the logic of the model is the following list of principles: the assumption of diminishing returns to accumulation of capital, the presumed negative impact of population growth on the use of savings, and exogenous technological progress as the only alternative mechanism for increasing per capita income. The model is an aggregate level model, sharing with the Keynesian framework an emphasis on aggregate demand, especially the role of savings. It assumes that the economy is closed, all investment flows being funded by domestic savings.

The Swann-Solow model is laid out in more detail in the Appendix to this chapter. There it is shown that the assumption of diminishing returns to each factor of production – a standard assumption in neo-classical theory – is used to argue that the level of output per worker (labor productivity) rises as the amount of capital per labor increases but at a diminishing rate (the increments of output per worker decreasing with given increments of the capital/labor ratio as the level of the capital/labor ratio rises). The savings rate (savings as a percentage of income) and the rate of population growth are used together with the diminishing returns relationship assumed to tie capital per worker to worker productivity to the equilibrium level of capital per worker, population growth working to lower the equilibrium, the savings rate working to increase it. As for population the key distinction is between capital deepening (increasing the capital/labor ratio) and capital widening (tooling up entrants to the labor force with the already existing capital/labor ratio). The higher the rates of population growth, the greater the bite capital widening takes out of savings per worker, thereby decreasing the amount of savings per worker that can be put into accumulation of more capital per worker. The higher the savings rate, the greater the possibility for increasing the capital/labor ratio. Finally exogenous technological progress, not generated within the economy but rather by "manna-from-heaven" improvements due to inventive activity, raises the level of output per worker at any given level of the capital/labor ratio.

It should be noted that one important implication of the Swann-Solow model is that enterprises within an economy can bolster the level of income per worker and per person by securing technology from enterprises in other countries. Admittedly allowing for this possibility means abandoning the strict assumption that the economy under consideration is totally closed. But allowing for this source of growth does not mean assuming that the country depends on foreign bank loans or foreign direct investment by multinational corporations outside the country.

The Schumpeterian model is quite different from the Swann-Solow model. It is not based on the equilibrium concept; it is not based on the idea of exogenous technological change. In the Schumpeterian framework members of an elite – the entrepreneurs – innovate, exploiting inventions made by other individuals to bring new products to market, to set up new production processes. Schumpeter believed that innovations tended to come in clusters – for instance during the industrial revolution in the latter half of the eighteenth century and the beginning of the nineteenth century the low cost harnessing of steam power, the development of relatively low cost methods for manufacturing iron and steel plate and bar, and advances in the mechanization of cotton textile production combined with the innovation of the factory system – driving up prices for raw materials and labor, setting in motion a wave of imitation as other producers adopt the innovations made by the entrepreneurs. Eventually widespread creative destruction sets in, the producers failing to adapt to the innovations losing out in the marketplace as their relative costs rise, as their products, now viewed as hackneyed and old, experience a fall off in demand. During the creative destruction downswing, bankruptcies increase, prices fall; with instability ensuing, lenders are unwilling to fund new innovations and reluctant to try to sort out the wheat from the chaff in the arena of entrepreneurship, trying to distinguish between crackpot ideas and those solidly grounded. Even though new inventions are coming online, innovation slows to a crawl, entrepreneurs being unable to secure financial backing for new projects. Only after creative destruction has run its course, clearing off the economic playing field as the economically weak, the unprofitable, are driven out of business does the economy move back to a position of relative stability during which a new innovation cluster can take root, launching a new wave of innovation, imitation and creative destruction.

Basing his empirical analysis on the work of the Russian statistician Kondratieff, Schumpeter believed each innovation wave ran its course over a period of approximately fifty years. Writing in the late 1930s he thought the first wave was associated with the innovations involved in the industrial revolution in England, the second with the spread of steam power and its applications to transportation (for instance steamships and steam railroads) and the third with the harnessing of electricity and the internal combustion engine.

In all of the models that we have considered so far, economies have basically been treated as closed. How important is international trade in shaping the course of a country's development?

The standard neo-classical theory of trade rests on the idea of comparative advantage. The logic of comparative advantage can be grasped most easily if we consider the following circumstances: a busy lawyer who put her way through college doing gardening is trying to decide whether to hire a youth in her neighborhood to mow her lawn, mulch her roses, and prune her fruit trees. If the lawyer does the work herself, suppose she saves $200 a week by forgoing the hiring of one of the teenagers along his street. However, doing the work ties her up with gardening chores at a clip of about ten hours a week. If she works as a lawyer for the ten hours she would have to give to gardening she makes an additional $1000. Clearly from a narrow economic perspective – ignoring the fact that she might enjoy doing the gardening and she might be tired of carrying out the tasks involved in being a lawyer and ignoring taxes she might have to pay – she is better off hiring a teenager to do the gardening. This is true regardless of the fact that she might be more efficient at doing the gardening (given her background in the field) than the youth she hires.

In short, even though the lawyer has an absolute advantage over any teenager she might hire to do the gardening (and an absolute advantage in being a lawyer), she has a comparative advantage in being a lawyer. The principle of comparative advantage in international trade follows this line of reasoning. A country should produce those things in which it has a comparative advantage, importing those goods and services which it has a comparative relative disadvantage producing.

One of the most important implications of the comparative advantage paradigm is a tendency for relative prices for commodities and services to converge globally. The basic idea is arbitrage. Exporting what you have a comparative advantage in – hence what is supplied relatively cheaply in your home market – causes the price of the exported item to rise in price in your domestic market. In the importing market the opposite occurs. Supply of the commodity that the country has a comparative disadvantage in producing (and that hence is relatively expensive) expands, driving down relative prices. If all goods and services are traded freely and without impediment all relative prices should converge to a common price structure. This is called the law of one price.

Comparative advantage is all fine and well as a pure static theory. However, as a practical matter, following it does tend to discourage countries from advancing

Law of one price

The law of one price refers to the tendency of relative prices in different jurisdictions to converge toward a common set of relative prices. The idea is that trade between any two jurisdictions – say between Japan and the United States – changes the relative supplies of different types of goods in the two national markets and therefore their relative prices.

For instance, consider the case where rice and automobiles are freely traded between Japan and the United States. Reflecting the relative availability of irrigated land (e.g. in the state of California), rice can be produced cheaply in the United States relative to automobiles. In Japan the reverse holds. When Japanese importers purchase rice from farmers in the United States, they increase the supply of rice in Japan, thus lowering the price of rice relative to cars there. Shipping Japanese manufactured cars to the United States has a parallel impact. It reduces the supply of cars in Japan, thus raising car prices in Japan relative to rice. It increases the supply of cars in the United States, exporting cars to the American market lowers the American prices for cars relative to rice. In this way trade between the two countries forces relative prices to converge.

Since most goods and services produced and consumed in countries with large domestic markets are not traded, there is a limit to how far relative price convergence can proceed in practice. Moreover, most goods are not traded free of regulation and duty. In addition transportation costs must be factored in considering the strength of the law of one price. For relatively small countries – Taiwan, Singapore, and Sweden – there is much to be said in favor of the law of one price. For Japan and the United States the logic of the convergence argument is less compelling.

It is useful to formulate the law of one price in terms of the relationship between the real exchange rate and the nominal exchange rate. Explaining this involves going through a few definitions and examples.

Let the market exchange rate between countries be denoted by "exAB" where B is the reference country, meaning that one unit of B's currency buys "exAB" units of A's currency. For instance if B is the United States and A is Japan and the exchange rate is 200, then one US dollar purchases 200 yen. Now let "repAB" be the price of a particular good priced out in market B relative to the price of the good in market A (repAB = pB/pA where pA is the price of the good in market A and pB is the price of the good in market B). The real exchange rate (rexAB) is

$$rexAB = (exAB) * (repAB). \qquad (1.1)$$

For instance if the good is priced at 400 yen in Japan and at 2$ in the United States, the rexAB = 1; if the good is priced at 600 yen in Japan and *at 2$ in the United States, the rexAB = 2/3; if the good is priced at 200 yen in Japan and at 2$ in the United States, the rexAB = 2.*

With these definitions we can formulate the law of one price as follows. The law of one price involving two countries A and B holds when the real exchange rate between the two countries is unity, one, that is

$$rexAB = 1. \qquad\qquad (1.2)$$

The logic of this statement can be illustrated using the principle of arbitrage and the numerical example considered above. If a musical recording, a compact disk, is priced at 6000 yen in Japan and at $20 in the United States and the exchange rate is $1 = 200 yen (that is the real exchange rate is 2/3), it pays Japanese importers to purchase the disks in the United States, bringing them to Japan for sale to consumers. If this process occurs on a grand scale for a wide range of goods, Japanese demand for dollars to secure goods in the United States increases, driving the yen down and the dollar up, thereby pushing the real exchange rate in the direction of unity. Alternatively, suppose the exchange rate is $1 = 200 yen, the compact disk is priced at 200 yen in Japan and at $2 in the United States (i.e. the real exchange rate is 2). How will arbitrage impact the nominal and real exchange rates?

As a completely theoretical proposition, the law of one price simply restates the arbitrage principle extended into the dimension of international trade. In practice, it only describes a tendency. In the real world, product labeling in national languages, imposition of product standards by governments, tariffs and duties, and transportation costs create friction that prevents the law of one price from operating. Moreover, bilateral trade involves many commodities, each having a different real exchange rate. The tendency of trade to establish a common real price level for copiers is quite likely to drive real exchange rates to a different level than does trade in apples and soybeans. Finally, as noted earlier, in large national markets most commodities produced and consumed are produced domestically.

This said, the real exchange concept, grounded in the arbitrage principle, contains useful insights that can help illuminate why the impact of movements in nominal exchange rates on bilateral trade flows is constrained by movements in price levels of the countries carrying on the bilateral trade.

Consider the impact of the appreciation of the yen relative to the US dollar between 1972 and 1996. In 1972 the dollar was worth 308 yen; in 1984 it was worth 231 yen; and in 1996 it was worth 106 yen. According to the theory of relative price, because Japanese goods were becoming more expensive relative to American goods, the demand for Japanese goods in the United States should have consistently fallen over this period and the demand for American goods in Japan should have steadily increased. True, measuring the bilateral trade in quantity terms it is apparent that this did happen. However, the impact of readjustments in the exchange rate was counteracted by differential rates of inflation in the two markets.

Using the consumer price index, for instance, we see that prices went up between 1972 and 1984 by a multiple of 2.38 in Japan and by a multiple of 2.46 in the United States; and between 1984 and 1996 by a multiple of 1.33 in Japan and by 1.49 in the United States. Since inflation was higher in the United States than in Japan, the real exchange rate moved less than the nominal exchange rate. Higher inflation in the United States worked against the rise in the yen relative to the dollar: the struggle of Japanese producers of automobiles, televisions and computer chips to stay competitive in the American market was aided by the tendency of prices to escalate faster in the United States than in Japan.

up the economic ladder, achieving development through import substitution, replacing goods manufactured in foreign lands with those produced domestically. For instance according to the logic of comparative advantage, an agricultural country should remain agricultural, trading its grain, its meat, and its fruits, for foreign clothing, machinery and consumer durables.

Economic nationalists usually reject static comparative advantage, arguing that dynamic comparative advantage offers an alternative that is better suited to national economic development. Dynamic comparative advantage implies changing comparative advantage, a country moving up the economic ladder by import substitution, beginning with relatively labor-intensive industries then moving on to increasingly sophisticated industries, at each step substituting domestic production for imports, then promoting exports in the new field so that the former import item becomes an export item.

An example would be starting out with cotton textiles, moving on to iron and steel, then to machinery, to shipbuilding, and eventually arriving at consumer durables like automobiles and technology intensive products like personal computers, each step of the process involving moving from net importing to exporting in successive stages of the process. This is known as the product cycle. Ultimately, a country that has moved up the economic ladder forgoes its comparative advantage in industries that it earlier on established a net export position in – say textiles – switching back from a net export position to a net import position in the industry. Thus the complete product cycle goes from net importing to import substitution to net exporting and finally ends up at net importing.

Another model of trade involves the gravity principle according to which countries trade in accordance with the relative size of their economies, their incomes per capita (that determine the structure of their demand) and the distance between them. As Feenstra (2004) shows this type of trade often emerges because of monopolistic competition within national markets. Country identification becomes important: Germany becomes famous for well machined luxury automobiles; Japan for building quality into its automobiles and trucks; the United States for creating technologically sophisticated computer software and motion pictures that exploit novel special affects. Consumers desire diversity. Because the few companies within their own country offer a limited menu of choices within a particular product line – say automobiles, say computer monitors, say television programs – consumers seek out options in foreign markets. In this way scale economies that engender monopolistic competition produce the intra-industry international trade associated with the gravity equation.

An important addendum to the argument made about monopolistic competition driving intra-industry international trade concerns the way business groups, like the *zaibatsu* and *keiretsu* groups that we shall be discussing later on this volume (see, for instance, Chapters 3, 6, and 8) create brand loyalty as a device for exercising market power. By joining a group a company acquires a brand name – say the identifying logo used by companies in the Sumitomo or Mitsui or Mitsubishi *keiretsu* – that may help it gain traction, credibility, in a new burgeoning market. Moreover, it may be able to purchase its inputs from other members of the group at below market price.

One other aspect of international trade deserves mentioning here. Trade can be a factor shaping technological borrowing. Suppose the enterprises within a country pursue a strategy of reverse engineering as a device for learning about foreign production techniques. The producers import products from abroad in order to carry this out. They may well decide to do so because they realize imports from abroad in a particular sector have established a strong niche in the domestic market, thereby spurring these producers on to attempt import substitution. Alternatively, trying to export to another country may encourage exporting companies to upgrade their product quality to meet standards imposed abroad, thereby improving their output marketed both at home and abroad. Because trade widens the sphere of competition a firm operates in, it acts as a prod, preventing firms from resting too long on their laurels, keeping them hungry, lean and mean.

This completes our survey of the principles governing markets.[2] Our next topic is a brief survey of the possible influence of values, norms and ideologies on economic development.

Values, norms and ideologies

Our focus here is on sociological theories. It begins with the notion of social class and class consciousness elaborated by Marx, turning to Max Weber-inspired theories – originally developed as a critique of Marx's approach – afterward. No attempt is made to be comprehensive. Rather our focus is on discussing those theories that seem to crop up frequently in discussing Japanese economic development.

Marx was one of the great classical economists, wedding a labor theory of value to a theory of social class, the basis for class structure rooted in the technologies governing economic production and military affairs. In Marxist analysis the attitudes – the consciousness – of social classes play a pivotal role in shaping historical evolution, history moving through a regular set of stages, from pre-feudalism to feudalism, from feudalism to capitalism, from capitalism to socialism, and from socialism to communism. Our focus here is on the transition from feudalism to capitalism because this has garnered the greatest amount of interest in the Japanese literature, Marxist stage theory dominating many of the economics and sociology departments in Japanese universities during the period between 1920 and the 1970s, and still occupying an important, albeit diminished, role in the Japanese higher educational system.

In analyzing the transition from feudalism to capitalism, Marx relied heavily on historical accounts of the process in England and continental Western Europe, believing that the transition Europe had gone through represented a paradigm, perhaps universal, for other countries and regions. His key concepts were the rate of exploitation, the primitive accumulation of capital, and the industrial reserve army of labor.

To simplify for the purposes of brevity, under early forms of feudalism there were two main classes, peasants and lords. Lords controlled manorial estates that were divided up in the lord's portion (the demesne), the portion that the peasantry farmed as a collective group (the open fields, usually farmed on a three year rotation cycle, the portion set aside for a spring crop becoming the portion utilized for a winter crop in the next year and for fallowing in the third year, returning to use as the spring crop field in the fourth year) and the commons open to everyone. Peasants were required to provide labor services on the demesne, perhaps helping to make the lord's wine, perhaps even providing domestic service. The rate at which labor services were extracted as a portion of the total labor time the peasants worked is the rate of exploitation. For instance if a typical peasant worked three hours on the demesne for every seven hours he or she worked on the open and common fields, the rate of exploitation would be thirty percent.

In this manorial feudal economy dominated by non-monetized exchange, and by concepts of fealty and obligation, emerged a nascent commercial sector. It emerged because manorial estates did tend to produce a surplus, the surplus largely accruing to the lord of the manor and his immediate retainers. With this surplus the lord purchased luxury goods – swords, armor, paintings, tapestries, silk clothing – filling their castles and estates with fineries that enhanced their prestige, their social standing. The lords and their retainers purchased these from cities, the goods worked up by members of artisan guilds who sold them to merchants who then sold them to the lords on the estates.

Over time the merchants acquired more and more economic power, exploiting their middleman status – small oligarchies of merchants tended to control city governments – to build up their assets. At the same time, the lords saw their relative economic position decline as they piled up debts to the merchants to meet their voracious demands for city produced luxuries. Over time the merchants used their enhanced economic prowess to gobble up estates, and to set up workshops where they employed skilled craftsmen. While not capitalists in the modern sense of the word, the merchants did have a strong commercial orientation, preferring to rent out land rather than being in a hierarchical position in a feudal exchange of labor services for military protection, preferring to hire workers rather than working with hierarchical guilds. As merchants acquired an increasingly strong hand in the rural economy, they commercialized the open fields, promoting enclosure of land which led to the carving out of individual farms from the fields once tilled and cultivated collectively, breaking up the commons as well. Since marginal squatters often occupied part of the commons, they were driven off the land as a result of enclosure, becoming a "reserve army of labor" for the workshops and factories being created by the merchants in cities. This process is known as the primitive accumulation of capital in Marxist theory.

As the bourgeoisie – the merchant class – gained increasing economic prowess relative to the feudal lords, it felt its economic interests were potentially threatened by the continuation of a political system that put overwhelming power in the hands of feudal lords who could repudiate their debts through a political process. Their consciousness – rooted in their class interest – was inconsistent with the ideology justifying feudalism. Thus the merchants pushed for political change, eventually promoting revolutions. According to the logic of this theory, the long parliament in mid-seventeenth-century England and the French Revolution in late eighteenth-century France are examples of violent political transformations brought on by the primitive accumulation of capital. As we shall see in Chapter 2, Japanese Marxists argue that the Meiji Restoration was also a revolution of a sort, ushering in capitalism.

Once the political transformation is complete, the stage of capitalism ensues. Under capitalism workers are paid a culturally defined subsistence wage just sufficient for their reproduction (for supporting themselves and a family), the remainder of output per worker going into profits accruing to the owner of capital whose historical role is to accumulate more capital. Exploitation under capitalism is the rate at which capitalists extract a surplus from the workers.

Marx made a crucial distinction between fixed and variable capital in elaborating his theory of the dynamics of capitalism. Variable capital is raw materials and intermediate goods used in higher stages of production, for example raw cotton in a cotton textile mill. The more variable capital, the greater the demand for labor, the more workers hired. Fixed capital is built up labor power, machines produced by workers substituting for workers themselves, for instance power looms and mechanical spinning machines substituting for factory workers. A compositional shift from variable to fixed capital implies a fall off in the demand for workers, potentially leading to an industrial crisis with unemployment. In this case automation and mechanization generate the unemployment.

Marx argued that the competition between capitalists would yield a compositional shift in the capital stock away from variable and toward fixed capital. He called this the organic composition of capital. He believed that the rate of profit under capitalism would be driven down as the organic composition of capital proceeded – unless technological progress or other forces exogenous to a country such as foreign trade could overcome this tendency – leading to a crisis in capitalism. Dismayed by being exploited and potentially unemployed under capitalism, the class consciousness of workers becomes the ideological linchpin of another revolutionary political change, capitalism giving way to socialism as the workers take power into their own hands, creating a political system consistent with their own working class interests.

In Marxist theory, the material world is the substructure, the norms and ideologies of social classes erected on top of this structure. Ideas are secondary, emerging out of materially rooted class relationships. The famous German sociologist Max Weber turned Marxism on its head, arguing that ideas and norms constitute the truest substructure, the material world adjusting to them. In particular he argued that Protestantism emerging in Europe in the twilight of the medieval period provided a new set of ideas and norms that justified capitalism, undermining Catholic ideas hostile to usury, accumulation of capital and rational calculation systematically relating ends and means. Ideas produced capitalist rationality that in turn changed the material nature of the world not vice-versa. Ultimately it is a web of beliefs that motivates people to act in the material world.

Weber noted that the hierarchical obligations outlined by Confucianism might also motivate people to perform well in the economic realm. Under Confucianism there are no absolute ethical precepts as there are under Protestantism, no black and white rules about what is required of the individual who is fortunate enough to earn a place in heaven. Rather society is best arranged, harmony best established, if the populace is virtuous.

Confucius listed a number of virtues that he thought would best contribute to social harmony. Key virtues in his system of thought were benevolence, loyalty, justice, ceremony, knowledge and faith. He believed that the virtues were best cultivated if they were based on the natural affection between parents and children, brothers and sisters, prevailing within families. Believing benevolence was the most important of the virtues, he believed that those who could feel a natural affection for humanity as a whole or at least for his or her countryman would be the best rulers for society. In the Chinese interpretation of Confucianism the mandate of heaven could be lost if the rulers lost the capacity to be benevolent. In this case a change of dynasty was justified. Indeed, in Chinese history changes of dynasty, while not frequent, did occur.

The Japanese did import Confucianism from China. But eventually, isolated themselves from China, they developed the doctrine along lines different from the Chinese. In particular, loyalty, not benevolence, emerged as the key tenet of Japanese Confucianism. Those governed were expected to be loyal to their ruler, in theory the emperor of Japan, although other individuals, like the *shogun* during the Tokugawa period, might stand between the emperor and the populace, actually making and executing policy. The key point is that loyalty could not be squandered by the emperor because the benevolence given by the emperor was inadequate, the mandate of heaven could not be lost.

This does not mean that benevolence was unimportant in the Japanese version of Confucianism. What it does mean is that a restive and unhappy segment of the body politic could express its dissatisfaction, could carry out demonstrations requesting benevolence, but it could not be disloyal even if the rulers were unable or unwilling to meet their demands.[3]

It can be seen that the Confucian view of the world gave primacy to politics, to arranging power relations so that society was relatively harmonious, rejecting absolute codes rooted in theories of good and evil, right and wrong as guides for social behavior. Rather networks of obligations governing the relationships between superior and inferior – between parents and children, between eldest son and younger sons, between husband and wife, between landlord and tenant, between owner of an enterprise and employees – were designed to regulate society so that harmony prevailed. These obligations were based on commitments running two ways, the inferior party being loyal to the superior party who in turn showers benevolence on the inferior in the relationship.

Economists often describe the resulting relationships as ones of gift exchange, the inferior working hard and loyally in anticipation that the superior is prepared to reciprocate, the employer arranging the marriage of the employee, or assisting him with a special family allowance if his or her parents fall on hard times. The benevolence granted the inferior is known as *on* in Japanese; its reciprocated service or good offered to the superior by the inferior party *hōon*. Loyalty and hard work are exchanged for acts of benevolence. Emotions appropriate to a ritualized formalized gift exchange underlie the relationships of landlords and tenants, factory managers and rank and file workers, politicians and their underlings, labor bosses and their subordinates.

An alternative non-Confucian view of how social norms and values condition Japanese behavior is due to Chie (1970). Chie rejects the Confucian notion that family ties, especially blood ties, explain why loyalty and hierarchy are important in Japan. She notes that the health of corporate entities created by families – for example farms in villages, shops managed by households – often takes precedent over maintaining harmony with the bloodline. As we shall see in Chapter 2, in-adoption of males as son-in-laws was not uncommon in prewar Japan. In some cases, if a biological son was incompetent or lazy, a household head was prepared to pass over that son in arranging for the passing down of the assets to the next generation, making the fictive in-adopted son the primary heir. As an alternative to Confucian hierarchy and loyalty Chie argues that frame is fundamental to Japanese society.

By frame Chie means a group – a corporation, a village, a faction within a political party – usually relatively small, to which an individual belongs. She differentiates between the frame for, and the attributes of, individuals, attributes being characteristics like gender, age, family of origin, or occupation. For instance a male electrical engineer employed by Hitachi has the attributes of a male engineering professional, perhaps even belonging to an electrical engineering professional association but is operating within the frame of Hitachi. In her view frame trumps attribute in Japan. Is this because Japan at one time consisted almost entirely of rice cultivating villages for which collective management of water, the opening and closing of irrigation lines was crucial to everyone in the village getting access to one of the key resources in rice farming? Did the necessity of getting along with other villagers make frame fundamental? Appealing as this thesis is, it does not explain why frame did not develop to the same degree in China and in those parts of India and Southeast Asia where rice farming is widespread.

While not denying that hierarchy occurs in the relationships of Japanese arising from attributes, for instance in professional societies, Chie argues that hierarchy is particularly important in frame settings especially in the relatively small groups that she believes dominate in Japanese society. In short she sees frame and hierarchy in small groups as a defining characteristic of Japan, using her argument to explain why all of the political parties in Japan tend to be factionalized. Along similar lines, one can argue that larger groups, for instance corporations and government bureaucracies, hiring thousands of workers, have to fight the tendency of small groups spinning out of control, adopting a strategy of constantly rotating employees around from group to group, thereby diluting loyalty to one particular unit with the enterprise or agency.

A third type of norm or value that is often put forth as key to Japanese society is homogeneity of tastes, preferences, that is culture. This argument usually assumes that the way children are socialized in Japan tends to be remarkably similar everywhere in part because until fairly recently the number of immigrants coming into Japan from diverse countries was fairly low. Indeed, the difficulty experienced by Japanese children who leave Japan when they are young, typically to accompany their parents who are going abroad to work or study, when reintegrating into Japanese society is usually offered as proof that being Japanese is well defined and is a byproduct of being reared within the country, the influence of school, neighborhood and family being overwhelming.

An extreme version of this homogeneity view is *nihonjinron*, the theory of the Japanese. Proponents of *nihonjinron* often make claims about the uniqueness of the Japanese – learning language on the side of the brain opposite to the side used by other nationalities in learning language, that their stomachs differ in size from those of other nationalities – that border on racism. Indeed, the kinds of arguments that eugenicists used to make about the crucial role of genetic transmission in perpetuating national, ethnic, and social class intelligence levels during the late nineteenth and early twentieth centuries in the United States, England, Germany and France are frequently echoed by authors writing in the *nihonjinron* tradition.

It should be emphasized that the homogeneity interpretation is predicated on the existence of a strong undercurrent of collectivism or nationalism in Japan. It would also seem to be somewhat inconsistent with the idea that small frames dominate the Japanese social scene. We will return to the nationalism theme shortly when we consider constraints.[4]

It should be noted that criticism of the Confucian, frame and homogeneity models of Japan crops up in much of the Western social science writing on Japan. It is pointed out that the theories tend to be based upon stereotypes that do not seem to apply to particular individuals, often the acquaintances or spouses of the writers. Or it is noted that strong-willed individuals in Japan are more common than is sometimes believed, finding ways of masking their emotions so that they appear to be less self directed and self seeking than they are. Indeed, some writers even turn to stereotypic concepts to counter the stereotypes, noting that there are two often cited Japanese words – the term *honne* signifying a real deeply rooted reality that is covered up or disguised by a *tatemae* indicating something standing in front – revealing the tendency of Japanese to hide their real feelings behind masks. A façade of Confucianism could be consistent with a reality of rampant individualism.

In closing out this discussion of norms, values and ideologies it is important to note that some of these arguments do have a bearing on how markets might work in Japan. For instance if Japanese society is extremely homogeneous transactions costs to negotiating informal non-written contracts – between employers and employees, between assemblers like Toyota Motors and its sub-contractors – may be low. Lawyers are not needed to the same degree as they are in the West to draw up and guarantee enforcement of agreements reached through talk, body language and profuse bowing. If Japan's homogeneous information may flow more freely than it does in other countries, reducing the friction to market clearing due to the existence of information asymmetry. If Confucian ideals shape the way enterprises are organized, both employers and the individuals they are seeking to recruit may share a similar value on the importance of forming a long-term relationship, the recruit expecting to stay with the enterprise until a mandated retirement age is reached. If Confucian ideals are important, we would not be surprised to observe paternalistic practices in Japanese companies, employers providing company housing and generous health care plans that look out after the wellbeing of employee, immediate family, and aged parents as well. These practices could be viewed as conscious attempts on the part of management to bind workers to their enterprises. Alternatively, they can be viewed as byproducts of deeply entrenched social values and norms, reflecting Confucianism, frame or homogeneity.

The discussion of homogeneity and nationalism is on the borderline between norms, values and ideologies and constraints. Let us explore the issue of constraints in greater detail now.

Constraints

By constraints I have in mind limits on the way markets operate imposed by politics and policies on the one hand, and by geography on the other. Let us start with geography.

The notion that Japanese geography conditions Japanese economic behavior typically boils down to four propositions. First Japan lacks raw materials. Therefore exports must subsidize imports. Naturally a political leadership concerned with national security is inclined to be neo-mercantilist, encouraging firms to export by carefully crafting incentives to seek out foreign markets. Second the land area of Japan is limited – especially the land area that can be inhabited by residential populations because Japan is mostly mountainous, the proportion of land with a slope of at least fifteen degrees being about 75 percent of the land area – driving up the relative price of land compared to the price of other assets. Third Japan is a rice producing nation because it is situated on the periphery of monsoon Asia, swept by the great rainstorms of early summer originating from the southwest of the archipelago, and by the mighty deluges of Siberian monsoons during the winter. Fourth Japan lies on the ring of fire, being heavily volcanic, thus a victim of frequent earthquakes, some, like the 1923 earthquake on the Kantō plain being especially destructive, rendering the Japanese unusually risk averse, addicted to long-run planning aimed at giving them a feeling of security in an often insecure world.

As for natural resources it must be pointed out that Japan is hardly devoid of all natural resources. In particular, Japan being about 75 percent mountainous, about the same percentage of its land area is in forest, mainly broadleaf, coniferous and mixed forests being intermingled. Of course the country could have been denuded of its forests, as much of England, parts of Sweden at one time, and swathes of China have been. For reasons that we shall discuss in Chapter 2, fear of soil erosion, and fear of losing timber for building the housing and structures of its many cities during its early modern period, encouraged Japanese rulers to limit logging and to plan for forest rejuvenation. As well, the fact that much of the soil was laced with volcanic ash probably helped the forests grow back reasonably quickly. Japan also enjoyed and to some extent still enjoys some domestic sources of coal, particularly in its northern island of Hokkaidō and in the island of Kyūshū just south of the main island of Honshū.

This said Japan imports most of the raw materials it uses. Figures for 1971 bear this out. In that year Japanese enterprises imported all of the lead ore, bauxite, wool and cotton that they used. And they imported over 99 percent of the crude petroleum, and iron ore that they consumed. For manganese ore the figure was 84 percent; for zinc ore almost 79 percent; and for coal about 58 percent. This is not resource abundance.

Crowding into densely packed conurbations reflecting a lack of flat plains is a reality of Japan. The nation is an island archipelago consisting of four main islands running in a chain from northeast (Hokkaidō) to the main island of Honshū, the smallest of the four Shikoku (lying off the main island becoming the eastern perimeter of the Inland Sea whose western perimeter is Osaka, Kobe and Wakayama prefecture on Honshū) and finally Kyūshū to the south. There are three main areas of the main island on which the six largest cities of Japan are located. The Kantō plain, gateway to the northeast, is the location for Tokyo, Yokohama and the other conurbations surrounding Tokyo Bay. In the Nobi plain, fronting out toward the Pacific in central Honshū, Nagoya is one of the great centers of the land, Toyota City being not too far from the great metropolis. In the Kinai region, home to the ancient capitals of Nara and Kyoto, lie Osaka and Kobe, the mighty Yodo River running through Osaka as it empties out in the Inland Sea. The degree of crowding should not be exaggerated. Very large numbers of Japanese live in small cities nestled in mountains or lying along train lines that bring them in and out of bedroom satellite cities surrounding the six biggest cities of Japan. As a perusal of Table A.2 reveals, the actual proportion of the population living in the six big cities has fallen short of 20 percent throughout the period after World War II.

Finally the importance of the monsoon rains and volcanic activity should not be underestimated. The threat of tsunamis that could overwhelm low lying sections of Tokyo, for instance, is a real danger whose enormity can not be discounted.

A second type of geographic constraint mixes politics and geographic position: geopolitics. The term "geopolitics" refers to the fact that the countries that are close to one another tend to be either potential allies or potential enemies. Many of the wars fought in history are between countries that are contiguous or nearly contiguous, in part because a large proportion of wars are fought over disputed territory. Thus international diplomacy is intimately connected to geographic location. Japan lies off the Eurasian landmass, facing China, Korea and Russia, lying not too far north of the island of Taiwan. It is also an island nation in the Pacific Ocean. Naturally this encourages its military to concentrate on building a navy and coast guard. As a Pacific naval power Japan's navy has measured itself up against two of the other great navies of the twentieth century, those of the United States and the United Kingdom. China has also built up its naval forces substantially since the early1990s.

Given these geopolitical issues, it should not completely surprise us that Japan's military destiny has been intertwined with the military destinies of the other large powers having geopolitical interests in the region. Between 1890 and 1945, Japan fought wars with China, Russia, the United States and the United Kingdom, colonizing Korea and Taiwan during the heyday of its period of empire building.

Nationalism plays a role in shaping the ability of political leaders to successfully negotiate treaties and agreements in the international sphere. Negotiation is all about give and take, reaching common ground through fashioning mutually acceptable compromise, trading off some goals to secure other goals. But diplomats have to come home and sell the fruits of their efforts to their domestic audiences. Xenophobic nationalism may make this very difficult, effectively tying the hands of diplomats. Geopolitical calculations may fall afoul of the passions of unrestrained nationalism.

Because trade follows diplomacy and empire building, geopolitical concerns have played an important role in shaping Japanese trade. For instance, Japanese enterprises directed sizeable chunks of their trade to Japan's empire during the period 1920–45, integrating Korea and Taiwan into its economy both as suppliers of rice, sugar and other foodstuffs and as locales for setting up overseas enterprises and subsidiaries. Again, after 1950, allied with the United States and operating under the shelter of American military prowess, Japanese companies directed sizeable shares of their exports to the United States market, a fact that eventually created considerable friction between itself and its ally.

International political constraints shape trade. Domestic political constraints shape domestic markets. From the theory of the second best, we know that there is a place for government intervention, whether it be in the realm of short-run stabilization (policy operating through monetary and fiscal avenues); or in providing externalities such as physical, financial or human capital enhancing infrastructure; or in regulating industries that pollute the air or the ocean; or in helping to coordinate firms in an industry through the monitoring of cartels or subsidizing certain designated industries through proactive industrial policy.

So policies matter in constraining the way markets operate. So do politics. Politics refer to those who make decisions and why they make the decisions they do. Do bureaucrats make economic policies arriving at them in relatively insulated circumstances, able to coolly study practices in other states, free of the pressures of an aroused electorate? Or are political priorities largely shaped by the voters, politicians in the Diet crafting legislation in response to pressures from their constituencies? Which state of affairs prevails matters since a model of Japanese policy making rooted in the political calculus of elected officials is one emphasizing pork barrel politics and the demands voiced by special interest groups who lobby the politicians. The bureaucratic insulation model, however, assumes an elite corps of bureaucrats can carefully study a variety of options, weighing them behind closed doors before rolling out proposals.[5]

Politics involve power: who has it and how they exercise it. On the question of who actually exercises power in Japan there is considerable and contentious debate. Does big business actually wield power in Japan? How powerful are the elite bureaucrats who head up the most important bureaus with the ministries? Van Wolferen (1989) suggests that power is actually widely distributed in Japan making it very difficult for an outsider negotiating with Japanese government officials to figure out who is actually in charge and can make binding deals. Holders of power often mask their influence, keeping a low profile lest they incite criticism from other power holders. Van Wolferen (1989) explains why this is the case in Japan by evoking the tradition of Confucianism, a tradition making politics and hence the securing of power of prime importance to those who carry on business on a grand scale.

Politics aside, policies affecting an economy can be readily classified. Table 1.1 provides a framework. The standard Keynesian-type policies are aimed at stabilizing an economy. They work through monetary and fiscal channels. Transfer policies involve redistributing income. Because they involve fiscal outlays they are sometimes included under the fiscal rubric. Note that sales taxes and duties on imports are classified under the fiscal rubric and standards that implicitly or explicitly keep out imports are classified under the regulation rubric. For the purposes of this book facilitating/coordinating policies are especially important. You will encounter them many times in the remainder of this text. To some authorities on Japanese economic policy making they are the most innovative, and important, of all of the policies shaping Japan's long-run economic development.

Competing or complementary paradigms?

We have reviewed the bare bones of three seemingly different paradigms for explaining Japanese economic development: those based upon market equilibrium

Table 1.1 Government involvement in economic affairs: modes and examples

Mode	Examples
Command and control	Military organizations relying on hierarchy and direct commands; central planning in which bureaucrats set production targets and quotas for farms and manufacturing firms
Stabilization – fiscal	Government spending for goods and services and for capital formation; setting taxation levels; collecting revenue from tariffs and user fees
Stabilization – monetary	Money supply management in which a central bank serves as a lender of last resort for other public or private banks; reliance on reserve requirements for, and/or the setting of discount rates offered to, member banks, open market operations involving the sale or purchase of bonds, and informal pressure; participation in the international economic order, for instance by adhering to the gold standard
Transfer	Welfare benefits, social insurance
Regulation	Setting standards for, and monitoring activities in, labor and capital markets; setting quotas on imports or quality standards for products consumed domestically
Facilitating/Coordination	Mediation and arbitration; industrial policy (monitoring cartels, subsidizing selected sectors or firms); promulgating rules for the enforcement of patents and the diffusion of technology; working together with firms in developing infrastructure, assisting firms in negotiating technology licensing agreements

principles, those based on norms and values, and those based on political and geographic constraints. Within each category we have considered a number of variants, noting that there are different schools of thought within fields. Is it possible to see these approaches as complementary, or are they truly competitive with one another, only one offering an accurate picture of what happened?

The view of this author – and I hope the view of the student who has absorbed this text – is that the paradigms are complementary, over-determination taking place in the economic and social realm. For instance, consider the possible inter-action of norms, policies and market forces in the fashioning of a family based welfare policy in Japan. We can explain why this occurred by evoking Confucianism, by evoking the market, and by evoking the nature of policy. In fact the emergence of the system is best seen as coming from all three forces, the existence of outcomes in one realm reinforcing the behavior observed in the other realms. As a result social scientists from different disciplines could offer equally valid but divergent interpretations of the phenomenon.

In the arena of markets big firms compete against small firms for the best workers. To secure the most gifted, the big firms pay a premium, attempting to bind the valued worker they are recruiting to the firm by paying high wages, and by offering extra side benefits designed to appeal to the family oriented values of Confucianism, such as lodging in company housing; or like generous health care benefits for the employee, his or her family including aged parents. Small firms offer something else: the emotional interaction that persons socialized in small frames seek, the opportunity to become the boss over time, learning by emulating the master so to speak. Thus family oriented paternalism developed out of the market as conditioned by the preferences of employees about the workplace.

A government strapped for resources, and a government wishing to encourage the expansion of big business (politicians receiving contributions for major corporations for instance) observes that the development of corporate paternalism in the private sector means less political pressure is being put on its coffers. So it promotes the further diffusion of paternalism within the corporate sector by drawing up tax policies that give an added incentive for firms to engage in this kind of practice, making the approach all the more lucrative. An alternative scenario sees the government putting forward the tax policies at the outset, trusting that firms will follow the incentives given and adopt family oriented corporate paternalism. What is the chicken? What is the egg?

The mutual interaction and mutual reinforcement of behavior in one realm by behavior in the other realms is the point that I wish to hammer home here. Social scientists coming from different disciplines, with different intellectual backgrounds, could honestly differ on what is the cause of the phenomenon, whether it arises from politics, from markets, or from norms. Each discipline offers some truth. Each discipline offers an incomplete explanation. As in Akutagawa's bleak tale, what we bring to the table influences what we take away from the table.

Key terms and concepts in Chapter 1

Mercantilism	Tragedy of the commons
Iron law of wages	**IS/LM** model
Marshallian scissors of supply and demand	Swann-Solow model
	Schumpeterian model
Aggregate demand analysis	Comparative advantage
Arbitrage principle	Gravity model of international trade
Cost/benefit principle	Labor theory of value
Information asymmetry	Marxist theory of social class
Scale economies	Confucianism
Barriers to entry	Frame
Oligopoly	*Nihonjinron*
Monopolistic competition	Geopolitics
Externalities	Pork barrel politics

Appendix to Chapter 1: Economic models

Economists work with stylized models, usually couched in the language of mathematics, often employing graphs to make points. Arguing in terms of this language gives precision to discussions. However, it can erect barriers to understanding, precluding mastery of economic arguments by persons not tooled up in mathematics. Recognizing this, I have tried to present arguments verbally in the main text of this chapter. However, I encourage the student to master slightly more formal presentations of some of the arguments presented earlier. I go through the elementary graphics of four models: the arbitrage/invisible hand model; the information asymmetry model as applied to labor markets; the **IS/LM** model with and without variable prices; and the Swann-Solow growth model.

In Figures 1.2A and 1.2B we present the elements of the invisible hand/ arbitrage models. In both graphs the demand curve slopes down – price being on the vertical axis and quantity supplied and demanded on the horizontal axis – reflecting the fact that there are more consumers willing to expend their scarce resources on cheaper products and services. The supply curve slopes the other way, producers prepared to put more resources, devote more labor and capital as a group, to making and marketing the good or service provided it commands a higher price on the market.

Suppose demand shifts out, increasing at every level of price. This could be because the country abandons autarky and begins to export abroad, or because incomes go up, or because a particular product becomes socially fashionable and faddish. As you can see from Figure 1.2A, this causes the price of the good – relative to the price of other goods – to rise. Alternatively, suppose supply expands outward, say because the country opens itself up to imports from abroad. This is the situation contemplated in Figure 1.2B. Supply shifting to the right drives down the price of the good.

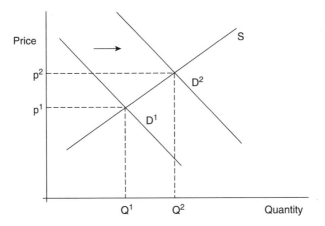

Figure 1.2A The arbitrage principle: demand shift dynamics.

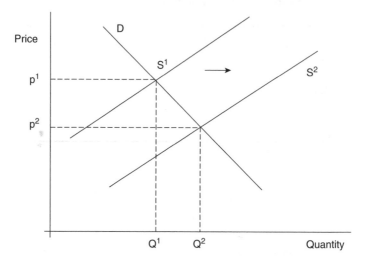

Figure 1.2B The arbitrage principle: supply shift dynamics.

The student should work out what happens when demand shifts in, and what happens when supply shifts in. What happens if both curves shift? Why might it be difficult to explain why the relative international price of a commodity like soybeans goes up over a period of time? What would we have to know to explain why this occurs? Now consider the active labor market for new recruits, large firms developing new technologies or securing them from abroad looking for particularly dedicated and enthusiastic hires, the cream of the crop so to speak. As we have noted before they have an incentive to offer a premium wage. Why? Because if they pay the market wage, $\mathbf{W_m}$, the worker is inclined to give minimal levels of effort and commitment, realizing that if he or she is caught shirking he or she can secure alternative employment somewhere else at the equivalent wage. From the firm's point of view this is precisely what it does not want, this is inefficient. Note that if monitoring costs were zero – and in small firms they may well be near zero – the incentive to offer a premium wage is nil.

So the large enterprise offers a wage (including a paternalist health package) above the market clearing wage. Call the value of this wage $\mathbf{W_e}$. In this case there are two wages prevailing on the market, one higher than the other. This is the situation envisioned in Figure 1.3. Note that because some firms pay premium wages, the supply of labor exceeds the demand for labor in the market as a whole. Young entrants to the labor market seek the highest paying jobs, joining a queue. But only a select subgroup of the persons looking for employment can actually land the position.

This is known as the efficiency wage theory of unemployment or underemployment. It can be used to explain why dualism exists within an economy, some firms paying high wages, others low wages. It can be shown that if the amount of

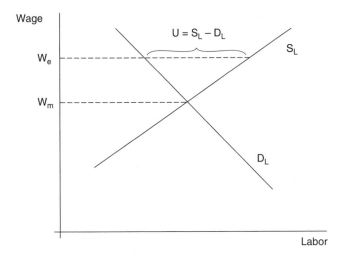

Figure 1.3 Efficiency wage equilibrium.

effort an employee gives rises but at a diminishing rate as fatigue sets in, there is an equilibrium point – the percentage increment in wage costs to ensure effort equaling the percentage increment in the value of the productivity of the worker at that point – where a wage level is set within the firm $\mathbf{W_e}$ that is efficient from the firm's point of view. It is illustrated in Figure 1.3.

One interpretation of this doctrine is the gift exchange interpretation. The firm is benevolent, offering compensation above what supply and demand in the market gives. The employee reciprocates by giving extra effort, by being especially diligent. This type of gift exchange could emerge from Confucianism.

Now let us consider the **IS/LM** model, beginning with reason why it is given the name it is. We start out with a closed economy and a fixed price level. We will relax the second assumption shortly.

The term **IS** refers to investment **I** equals savings **S**. Underlying this is the identity in the market of goods and services, aggregate demand $\mathbf{D_A}$ equaling the sum of consumption demand, investment demand, and government spending. Let us assume that consumption demand depends positively on the level of income (**Y**) and investment demand on the level of interest rates, higher borrowing costs of securing capital deterring new capital acquisition projects according to the logic of the cost/benefit principle. Then:

$$\mathbf{D_A} = C(Y) + I(i) + G = C(Y) + S(Y) + G \tag{1.2}$$

Where **C** stands for consumption demand, C_T for governmental demand for goods and services. Note that savings **S** depends upon income because it is simply the difference between aggregate income received and the level of consumption demand. By subtracting consumption and government spending demand from both sides of the equation we get:

$$I(i) = S(Y) \qquad\qquad (1.3)$$

or I/S, investment equals savings in the goods market.

We draw the resulting graph in Figure 1.4A, income demanded falling as interest rates rise because investment demand is inverse to interest rates.

Now consider the financial market in which governments and firms secure resources, either tapping banks where the public makes deposits or the bond market, issuing debt as an option. From the public's point of view it has two choices as to where to put its financial assets, either in liquid but risk free money (bearing no return but not losing or gaining value as long as the price level remains fixed), or in bonds that are risky, their price fluctuating, offering potential returns in the form of interest paid **i.**

At this point in our story it is important to appreciate the linking of bond prices and interest rates. If a bond with a face value of $100 payable at the end of one year sells for $90 at the beginning of the year, the annual interest rate on the bond is 10 percent. Thus bond prices and interest rates move inversely to one another. For example what is the price of a one-year bond paying 20 percent interest if its face value at the end of the year is $100?

Assume the public holds its financial assets in a mixed portfolio of bonds and money, increasing their share of bonds relative to money when the interest rate is higher, thus the price of a bond lower. After all, the more attractive are bonds, the more willing is a typical household, a typical mutual fund, a typical corporation awash in cash, to diversify out of liquid money into bonds. However everyone needs liquidity, mainly in order to make transactions on the market. Thus there are

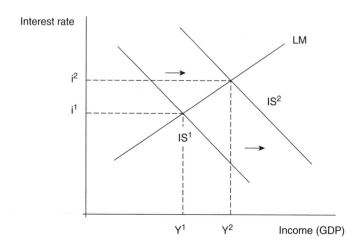

Figure 1.4A The IS/LM model: IS shift dynamics.

two reasons why households demand money: to hold it as a financial asset competing with bonds in this regard – this is known as the speculative demand for money – and to effect transactions. Given the supply of money **M** available at any given time, **M** must equal the sum of speculative demand (that varies inversely to the interest rate **i**) and transactions demand that is a positive function of the level of income **Y** generated in the aggregate economy. Assuming a linear form to the demand for liquidity **L** we can write:

$$\mathbf{L(Y,i)} = a\mathbf{Y} - b\mathbf{i} = \mathbf{M} \tag{1.4}$$

the demand for liquidity equaling liquidity supplied, thus the term **LM**.

Both the **IS** and the **LM** curves appear in Figure 1.4A. Note that the **IS** curve slopes down and the **LM** curve slopes up. You should convince yourself that this is the case by working through the logic of each curve one more time. The key point is that there is an equilibrium level of income and the interest rate that results. At this equilibrium there is no guarantee that income is equal to full employment income. It could fall short, thereby generating unemployment, some workers being thrown out of work due to deficient demand. For instance demand might be deficient because entrepreneurs are pessimistic about future returns on investment in new plant and equipment, therefore unwilling to spend on new machines, structures and transport vehicles. If this is the case – operating under the assumption that wages and prices do not fall when there is unemployment for the present – there is an argument in favor of government intervention, either employing expansionary fiscal or expansionary monetary policy, or some mix of the two.

Consider fiscal policy, bolstering government purchase of goods and services, cutting personal income tax rates in order to stimulate consumption demand and so forth. This is contemplated in Figure 1.4A, the **IS** curve being shifted out because **G** is boosted or because **C** is boosted. Note that income increases the expanded level of economic activity drawing down unemployment in its wake. Also note that interest rates rise as the economy moves along an upward path. Why?

Now consider what happens if the government eschews fiscal policy, employing expansionary monetary policy instead, increasing the liquidity supplied to the public **M**. The **LM** curve shifts out to the right, output being pumped up in tandem with plummeting interest rates. This is the case illustrated in Figure 1.4B.

There are two special cases that need to be considered. Suppose the **LM** curve is completely vertical. This is the situation captured in Figure 1.4C. It is known as the classical case. In this case fiscal policy is useless. Indeed it could be argued that it is actually counterproductive in a capitalist economy. A rightward shift in the **IS** curve simply drives up interest rates, reducing investment demand at the expansion of either consumption demand or government spending demand. Investment demand is crowded out so to speak.

Another pathological case is illustrated in Figure 1.4D. In this case the **LM** curve is flat. Monetary policy is useless, a shift in the **LM** curve being impossible (the curve would have to move on top of itself like a snake wiggling along its

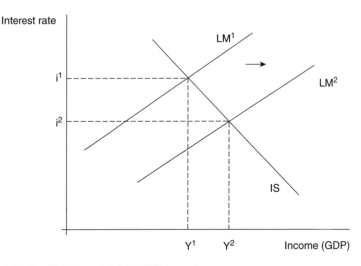

Figure 1.4B The IS/LM model: LM shift dynamics.

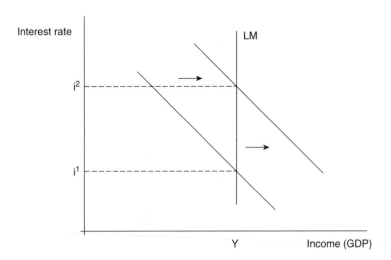

Figure 1.4C The IS/LM model: crowding out in the classical case.

own belly). This is sometimes called the Keynesian case – because it corresponds to his advocacy of expansionary fiscal policy during depressions – and it is also known as the liquidity trap case. In a liquidity trap interest rates cannot fall any lower. Alternatively monetary policy is not a panacea.

The problem with the **IS/LM** model is that it assumes the general price level is fixed. This is unrealistic in the long run. For example if there is unemployment

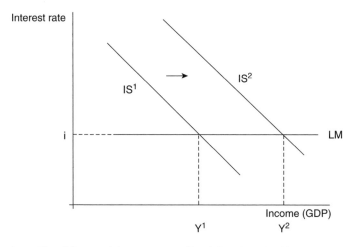

Figure 1.4D The IS/LM model: monetary policy fails with a liquidity trap.

we would expect wages, hence production costs, hence prices in a competitive setting to fall, eventually. This is the scenario contemplated in Figure 1.4E, the aggregate demand levels of equilibrium output shifting the economy out as the price level drops. Diminished prices generate an increase in the value of real money balances (**M/P**). As far as transactions are concerned the public requires less money since prices have fallen. The **LM** curve should shift out to the right, thereby moving the economy back to full employment levels Y_f. In theory pure reliance on market forces should eliminate unemployment. This tendency is illustrated by arrow # 1 in Figure 1.4 E. This is a long-run property of the system. However as Keynes pointed out in the long run we are all dead. The theory that posits a long-run equilibrium might be useful as a theoretical possibility – an implied benchmark – but absolutely useless in a practical sense, for instance in a politically unstable world where sustained unemployment can trigger revolution. Indeed, at the time when Keynes was writing, Marxist inspired revolution was a dark possibility stalking the entire world, in both industrial and also in predominantly agricultural societies. And there are some good reasons to think that wages and prices might not fall for quite a while. First within the ranks of the labor market there might be a large number of efficiency wage type workers, employers being reluctant to cut wages at least in the short run. Alternatively, there might be entrenched oligopoly or monopoly in the capital goods and consumer goods sector for instance. In this case competitive forces driving down prices in some sectors of the economy – for instance in agriculture and light consumer goods production – might not force down price levels in the capital goods and consumer goods sectors. Or the economy might be in a liquidity trap rendering the expansion of real money balances due to falling prices useless as a mechanism for reducing unemployment, returning the economy to full employment levels of activity.

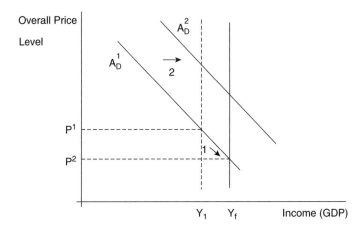

Figure 1.4E The natural rate property of an aggregate economy.

The possibility that an economy might reach a long-run equilibrium short of full employment – everyone seeking a job securing a position instantaneously – is known as the natural rate property of an economy. The idea is that there may be some unemployment at the point where an economy is not generating inflation. This could be because the efficiency wage equilibrium might involve some unemployment. Or it might be because some workers are switching voluntarily or involuntarily and it takes time for them to find a new placement. It might stem from the existence of unemployment insurance programs that subsidize protracted job searches. In Figure 1.4 E the level of output consistent with no inflation is Y_1. If the government counteracts the unemployment by expanding aggregate demand it drives up prices. It may or may not reduce unemployment in so doing. The case where the entire impact takes the form of price increase is illustrated with arrow # 2 in the figure.

More generally suppose a government is using monetary policy to expand aggregate demand. The expansion in the money supply is likely to impact both growth of real output and the growth of the price. In the equation (1.5) we see that an expansion in the money supply ($G_M = \Delta M/M$) can drive up both the overall price level (P), causing inflation ($\pi = \Delta P/P$) as well as growth in real GDP ($G_Y = \Delta Y/Y$):

$$\pi = G_M - \theta(G_Y) \qquad (1.5)$$

where the parameter θ captures the impact of a percentage increase in demand for money associated with the surge in transactions (both for goods and services and for assets like land) stemming a given percentage increase in real output.

The last model we consider in this Appendix is the Swann-Solow growth model. In this model we assume, as we have with the **IS/LM** model, that we are operating in a closed economy, domestic savings equaling domestic investment.

We also assume that constant returns to scale obtain at the level of aggregate production (defined below) and that the economy is operating at "full employment" (where there might be some equilibrium unemployment generated through the natural rate property of the economy).

In the Swann-Solow model, the economy is assumed to generate output with constant returns to scale according to the following production function:

$$Q = A \ f(K,L) \tag{1.6}$$

where **A** is an index for the level of technology, organization, institutions and any scale economies that might be associated with the level of output, **Q** is output, **K** is the capital stock, and **L** is the size of the labor force (technically **K** stands for the flow of capital services reflecting the capital utilization rate and **L** the flow of labor services).

"Constant returns to scales" means that multiplying both inputs by any constant μ multiplies total output by the identical level μ, namely:

$$\mu Q = A \ f(\mu K, \mu L) \tag{1.7}$$

Under this assumption we can derive a simplified relationship between the level of average labor productivity (q = Q/L) and the level of the capital/labor ratio (**K/L**) namely:

$$q = A \ f(k) \tag{1.8}$$

by setting μ equal to **1/L** in equation (1.7) above.

One production function that satisfies the condition of constant returns to scale is the Cobb-Douglas form:

$$Q = A \ K^{\alpha} \ L^{1-\alpha} \tag{1.9}$$

This form is commonly used in mainstream neo-classical growth analysis.

The basic dynamics of the Swann-Solow model appear in Figure 1.5A. The model uses the following variables: the capital/labor ratio **k**, the level of worker productivity **q**, the rate of technological and organizational progress $g_A = \Delta A/A$, the rate of population growth **n**, the rate of depreciation on capital stock δ and the rate of savings out of income, **s = S/Y**.

As you can see from the diagram, the model generates equilibrium. At the equilibrium the levels of the capital/labor ratio (**q***) and the level of labor productivity (**k***) are determined. To the left of **k*** the demand put on capital accumulation by labor force growth (known as capital widening) and depreciation is less than savings per worker. At any of these points the capital/labor grows (capital deepening). To the right of **k*** the reverse happens. Capital "shallowing" (negative capital deepening) takes place, the demands put on capital by labor force growth and depreciation exceeding savings per worker.

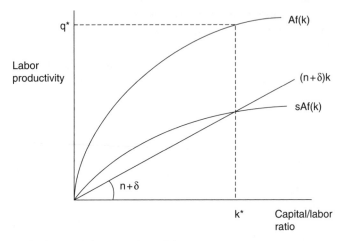

Figure 1.5A The Swann-Solow growth model.

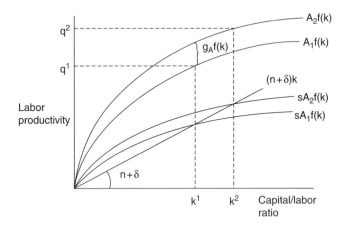

Figure 1.5B The Swann-Solow growth model: technological and organizational progress bolsters labor productivity.

Intuitively the idea driving the model is as follows. At any given level of technology and organization **A**, there are diminishing returns to increases in the capital/labor ratio **k**. If you increase the number of robots, digitally controlled machines, the size of the workshop, on a per worker basis, output per worker does rise, but at a diminishing rate. At some point the worker could actually get lost in the factory oversupplied as it is with capital equipment.

Savings per worker is the product of the savings rate **s** and the level of worker productivity. On Figure 1.5A it appears as the curved line marked **sAf(k)**. It intersects the straight line **(n+δ)*k** at one and one point only. This is the equilibrium

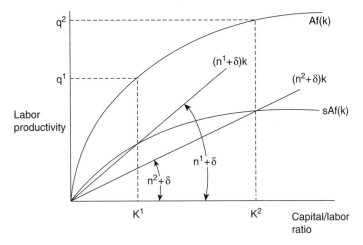

Figure 1.5C The Swann-Solow growth model: a slowdown in population growth promotes capital deepening.

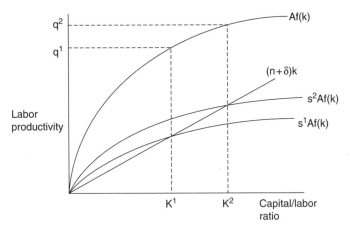

Figure 1.5D The Swann-Solow growth model: raising the savings rate promotes capital deepening.

of the system. In the long run, absent technological and organizational progress, absent any change in the savings rate, and absent any change in population growth or depreciation on capital, there is a steady state for the economy.

Now suppose there is exogenous, "manna-from-heaven," technological or organizational progress, innovation occuring (the index of technology and organization expanding). In this case you get the situation illustrated in Figure 1.5B. Worker productivity rises because the production process has become more efficient in extracting output from of the raw materials, labor and capital equipment. Note that savings per worker rises in this case not because of the savings rate but simply because per worker productivity has been enhanced.

Alternatively suppose the rate of population growth decreases, falling from n^1 to n^2. This is the situation contemplated in Figure 1.5C. The level of capital per worker rises. Why? Because less of the savings per worker is going into tooling new entrants to the labor force with equipment and structures, capital widening, and more is going into increasing the capital/labor ratio, capital deepening.

Finally consider what happens if the savings rate is increased from s^1 to s^2. This is the situation envisioned in Figure 1.5D. In this case the level of capital per worker goes up and the level of productivity per worker goes up as you move from the first equilibrium to the second equilibrium of the economy.

To summarize: the key points of the Swann-Solow model are that an economy generates a higher rate of growth in per worker productivity – and hence a higher rate of growth for per capita income (assuming the proportion of the population engaged in the labor force is constant) – the higher is the rate of technological and organizational progress, the higher is the savings rate, and the lower is the rate of population growth.

2 Before industrialization

The *bakuhan* system

One of the great puzzles of late nineteenth-century history can be captured in a succinct phrase: why Japan? Out of all of the Asian countries – China, Korea, Thailand, India – grappling with the penetration of European imperialism in the nineteenth century, why was it Japan, and Japan alone, that managed to respond comprehensively to the Western onslaught, to simultaneously industrialize rapidly and build up its military prowess, forcing the Western powers to grudgingly acknowledge its growing hegemony in Northeast Asia and on the Pacific?

The answer lies in the economic development of Japan between the early seventeenth century and the mid-nineteenth century. During this period there were four major economic transformations, each proceeding through slow but persistent evolution. First an institutional framework for fiscal and monetary was established, more centralized in the monetary realm than in the fiscal realm. An understanding of how to use the instruments of stabilization policy – even though it was not actually directed to reducing unemployment – diffused through the administrative circles of the country. Second powerful externalities were created involving physical infrastructure, most prominently towns and metropolitan centers, roads, "canalized" rivers (the term is explained later), and education. Third, a political regime emerged that solved the tragedy of the commons in two important environmental dimensions: management of the water drenching the countryside during the monsoon rainfalls; and management of forest and mountain slopes alike, learning how to carry out plantation forestry that preserved the soils in the highlands, preventing their natural erosion from excessively silting up the river beds below, guaranteeing sufficient forest rejuvenation at the same time. Fourth, the economy evolved from one that I characterize as Organic Economy stage B operating at a medium level to Organic Economy Stage B operating at a high level. Since the last point involves new concepts, let us begin with it, turning to a discussion of the political transformation that set the stage for the other key elements of our story after.

By an organic economy I mean one that utilizes the natural energy sources of wind, water and fire, combining these with the muscle of humans and domesticated animals. By the early seventeenth century most of the population residing in the main islands of Japan had progressed from an exclusive reliance on hunting and gathering to settled agriculture. The prominent exception were the Ainu, who had largely been driven off the northern tip of Honshū by 1600, pushed up in the northern island of Hokkaidō where they carried on trade in fur, fish and timber with one of the Japanese fiefs (see below) that occupied the southwestern tip of Hokkaidō.

Table 2.1 Broad stages in long-run economic development

Organic economy A (natural energy sources – wind, water, fire, human physical exertion)
    Hunting and gathering

Organic economy B (natural energy sources – wind, water, fire, human and animal physical exertion)
    Settled agriculture with domesticated animals

    Crops – **cereals** (wheat, barley, rice, corn, sorghum, millet, sugar cane); **pulses** (pea, lentil, bean, peanut); **fibers** (flax, hemp, cotton); **roots, tubers** (yam, potato, taro); **melon** (melon, cucumber, squash)

    Animals – Major 5 (sheep, goat, cow (ox, cattle), pig, horse); and minor 9

    Gradual development of natural immunity to diseases spread from animals to humans (**measles** – cattle, rinderpest; **tuberculosis** – cattle; **smallpox** – cowpox or other livestock pox; **flu** – pigs and ducks; **pertussis** – pigs, dogs; **Falciparum malaria** – birds)

    Approximate dates of "stages" of organic economy B in China:
        Plant domestication – by 7500 BC
        Animal domestication – by 7500 BC
        Pottery – by 7500 BC
        Villages – by 7500 BC
        Chiefdoms – 4000 BC
        Widespread metal tools – 2000 BC
        States – 2000 BC
        Writing – by 1300 BC
        Widespread iron tools – 500 BC
    At higher stages of the organic economy (e.g. Japan between 1700 and 1850)
        Extensive spread of proto-industrial (craft) production
        Formal education spreads and basic literacy/numerical skills develop in
            broad segments of the population
        Urbanization and infrastructure (roads, canals, harbors) expansion

Inorganic economy (exploitation of energy sources pent up in stocks of natural resources, e.g. in fossil fuels)
    First industrial revolution – fossil fuels, steam power, iron and steel production streamlined, factory system, applications of steam to transport (ships, railroads)

    Second industrial revolution – hydroelectric power, internal combustion engine (cars and airplanes, diesel engines), synthetic materials, applications of the germ theory of disease – growing demand for education and physical and financial infrastructure.

A stripped down stage theoretic scheme can usefully be employed to describe the three main stages in long-run economic evolution. The scheme appears in Table 2.1.[1] According to the table, there are higher and lower stages of the Organic Economy B when settled agriculture takes over from hunting and gathering. In the earlier phases, pottery and village life emerge. Later on more complex political forms emerge, chiefdoms giving rise to states ruled by kings, emperors or republican senates. Writing and the widespread use of iron tools follows, albeit with a long lag.

At higher stages – the stage Japan achieved by the early nineteenth century – education and proto-industrial craft production (exemplified by the making of cotton and silk fabrics, the processing of rice wine, the drying out of small fish and working up of soybean cakes for fertilizers) become sufficiently diffused throughout the economy so that one can refer to it as a highly diversified organic economy.

Why did the Japanese economy make the institutional and structural leaps and bounds it did between 1600 and the 1850s? While it would be simplistic to argue that political change was at the root of the transformations – after all the political changes were partly the result of merchants becoming an increasing presence in the economy as they flocked to urban centers under the protection of powerful warlords (*daimyō*) – the political change was crucial. So we begin with it.

Under the *bakuhan* system that emerged in the late sixteenth century and was solidified in Japan between the great battle of Sekigahara (1600) and the destruction of Osaka castle a decade and a half later (which had become the rallying point for those loyal to the Toyotomi family that had been hegemonic before Sekigahara), a confederation style of governance was created, warlords being assigned fiefs as local power bases, at the same time surrendering considerable power to a central authority, known as the *bakufu* or the shogunate. The very term "*bakuhan*" conveys the point of the system: "*baku*" stands for tent, symbolizing the center's predominant position; "*han*" stands for fief, the other, far weaker, pillar of the political system.

Hideyoshi Toyotomi, Tokugawa Ieyasu and the bakuhan system

The confederation "divide and rule" style of governance perfected by the Tokugawa shogun and his advisors was the product of protracted struggle to establish hegemonic rule over Japan wracked by the ravages of civil war between the 1460s and the 1560s. Prior to Hideyoshi Toyotomi, the most successful unifier of Japan was Oda Nobunaga, a minor warlord who emerged out of the province of Owari in the Nobi plain to eventually take control of the capital, Kyoto, during the 1560s. Assassinated in 1582, Oda's grip over most of Japan gave way to the drive to hegemony initiated by Toyotomi Hideyoshi who brought even eastern Japan under his heel in 1590.

Hideyoshi carried out a string of political innovations that paved the way for the pax Tokugawa: *he demilitarized the countryside by carrying out a sword hunt aimed at removing weapons from farming villages; he ordered a land survey be carried out so that systematic taxation on land could be implemented; and he shared power with the other powerful warlords through the fashioning a system of federation government, the warlords (daimyō) being control over the populations within their domains.*

Unfortunately for the dynastic rule carved out by Hideyoshi, an ambitious warlord, Tokugawa Ieyasu, whose fief was located in the Kantō plain in eastern Japan and who established a castle town in the sleepy fishing village of Edo, put together a military coalition that defeated the allies of Hideyoshi at Sekigahara in 1600.

Building upon the innovations pioneered by Nobunaga and Hideyoshi, Ieyasu created the bakufu ("military tent" rule) regime that kept the country free from major civil unrest until the 1850s, adopting the title "sei-i taishōgun" (Commander-in-chief of the Pacification of Savages), shōgun for short.

The bakufu extended its immediate control over a substantial swath of territory throughout many of the 68 domains established in the wake of Sekigahara – including control over silver mines, and the major metropolises of Kyoto, Osaka, and Nagasaki in addition to its capital in Edo – and worked out an effective strategy for keeping the daimyō at bay, that is a strategy for preventing rival regional military coalitions from forming.

Key to the bakufu's approach was the introduction of the sankin kōtai system of alternate attendance whereby most daimyō were forced to come to Edo on a regular schedule, residing in the capital with their wives and children (who remained as prisoners in the capital when the daimyō returned to their domains) for a year at a time. Forced to attend the bakufu court in Edo, the warlords and their attendants were kept under constant observation by spies of the Tokugawa shōgun. Also central to the "divide and rule" approach was the isolation (sakoku) policy implemented in the mid-seventeenth century. Preventing Japanese from going abroad or having contact with foreigners unsupervised by the bakufu denied individual daimyō the capacity to forge alliances with foreign powers, or to send military emissaries abroad where they could plot the overthrow of Tokugawa hegemony.

The system that evolved through the agency of Nobunaga, Hideyoshi, Ieyasu and his descendants is known as the bakuhan system, the system that shared power between the bakufu shōgun and the daimyō who ruled over individual fief domains known as han ("bakuhan" = "baku" plus "han").

The center was reasonably strong, far stronger than had been shogunates established at earlier points in Japanese history. The new Tokugawa *bakufu* controlled directly about 30 percent of the land area of Japan including the four great conurbations, Edo (later Tokyo), Osaka, Kyoto and Nagasaki. In addition the immediate collateral lines, branch families, of the shogun controlled another 10 percent or so of the territory of the country, including the castle town of Nagoya on the Pacific edge of the Nobi plain. Finally, clustering around the territory of the *bakufu* were the fiefs allocated to the *daimyō* who had been allies of the Tokugawa family that held the shogun's position, the so called *fudai* (or inner) *daimyō*. Taken as a group, the land area occupied by fiefs headed up by *fudai daimyō* was about 20 percent of the land area of Japan – generally the fiefs granted to these warlords were relatively small, testifying to the desire of the shogun to stand far above his immediate allies in the pecking order, to accentuate their dependence on him. All together, about 60 percent of Japan was controlled by the *bakufu* center – by the shogun and his advisors – the immediate relatives of the shogun and the warlord allies he trusted and consulted.

On the outer reaches of the Japanese territory were the fiefs assigned to the *tozama* or outside *daimyō*, those who had opposed the Tokugawa alliance at Sekigahara. Typically bigger than those given over to the inner warlords, these fiefs were given to those warlords whose lineages were too powerful to extinguish. To say that contact between the shogun and the *tozama* warlords was suffused in tension and strain would be an understatement. Even hundreds of years later – during the 1860s – the resentment that the *tozama* fiefs felt towards the *bakufu* center continued on. It was no accident that the two fiefs most instrumental in the destruction of the *bakuhan* system in the 1860s were Chōshū and Satsuma, two of the largest and most powerful *tozama* fiefs located in the southwest.

Successive shoguns did what they could to weaken the power of the warlords, ultimately sealing off the country to most interchange with foreigners, exceptions being made for the *bakufu* itself, which basically monopolized the limited trade that continued, giving over the island of Dejima in *bakufu* controlled Nagasaki harbor (on the southwestern island of Kyūshū) to a small community of Dutch merchants and assistants, otherwise carrying on desultory commerce and diplomatic intercourse with China and Korea. By virtually sealing off the country the *bakufu* guaranteed that the warlords would not be able to form alliances with foreign powers, with the Spanish, Portuguese, Dutch, British and French who had been making strong inroads into the shipping of goods in the Indian Ocean and the South China Sea since the early fifteenth century.

To ensure that the Western Christian powers – especially the Catholic powers, Spain and Portugal that put a strong emphasis on converting populations that they came in contact with to their faith – did not make any further inroads into the Japanese populace than they had already done during the Warring States period when the Catholic religion did establish a base in southwestern Japan, particularly in Nagasaki and its surrounding environs, the *bakufu* prohibited Christianity in Japan. To strengthen this policy, attempting to promote religious homogeneity throughout the land, the shogunate required households to register with their local Buddhist temple.

Nor was the drive of the *bakufu* to establish intellectual and spiritual conformity restricted to Buddhist registration. To hammer home the importance of class hierarchy and loyalty to superiors – the *daimyō* and the court nobles at the apex, their samurai military retainers next, then the peasantry, and finally non-samurai urban dwellers (merchants, artisans and common laborers) – the *bakufu* promoted Neo-Confucianism as an idealized theory of government and a code for social behavior.

To bind the samurai to his ruler, loyalty and service to the lord of the realm became the official ideology of fief and *bakufu* controlled territory alike, the concept of *hōon* that taught that a subordinate's primary commitment was to carry out tasks for one's superior in exchange for benevolence received. To die for one's lord was considered the most sincere expression of loyalty, an act offering the warm embrace of sacrifice repaid with salvation for the soul of the martyr. Combining elements of Neo-Confucianism and Buddhist thought, the code of behavior for the samurai that emerged during the early Tokugawa period, further refined later, was known as *bushidō*, the way of the warrior. Over time the main duties of the samurai evolved from mastering military skills to being bureaucrats, managing fief political and administrative affairs, managing fief run business enterprises. Still, even then, the tenets of *bushidō* remained central to the ethos of the samurai.

To strengthen the "divide and rule" system checking the potential economic and military power of *daimyō* relative to the shogunate, the *bakufu* developed a policy of requiring compulsory attendance of the *daimyō* in Edo on an alternating basis, Edo being the capital/castle town established by the *bakufu* on the mouth of the Kantō plain. When they were residing in their Edo estates and when they were coming and going in and out of Edo the warlords could be closely monitored by the shogun's spies at least in theory. Maintaining lavish compounds in Edo, staffed by servants, housing some of their samurai military retainers, drained the warlords of their financial resources. Moreover under the "guns out/women in" policy of the *bakufu*, the children and wife on the *daimyō* had to always remain in Edo, virtual hostages, and the *daimyō* had to submit to regular checks for concealed weapons on the journeys that he and his accompanying retainers took back and forth from fief to Edo.

Reining in warlord power that had run rampant during the Warring States period that preceded the establishment of the hegemony of Hideyoshi and then the Tokugawa dynasty was one of the chief aims of the shogunate administration. A second aim was to demilitarize the countryside by removing the samurai, the warriors who played a leading role in village life during the Warring States period, from their power basis in the countryside, forcing them to move to castle towns which served as the capitals, the administrative centers, for the individual fiefs. Accomplishing this extended the reach of peace, however artfully contrived through the "divide and rule" approach of the *bakufu*, to village Japan.

Though removed from the villages, the samurai, typically accounting for about 5 to 7 percent of a typical fief's populace, had to be given resources for feeding, housing and clothing their families; they had to be compensated for being uprooted from their opportunity to farm with some form of stipend. Since rice was the main crop produced in village Japan, taxing the villages collectively, taking a percentage of their rice output that could be transferred to the samurai and to the private coffers of the *daimyō* placed in charge of a fief by the shogun, represented a logical and obvious solution to the problem of securing samurai loyalty to the fief's authority and to the *bakuhan* system as a whole. Indicative of the fact the loyalty was often grudgingly and angrily offered up by the samurai is the fact that samurai rebellions during the seventeenth and early eighteenth centuries were not uncommon. Not all samurai embraced being removed from their power bases in the villages of the newly laid out fiefs with equanimity and enthusiasm. Just as resentment against the center festered in the *tozama* fiefs, so did resentment against the fief administrations fester amongst some samurai, especially in the ranks of those whose rice stipend was minuscule.

To secure rice from the villages that were emerging as the linchpin of fief and *bakufu* fiscal policy alike, carefully surveying village land area became crucial. First surveyed by Hideyoshi, assigning a certain number of rice produced in *koku* – *koku* being the unit of measure for rice volumes – to each village yielded a fiscal system known as the *kokudaka* system as the basis for fiscal affairs. Each village was assigned a requisite tribute of rice on the basis of the number of *koku* it was expected to produce according to the *kokudaka* survey in use by fief and *bakufu* officials alike.

As the reader can see the resulting fiscal system was not completely centralized, not completely decentralized. Since by far the largest number of *koku* ended up under the direct control of the shogunate, there was a significant degree of central control. On the other hand, fiefs had their own independent fiscal bases, collecting their own rice tribute, employing officials who lived in local areas to make certain the rice mandated for collection came into the fief's coffers. In this sense the system reflected the confederation style power sharing between center and fief.

It is important to understand that the relative standing of a fief, its position in the pecking order, was partly based on the number of *koku* it was expected to generate, in part on whether it was *fudai* or *tozama*. Rank being jealously guarded by fiefs that had relatively large numbers of estimated *koku* in initial surveys, there was strong resistance to changing the *kokudaka* estimates with new surveys, even when the productivity of the land was going up.

Monetary control was centralized to a greater degree. By monopolizing control over the mining of silver, gold and copper the *bakufu* controlled the manufacture of coins that was used by fief and shogunate alike to back up paper money issued. Ultimately, it was the management of the coinage base by the *bakufu* that was crucial to the expansion or contraction of the money supply insofar as government was able to control the money supply. What happened in village isolates where local barter arrangements might take place was an altogether different matter.

Further acting to centralize the monetary and fiscal system that emerged during the seventeenth century under *bakufu* rule was Osaka, known popularly – though perhaps only colloquially – as the "kitchen of the *bakufu*" – a Venice-like conurbation crisscrossed with canals carved out of the silted up islands built up where the Yodo River debouches into the ocean. At Hideyoshi's behest the merchants of Sakai, also in the vicinity of the Inland Sea moved into Osaka where he was building his forbidding castle town designed to be the capital of his hegemonic rule. Many of the fiefs of Japan – especially the fiefs in the southern reaches of the country – opened bailiff managed warehouses in Osaka where they could store rice and other fief produced commodities, exchanging them for luxury goods, food in times of dearth in the fief, and other goods. Exchange in Osaka became crucial to the way the fiefs managed their fiscal and monetary affairs, the credibility of their fief notes hinging on their fiscal solvency and the wherewithal that they mustered in their Osaka dealings. Controlled by the *bakufu* Osaka emerged as the major trading, financial and merchant metropolis of Japan during the seventeenth century while Edo emerged as the political and cultural capital, its growth fed by the system of compulsory attendance of the *daimyō* in Edo.

To meet the needs of carefully regulated and choreographed processions of *daimyō* on their way back and forth to Edo, the *bakufu* established a famous road network consisting of five major roads and eight auxiliary roads. This system of roads replete with check points at which documents and trunks carrying clothing could be carefully scrutinized by *bakufu* officials concerned by whether traveling entourages were concealing banned weapons is known as the Gokaidō road network.[2] Originally designed for political purposes, soon enough it was turned to commercial ends, either for transporting goods or for tourism and/or religious pilgrimages of the common folk. This created a powerful externality reducing the costs of shipping goods and information from one part of the country to another.

The road network was hardly the only major physical infrastructure project ushered in by the new *bakuhan* rule. Three other types of externality-creating infrastructure arose from the vortex of demilitarization of the countryside: cities; "canalized" rivers; and irrigation lines reaching out deep into valleys that had hitherto been untouched by regular irrigating water flows.

Urban centers flourished as the two hundred and fifty or so fiefs each created administrative centers replete with a castle, populated by samurai now displaced from rural villages and merchants anticipating business in the new cities. Adding to the urban building boom was the rapid growth of the *bakufu* controlled metropolises, Edo and Osaka growing from modest roots to mammoth size, while the ancient city of Kyoto where the imperial court was located and carefully monitored by the *bakufu* and the important Kyūshū port of Nagasaki where Chinese, and later Portuguese and Spanish, merchants had traditionally congregated. This massive building boom put immense pressure on the forest resources of Japan, the Kinai being the first region effectively denuded of trees. Adding to the demands placed on the forest reserves of the land were frequent fires, not uncommon in a country experiencing frequent earthquakes stemming from its volcanic activity. For instance the Meireki fire that burned almost half of Edo in 1657 probably extinguished over one hundred thousand persons in its conflagrations.

In the interests of reducing the incidence of flooding and the building up of silt that was torn from mountainsides, brought down in massive quantity in the aftermath of the violent monsoon rains, both *bakufu* and fief alike worked on "canalizing" rivers. River beds were built up with rocks, their sides also consolidated with rock enfacements designed to regularize their water flow, preventing overflowing in times of torrential rain, preventing rivers from jumping their normal paths of flow.

Finally, demilitarization of the countryside ended the marauding of villages by roving bands of samurai warrior-farmers. No longer could villages located near rivers resist the demands of villages further upstream for water through force of arms. Disputes over water flow along irrigation ditches now had to be settled, negotiated to a consensus amongst aggrieved parties, by officials, either fief officials or *bakufu* officials. The result was an end to the tragedy of the commons in the use of monsoon rainfall. Henceforth the flow of water into irrigation ditches was regulated. It was no longer a pinball bounced about by the violent actions of armed villagers. Irrigation lines were not pushed further and further into the remote reaches of river basins and even up along the sides of valleys. Land reclamation – conversion of dry fields, conversion of marshes and the shores of lakes and ocean alike to new paddy fields known as *shinden* – became a driving force behind the expansion of fief and *bakufu* controlled rural village life alike, offering an attractive avenue for expanding their *koku*, their rice tax bases.

Growth in rice output and population

Between 1600 and 1720 Japan experienced extensive growth. By this term I mean the expansion of the size of the economy – its population in particular – unaccompanied by substantial gains in per capita income. I differentiate this type of growth from the intensive growth that characterized the next 130 years of Japanese economic history – from 1720 to 1850 – when per capita income expanded in at least parts of the country while national levels of the population remained largely unchanged. Using the simple approximation

$$G(Y) \cong G(P) + G(y) \tag{2.1}$$

Where $G(Y)$ is the growth of total income or output, $G(P)$ is the growth of population and $G(y)$ is the growth of per capita income, we can define extensive growth as growth such that $G(Y) \cong G(P)$ and intensive growth as growth where $G(Y) \cong G(y)$.

Estimating population totals for Tokugawa Japan is a tricky business. The main documentation that can be utilized to secure aggregate level population estimates are the *kokudaka* counts (so many *koku* being produced nationwide) and occasional estimates by the shogunate as to the size of the national populace.

To go from the number of *koku* to the number of persons you need a ratio, the number of people per *koku*. What assumptions about the ratio do we make? As Hayami (1997) and Hayami, Saitō, and Toby (1999) point out, the old assumption – a ratio of one – yields a figure of around 18 million for the population in 1600. Linking this up with a slightly modified figure made by the shogunate *c.* 1720 that suggests the number of Japanese had increased to around 26 million in that year, implies relatively strong increase in human numbers over the course of the seventeenth century. Hayami (1997) argues that the person per *koku* ratio should be closer to one-half, arriving at an estimate of rice producers of around 9 million in 1600. To this total he adds estimates of urban dwellers and samurai, reaching a figure of around 12 million for 1600. Assuming the 1720 figure is more or less accurate – estimates as high as 31 million exist – one finds the population more than doubled over the 120-year period from 1600 to 1720. Since the country was closed off to immigration or emigration, all of this considerable increase must have come from the excess of births over deaths.

What specific forces led to the expansion of cultivated acreage, either through increasing the number of paddy fields within a village or through establishing new villages? To what extent did the fief administrations play a role in promoting the increase? On these issues there is controversy. Some Marxist historians argue that the fiefs and the *bakufu* acting in concert fashioned a new class of "independent peasant proprietors" who were basically given private property rights over land in exchange for paying rice taxes, the theory being that marginal farmers and the landless could never serve as the basis for a stable fiscal system. To support the "independent peasant proprietors" the fiefs and the *bakufu*, joined in this venture by powerful village heads, used the *corvée* labor of the peasants to reclaim land – to convert it from dry field to paddy; to secure it from marshes, and the banks of lakes and bays – the peasants constructing vast networks of irrigation ditches and canals under the watchful eyes of administrators.

Ultimately the burden of supplying this uncompensated labor proved to be too great, leading to growing resentment and friction between village heads and the peasants, the peasants withholding taxes to a degree, thereby undermining the "independent peasant proprietor" system. In this line of analysis the rank and file peasant plays a relatively passive role, only reacting, perhaps rebelling, in any event demanding benevolence from those in power, once the rate of exploitation becomes too burdensome.[3] One of the tenets of the exploitation view is that the rice tax rate was high. Assertions made perhaps out of ruler bravado or arrogance that the peasants only got to keep 40 percent of their crop, perhaps 50 percent, are taken at face value by advocates of the exploitation theory.

A second analysis working with the assumption that the typical peasant played an active, not a passive role, is that of Smith (1966, 1988). According to Smith during the early Tokugawa period those households with relatively large holdings carried out their farming operations with the assistance of servants, hereditary and non-hereditary, and of subordinate households attached to the main house. In exchange they gave their dependent households access to land, showering benevolence on them in times of dearth with presents of food. Exchange was not monetized. Rather a kind of barter system – perhaps best conceptualized as gift exchange taking place between hierarchically superior and inferior parties – prevailed. Exchange was deeply informed by hierarchy, inferior servants and branch families depending upon the largesse of powerful mainline families in the village. The rituals of hierarchy were even carried over into religious ceremonies, subordinate households assisting their mainline families. Village politics revolved around the interests of the powerful mainline households.

Over time technological changes and new opportunities – learning how to plant rice seedlings in more even rows, how to improve irrigation, how to raise cotton, hemp tea and mulberry plants in dry fields (crops flourishing in regions like the Kinai where merchants were active and soil conditions favorable) – transformed the demands placed on particular workers in farming, effectively ratcheting up the skills required to be competitive. Creating new rice fields, either through the hiving off of villages and the settling of new villages or through land reclamation within the village's territorial expanse, was integral to this process of reorganizing production on the land so that more rice could be squeezed out of a given hectare of paddy.

To better address the increasing demand for skills, larger landowners jettisoned the practice of labor exchange realizing that smaller production units – individual families as opposed to groups of families – were better equipped to motivate and train workers than a sprawling network of households centered upon a mainline unit. Gradually they switched over to the types of commercial exchange we associate with markets calibrated in terms of price. They broke up their landholdings into those parcels of land they farmed directly and those that they put out to rent or worked with hired labor. Reducing their reliance on labor services provided by subordinate households, those in control of substantial holdings increasingly came to secure workers by offering wages on a short-term basis or by drawing up longer-term contracts of employment. Wages, land rent – fixed or based upon sharecropping – gradually but inexorably supplanted the hierarchical social and political bonds that organized production in the seventeenth century. This process was well established in certain districts of the country by the late seventeenth century, especially in the Kinai where merchants were active, later spreading out across much of the rest of the country.

Not surprisingly, scholars who accept the notion that the typical peasant acted with a relatively wide choice set, taking carefully calibrated risks for personal gain, tend to reject the notion that the tax rate was set at cruelly elevated levels. Indeed, the "active peasant" school of thought rejects as mythology the notion that rulers took over 50 percent of the rice in tribute, arguing that the rates were considerably lower and – for reasons that we shall discuss shortly – tended to decline over time, perhaps falling as low as a third of the rice yield by last decades of the Tokugawa period.

To repeat: there are two sharply conflicting interpretations of Japanese peasant behavior: the "passive, exploited" version favored by various schools of Marxist historians, and the "active" version. Is the typical peasant, not the wealthy landowner, master of his or her own destiny, making his or her own choices, taking his or her own chances in arriving at decisions? Understanding that there are two very different ways of viewing peasant behavior is crucial to an appraisal of rural life in early Tokugawa Japan. Moreover, as we shall see, the gulf between the two views informs analysis of agrarian Japan in later periods, between the world wars, and even after.

On one thing both schools agree. The merchants played an increasingly important role in the economic behavior of peasants, at first mainly in the rural hinterlands surrounding the major metropolises, especially Osaka, later on in distant villages remote from the great centers of Japan facing out onto the Pacific Ocean. At first the merchants were mainly concentrated in cities, in castle towns, in the great *bakufu* conurbations like Osaka, Kyoto, and Nagasaki. Merchants penetrated village life through the putting-out system. Organizing networks of craftspeople, tapping the seasonal labor supplied by farming families who had substantial downtime between fall harvesting and spring transplanting of rice seedlings to the paddy fields, merchants played a key role as intermediaries in a decentralized system of craft, proto-industrial production.

Consider cotton textiles. Merchants purchased raw cotton from farmers (cotton was grown throughout the mountains of the Kinai for instance), taking it to households that wove it into thread, effectively selling them the cotton at a price below what they paid to get the thread once it was spun by the household. Buying back the thread, the merchants delivered it to households specializing in weaving, owning a loom, contracting with the household for finished cloth, paying a price for the finished product greater than the price the household paid for the thread. From the weaver, the merchant proceeded to the dyer who applied natural dyes to produce colored fabric. The merchant then proceeded to take the dyed fabric to a finisher who worked it up into clothing that the merchant could market. At each stage in the process, the merchant "put-out" the raw material for further processing.

By the late seventeenth century proto-industry organized mainly along putting-out lines had spread to the making of a vast array of craft products – silk cloth, rice wine, *tatami* mats, swords for samurai, beautifully crafted screens, fish fertilizers – that were marketed locally at first, eventually spreading out across the countryside, penetrating into rural isolates. At the top of the hierarchy of early Tokugawa craft products were the luxuries sold to the *daimyō* and their most favored samurai retainers – there was an elaborate pecking order amongst the samurai, some receiving more *koku* of rice than others – many of which ended up in the Edo estates of the *daimyō* where the carefully choreographed rituals of compulsory attendance were carried out.

In the exchange of the rice tax for craft products produced by the proto-industrial sector merchants played a crucial role, nowhere greater than in Osaka where merchants established houses along the canals carved out from the flow of the Yodo River. Gradually large and powerful merchant houses emerged in Japan – Sumitomo that owed its initial surge to prominence to its dealings in silver, Mitsui to its dry goods business – developing an ingenious system of franchising, the hiving off of new outlets through the process of *noren-wake*. The term "*noren*" refers to the fabric hung at the front of a store or merchant house headquarters that bears the seal of the house; the term "*wake*" indicates division deriving from the verb *wakeru* to divide. Literally, the term "*noren-wake*" means to divide up the merchant house's operation, effectively creating new franchise operations where its products could be sold, its putting-out activities organized, its dealings with fief and *bakufu* officialdom handled.

To staff merchant house operations, to recruit and train persons who could carry on the daily activities of transporting goods, handling accounts, managing franchise operations the houses gradually developed a system of apprenticeship. Economists like to refer to this type of system as an internal labor market because young recruits are brought into the operation, trained in the practices and codes of behavior integral to the particular merchant house, promoted over time, and eventually retired at the end of their careers (given the life expectancies that prevailed at the time retirement was probably not uncommon). The recruit – often brought into the house from a rural village, the recruitment arranged by powerful members of the village or through putting out connections – spent his or her entire career within the internal confines of the firm, advancing through an internalized system of promotion.

In the standard model of recruitment and promotion, an apprentice – *detchi* in Japanese – was brought into the enterprise as a teenager, housed, clothed and fed by the merchant house but not paid a wage, compensated in kind and in the training provided by higher level, already experienced, members of the house. Eventually promoted to clerk (*tedai*) status which was paid a salary, the employee would depart the merchant's quarters, now being able to marry and support a family. For many employees brought into the internal labor market of a house, making clerk status might well mark the end of the promotion process, might well indicate the highest rung on the advancement ladder. Some could go further. Clerks unusually gifted could aspire to further advancement, being put in charge of franchise operations spun off by *noren-wake*. Persons put in charge of the subsidiary units in the house were known as chief clerks, *bantō* in Japanese terminology.

One of the interesting aspects of the Tokugawa Japanese merchant house that differentiate it from merchant houses that emerged in Western Europe was the practice of separating the ownership of the firm from the management of the firm. The family that "owned" the firm, originally creating the enterprise – for instance the Mitsui family – did not usually manage the enterprise. Management was typically carried out by the chief *bantō*, the most powerful of the head clerks engaged in working for the house.

In this sense Japanese merchant houses separated management of corporate assets from ownership of corporate assets at an early stage in economic development, something typically not achieved in the West until the nineteenth century. That Japanese merchant houses were not carbon copies of Western merchant houses testifies to another important point: the Tokugawa system, often described as feudal (especially by Marxist historians arguing that Japan passed through feudalism on its road to capitalism just like Western Europe) was not the same as the feudal system that emerged in Western Europe.

In both environments, merchant houses emerged, in both environments putting-out and proto-industry flourished under political regimes dominated by local military rulers who owed allegiance to a central political authority. But the two systems were not identical. In Western feudalism the power of lords resided in their direct control over their manorial estates. They could not easily be dislodged from their bailiwicks, from their manors. By contrast the *bakuhan* system was basically an administrative system. The *bakufu* could and did remove *daimyō* from their fiefs, throwing their samurai out into society as master-less samurai (*rōnin*). Managing the fief so that it did not break apart in civil conflict or collapse in bankruptcy was an obligation imposed on, expected of *daimyō*, by the administrative center of the system, the shogunate.

By the same token the great merchant houses of the Tokugawa period were not identical to those that built up their corporate activities under Western feudalism. Those steeped in arguments based upon social norms and values would attribute this to the idealized codes of behavior dictated by Neo-Confucianism, the importance of politics and power, and hierarchy. Those more inclined to ferret out purely political constraints as an intellectual guide for analyzing market activity tend to point to the difference between Tokugawa feudalism and Western feudalism as formal systems for regulating and organizing the body politic.

Reform and rebellion

In the early eighteenth century extensive growth reached limits, pressing up against geographic constraints. One of these constraints involved the amount of cultivable land area in so far as it could be reclaimed and made increasingly productive in paddy rice farming. Given the technological advances in rice farming that had evolved, especially in the southwest where rice was double cropped because of the benevolent climate (the growing season in the southwest was around 250 days a year, almost double that in the northeast where the winter was far longer), rice yields did improve in certain favored districts. Had the political system been different, had it not created barriers to regional interaction and diffusion of ideas developed in different parts of the country, it is possible that the land reclamation and improvement of per hectare yields characteristic of the seventeenth century could have continued on into the late eighteenth century. However the *bakuhan* system created barriers to mobility of persons, bottling up innovations developed within domain borders. *Daimyō* were jealous of one another. Is it reasonable to think that they would willingly share secrets of how to bolster rice yields or manage fief licensed commercial monopolies and oligopolies with one another?

In the southwest new seed varieties were developed. Peasants could afford to experiment boldly since they enjoyed the implicit insurance of being able to plant a winter rice crop as well as a spring rice crop. Ironically, this bolstered the fortunes of the *tozama* fiefs that nursed hostility towards the *bakufu*. Thus by the 1720s in most of the country the process of reclaiming fields, wresting *shinden* from land hitherto given over to dry fields, marsh or low lying woodland, came to an end. This put a limit on the amount of rice, the total volume measured in *koku* that could be generated from the plains, river basins and mountainsides of Japan.

The same limit involved the forests. The building boom of the seventeenth century put a strain on the timber reserves of the country, denuding the hills and mountains of the Kinai district of trees, causing mud to slide off their steep slopes, silting up the rivers below, churning up mud and trees during the torrential monsoon rainfalls. That an earthquake prone country experienced frequent fires only contributed to the environmental problem. The urbanization of Japan was running up against limits. With the *bakufu* taking the lead, the various domains gradually developed and refined a system of forest management, appointing professionally oriented experts knowledgeable about trees to oversee particular forests, systematically planning forest rejuvenation, effectively creating plantations. In this way the Tokugawa political leadership managed to solve a second major tragedy of the commons, preventing the decimation of Japan's timber reserves. This said it is apparent that there were limits to urban growth imposed by available forest reserves. To sustain a massive urban complex fashioned from wood that was also utilized in the building of ships that plied the seas off of Japan and the rivers spilling out into the ocean, generous forests reserves were required. Eventually, as more and more trees were cut down, the costs of getting good timber rose, escalating price signaling serious constraints on further urban expansion. The only way to release this constraint on growth was to substitute other materials – such as iron and steel, synthetics like plastics – for wood.

Once the country embraced the inorganic economy – exploiting European developed technologies in iron and steel making, in generating steam power from fossil fuels like coal and so forth – breaking out of the constraints imposed by forest reserves became possible. But this did not happen during the eighteenth or early nineteenth centuries, the country remaining virtually sealed off to intercourse with the West.

Given the limits to growth reached during the early eighteenth century, extensive growth ended. Taking its place was intensive growth, income per capita gradually expanding as a combination of accumulation of capital, diversification away from rice farming into proto-industrial production in the countryside, and the virtual cessation of population growth at the national level gained force.

Before getting into the details of this intensive growth dynamic it is useful to illustrate what is involved analytically by invoking the Swann-Solow growth model discussed in Chapter 1. Consider Figure 1.5 C in the Appendix to Chapter 1. As can been seen rotating the line that captures the demands placed on savings per worker by the need to accommodate capital widening due to population growth to the right – due to a fall in the population growth rate – increases the equilibrium level of the capital/labor ratio, contributing to a rise in per capita income. To this source of growth in income per head we can add technological progress whose impact is diagrammed in Figure 1.5 B. Taken together an increase in the use of savings per worker to fuel capital deepening due to a slowdown – actually an end to – population growth coupled with a modest but ongoing technological progress can account for a gradual improvement in income per capita, the hallmark of intensive growth.

It is important to understand that the rise of income per capita might not be experienced by all sectors of the population. Indeed, the central thrust of the

Marxist interpretation of late Tokugawa development is that the peasantry (and many of the lower samurai) became poorer, increasingly forced into economic misery and distress, as a merchant and rural elite improved its economic standard of living, exploiting most of the downtrodden villagers in their insatiable drive to amass capital. This, recall, is the crux of the "passive exploited" peasant interpretation. By contrast the "active peasant" view emphasizes the rational directed behavior of the typical rural villager, taking advantage of every avenue to reap success, improving the fortunes of the household for the present generation and its successor generations. Whether one believes that the distribution of income worsened, stayed the same, or improved makes an essential difference in interpreting late Tokugawa economic development.

Despite disagreements over the broad based interpretation of late Tokugawa period dynamics there is general agreement on a number of points: the reform of fief fiscal management, the spread of proto-industrial production to remote rural districts, and an intensification of merchant activity sometimes described as the commercialization of the countryside, the cessation of population growth at the national level, the occurrence of three major famines, and an upsurge in peasant rebellions.

To begin with, the fiefs found their fiscal resources were squeezed, mainly because the expansion of rice cultivation came to an end, partly because forest management became increasingly expensive, just cutting down trees and selling them to agents who shipped them down rivers to be used in building construction no longer being an option in most parts of the land. As a result the fiefs carried out a number of reforms, including streamlining the training of samurai bureaucrats in fiscal management through the aegis of the fief academy. During the eighteenth century the number of fief schools proliferated rapidly. By the end of the eighteenth century almost all samurai were literate, versed in the Chinese classics to a degree, schooled in the principles of Neo-Confucianism, aware of the importance of carefully monitoring fief outlays with an attempt to balance fief budgets.

It goes without saying that a fief pressed up against its fiscal limits, burdened with the demands placed on it of maintaining an opulent lifestyle for the *daimyō* and his immediate entourage in both castle town and Edo, would press upon the merchants residing in its domain and upon its villages, forcing the merchants to pay "thank you" money for the right to carry on commercial activity within its border, forcing the villages to pay higher tax rates. It would also press upon its less powerful samurai retainers, cutting their stipends. This is a key element in the Marxist exploitation story about the later Tokugawa economy. One thing is certain: the domains began to experiment with licensing domain monopolies to merchants, even managing some of these as domain businesses. They definitely became more commercial in their orientation.

Marxist historians extend the exploitation thesis to the village as well. They argue that large landowners in the countryside began to diversify out of farming, emulating the merchants active in Osaka, Edo and the castle towns. Organizing putting out proto-industrial production, buying up land from destitute peasants falling upon hard times, powerful farmer-cum-merchants took control of the economies in the countryside, exploiting their brethren. This was the way the primitive accumulation of capital played out in village Japan.

According to this logic famine, peasant rebellion and the cessation of population growth are all symptoms of a worsening income distribution, indicators of the extreme desperation into which the great mass of the peasantry was consigned. Famines occurred because many peasants were rendered landless or forced onto marginal plots. Rebellion occurred because the hunger driven peasants had no choice but voice their discontent and dismay through violent disruption aimed at securing food and other resources from "benevolent" fief and *bakufu* administrations. Population growth ceased because mortality rose due to increased misery and because peasant households were forced to practice infanticide in order to survive as family units in the village. The Marxist interpretation emphasizes the negative, painting a picture bleak and dark in its main tones, hues and contours.

It will probably come as no surprise to the reader that the "active peasant" interpretation paints a radically different picture, one steeped in the belief that opportunities were proliferating in the countryside as proto-industrialization spread there, offering more chances – not fewer – for the typical villager to earn income, to pull him or herself out of the trammels of poverty. To argue this is not to claim that every peasant improved his or her circumstances during the late Tokugawa period, only that the vast majority did so. The debate is not about particular households, only about the great mass of the farming population that constituted about 85 percent of the Japanese populace during the Tokugawa period.

According to the "active peasant" or optimistic portrait of late Tokugawa Japan, the three great famines of the late eighteenth and early nineteenth centuries were brought on by unfavorable environmental and epidemiological circumstances. In accordance with this line of analysis, it is pointed out that the Temmei famine – ravaging northern Japan from time to time, in three nonconsecutive years, during the 1780s – was brought on by a lack of sunlight and the absence of warm temperatures during the growing season. Not only were these famines devastating on their own, they came in the wake of the Horeki famine of the mid-1750s from which northern Japan was just recovering. The eruption of Mount Asama in 1783 compounded the problems visited on the region, volcanic ash absorbed by the soil raising the levels of acidity in the ground, thereby weakening yields in the Kantō regime. The final great famine of the late Tokugawa era, the Tempo famine, struck during the 1830s, perhaps brought on by an epidemic that sidelined many farmers in central Honshū.

The "active peasant" thesis interprets the practice of infanticide – the term *mabiki* evoking the practice of winnowing out the rice plants, pulling out some so that the remainder can better get access to the rays of the sun – in a more positive light than is offered by the pessimism of the Marxists. The technique of family reconstitution originally developed by French demographers during the 1950s and 1960s interested in analyzing Catholic parish records from the pre-industrial period has been applied to village data for Japan, yielding a picture of village life very different from that put forth by the Marxist historians.

Family reconstitution studies, basically sophisticated genealogical reconstructions of the life cycles of households in villages, have been carried out on a number of Tokugawa villages throughout Japan. These studies utilize extant Buddhist temple registers that were generated by the mandate of the *bakufu* that every peasant household register births, deaths and marriages in the local Buddhist temple. While the details involved in these reconstitutions are manifold and technical their basic logic is clear enough: they link up individuals according to when they were born, when they married, when their children were born, and when they died, thereby giving a complete life cycle picture of the vital processes. What these studies show – see *inter alia* Hayami (1997); Hayami, Saitō and Toby (1999); Mosk (1983, 1996); and Smith (1988) – is that life expectancy was quite high – the high 30s or low 40s are not uncommon – and fertility was fairly low despite marriage for females being comparatively early.

Analysis of sex ratios for successive births in at least one village (Nakahara) suggests that infanticide was used to secure sex balance for the children allowed to survive, and/or as a strategy to lengthen the intervals between births so that sufficient resources of food, clothing and time could be lavished on each surviving child. In other villages there is a suggestion that infanticide was mainly directed at female births, distorting the gender balance amongst births.

Evidence supporting some of these points appears in Table 2.2. Particularly notable are the relatively low levels of completed reproduction within marriage, the marital total fertility rate reported in the fifth column in the table. To put this in perspective the reader should keep in mind that total marital fertility rates of over ten are not uncommon in agrarian societies. Also notable are the relatively low levels of infant mortality. In many agricultural settings these rates are far higher, often over 400 per 1,000 live births. However the reader should not forget that if births that were eliminated through infanticide were not recorded – and under the system of registration maintained at Buddhist temples births were usually only recorded in the registers on the Chinese New Years day – the infant mortality rates reported here do not take into account births and deaths for offspring deliberately killed by the parents. By the same token life expectancy estimates based on linking up birth dates of persons allowed to survive to the date of their demise excluded those births deliberately eliminated prior to registration at the temple. If parents tended to direct infanticide at the physically weakest children born, for instance those with low birth weights or those born sickly, they could have effectively removed the most inherently frail persons at birth, thereby enhancing the survivability of the population permitted to live. But this is just speculation; we really do not have direct evidence of the point one way or another.

In short, on the basis of family reconstitution analyses it appears that the cessation of growth of the Japanese populace after 1720 or so was mainly due to a drop in fertility, not to a rise in mortality. Not all regions of Japan were the same

Table 2.2 Fertility and mortality in selected Tokugawa villages

Village	Period	MAFM[a]	ALB[b]	TMFR[c]	LEM[d]	LEF[e]	IMR[f]
Asakusanaka	1717–1830	19.6	37.5	6.5	n.e.	n.e.	n.e.
Kabutoyama	1675–1780	18.3	39.8	6.1	n.e.	n.e.	n.e.
Kandoshinden	ca. 1800	21.6	39.2	7.3	33.2	31.6	n.e.
Minami Oji	1700–1899	17.9	n.e.	n.e.	37.1	38.4	n.e.
Nakahara	1700–1899	19.6	37.5	n.e.	46.1	50.5	165
Ogenji	1776–1875	n.e.	n.e.	n.e.	32.3	32.0	288
Shibuki	1826–1871	23.4	36.0	4.7	n.e.	n.e.	n.e.
Shimoshinjo	1828–1847	20.4	37.8	6.2	n.e.	n.e.	n.e.
Shimoyuda	1737–1870	15.6	29.9	2.6	n.e.	n.e.	n.e.
Toraiwa	ca. 1815	n.e.	n.e.	n.e.	36.8	36.5	229
Yokouchi	1700–1899	19.4	37.1	5.0	36.8	29.0	n.e.
Yufunezawa	1731–1765	20.2	39.3	5.0	n.e.	n.e.	n.e.

Source: Mosk (1996): Table 15, p. 70.

Notes
a MAFM = mean age at first marriage for females
b ALB = age of marriage at last recorded birth
c TMFR = total marital fertility rate (estimate of number of live births over married life of the mother)
d LEM = life expectancy for males at age one
e LEF = life expectancy for females at age one
f IMR = infant mortality rate (males) = deaths to males aged one per 1,000 live births
n.e. = not estimated

however. In southwestern Japan fertility probably exceeded mortality, generating some positive growth; in central Japan that was relatively highly urbanized (particularly in the Kinai district), mortality was probably fairly high in cities, so population growth was basically checked; in northeastern Japan where the climate was relatively harsh upward spikes in mortality probably produced negative population growth. For the country as a whole the population appears to have oscillated around totals in the higher twenty millions, say between twenty five million and twenty nine million.

What motivated households to limit their family sizes? One story is that they did so because they wished to maximize survivorship and at the same time adjust their family sizes to their demand for labor. As population filled out on the land during the seventeenth century the scale of rice farming, the area in paddy fields that each family worked, fell, reducing the demand for child labor. A second interpretation relates the change to the diffusion of the stem family system in Japan. But why did the stem family system take hold with such force during the early seventeenth century? The argument here is that it did so because the availability of new rice fields was falling after the sustained population explosion of the 1600s. It was no longer possible to place children on freshly developing rice paddy farms. Thus parents concerned about potential conflicts over who would inherit the family farm felt they had little choice but to cut their birth rates dramatically, thereby restricting the numbers of both male and female children that they raised.

Ideal types for family systems

Households are units based upon who co-resides, who shares a common cooking pot; families are units linked through marriage, procreation, and adoption.

Anthropologists and historians have worked out systems for classifying households, dividing them into groups according to idealized rules about how they are formed, how they evolve from one type to another, and how they are related to family formation.

One such system is the Hammel-Laslett system. It is based on five major types of household units:

1   *Solitaires (widowed persons; single persons; or persons of unknown status).*
2   *Households that are not families (co-resident siblings; co-resident relations of other kinds; or unrelated persons co-residing).*
3   *Simple family households (married couples alone; married couples with children; widowers with children; or widows with children).*
4   *Extended family households (extended upwards; extended downward; extended laterally; or combinations of these three types).*
5   *Multiple family households (secondary units up; secondary units down; secondary units lateral; frereches; and other multiple family households).*

It can be seen from the above list that families can pass through life cycles that push the household structure from one form to another.

For instance in the stem family system type that became dominant in Japan during the eighteenth century, households moved back and forth between a conjugal phase and a stem phase in which junior and senior conjugal units co-resided. A stem family system is a system characterized by the following rules: (1) a spouse is brought into the family by one and only one offspring in each generation; (2) succession of the family headship falls on the offspring who has married within the family; (3) inheritance, which is unequal, favors the single heir/successor; and (4) the family's organizational form passes through an alternating cycle, conjugal phases resembling nuclear families followed by a stem phase and then back to the conjugal phase. The transition from the stem to the conjugal phase is marked by the death of the last member of the senior couple. The transition from the conjugal to the stem phase is marked by the marriage of the heir.

In practice the distribution of households according to their type depends not only on the degree to which the rules of family formation are followed by everyone, but also on the demography of the population. If lives are brief, life expectancy low, the probability of forming three-generation households in which a married male heir co-resides with his parents and his children is low. Ideal types are ideals; in the real world the incidence of families realizing all phases of the idealized system may be insignificant.

But demography conditions the operation in other ways. What happens when a Japanese family finds itself unable to biologically produce an heir, or produces a potential heir who is too young to assume the family headship at the time when the older couple wishes to "retire" and commence the stem phase of the cycle? To secure a successor under these circumstances was ingeniously dealt with by Japanese families through the fiction of creating "sons" through in-adoption, securing a male heir from another family, turning over responsibility for carrying out the rituals of ancestor worship for the family as a lineage extending through generations to the in-adopted male. For families who gave birth to daughters but not to males, the option of bringing in a male to be the husband of the daughter and the "son" for the daughter's parents generated yet another form of in-adoption.

It should be stressed that the economic viability of the Japanese family line could, and often in practice did, take precedence over blood. Families whose male offspring were deemed incapable of effectively managing the resources of the family – the paddy fields and physical structures passed on from generation to generation in rural villages – due to infirmity, indolence or mental incapacity, could and did pass over their own blood offspring in designating a "son" to take over the family headship, reaching outside the family for an in-adopted heir.

It is sometimes argued that peasant households concerned about passing on their farms to the next generation, thereby securing support from their offspring for their old age, tend to err on the side of having too many children, thereby gaining insurance against the possibility that one or more of the children will die young or abandon the family farm out of disgust or ill will. That Japanese households could in-adopt fictive heirs meant that they did not have to resort to such a strategy. Moreover, families that were childless or were unable to attract an in-adopted heir had the option of affiliating with a group of households that pooled labor services known as a *dōzoku*. Thus Japanese peasants had a rich menu of options to choose from in managing their old age and finding ways to pass on their assets. To say this is not to deny that the preferred strategy was to give birth to children raised in the norms and values of the house with an expectation that one of the children would inherit and take care of the parents in old age. Rather it is simply to say that a strategy of restricting fertility was a relatively low risk strategy in late Tokugawa Japan.

Dōzoku

A dōzoku is a collection of households that form a local corporate group, typically located in a rice-producing village or group of villages. Anthropologists and sociologists are divided on how to characterize a dōzoku. Some scholars emphasize the importance of kinship ties, seeing the dōzoku as the resultant of a hiving off of branch lines (bunke) from the original stem family (the honke) that spanned these branch lines. Other scholars, most notably Nakane Chie, view the dōzoku as an cooperative economic unit involving power of superior mainline over branch line, not a kinship unit.

The idea that the dōzoku is based upon kinship is appealing. Under the rules of the stem family system, sons and daughters who are not in the direct line to succeed to the headship of the family must marry outside the family. If the land and other farming resources controlled and owned by the stem family are extensive, the head of the stem family may set up some of the non-inheriting offspring on its fields, renting out land to these branch households who remain subservient to the main stem family. For instance the main line family may want to in-adopt a son for a daughter, situating the resulting new household so created by marriage a portion of its rice fields.

Students of Japanese folk religion point out that dōzoku manifest their solidarity through their religious rites: each dōzoku having its own particular shrine and its own cemetery. It operates as a cooperative unit, mobilizing its members when a building requires thatching, a well sunk or births, deaths and marriages acknowledged through ritual. Gifts are exchanged within the confines of the dōzoku, the mainline family typically giving lavish presents to their branch families who reciprocate with their own crafted offerings to the mainline.

According to Nakane Chie, the problem with the anthropological arguments emphasizing religion and family ties, is that they ignore the fact that a dōzoku is only created when an economic relationship exists, rooting the institution in the exigencies of farming. If a non-inheriting son continues to reside in the village of the stem family into which he was born, but does not rent land or provide labor services to its family of origin, the common practice is to not refer to the family created by the son as a branch family (bunke).

In Nakane's eyes, the ultimate logic of the dōzoku system lies in the nature of rice production requiring extensive cooperation within a village lest that the village's collective management of water for irrigation, its capacity to carry out transplanting of rice seedlings in the spring and harvest in the fall in a systematic fashion, be compromised. Family ties, whether real or fictive in the sense that they are created by in-adoption, help create solidarity in the village. By the same token these ties that intertwine the ideology of the family system with corporate economic activity in the village make for village exclusiveness, for strong within-village identification and reluctance to admit individuals or households from distant places unknown by members of the village community.

One of the most important consequences of keeping family sizes small was the freeing up of resources to put into each child, (a mainstream economist would call this substituting quality for quantity), and the freeing up of resources to put into improving farm equipment, structures and the like. This is the analogue at the level of the family to the analysis we carried out with the Swann-Solow model when we considered the impact of a drop in the population growth rate on the capital–labor ratio.

Testimony to peasant households' substituting quality for quantity is the growth in the demand for schooling in rural villages during the later Tokugawa period. Emulating the popularity of fief academies to some extent but more focused on practical matters like carrying out computations on an abacus or mastering basic literacy so one could read a book recommending improvements in rice farming or the raising of silk cocoons, schools proliferated in the countryside during the eighteenth and early nineteenth centuries. Known as *terakoya* schools because they were often housed in temples (*tera*), these schools served as a springboard for promoting literacy throughout the nation.

How literate was the Japanese population by the middle of the nineteenth century? Estimates vary: samurai were expected to be literate. Many merchant houses promoted it as it was essential for carrying on business. Finally, at least the more prosperous peasants were literate, taught their basic Chinese characters used for writing Japanese in temple schools. Perhaps the literacy rate was as high as 40 percent. Probably the rate was actually lower. In any case it was impressive for an organic economy.

What impact did the diffusion of proto-industrial production to the countryside have on the financial wellbeing of the typical peasant household? Contrary to the claims of Marxist economic historians, the "active peasant" school of thought emphasizes the opportunities afforded by participation in craft production including – ironically – the opportunity to reduce the household's tax burden. By diversifying out of rice that was taxable into proto-industrial production that was not covered in the *kokudaka* system, peasants were able to reduce the effective tax burden on their total economic activity. This is one of the arguments used to bolster the thesis that the tax rate actually declined over the course of the Tokugawa period, perhaps reaching a level as low as a third of earned income by the nineteenth century.

Hida Takayama

Are museums, especially "living museums" that employ individuals simulating the lives of persons in days gone by – spinning yarn on spinning wheels, drawing water from deep wells by hand, employing ancient wooden plows to break the soil – purveyors of nostalgia or teachers that inform us about the grand changes that separate ourselves from our ancestors?

In the United States Colonial Williamsburg in Virginia and Sturbridge Village in Massachusetts attempt to bring the craft making and farming practices to persons of the twenty-first century in a vivid and instructive manner. Contemporary Japan has its own impressive collection of open air museums – including a historic village in Hokkaido, Meiji Mura in Inuyama that boasts of about 60 buildings constructed during the Meiji period – no one better equipped to take the tourist on a trip into the past than the Hida Minzoku-mura (Hida folk village) located in Hida Takayama, a small town of around sixty thousand nestled in the Japan Alps region, located in Gifu prefecture.

To be sure the Hida folk village is artificial: its remarkable thatched or wood-shingled roofed houses and tools were assembled from all over the Hida region. They were not located in Hida Takayama before the museum was created in a bid to generate tourist revenue in Hida Takayama. Nevertheless, the farmhouses assembled in the village do instruct; they do have a story to tell.

Famous as illustrations of the "gassho-zukuri" (meaning "the style of a steep-rafter-roof mimicking the joining of hands in prayer"), the massive two and three story farm households assembled in Hida Takayama remind us of what it was like to raise silk cocoons on mulberry, to dry the cocoons in attics, and to draw out silk thread for textile making. In the mind of this author who visited Hida Takayama during the 1970s, the strongest impression culled from a viewing of the Hida folk village farmhouses was the conviction that many farm households in late Tokugawa and early Meiji Japan were managing mini-factories, carrying out proto-industrial production for far flung markets throughout Japan, later on satisfying demand for raw silk in the United States and Europe. That the remote recesses of the Hida region in Alps appear to have been tapped for local proto-industrial output of silk, and that farming families were responding to demand by organizing all stages in the preparation of raw silk within their homes during the nineteenth century, was striking proof, convincing this author at least, of the diffusion of proto-industrialization throughout rural Japan in response to wide ranging market forces.

If economic conditions for the great mass of the Japanese peasantry were actually improving during the course of the later Tokugawa period, why did peasant rebellions break out with such frequency during this era? Vlastos (1986) cites Japanese authorities who have compiled lists of peasant rebellions, demonstrating that about three thousand rebellions against fief and *bakufu* regimes took place. In addition approximately three thousand conflicts involving disputes within villages occurred, yielding a rough annual estimate of approximately twenty protests and disputes per year. Moreover, protest occurred everywhere in the country, in all regions, in the southwest, in central Japan, in the northeast. The commonality of belonging to a well-defined class – the peasantry – undoubtedly fueled some sense of solidarity of the sort emphasized by Marxists. That protests broke out during times of famine is not surprising. This might explain why peasant restiveness in the northeast became a problem during the period 1780–1850. But why protest everywhere, even in the relatively prosperous parts of the southwest and the Kinai?

One answer lies in the diversification of peasant economic activity brought on by the growing penetration of the proto-industrial economy in village life. As this occurred more and more peasants relied on exchange in the market to cover their acquisition of foodstuffs, selling raw cotton or raw silk or tea or hemp, generating cash incomes with which they could purchase rice and barley. In so far as this shift took place peasants became increasingly dependent on the vagaries of the market. If the terms of trade – the prices of the goods that they were selling relative to the prices of the goods that they were buying – deteriorated, they were temporarily worse off. For instance falling prices for raw silk and rising prices for rice could seriously impact farmers living in the Japanese Alps who were specializing in silk. How could they get the attention of their domain authorities who could – if the will was there – either reach into their warehouses or purchase rice on the Osaka market and distribute it to the badly affected regions of their domain? To lobby for that benevolence, peasants banded together in organized protests. It would be incorrect to say that they were driven to these acts out of desperation. Rather it might be fair to say that they adopted the protest as a device for spurring on their rulers to take into account their desire to remain solvent as members of the peasant class, as a device for crying out for the benevolence that was embedded in Neo-Confucian doctrine.

All of this implies that the rural economy of Japan was expanding vigorously. Did this rural expansion take place at the expense of urban Japan? Estimates of city sizes by Smith (1988) suggest that many castle towns experienced significant population decline as proto-industrial and merchant commercial activity moved out to the villages. Estimates for Osaka's population in the early nineteenth century suggest that it also lost people, declining from around 374,300 in 1830 to approximately 321,200 in 1855. To put this in perspective, the reader should bear in mind that Osaka's population in 1740 was probably around 403,700 persons. So even the great metropolis that Hideyoshi marked out to become the commercial hub of the *bakuhan* system, a policy acceded to the Tokugawa shogunate that anticipated Osaka would be the "kitchen of the *bakufu*", was losing its population growth potential as urban merchant houses lost business to rural merchants and to rural based fief monopolies. Was this due to the fact that slowing growth, perhaps declining growth, of merchant house business reduced the rate at which new apprentices were recruited and the rate at which they were promoted to clerk status, thereby delaying marriages for younger members brought into the merchant houses? Were more and more apprentices becoming resigned to not being married at all?

Interestingly, Edo continued to grow in numbers during the early nineteenth century. Estimates suggest that its population jumped to 574,000 in 1855 from 546,000 in 1830. Why was Edo's fate different from Osaka's? Some scholars argue the labor markets in the two great *bakufu* controlled cites were fundamentally different. In Osaka merchant house employment was a dominant sector. Employment was highly internalized by the promotional ladder characteristic of the houses. In Edo common laborers and servants, moving around from job to job, in short casual as opposed to highly internalized labor markets, dominated. Growing rural merchant economic muscle did not undercut this market.

In sum there are two major views about the economic dynamics of the late Tokugawa period: the Marxist "passive peasant" pessimistic view and the more optimistic "active peasant" theory. In many ways the two interpretations are diametrically opposed. But in one sense the two views are similar. Both agree that accumulation was important. Adhering to the notion of the primitive accumulation of capital, Marxists emphasize exploitation of peasants and lower samurai in locating this accumulation in the ranks of the merchant class. Those who reject the pessimism of the Marxists see the accumulation of capital as a broad based movement sweeping across rural Japan as proto-industrialization penetrated more and more deeply in the countryside. Both frameworks also accept the notion that population growth slowed down, although the pessimists see the source of this retardation in an upward surge in the death rate, while optimists see its source in suppression of the birth rate. In this sense both views support the idea central to the Swann-Solow model that puts strong weight on the twin principles of limiting population increase and raising the savings rate.

Western intrusion, *bakuhan* collapse

The *bakuhan* system emerged out of a complex of political and economic challenges, the political challenges involving domestic issues first and foremost – demilitarization of the countryside, hemming in the power of local warlords – but international constraints as well. One of the biggest constraints operating on the international stage was the Western intrusion into Asia that gathered force in the fifteenth and sixteenth centuries as the Spanish, Portuguese, Dutch, English and French flexed their commercial and seafaring muscle in the South China Sea. Symptomatic of the ambivalence of the *bakufu* towards the West was its willingness to carry on carefully regulated and controlled trade with the Dutch who were allocated space on the tiny island of Dejima lying off of Nagasaki harbor. As Japan's ability to fend off growing Western pressure to open up to Western commerce and the presence of Westerners on Japanese territory eroded over the course of the early 1800s, more and more samurai took an interest in learning Dutch, studying in schools that taught "Dutch learning" (*rangaku*) as a vehicle for understanding better the technologies and philosophies of the West.

But history has a way of reshaping the realities of international power. Once a great power in the seventeenth century, the Netherlands was in relative decline in the eighteenth and early nineteenth centuries. Center stage was now being taken by the United Kingdom. It was emerging as the world's most powerful economy as it industrialized in the late eighteenth century, embracing the inorganic economy with its growing adherence to steam power in cotton textiles and its massive buildup in iron and steel production through improvements in the furnaces used to handle molten iron ore. Economic prowess can be channeled into military force although this does not necessarily have to occur. In the case of the United Kingdom a succession of conflicts had conspired to encourage military buildup commensurate with its growing economic power, most importantly the Napoleonic Wars. By 1815 the United Kingdom had the world's strongest navy. Moreover as its merchant marine began to switch over to steamships during the post-1820 period, it had a growing capacity to extend its military force across the oceans.

Key developments of the industrial revolution

The industrial revolution is a term normally applied to developments that took place in the United Kingdom between 1760 and 1830. These developments include the shift towards inorganic energy production; technological improvements in certain sectors of manufacturing, especially in textiles and iron and steel making; and development of the factory system.

Key to the energy revolution was invention in the steam sector. Especially important were the inventions of James Watt, who pioneered the separate condenser, the idea of double-acting expansion, and the use of improved gears for harnessing the pumping of the engine facilitating the harnessing of rotary motion exploited in industrial machinery and in transportation. As a result of the innovations in steam production, the cost of extracting coal from mine shafts fell, and the use of coal (a fossil fuel that stored up energy rather than a flow source of energy like water power or wind power) to efficiently produce energy boomed.

Manufacturing technology was given a strong fillip with the steam engine: the mule combining the spinning jenny and the throstle was harnessed to steam, giving rise to the first truly modern factories in the cotton textile industry. But harnessing steam was hardly the full story. Weaving was revolutionized with the flying shuttle during the first half of the eighteenth century. But even in weaving steam power ultimately became a factor. By the 1820s effective weaving on power looms allowed for the mechanizing of the weaving process. Carding and ginning that removed impurities from the raw cotton were also mechanized toward the end of the eighteenth century.

In iron and steel making, smelting of iron ore in blast furnaces reduced costs. The development of puddling and rolling by Henry Cort in 1785, refining the process of making malleable wrought iron and handling the molten ore as it came out of the furnace, cut dramatically costs of making high-quality iron and steel plates and bars. In the nineteenth century blast furnaces became larger and larger, and ultimately more energy efficient when processes that recycled the hot gases generated out of the furnaces into the blasting process were developed.

As a result of the technological breakthroughs in energy production and mechanization, the drive to centralize production around a central energy source in factories gathered force. Factory production went head to head with proto-industrial production. Artisans in a variety of sectors organized through the putting-out system in which merchants served as crucial intermediaries in the production process – in spinning, in weaving, in iron making, in brewing – now faced the competition from mechanized factories. Over time the superiority of the factory in throughput and in driving down production costs won out over proto-industry. Some artisans participated in rebellions – Ned Ludd is famous as the imaginary leader of groups of artisans that attacked and destroyed textile machines installed in factories throughout the new industrial towns springing up throughout the midlands of England – but ultimately the artisan ranks dwindled as younger recruits to machinery entered factories rather than entered artisan guilds.

In short, the industrial revolution transformed the production and harnessing of energy, allowing for the systematic substitution of coal for charcoal and timber; it transformed textile manufacturing by making mechanization of spinning and weaving possible and cost effective; it transformed iron and steel making with the blast furnace and the puddling and rolling process; and it transformed the social landscape by concentrating increasingly large shares of the industrial labor force in factories, thereby reducing the importance of the proto-industrial sector.

Note: This discussion draws heavily upon Mokyr (2003).

So the obsessive concentration on Dutch learning by the samurai and the *bakufu* officialdom is typically judged by historians enjoying the advantage of knowing full well what happened later as anachronistic, almost pathetic. Without a realistic and informed appraisal of the sea changes revolutionizing the system of international diplomacy in the West, the Dutch declining and the British aggrandizing power, the political leaders of fief and *bakufu* alike had little concrete knowledge to go on in understanding what they had to contend with, at least at first.

But then affairs transpiring in China alerted them. Tension between China and the United Kingdom had been building during the 1820s and 1830s over the issue of what goods the British could export into China, the British purchasing tea and ceramics, operating through the one port left open to trade by order of the Chinese emperor, namely Canton (like Japan in the seventeenth century China established a policy of almost complete autarky as the Europeans expanded their trade activities in the South China Sea, carefully regulating by only allowing officially designated monopolies to handle the commercial transactions involved). The Chinese position was clear. The British could pay for the tea they were buying with silver that was used as the standard, the basis, for the Chinese monetary system. But this was not acceptable to England which was gradually moving onto a gold standard during the first half of the nineteenth century. Her merchants had to secure silver on the European continent as they did not normally carry on commerce with it.

Struggling to come up with a commodity with which they could make inroads in the Chinese market, the British traders hit upon opium. This they acquired in Bengal. Establishing a monopoly to produce the drug for the exclusive purpose of trading with China, the British shippers vastly expanded their opium exports to China between 1821 and 1837. This angered Chinese officialdom concerned about growing addiction to the drug amongst the Chinese population especially amongst those who moved around the Chinese coast from domestic trading port to trading port. Chinese authorities seized some of the opium, precipitating a riot by British sailors in the summer of 1939. War between the two powers broke out in late 1939. By 1842 the British navy had seized Hong Kong which they used as a military base, sunk many Chinese ships, captured the ports near Canton guarding the mouth of the Pearl River delta, and had decimated Chinese naval forces at the mouth of the Yangtze River.

Forced to sign the humiliating Treaty of Nanjing in 1842, the Chinese ceded Hong Kong to England. China also had to open five designated treaty ports to the British who were granted extraterritorial rights – their nationals not subject to Chinese law, being tried for crimes committed in special British courts set up in the treaty ports – and to grant most favored nation trade status to England. Under that policy any tariffs applied to British goods could not exceed the lowest tariffs accorded to any other trading partner of China. In effect England was granted special almost colonizing status in China.

The French and Americans, also eager to increase their commercial and diplomatic presence in Asia, also negotiated treaties with China, spurring the English on to request even greater privileges from the Chinese. Their demands included opening up of all of China to British merchants, legalization of the opium trade, and permission for a British ambassador to reside in Beijing. Rejecting the demands of the British, and the separate pressure of the Americans and French to reopen negotiations regarding their trading rights in China, the Chinese empire was once more brought to the brink of war. After officials of the Chinese empire boarded a ship in Canton that was flying a British flag and was registered in England, the second Opium War broke out. Ultimately going down in defeat to a combined British–French military onslaught, Chinese officials negotiated the Treaty of Tientsin in 1858 with representatives from Britain, France and the United States. Under the terms of the 1858 arrangement all three

Western powers were allowed to open embassies in Beijing and more treaty ports were created.

While the urge to open up trade and to secure coaling ports for steamships was an impetus to the Western military push into Asia during the first half of the nineteenth century, bringing Asian countries into the system of Western style diplomacy in which representatives of nation-states resided in each other's capitals was also on the agendas of the Western powers. From an East Asian perspective the system of Western diplomacy was novel, completely foreign. For centuries, East Asia had operated under a kind of Sino-centric tribute trade system. According to the rules of that system, subordinate lands – Japan and Korea for instance – dispatched emissaries to the Chinese court, bringing gifts with their entourages, kowtowing to the Chinese emperor in exchange for the right to carry on trade with the cultural and political hub of their world, China. Without a doubt the first major penetration of Europeans into Asian waters in the fifteenth and sixteenth centuries eroded the tribute trade system to a degree. As more and more East Asian lands limited the scope of their international commerce – Japan in the mid-seventeenth century for instance – trade, and hence diplomatic interaction, between the East Asian powers deteriorated. Still, the notion that China was the center, the notion of securing the right to trade with the center through tribute, was the cornerstone of the East Asian system of diplomacy and interchange between the various countries in the region continued on that basis until the Opium Wars broke out.

States and nations

The modern state system is commonly said to have originated in Western Europe with the Peace of Westphalia agreed to in 1648 by the major belligerents who had participated in the Thirty Years' War that ravaged Germany especially between 1618 and 1648. Signatories to the treaty (France, Sweden, Spain, the Holy Roman Empire, and the Netherlands) recognized a variety of principles considered fundamental to modern diplomacy: sovereignty of states; the balance of power; and the importance of diplomacy among representatives of states that might potentially be drawn into war with one another.

Birth of the ideology of nationalism that gave rise to the term "nation" is usually associated with the late eighteenth and nineteenth centuries. Three political developments are associated with the emergence of nationalism in Western Europe: the French Revolution; the unification of Germany and Italy; and the partial breakup of old empires like the Austro-Hungarian and Ottoman Empires.

The French Revolution (1789–1799) gave rise to the idea of a republic in which all citizens participated in the national body through a common set of principles (e.g. liberty and equality). Germany and Italy in the latter half of the nineteenth century were each unified along lines of common language and culture that provided the cement binding together disparate economic and social zones into national unities. In the Balkans, Greece secured independence from the Ottomans, and in 1878, great power diplomacy freed Romania, Serbia and Montenegro from Ottoman rule. In 1867 Hungary gained virtually complete independence from the Hapsburgs who ruled the Austro-Hungarian Empire.

In the Americas, nationalism had earlier historical roots. The American Revolution (1776–1783) that freed the British colonies, but not Canada, from British imperial rule, was based upon a set of natural law and radical anti-monarchist principles set forth in the Declaration of Independence and instituted in the idea of the Bill of Rights and the separation of powers written into the Constitution of the United States (between the executive, legislative and judicial branches at the federal level; between states and the federal authorities) setting up the new nation. Subsequent rebellions in Latin America freed from domination by Spain, Portugal and the other European powers the entirety of the continental American landmass with the exception of British North America, spawning a host of new national entities grounded in national constitutions in Central and South America. Even Canada achieved partial independence from the United Kingdom with initial confederation in 1867, gaining some latitude of home rule with the British North America Act.

As can be seen from the examples sketched out here, nationalism is often associated with particular ideological principles: with republicanism in the case of France; with the natural rights philosophy and a desire to limit abuses of the powerful through the separation of powers in the case of the United States; and with the idea of language as a unifier in the case of Germany.

In the West, the earlier development of the Westphalia system of sovereign states with the eighteenth and nineteenth century ideas inherent in nationalism, gave rise to the idea of a system of diplomacy and the balance of power operating amongst nation-states. This idea, integral to the political evolution of Europe and the Americas, was foreign to East Asia which had operated under a Sino-centric system, the tribute trade system, according to which trade and political intercourse with the traditional dominant power of Asia, China, provided a framework for diplomacy and negotiation between cultural zones of Asia. As the nineteenth-century Western powers expanded the thrust of their military power – its growth nurtured and fueled by new technological and economic prowess garnered in the crucible of the industrial revolution – into Asia, they attempted to fit the Asian powers with whom they were negotiating into the nation-state system that had been evolving in Europe since the mid-seventeenth century. This led to a vigorous and sustained clash between the two systems within Asia, some countries adopting the European model (Japan) earlier than others (China).

Watching China wrestle with the Europeans and Americans – the Taiping Rebellion, which broke out in 1851 in the aftermath of China's humiliating defeats in the Opium Wars, became one the bloodiest civil wars in Chinese history – put the Japanese political elite on notice that a major external threat was looming. Three lessons were certainly impressing themselves on the most perceptive political figures in fief and shogunate alike: the tribute trade system of East Asian diplomacy was crumbling; increasing military power was being linked to economic prowess, and it was the West that appeared to being making major advances in both military and economic affairs, not the Chinese; and there was little chance that Japan could escape being opened up by the Western powers.

Economic power and military power

For the political elite of a nation-state, the overriding consideration in formulating a foreign policy is obtaining security for the nation's population and territory.

To maximize security, governments allocate portions of their budgets to military expenditure; sign treaties of alliance with other powers with the aim of deterring foreign aggression directed against them; and participate in multilateral architecture aimed at guaranteeing collective security. Examples of multilateral architecture are the balance of power and diplomacy systems established at the Peace of Westphalia, the League of Nations created at the Paris peace conference negotiating the conclusion of World War I, or the United Nations that emerged from the carnage of World War II.

There is a fine line between the drive to maximize security and the drive to establish regional or global hegemony. Major powers within a region, those with the grandest armies and navies, are more secure when they dominate their neighboring states, fashioning buffer zones between themselves and other powerful states. Since 1800, Western Europe has witnessed two major drives aimed at establishing regional hegemony: Napoleon's and Hitler's. In the Americas, the United States became the de facto *regional hegemonic power during the nineteenth century, expanding out to the west through a series of land purchases, and wars with Mexico, under the ideology of manifest destiny. Since the early nineteenth century one of the chief pillars of the foreign policy of the United States has been the Monroe Doctrine that warns off European powers from meddling in the affairs of the Americas, leaving the cleaning up of regional conflicts to the foreign policy establishment of the United States.*

To exert hegemonic power over neighbors or distant lands, leaders of a nation-state require a strong economic base, a rich coffer of revenues and numerous suppliers of armaments which they can draw upon in financing and equipping armies, navies and coast guards. Since the industrial revolution the requisite economic base has been a productive industrial sector, one churning out iron and steel, ships and land transport vehicles that can be turned to military purposes, and chemicals that can be utilized in manufacturing explosives.

The link between modern industrialization and military power became increasingly evident in the nineteenth century as the United Kingdom, the workshop of the world, emerged as the dominant global hegemonic power in the aftermath of the Napoleonic Wars. Building a massive navy, the United Kingdom dominated a growing empire that including dominions like Canada, Australia and New Zealand that enjoyed some form of home rule, and colonies like India that enjoyed far less political leverage within the empire.

Testimony to British economic and political dominance was growing international adherence to a British pound based gold standard, the pound (its price linked directly to gold) serving as the reserve currency settling balance of payments adjustments between most major trading partners, London being the dominant international capital market. Under the gold standard system other major trading nations established fixed exchange rates between their currencies and gold, thereby fixing the exchange rate between their currency and the British pound.

The theory of hegemonic stability is often used to explain why global hegemonic powers like the United Kingdom eventually see their hegemonic power slip away. To a degree it is in the interests of a hegemonic power to provide public goods that sustain the international trade system. This is because hegemonic powers have large economies, therefore carrying on substantial trade with other countries by dint of sheer size. They require markets for their exports; raw materials produced abroad; and foreign opportunities upon which their banks and merchants can pour capital, anticipating higher returns for their capital in lands where it is less abundant than it is at home.

For these reasons the hegemonic power shores up the international economic order with its own currency; and uses "gunboat diplomacy" when attempts are made to seize the capital assets acquired by the citizens of the hegemonic power in foreign lands.

According to the theory of hegemonic stability, countries other than the hegemonic power can "free ride" off the military and financial security provided by the leading country. Free riders can seize the opportunity to catch up with the hegemonic power by borrowing the latest technologies generated in the most advanced country, by borrowing in the capital markets of the leader. Countries that catch up threaten the global dominance of the hegemonic power. As the economies of the countries that catch up grow, so does their capacity to fund and field armies and navies.

During the period 1860–1900, Germany and the United States caught up with the United Kingdom, thereby becoming regional hegemonic powers that challenged the dominance of the United Kingdom. This argument is often used to explain why there was a race for colonies in Asia and Africa after 1880, why World War I broke out, and why the British pound based gold standard ceased to operate effectively after World War I.

For these reasons the infamous visits of Commodore Perry's black ships during the mid-1850s that forced the *bakufu* to accede to the opening of the country through the granting of treaty ports and the acknowledgement of the principle of extraterritoriality already imposed upon the Chinese empire did not come as a completely unexpected set of unpleasant surprises to the most astute and best informed Japanese. Was Japan now going to go the way of China, ravaged by civil conflict, its coastlines to be gradually carved up by the aggressive Western powers? Worse yet, was there a possibility Japan could end up completely colonized by one or more of the Western powers?

The race for colonies

After 1880 the drive to imperialism, which had been on the wane during the early nineteenth century as Latin America broke away from Spain and Portugal and nation-states proliferated in the Americas, gathered momentum once again. Africa was largely divided up by the European powers that also established new, or consolidated old, outposts in Asia. The United States joined the fray after the Spanish-American War of 1898, securing the Philippines and Hawaii.

Despite the fillip to nation-state development laid forth at the Paris peace conference, the Treaty of Versailles, and the establishment of the League of Nations occurring in the wake of World War I, and despite the demise of some empires (e.g. the Ottoman and Austro-Hungarian empires), European colonial empires survived the aftermath of the great conflict. Between World War I and World War II, it is estimated that the British colonial empire – upon which the sun never set – was populated with around 470 million persons; the French colonial possessions housed 65 million individuals; the Belgium empire controlled 13 million persons in its colonies (most infamously in the Belgian Congo); and the Dutch empire, holding onto Indonesia, incorporated 66 million persons. Not surprisingly the ideology of nationalism spread from its crucible in the Americas and Europe to the colonies, generating strong local opposition to colonial rule.

Why was there such a strong drive to colonize Africa and Asia at the end of the nineteenth century? One answer is geopolitical competition. As regional hegemonic powers emerged challenging the global supremacy of the United Kingdom, the race to secure strategically useful territory for global military operations intensified. This argument can be used to explain why Germany, France and the United States sought colonies throughout Asia-Pacific waters.

One of the implicit ideological pillars relied on by advocates for colonialism that fed into the geopolitical logic was eugenics, sometimes known as scientific racism. A theory of racial superiority or inferiority rooted in the logic of social Darwinism – the so-called survival of the fittest where fitness was associated with achievement in economic and political affairs – was used to justify the "white man's burden". The new fields of genetics and biometrics (the study of height, weight, cranium size, and intelligence) were called upon to provide scientific justification for the idea that distinct races existed and passed on their characteristics through reproduction. It was natural for social Darwinists to hitch theories of racial superiority and inferiority to justifications for colonialism.

A second set of arguments is based upon economic rationality. The British economist John Hobson advanced a theory of underconsumption in the advanced countries to explain the impetus to establish colonies that might absorb the products of the metropolitan power and provide foodstuffs and raw materials for industrial production to the metropolitan economy. Hobson believed that the development of the nascent welfare state – establishing a minimum wage by legislation, legalizing unions and the right to strike – might give a boost to the aggregate consumption demand of the masses of the populations in the advanced countries. Short of that, forced creation of captive markets for the excessive production of the advanced industrial countries in foreign lands through military action and colonialism seemed inevitable.

The Leninist–Marxist theory of imperialism rejected Hobson's belief that amelioration of the economic condition of the masses in the advanced nations through legislation could counteract the drive of the advanced industrial powers to colonize the less developed countries of the world. The Leninist theory rejected underconsumption as the basis for the economic drive to empire, substituting a theory based on a tendency to monopoly and oligopoly that was viewed as a concomitant of advanced capitalism. Economically powerful monopolists and captains of industry in oligopolies, wielding their financial clout to bribe monarchs, parliamentarians, and executive authorities in the advanced countries would and could influence the military policy of their governments, directing them along lines that suited their desire to create new markets in the colonial world.

As nationalist resistance to European and American colonialism gathered force in Africa and Asia a variety of arguments – some rooted in Leninist Marxism, some rooted in Hobson's logic, some rooted in

> *geopolitics – spread amongst the intellectuals, writers and journalists who sprang out of the colonized populations. For this reason nationalist movements to overthrow colonial masters were often characterized by a diverse and contradictory set of ideologies and theories about the nature of the colonial rule that had to be overthrown. The crazy quilt nature of these contending ideologies could and did condition, and sometimes confuse, the political regimes that emerged in former colonies securing independence from their colonial masters, becoming newly minted nation-states.*

The urgency of the potential threat to Japan's sovereignty was something that no politically sophisticated Japanese could disregard. Moreover there were practical economic problems with opening the country up to widespread trade with the Westerners. One involved the demand of the Western commercial community to establish a fixed exchange rate between Japan's domestic currency and the currency that most of them were using elsewhere in Asia, the Mexican silver dollar. The problem with doing so was this: the exchange rate between gold and silver established in the Western economies was one to fifteen, that is one ounce of gold purchased fifteen ounces of gold; in Japan's long insulated domestic monetary system one ounce of gold exchanged for five ounces of silver. Arbitrageurs – Western merchants operating in the treaty ports for example – could purchase gold in Japan with their silver, convert it to silver back in their home countries, returning to Japan to buy more gold – could and did profit from the discrepancy between the exchange rates. Gold flowed out; silver flowed in. Moving to consistency between the exchange rate system prevailing outside of Japan reflecting global supplies and demands for the precious metals and that which had been established domestically within Japan which had closed itself off from most international exchange for over two centuries dictated reorganization of the exchange rates between gold and silver within the country. In effect the value of silver had to deteriorate within Japan, hurting the interests of those holding silver, benefiting the interests of those parties who could exploit the opportunity arbitrage opened up. The *bakufu* itself was largely protected from the adverse drop in the value of silver, its coinage being a mélange containing a variety of metals. But the positions of many of the Osaka houses, committed to silver, were seriously compromised by the adjustment in silver/gold exchange rates.

The *bakufu* actually managed to benefit from the shock imposed upon Japan's monetary system because it was gobbling up foreign silver as trade was being opened up. Using these enhanced reserves of silver, the *bakufu* adopted a policy of recoinage, dramatically increasing the volume of its coins in circulation. This benefited the shogunate's fiscal position in the short run, but set in motion hyperinflation in the 1860s, domestic prices shooting up as the money supply increased far faster than the volume of transactions in the domestic economy. The discussion in the Appendix to Chapter 1 concerning the impact of growth in the money supply upon inflation rates (see the text discussing Figure 1.4E) is relevant here. Under the assumption that there was little if any growth in real output, inflationary tendencies should take over. This appears to have happened.

As noted the big losers in this episode were the merchant houses, especially those based in Osaka that held substantial amounts of silver. Many of them were bankrupted by the debasement of silver.

All of these developments, international and domestic, called into question the credibility of carrying out business as usual. Was the *bakuhan* system up to the task of confronting the Western powers? Would the shogun not do what the Chinese emperor was doing, moving along a path of capitulating to ongoing Western demands and Western military pressure? Out of the controversy and ferment swirling around amongst the most politically engaged samurai, farmers and merchants, two diametrically opposed options emerged: continue with the *bakuhan* system, remaining loyal to the shogun; or abandon the shogun.

Given the Neo-Confucian ideology informing Tokugawa Japan, the problem posed by jettisoning loyalty to the shogun was substantial. To whom, if anyone, was loyalty to be transferred? In countries adhering to the values of liberalism emerging out of England – England itself, the United States, Canada, for instance – loyalty was directed to the nation-state representing the people through the principle of democracy. This was not a concept of loyalty that could easily be made compatible with the hierarchical concepts of loyalty central to Neo-Confucian and *bushidō* ideology. For samurai in particular the only solution to the problem that made sense was to transfer loyalty to the emperor. After all, the shogun claimed that its power was based on protecting and serving the emperor, who somehow symbolized the collectivity of the Japanese people as a whole.

Thus a kind of ideological civil war broke out within most of the fiefs. Support the emperor or support the shogunate. In some of the fiefs the intellectual civil war became an actual civil war, opposing factions fighting each other tooth and nail. While it is fair to say that most of the samurai in most of the fiefs remained disengaged, at least in a military sense, debate in the political arena swept across the country as a whole. But in some of the *tozama* fiefs, where hostility to the *bakufu* had festered for centuries, samurai opposed to staying loyal to the shogunate were willing to throw caution to the wind. In two of the southwestern fiefs in particular – in Satsuma and Chōshū – internal war between opposing factions broke out. Ultimately those advocating loyalty to the emperor emerged triumphant, now carrying their battle beyond the boundaries of their fiefs, into the national arena. The twilight of the shogunate – known as *bakumatsu* in Japanese – was rapidly coming to a conclusion.

Mounting an anemic political and military campaign to stay in power, the *bakufu* quickly collapsed. In 1868, the last shogun abdicated. Power now passed to the emperor or rather to the emperor as advised by key samurai from the two fiefs that had spearheaded the attack on the *bakufu*, Satsuma and Chōshū. This is known as the Meiji Restoration because the nominal power of the emperor over Japan was restored, wrested away from the shogun.

Was the Meiji Restoration a revolution – akin to the French Revolution – that emerged out of the primitive accumulation of capital and the conflict between social classes predicted by Marx in his stage theory of history? Was it a bourgeois revolution? Does Japan's economic development follow along the lines set forth by Marx, feudalism dying, as capitalism emerged from its death throes? A huge Marxist inspired literature whose arguments we have briefly touched on earlier in this chapter emerged after World War I, basically defending the view that the Meiji Restoration does fit into a close variant of the Marxist stage theory that, after all, was developed to explain what had happened, and was happening, in Western Europe. In writings in English, perhaps the most widely cited English language account of this Marxist interpretation is due to Norman (2000). Norman basically argues that a coalition of merchants and lower samurai emerged during the period after Perry's forcible opening up of Japan, the merchants financing the military activities of the restive samurai opposed to the continuation of the *bakuhan* system. Moreover, he argues, the most powerful of the merchant houses provided the contributions and forced loans that shored up the new Meiji government established in 1868.

Critics of this view abound. Indeed, as we have seen in this chapter, there is a large literature that rejects the Marxist interpretation of Tokugawa economic development. Moreover, there is a large body of scholarship arguing that many merchants did support the *bakufu*, and that the samurai opposed to its continuing were largely motivated by loyalty to their (*tozama*) fiefs that had been placed on the outside rung of power by the *bakufu*.

What is clear is that a daring and fairly small group of samurai committed to restoring an early form of government – rule by the emperor – a reactionary idea in many ways, spearheaded revolutionary change, destroying along the way the very samurai class that they were born into. Understanding how this apparent paradox came about is the subject of our next chapter.

Key terms and concepts in Chapter 2

Bakuhan system	*Noren-wake*
Organic Economy stages A and B	Internal labor market of a merchant
Proto-industrial craft production	house
Baku and *han*	*Mabiki*
Fudai and *tozama daimyō*	Family reconstitution studies
Bushidō	Primitive accumulation of capital
Shinden	Dutch learning (*rangaku*)
Rice tax rate	Extraterritorial rights
Putting-out system	

Part II

Industrialization, 1870–1945

3   Meeting the Western challenge

The politics and policies of the Meiji Restoration

Proceeding forward and backward at the same time, lurching between eclectic borrowing from the menacing Western powers and celebration of ancient domestic traditions, Japan successfully embraced industrialization and emerged as a power to be reckoned with in the Eurocentric nation-state system between the Meiji Restoration and the onset of World War I.

Paradox abounds. The period 1868–1914 saw intense innovation and restless experimentation in polity and economy, deep divisions over policy hovering over the wrenching changes. A foreign observer residing in Japan during the 1870s might well have predicted a dismal conclusion to the process, the new regime ending up as a failed state. The country might have been carved up, or at least dominated, by one or several Western powers. That the nation actually emerged stronger and wealthier through its transition is in no small degree attributable to the Tokugawa legacy that continued to inform its politics, policies and economic growth during its first four decades of steam power centered industrialization.

Debate over what belongs on a short list of Tokugawa period contributions to Meiji period development will never cease.[1] Still, there are at least eight characteristics of late Tokugawa period Japan that most informed opinion would emphasize: national integration grounded in well developed within-transport networks on the water and on the land supporting substantial specialization and division of labor; accumulation of physical capital including infrastructure maintained and managed by governments (e.g. canalized waterways, roads, irrigation ditches, urban centers) and structures and machines privately utilized by peasant households in the agriculture and proto-industrial sectors; human capital enhancing infrastructure, namely fief academies and temple schools; financial infrastructure including money – *bakufu* coins, paper notes issued to fiefs and shogunate alike – and instruments for handling debt and insuring risky activity; a relatively strong commitment to the principle of private property rights, in land, in structures and transport vehicles for merchants and peasants; relatively high productivity levels in rice farming, especially in the southwest of the country; a widespread diffusion of proto-industrial production penetrating urban centers, rural hinterlands and even remote rural districts high up in the mountains; and a bureaucracy largely staffed by warriors well versed in dealing with and coordinating the economic activities of farmers, merchants and artisans alike within fief boundaries and *bakufu* controlled territories.

Drawing upon Tokugawa era established principles of promoting national integration through markets and the diffusion of innovation, of developing infrastructure in all its main facets (physical, financial and human capital enhancing), of coordination of private economic activity by bureaucrats, and of respect for private property rights, the entrepreneurs, political leaders and bureaucrats of the Meiji era drew upon Western models in refining and improving upon their legacies. There was impressive continuity between the late Tokugawa period and the Meiji period. The notion of path dependence captures this idea: the choices made by, the paths traversed by, the innovators of Meiji, were profoundly shaped by the fact that they had all been born, raised and socialized under Tokugawa rule.

To argue this is not to deny that much was new in Meiji Japan. Indeed the most important rallying cry of the Meiji period – the political cement affording a "big tent" housing and accommodating militarists, economic nationalists, profit seeking entrepreneurs, struggling merchant houses, well to do peasants lobbying for improvements in their districts – *fukoku kyōhei* ("enrich the country, strengthen the military") was explicitly aimed at absorbing Western technology and institutions in political, economic and military affairs with the ultimate aim of resisting, repelling, Western power, Western pressure.[2]

From politics and economics predicated upon closure – the country virtually sealed off from all but the scantiest contact with the West and indeed with Asia as well during the long period of Tokugawa rule – Japan's new breed of political and economic elites now oriented themselves around being open, at least to a degree. They were now adjusting to political constraints imposed by Western powers that they simultaneously distrusted and admired. They were now wrestling with openness in trade. Under the terms of the unequal treaties signed with the Western powers the level of tariffs the Japanese government were allowed to charge was capped at a low rate so Japanese merchants working through the putting-out system were now forced to adjust to harsh competition from importers bringing in cotton textiles, spirits and furniture. At the same time producers of tea and silk thread could tap freshly opened up opportunities to sell the fruits of their labors in the voracious markets of Europe and North America.

The genrō

The term "genrō" refers to a small group of Meiji leaders who came to be recognized as elder statesmen from the 1890s through the early 1920s. Their power was partially rooted in their access to the emperor who they advised on matters of public policy.

Many of the genrō worked their way up the political ladder as state councilors under the Dajokan (Council of Government) system of government that held sway from 1869 until 1885 when it was replaced by a cabinet system. Most of the genrō had been lower ranking samurai in Satsuma and Chōshū fiefs – thus becoming embroiled in the fief clique factionalism under so-called Sat-Chō rule – although some were recruited from other fiefs, for example from Hizen and Tosa.

Disputes between the genrō played a prominent role in some of the most important events in the early Meiji period. Saigō Takamori, one of the most charismatic leaders to emerge from Satsuma fell out with Itō Hirobumi, also from Satsuma. Ultimately falling into policy disputes over a possible military campaign directed at Korea and government subsidies for the former samurai, Saigō organized a revolt against the new Meiji government from his base in Kagoshima, only to fall in defeat to the conscription army directed by his old nemesis Yamagata Aritomo of Chōshū, who had competed with Saigō for influence within the new army. The so-called Western War of 1877 in which Saigō himself perished (and 5,000 of his men died) represented the last gasp of the samurai as a military force.

A second major political crisis that sprang from divisions between the genrō broke out in 1881, this time over how to write constitution for the new Meiji government. Ōkuma Shigenobu, one of the few state councilors to emerge from a fief other than Satsuma or Chōshū (he was originally a samurai in Hizen) was a strong advocate of British parliamentary practice, arguing that the constitution should establish a framework in which political parties represented in parliament made national policy. Opposed were men like Itō who favored a system more akin to that prevailing in Bismarck's Germany, an elite clustered around the throne keeping a tight monopoly over policy making.

As vigorous competition between the genrō caused them to spin off into different directions in search of bases for political power – Ōkuma in helping to found the Constitutional Reform Party, developing the skills of a charismatic political campaigner and advocate for party rule; Yamagata in placing men loyal to him in the army thereby making it his political bastion – the capacity of the genrō to keep power within their small circle withered.

Nonetheless, of the eighteen prime ministers who formed cabinets between 1885 and 1921 when Hara Kei headed up what is generally believed to be the first true party cabinet, Itō held the post four times, Yamagata held the post twice, and Ōkuma twice. Moreover, Yamagata left a heavy imprint on the way the military was treated within Japan's pre-1945 government – the army and navy circumventing the civilian cabinet by directly reporting to the emperor – thereby paving the way for an environment in which the army, in Manchuria and elsewhere upon the Chinese mainland, was able to operate independently of the desires and designs of the cabinet in Tokyo.

Who constituted the new political elite? The key figures were all samurai, most of them born and raised in the Satsuma and Chōshū fiefs, all of them active in overthrowing pro-*bakufu* governments in their own fiefs, then spearheading the restoration of imperial rule and the destruction of the *bakufu* regime at the national level. That they came from the ranks of the samurai, typically from the ranks of the lower samurai whose fortunes generally had been in decline during the late Tokugawa period, rendered them ambivalent about the course of action that they felt they had to take lest champions of the *bakufu* system attempt to wrest back power from them by dint of arms or by dint of political maneuvering. Taking on the role of creative destroyers they proceeded to dismantle the *bakuhan* system, including the confederation style of power sharing and the class system, including the samurai class itself.

Why were samurai willing to ruthlessly attack and dismantle a system that they had been beneficiaries of? Several reasons seem plausible. The Tokugawa system of so-called feudal rule was quite different from feudal rule in the West. The Tokugawa system was an administrative system. The connection between the land and the ruler of a fief was weak at best: the *bakufu* could and did move *daimyō* around, could and did disband the samurai loyal to a *daimyō* who was being forcibly removed from power. By the later half of the Tokugawa period samurai had become bureaucrats, managing fief businesses in some cases, having no claim to particular parcels of land from which their fiefs secured rice taxes. Their self interest lay in either becoming administrators or political players in the new regime, or in exploiting their connections as samurai with the oligarchy taking control of the country to make money, in finance or in business.

That there was continual pressure on the Japanese political elite from demands placed upon them by the European powers and the United States did make it easier for the small clique of samurai taking charge of national affairs to have their way. After all, active domestic opposition to the new regime was likely to play into the hands of the Americans, British, French, Germans and Russians who had forced Japan open. Still, there were bitter disputes over policy priorities and at least one civil war broke out, known as the Satsuma Rebellion or the Western War, in 1877.

To an important degree the politics of the early Meiji period – from 1869 until the mid-1880s – were dominated by the need to stamp out domestic opposition to the policies undertaken by the government. Until domestic unrest could be squelched, the fragile character of the government's authority made it difficult for it to effectively institute policies that the public at large would comply with. As it transpired two main sources of opposition to the government surfaced. One came from the ranks of the samurai, that is from the beneficiaries of the old order now crumbling before their eyes. This signified the death rattle of the past. The other came from the penetration of liberal Western political philosophies into Japan. This signified the first steps of a march into the future.

Forming a council of Government, the *Dajokan*, in 1869, the key players in the political realm invested themselves with the formal mantle of power by becoming *sangi* (state councilors), advisors to the emperor in whose name, on whose behalf, they issued the directives that did away with the formal political apparatus of the Tokugawa state. In 1871 the *Dajokan*, committed to a unitary state model in which regional administrations would be weak relative to the center, ordered the fiefs abolished, groups of contiguous fiefs being consolidated into prefectures (*ken* in Japanese), initially fashioning seventy-five prefectures out of the several hundred fiefs (in a subsequent administrative reorganization these fiefs were further consolidated). In doing this they had to contend with the loyalty many samurai felt toward their old domain. Thus they carefully avoided appointing as the administrator of a prefecture an individual who came from the fiefs that were consolidated into the prefecture. This attacked the fief loyalty of the samurai whose right to carry and brandish swords was also curtailed.

In 1876 the *Dajokan* issued an order further eroding the fortunes of the former samurai, especially the former lower samurai. The *Dajokan* ordered the hereditary stipends paid to the samurai to be commuted into government bonds capitalized at between five and fourteen times the annual value of the stipend. These bonds were designed to bear interest ranging between 5 and 7 percent. Under the terms of the arrangement the fiscal burden of paying the stipends imposed upon the government was dramatically cut, by around a third. Moreover, while those samurai who had enjoyed higher rank and higher incomes under the *bakuhan* system actually emerged from the arrangement with decent prospects – they were encouraged to use their bonds to invest in the National Bank system that was being created – the lower samurai generally faced very bleak prospects indeed. This was one of the triggers fueling the Satsuma Rebellion, lower samurai angered over being impoverished flocking to the banner of Saigō Takamori.

Resentment over the commuting of the stipends was not the only issue inflaming Saigō and his followers. A second major issue involved foreign policy, especially relations with Korea. Throughout the 1850s and 1860s, Korea tried to retain its status as a vassal of China, not an independent country. Refusing to recognize the new imperial government in Japan further inflamed tensions between the two countries. Korea's stubborn stand angered many of the leaders of the new Meiji government who professed, after all, to equally support promoting economic development and a strong and assertive military. Under the political rubric of *fukoku kyōhei* both militarists and businesspeople were supposed to find common ground.

Tensions erupted in violence in 1875. Japan sent a gunboat up the Han River, dispatching the fleet after the boat was fired upon. Forced to become independent of China, Korea reluctantly signed a treaty of commerce with Japan in 1876, gaining recognition by the European powers and the United States during the 1880s. To the more vocal advocates of military action like Saigō the actions taken by Japan were insufficient, displaying a flaccid weakness. From their point of view there was too much emphasis on enriching the country, too little on strengthening the military. Nor was he alone amongst the oligarchy in taking this position. Most did support a more aggressive stance by Japan. But the arguments of the foreign policy moderates won out.

Angered by commutation and the Korean policy, Saigō retreated to the Satsuma region that had been absorbed into Kagoshima prefecture. There he and his followers built up an arsenal lest they require it in the future if they decided to take up military action against the government. Was Saigō tricked into open defiance through the machinations of the other Meiji oligarchs who feared his charismatic appeal? In any event the authorities in Tokyo had no choice but to send out the freshly established conscription army to take control of the arsenal. The Satsuma rebels went down to defeat in 1877, Saigō perishing in the debacle. With the defeat of the Satsuma Rebellion in 1877, the samurai were a spent force. In a sense this represented the last gasp of the *bakuhan* class system. Had the lower samurai who flocked to Satsuma been the only opponents of the Meiji oligarchy, 1877 might have marked the end of a period of transition between late Tokugawa *bakuhan* rule and a Meiji consensus.

However, the military's defeat of the Satsuma Rebellion did not bring to an end potential domestic unrest. Informed by Western concepts of democracy and republican rule, the People's Rights movement demanded the convening of representative assembly emerged, mainly organized amongst rural elites. Whatever their views on adopting Western constitutional principles into Japan – and the oligarchs had widely diverging opinions about the desirability of doing so, and which course of action would be best suited to meet their needs – the People's Rights movement threatened their power, bringing on a political crisis in the early 1880s. From 1881 to 1885 Dajokan rule continued – and continued to be criticized by the People's Rights movement – finally giving way to governance by the first cabinet in 1885 as the oligarchs argued amongst themselves about how best to manage the transition to governance under a constitution, namely the Meiji Constitution of 1889.

The Meiji Constitution

The Meiji Constitution of 1889 was a document of momentous significance for Japan's political development, prepared for with one of the most delicate political minuets danced by the genrō and their advisors. Trusted to the powerful genrō Itō Hirobumi in the early 1880s, the task of creating a constitutional form of government showcasing a national parliament fell into the hands of an oligarch enamored of the German model of limited popular democracy, of parliamentary governance relatively free of party politics, as opposed to the British model based upon party cabinet.

In anticipation of writing the key political clauses for the constitution, Itō engineered three administrative reforms: creating a peerage out of the nobility, former daimyō and meritorious samurai who would sit in the putative upper house of parliament; creating a cabinet, the offices of Prime Minister and Ministers of State being established; and the formulation of an examination system for the civil service, thereby transforming the appointment of bureaucrats from a "spoils system" to a merit system.

Entrusting the drafting of the constitution to a subordinate who had studied in Germany, Itō directed the crafting of the document along lines which wedded Sat-Chō attitudes about the proper role of the emperor in the political life of Japan with German practice. Crucial was the idea shared by both the Japanese and Germans who wrote the detailed clauses of the constitution that the emperor was to be the source of political power. Thus the clauses outlining the role of the emperor state that the "Emperor is sacred and inviolable," "... is head of the Empire, combining in Himself the rights of sovereignty...," "exercises the legislative power with the consent of the Imperial Diet...," and "... has the supreme command of the Army and Navy".

Left ambiguous in the document was the question of who was to appoint the cabinet: the parties enjoying majorities or substantial minorities in the upper and lower houses of the Diet; or the emperor. This ambiguity was Janus-faced: it allowed for flexibility; at the same time it opened the door for ongoing, bitter, struggle between advocates of party rule and those favoring concentration of power amongst the few.

Consistent with an approach that viewed imperial power as crucial to government – denying that sovereignty rested in the people – the rights accorded to Japanese citizens were limited, hemmed in by qualifications. True, ordinary Japanese were allowed "liberty of abode" and "right of property". Yet freedom of religious belief was allowed "within limits not prejudicial to peace and order", and the liberty of speech was permitted within "the limits of law".

How was the new document to be promulgated? A majority of the genrō favored approval by the emperor. However in 1887 leaders of the popular rights movement organized demonstrations in Tokyo demanding freedom of speech and reduction of the land tax. Pressed by the politics of mass protest, Yamagata, then Minister of Home Affairs, ordered the police to restrict the right to hold public meetings, the oligarchy following this up with the drafting of the Peace Preservation Law that restricted public protest. Realizing that reliance on the emperor's assent might foment further ongoing dissent, Itō created a special organization, the Privy Council, that considered the document for the constitution in secret sessions, approving its various clauses in order. On 11 February 1889, the anniversary of the accession of the Emperor Jimmu, the emperor read a statement granting the constitution to the nation before a select audience of high government officials, foreign diplomats, and prominent citizens.

Fukuzawa Yukichi

The second son of a low ranking feudal official, Fukuzawa Yukichi (1835–1901) became a pivotal figure in the intellectual ferment of the Meiji period, an ardent advocate of true learning – as opposed to false learning that trained people to be disciplined subordinates and vassals – rooted in promoting freedom and independence. The founder of the Keiō Gijuku that ultimately became Keiō University, one of the most prestigious private universities in Japan, and the founder of a newspaper, "Jijishimpō," Fukuzawa's writings were fundamental to the Westernization movement that gathered force during the late Tokugawa and early Meiji periods.

Initially bitterly opposed to the Sat-Chō style of government out of fear that the former samurai from Satsuma and Chōshū would follow the ideological sloganeering of late Tokugawa samurai to "honor the emperor and expel the foreigners", establishing a regime hostile to Western learning, Fukuzawa was pleased to see the Meiji oligarchs embrace things Western, in business, finance, political organization and government, and education.

In his "Theory of Civilization" (first published in 1875) Fukuzawa argued that Japanese should assiduously learn from the West, embracing the spirit of independence crucial to Western progress, thereby guaranteeing that Japan as a nation could maintain its independence from the Western powers. At the time when he was writing, Fukuzawa felt that the West and the West alone had achieved a state of 'civilization', this achievement resting not only on the shoulders of elites in Europe and North America, but also upon the shoulders of the masses, everyone contributing to the improvement of the "spirit of the times".

Given these views, it is not surprising that Fukuzawa opposed the politicization of education, the focus of school textbooks on promoting national unity through glorification of the cult of the emperor. In this respect his liberal views that emphasized the importance of separating politics from learning clashed with the views held amongst key Meiji oligarchs who believed that compulsory education should be bent to the needs of nation building.

It would be misleading to view the People's Rights movement as a groundswell emanating out of the masses. The ranks of the movement demanding a widening of the scope of political voice were dominated by elites. Particularly influential was a rural political elite (known as the *meibōka* in Japanese). They wanted a share of the power that the oligarchs were jealously monopolizing. They wanted a piece of the action. Most of them were not opposed to elite political rule.

While the oligarchs wrestled over the character of the constitution and the relationship between the emperor system whose power they had campaigned to restore in the 1860s and the rights of commoners as guaranteed in the constitution, the People's Rights movement ushered in the beginning of Western style party politics. In 1880 various representatives of liberal thought – including Tokyo intellectuals associated with Fukuzawa Yukichi's Keio academy – met with the aim of establishing a national party.

In 1881 they cobbled together a committee and an office, dubbing their party the "Jiyūtō" (Liberty Party). Giving a push to the new party was one of the oligarchs, Itagaki Taisuke, who had fallen out with the other oligarchs over policy and power, perhaps more heavily motivated by political opportunism than by a commitment to democracy rooted in Western style individualism.

From the oligarchs' point of view party democracy threatened their program of limiting decision making to a small clique of elites whose power ultimately derived from their access to the imperial court. To limit the spread of the pro-democracy movement the *Dajokan* issued Regulations for Public Meetings and Associations. These regulations mandated that organizers of public meetings secure official permission before holding them, forbade advertising of meetings by associations, and permitted the police to intervene if they felt disruption to public order might emanate from a meeting. In short, the *Dajokan* was reaching back into the Tokugawa past in restricting freedom of speech and assembly, using techniques developed by the shogunate to quell dissent and open discussion of political ideas. Whether the oligarchy had a real peril to its power remains an open question: most of the People's Rights representatives in the countryside came from the ranks of well-to-do peasants and merchants who were hardly interested in fomenting rebellion. After all, they did not want to see their the poorer strata of their villages recruited to a revolutionary movement bent on overthrowing the market oriented approach promoted by the majority of members of the *Dajokan*.

In short, the politics of the 1870s and 1880s were dominated by the oligarchy's efforts, ultimately successful, to achieve domestic political stability during its transition from Tokugawa to Meiji political regimes. In light of the fact that many of the newly minted nation-states created during the 1950s and 1960s failed – hopelessly bled by domestic unrest, corruption and ongoing political crises – this is not an unimpressive achievement. Moreover, during its wrenching transition from one regime to the next Japan had to contend with the Western powers which had extracted extraterritorial rights from it, imposing restrictions on the level of tariffs the Japanese state could impose on imports. Consider the inability of the Chinese government to mount a successful campaign of reform during the late nineteenth and early twentieth centuries under pressure from the Western powers. By comparison, Japan's record seems quite remarkable. With this in mind, let us consider how the new Meiji government – building upon the Tokugawa legacies in infrastructure construction, national integration, coordination of markets by bureaucrats, and private property rights – created a host of economic policies shaping economic incentives and outcomes.

We begin with the Land Tax Reform of 1873.[3] With the demise of the fief form of government, the authorities had to change the way they taxed farming, hitherto extracted as a percentage of the rice output produced by the villages within a fief. The solution hit upon was to establish legally sanctioned property rights in land, the government issuing certificates of ownership for every parcel of land throughout the country; to allow people to freely buy and sell the land; and to require the tax be paid in monetary terms. Each piece of land was assigned a market value – estimated by capitalizing the net revenue from rice production (gross revenue net of purchases of seed and fertilizer and net of national and local property taxes on the land) – and this value was taxed at a fixed rate t.

That is land value was determined by the equation:

$$V = \frac{R - C - TN - TL}{i} \tag{3.1}$$

Where V is the estimated land value, R is the gross revenue generated from the use of land, i is the interest rate prevailing at the time (6 percent), C is the sum of seed and fertilizer costs, TN is the national land tax paid on the land, and TL is the local surtax on the land. And total taxes were then assessed by multiplying land value through by fixed rates for national (t_N) and local surtaxes (t_L), namely:

$$TN = t_N * V \quad \text{and} \quad TL = t_L * V \tag{3.2}$$

In this way, taxation was monetized.

Under the law the rate could be modified from time to time as could the measure of land value. However these changes were not made on a regular annual basis. They were only undertaken occasionally. Thus the rate of taxation on farmland became a political variable. Farmers wanted a lower rate; government officials wanted a higher rate. Not surprisingly a government that was under political duress and terrified of peasant rebellion set off by what farmers perceived as unfairly high land taxes was prepared to lower the rate and collect less in the way of land taxes which were the bulk of taxes it collected in the first two decades of the new Meiji government. In 1877 the land tax was reduced, falling by one-sixth.

The fact that the land tax was based upon fixed monetized values for farmland and was calibrated in monetary terms became an issue during the famous – or from the farmers' point of view, infamous – Matsukata Deflation. The background to the deflation is as follows: to pay for the costs of suppressing the Satsuma Rebellion, the government issued a large number of paper notes, much of its note issue not being convertible into specie (Japan was still on a *de facto* silver standard at this time). This issue of money triggered inflation, the wholesale price index spiraling upward between 1877 and 1881 (one estimate suggests that the index jumped from a level of 106 in 1877 to a level of 164 in 1881). Once inflation gets deeply entrenched in an economy, the public begins to expect that it will continue. Expectations about price increases generate further price increases because producers anticipate that they will continue, building price increases into their marketing strategies. In no time at all, disruptive hyperinflation can take over, endangering orderly economic activity.

To rein in this headlong surge in prices, the new Finance Minister Matsukata Masayoshi pursued a policy of running a surplus, drastically slashing outlays, selling off model factories originally built by the government to the private sector. Government revenues exceeding expenditures, Matsukata was able to basically "burn" money, taking the currency surpluses that the government received out of circulation. The money supply dropped. So did the wholesale price index. By 1885, price stability returned. The problem from the farmers' point of view was that the prices of their rice output fell between 1881 and 1885, the nominal values their output commanded on the market plummeted, but the nominal taxes that they were required to pay did not. They found themselves squeezed. By all accounts some of the less well-to-do farmers had to sell off their land holdings in order to pay their taxes, thereby sinking into tenancy.

To Marxist historians the Matsukata Deflation is infamous because they believe it laid the foundations of parasitic landlordism in rural Japan. To be sure by the early 1900s about 45 percent of the paddy land was held in tenancy, mostly farmed under sharecropping arrangements. Was the drift towards increasing concentration of land in the hands of rural elite – landlords – an outgrowth of the deflation due to the fact that many of the poorer farmers had to sell off their fields in order to pay their taxes? Or was it simply due to the fact that rural merchants and better off peasants aggrandized land by offering to buy holdings from less efficient peasant households who mismanaged their plots? Was the village of the countryside falling into the hands of powerful landlord elites promoting limited political liberalization in so far as it accorded them political voice that they used to secure resources for their communities – roads, railroad lines, improved drainage – because these projects benefited them? Were these elites distrustful of their less prosperous brethren? Did they wish to simultaneously oppress the poorer strata of their villages while protesting political oppression by the *Dajokan*?

The ramifications of the Matsukata Deflation were hardly limited to agriculture. In order to raise revenues, Matsukata decided to sell off a number of the "model" state owned enterprises that had either been set up by fiefs prior to the Meiji Restoration or had been built with the aid of foreign advisors in the wake of the Restoration. State owned enterprises included the Tomioka Silk Works; the Miike mine; the Naval Weapon Factory and Mita Manufacturing located in Tokyo; and shipbuilding establishments located in Nagasaki and Kawasaki. Purchasing machinery from Europe and the United States to equip the state owned enterprises, hiring foreign advisors to train Japanese workers, the government created the model enterprises that it hoped the private sector would emulate and learn from. For instance, many Japanese managers and engineers who graduated from technical vocational schools did a stint in the state owned factories before moving to the private sector. So there were important externalities flowing from the enterprises. But in the wake of the inflation of the late 1870s, Matsukata felt it was time to liquidate most of the facilities, a prominent exception being military arsenals that it continued to manage. Many of these enterprises ended up in the hands of the *zaibatsu* (financial cliques) that we shall discuss shortly.

Matsukata's imprint on the Japanese economy was not limited to stemming inflation and privatization of the nascent Western technology using industrial sector. It was under his leadership that the financial infrastructure was substantially reworked. In 1872, before Matsukata assumed the position of Minister of Finance, the *Dajokan* brought in the National Bank Act, establishing a system of national banks. Impressed with the fact that the United States federal government, wrestling with problems of financing the Civil War and concerned about how to bring down the supply of inconvertible notes, had created a system of national banks in 1863, those making policy on banking decided to emulate the American banking system at least initially. They felt that it offered a panacea to Japan's currency crisis, brought on by the fact that the Japanese public was making use of a variety of paper currencies inherited from the Tokugawa period, including fief and *bakufu* issued notes that were generally not convertible into silver or gold. One of the characteristics of the American banking system of the 1860s was that it operated without a central bank, the charter for the Second Bank of the United States falling victim to hostility against East Coast moneyed interests during the presidency of Andrew Jackson. So the initial experiments of the Meiji government in setting up a banking system, creating an infrastructure of financial intermediaries, were based on avoiding the creation of a central bank, a lender of last resource backing up private banks.

To some extent the drive to charter national banks was tied in with the government's desire to ease the transition of the samurai, weaning them from their dependence on fiscal largesse through the issue of bonds that capitalized their hereditary stipends. The idea was to encourage the samurai to place their bonds in the national banks as paid in capital. Thus in 1876, the same year the samurai bond program was initiated, the National Bank Act was modified allowing the national banks to hold up to 80 percent of their capital in the form of government bonds.

Were the samurai the crucial linchpin for the nascent national bank system? This view has been contested. For instance Yamamura (1967) rejects the samurai centered interpretation. Analyzing the records of a number of the 153 national banks chartered under the 1872 and 1876 legislation, Yamamura argues that most of the deposits and paid in capital emanated from those circles who had accumulated capital during the late Tokugawa period – merchant houses, rural landlords and rural merchants – and from nouveaux riches who prospered by carrying on exchange with Westerners in the treaty ports, especially in Yokohama. Indeed at its founding 60 percent of the paid in capital for the First National Bank came from the merchant houses of Mitsui and Ono, the prodigious Meiji entrepreneur Shibusawa Eichi serving as its first president.

In this context the fact that Meiji Japan inherited an impressive legacy of financial infrastructure from the Tokugawa period must be kept in mind. Not only did merchant houses and the rural wealthy hold currency and coinage. A system of rotating savings and credit associations (*mujin*) with a long pedigree going back to the thirteenth century operated alongside the accumulation of financial capital by merchants rural and urban alike. According to Deckle and Hamada (2000) relatively small groups would create the *mujin*, placing their money into a pot, the accumulation of which was paid out either through a draw from the pot (the lucky drawer thereafter being barred from further draws from the pot) or through a process of competitive bidding. Interestingly enough these *mujin* have survived, being formally recognized and regulated by the Ministry of Finance around World War I, becoming the base upon which many of the mutual (*sōgō*) banks of the mid-1950s were created.

Moreover rural banks largely operated through the wealthy merchants and landowners, the *meibōka*. The banks made loans to the elite landowners and merchants who in turn made loans to less influential less fortunate colleagues. The hold of the Tokogawa rural economic elite over rural economic activity tended to continue. Additional testimony to the importance of the legacy of Tokugawa financial infrastructure is the decision of the government to permit the establishment of private banks (*ginkō*). The merchant house of Mitsui that had helped fund the armies overthrowing the *bakufu* had lobbied for that right to open a private bank. They were rewarded for their loyalty to the oligarchy in 1876, the same year the samurai stipends were capitalized into bonds that the government hoped would shore up the national banks.

Under Matsukata's direction steps were taken to jettison the experiment with American style banking. Matsukata saw to it that the rules governing the chartering of the national banks were rewritten, their charters reduced from thirty years to twenty years. Influenced by his discussions in continental Europe with economists, Matsukata promoted the central bank favored by the French and Belgians in particular. In 1882 directives were issued to create the Bank of Japan that was to operate under the careful supervision by the Ministry of Finance, the bank assuming its role of creating a lender of last resort system based on reserves – bank accounts earning interest – placed into its coffers by the banks that had been chartered. The Bank of Japan actually began its operations in 1885, the last year of the Matsukata Deflation.

In creating the Bank of Japan the oligarchy had to sidestep around the growing importance of Yokohama as a burgeoning financial center, fueled by the active trade and commerce going on between Western merchants and trading companies and Japanese who operated in the treaty ports. Indeed as Reed (1980) points out the first Japanese city to become a major international banking center was Yokohama not Tokyo; throughout the period 1880 to 1940 Tokyo shared its role as a global financial center with Yokohama first and then with Yokohama and Osaka. Under the 1882 legislation, the Yokohama Specie Bank created in 1880 was allowed to have a monopoly in foreign exchange dealings and the Bank of Japan agreed to provide cheap deposits for the Yokohama Specie Bank.

The continental European models favored by Matsukata also served as inspiration for the Meiji bureaucrats and oligarchs who designed government managed specialty banks to accommodate the Meiji expansions of both agriculture and industry. For instance the Hypothec Bank of Japan which focused on making loans for improving land and for funding non-residential construction projects was modeled after the French Crédit Foncier; the Industrial Bank of Japan that made long-term loans to manufacturing concerns, including the cotton textile enterprises whose growth fueled the first major boom in Japanese manufacturing, on the French Crédit Mobilier.

How important was Matsukata himself to the creation of Japan's financial infrastructure? To some scholars his stature is equal to that of Alexander

Hamilton in the early history of the United States. Secretary of the Treasury in the presidency of George Washington, first President of the United States, Hamilton promoted the development of a national currency backed by silver and gold. He stabilized national fiscal affairs, centralizing tax collection and establishing a system of federal government debt issue. The First Bank of the United States emerged out of Hamilton's program of responsible currency issue and responsible government finance. Once rules and channels through which government could finance its affairs were established, the groundwork was laid for a largely private sector banking system that could and did lend to both government and the private sector. Was Matsukata the Hamilton of Meiji Japan? By establishing the principles of lender of last resort and responsible management of the government's fiscal affairs did Matsukata set in motion the institutional changes that served as the cornerstone for the elaboration of Japan's financial infrastructure?

Debunking the myth of Matsukata's crucial contribution to Meiji financial development is the burden of Miwa and Ramseyer (2006b) who place the responsibility for the development of Japan's banking system squarely on the shoulders of the private sector. The evidence Miwa and Ramseyer assemble suggests that the main reason entrepreneurs created banks was to lend to commercial firms, not to government; and the government did not depend upon banks for most of its funding.

While banks played a crucial role in the funding of capital accumulation by the Meiji agriculture and manufacturing sectors, it is important to keep in mind that the oligarchs who traveled to Europe and the United States were impressed by the existence of equity – stock and bond – markets in Europe and North America, writing regulatory code that authorized and buttressed the operation of these markets in Japan. As Ott (1961) points out during the early Meiji period, the relative position of equity financing (as opposed to bank financing) was substantial, declining later on during the 1920s, 1930s, 1940s and 1950s.

In sum, the fashioning of Meiji financial infrastructure was eclectic, spawning novel hybrid forms of financial intermediation that brought savers and investors together, drawing upon American, European and Tokugawa inherited forms. It reached backward; it reached forward. By the mid-1880s it was sufficiently well developed to support the financing of a nascent private Western technology using manufacturing sector. While it would be an exaggeration to say that creating a viable financial sector was a precondition for Japanese industrialization, it is fair to say that Japan's economic development was finance led – a point emphasized by Patrick (1965, 1966) – the basic foundations of the financial infrastructure being created through a combination of government policy and private market pressure prior to Japan's first great manufacturing surge that commenced in the latter half of the 1880s.

Indeed, one can go further and argue that Meiji economic expansion was infrastructure-leading – or at least put an equal emphasis on infrastructure expansion and expansion in agriculture and industry – in all three dimensions: physical, human capital enhancing, and financial. In so far as this was the case the importance of the legacy inherited from the Tokugawa period must not be forgotten. Consider human capital enhancing infrastructure, in particular education. That schools had proliferated in the second half of the Tokugawa period – fief academies, rural temple schools – that samurai during the *bakumatsu* period had flocked to Nagasaki to study "Dutch learning", is testimony to view that Japanese, elites and non-elites alike, saw developing education as crucial to informed policy making, as crucial to developing human skills employed in agriculture and industry. Perhaps more important was the fact that there was a plethora of teachers, instructors, whose services could be tapped by a government intent on creating a publicly funded education system, consisting of a mix of compulsory and voluntary elements.

Indicative of the priority the Meiji oligarchs attached to education is the fact that the *Dajokan* created the Ministry of Education in 1871 (*Dajokan* order #361), a mere three years after the Meiji Restoration. In 1872 the Ministry issued the Fundamental Code of Education, consisting of 109 articles; a year late the number of articles in the code reached 213. The code laid out a comprehensive scheme governing the way the educational infrastructure was to be structured, four years' compulsory schooling for boys and girls in common schools serving as the base, the remainder of the system consisting of middle and higher schools, vocational schools, private academies like Keio, and at its apex the University of Tokyo which was created in 1877 out of an amalgam of the *Shoheiko*, the Tokugawa *bakufu*'s university, the *Kaiseijo* (Institute of Western Learning) and the *Igakushō* (Institute of Western Medicine). From the outset the government's dualistic two-track concept was clear: promoting mass education emphasizing basic numerical and literacy skills on the one hand through a compulsory component of the infrastructure; providing advanced specialized training aimed at elites and/or those wishing to master vocational skills needed for farming or for working in a factory in a voluntary component of the infrastructure.

That teachers were elastically supplied – presumably mainly drawn from the Tokugawa schools now defunct – is indicated by the fact that the number of teachers in elementary schools jumped at an annual rate of almost 12 percent, middle school teachers increased by almost 46 percent, the ranks of normal (teacher training) school teachers expanded by about 14 percent, and the number of vocational school teachers leaped by a whopping 584 percent over the period 1873–1885.

At first the direction that the compulsory component of the educational system was going to take was up for grabs. There were differing views on this in the oligarchy and in the Ministry. In 1879 changes made to the code suggested that the Ministry was struggling to create a nationally unified system with a standardized curriculum set by bureaucrats and political leaders in Tokyo. By 1890, when the Imperial Rescript on Education was promulgated, the drive to create a standardized compulsory system was reaching fulfillment. Key to the system that emerged in the 1890s was its focus on promoting the cult of the emperor, seen as a device for cementing a feeling of nationalism and national identity in Japan. Politics were important. The Meiji oligarchy was determined to stamp out the legacy of loyalty to local region, to fief, that characterized Tokugawa Japan. What better way to do this than to stress obedience to the emperor, steeped in the Confucian value placed upon loyalty?

At the highest level of the system, promoting a sense of Japanese identity was irrelevant. The focus was on knowledge in science, engineering, and law that would be useful for future national bureaucrats and for recruits into major industrial enterprises. At the pinnacle of the academic pecking order was the University of Tokyo, mainly staffed in the early years of the Meiji period by non-Japanese who taught in their own native languages, in English, in German, in French. This was specialized education for the elites; this was education designed to facilitate the transfer of technology and institutions from the West into Japan.

Recognizing the importance of roads, harbors, canalized rivers, irrigation, and communication through written documents for integrating Tokugawa Japan, for creating national markets and a sense of national identification, the Meiji oligarchs set out to harness Western knowledge and Western technologies. This meant coming to terms with the exigencies imposed by use of steam power on the water. Japan had only a few natural deep water ports. Yokohama and Kobe were. Thus accommodating deep hulled steamships was easy in these two ports, improvements largely limited to constructing massive breakwaters. In ports in which great rivers debouched into the ocean – Osaka laced through by the Yodo River, Tokyo by the Edo, Sumida and Tama Rivers – silting was a huge problem that could only be solved by systematic dredging and shoring up of embankments. Realizing these kinds of improvements took years for a government wrestling with many competing priorities. For instance the national government did not commence its reconfiguring of the Yodo River until 1887, ultimately building two giant breakwaters and a gigantic iron pier in Osaka harbor, a project that dragged on until 1929. Slowly but steadily then, the harbors of Japan were rendered compatible with the demands placed on them by steamship transport.

On the land harnessing steam power was also given priority, although perhaps less than it might have been had Japan not been an island archipelago surrounded by oceans upon which sailing and steam driven ships could operate. Even before the *bakufu* was overthrown, the Japanese authorities employed over ninety British technicians in designing a steam railroad network for the country. Given the limited resources available to the new Meiji government, and the competition from steamships, actual steam railroad construction as opposed to planning did not really get off the ground until the 1883, private investment being brought in for parts of the system, national government investment on other legs of the rail network. Setting the mileage of track completed as of 1883–84 at 100 (260 miles of track had been laid down as of that year), the index of track laid by 1891–1900 is 1038, and by 1901–1905, 1755. By 1907 there were about 5,000 miles of track for steam railroads put down throughout the country. Perhaps this was not too impressive. Nevertheless it was a good start.

That the effort to utilize Western technologies to speed up and make more efficient transport was relatively successful is borne out by comparing a price index for transport against the general consumer price index set at 100. In 1874–79 the relative price of transport was 154; by 1880–89 it had dropped to 116.5; and in 1900–1909 it stood at 120.5.[4] As with financial and human capital enhancing infrastructure, the Japanese government was promoting the foundations for future industrial expansion by direct investment, and by encouraging private enterprises to join the effort, hoping to generate profits from the capital they threw into the fray.

In sum, the politics of the early Meiji Restoration were focused on destroying the most important political vestiges of the Tokugawa era – eliminating fiefs and the feudal class system, streamlining demands placed on fiscal expenditure by doing away with stipends for the samurai – while at the same time exploiting the emphasis on infrastructure that was an outgrowth of the Tokugawa system. In this sense the modernization program of the Meiji oligarchy was Janus faced. It selectively destroyed the past; it selectively drew upon the past. It was both reform and renewal. Perhaps in that combination of past, present and future it drew considerable strength, perhaps it gained credibility amongst a people now exposed to foreign threats and foreign influences after centuries of enforced isolation.

Raising the productivity of agriculture, 1870–1915

One of the most important payoffs to the dismantling of the *bakuhan* system was the rise in the productivity of Japanese agriculture. Under the confederation system of fief/shogunate rule, techniques developed in one district of the country diffused slowly if at all to other districts of the country. To say this is not to assert that there was no mobility within Tokugawa era Japan, that there were no ways of communicating ideas developed in one fief of the country to the inhabitants of other fiefs. Indeed there was an important body of published writings on farming techniques during the Tokugawa period. So diffusion did occur – slowly, in a haphazard fashion – without propulsion or direction from political authorities. Indeed, the *daimyō* competed with each other. Having a more elegant compound in Edo, bearing more splendid gifts to the *bakufu*, were status symbols that depended on extracting rice taxes and proceeds from fief monopolies out of the villages and the towns under the lord's control. Better not to share any important innovations with other fiefs, better to keep them as secret as possible.

With the abolition of the fiefs the dams restraining diffusion of techniques burst. Techniques for irrigating and fertilizing land and new seed varieties, largely developed in the southwest where the number of growing days was substantial permitting planting of both spring and fall rice crops (the resulting relatively high productivity of an hectare of land permitting more aggressive experimentation) now spread throughout the country, encouraged by the new national government. Indeed the national authorities pinpointed the districts where productivity was unusually high, plucking farmers out of these villages, designating them "veteran farmers," sending them around the rest of the country to teach farmers elsewhere how to improve their yields. In this way the "veteran farmer" seed varieties – Omachi, Shinriki, Asahi, Aikoku, Kameno-o – spread throughout the rice fields of the nation.

In promoting the "veteran farmer" campaign the *meibōka* played an essential role. They had clout in their districts. They could cajole and direct, encouraging less well to do farmers to follow their lead.

An additional factor that might have bolstered yields was the effort on the part of the government to nail down once and for private property rights over land. By clarifying who owned exactly what the Land Tax Reform of 1873 may have indirectly contributed to productivity growth by changing incentives.

These Meiji era reforms raised the yields of farming areas, especially in the Kantō district and in the northeast. Land hitherto unutilized – wasteland – or devoted to dry field production was now being reclaimed in the northeast. Output rose. The exact extent of the expansion has been much contested. Some scholars argue that the official statistics on paddy fields and rice yields generated during the 1870s and 1880s were seriously flawed, the government allowing peasants to underestimate their yields and the amount of land they cultivated out of fear that comprehensive and complete reporting would spawn peasant unrest, perhaps outright rebellion. It must be kept in mind that the data on yields per hectare and land in cultivation are byproducts of the land taxation system. As the tax burden was cut back and as incentives to register land under cultivation changed the reported figures become more believable.

In any event, there was land reclamation and improvements in yield per hectare, particularly in the northeast. Land area under cultivation increased and so did the number of farm households that could be supported on the land. For instance in the prefecture of Tokyo the index of the number of farm households (set at a level of 100 in 1880–82) jumped to 184.8 for the decade 1900–1909. In the period 1870 to 1910 or so investing in land improvement might well generate substantial returns, especially in the northeast. For this reason many rural merchants bought up land to develop it; for this reason farmers often sent their children to agricultural vocational schools; for this reason overall economic growth was balanced in the sense that returns to investing in agriculture stayed on a par with returns to investing in manufacturing.

The most important drive to reclaim land, putting it into rice cultivation did not occur in northeastern Honshū however. It occurred in Hokkaidō. During the Tokugawa period most of Hokkaidō was not under the direct control of the *bakufu* or under the control of a particular fief. Rather it was largely occupied by various Ainu groups who carried on hunting and gathering, catching fish, killing birds, cutting down trees for shelter and to make fires. The Ainu had originally occupied huge swathes of territory in northern Honshū, gradually being driven northward by the Japanese who took over the main island completely by the early Tokugawa period. In addition, one fief – Matsumae – established an enclave in the southeast corner of Hokkaidō, securing from the *bakufu* the exclusive right, the monopoly, to trade in firs, fish, timber, and so forth with the Ainu. The small slice of land they carved out was known as the *wajinchi* (literally the land occupied by the "wajin," the Japanese people).

As the Western powers moved in to force Japan open in the first half of the nineteenth century, Russian ships made their way along the coastline of Hokkaidō. To ward off any designs that the Tsar might have on Hokkaidō the *bakufu* negotiated the Treaty of Shimoda with the Russians, agreeing that the Kurile Islands north of Etorofu would be Russian territory, Hokkaidō and the southern Kuriles being Japanese territory. In addition, the Russians secured the right to land ships at Hakodate in Hokkaidō.

With the Meiji Restoration, the political posture of the Japanese government towards foreign threats took a decided turn. Under the banner of *fukoku kyōhei* the oligarchs set out to make unmistakable, unambiguous, claims to various island territories in the vicinity of the main islands of Japan, promoting colonization where these regions were sparsely settled. This being the case for Hokkaidō, the Restoration government decided to aggressively colonize the entire island, making it a keystone of the "inner empire" of Japan, creating a colonial office to run the island in 1869, dispatching a former military officer, Kuroda Kiyotaki to manage the consolidation of Japanese rule over the territory. Impressed with the fact that Hokkaidō was a frontier area with a short growing season, being far north, Kuroda enlisted the assistance of a former Commissioner of Agriculture in the United States, Horace Capron, in planning for the settlement of the island.

Capron recommended and Kuroda and his colleagues ignored. Capron advocated growing Western crops, not rice. The Japanese worked on developing strains of rice that would grow. Capron recommended settling Americans and Europeans on the land. Kuroda and the government opted for Japanese settlement, bringing in ex-samurai first, in part to farm, in part to serve as a colonial militia.

The strategy of the Japanese government was to carry out in Hokkaidō what the Americans and Canadians were doing on the plains and prairies. Subjugate the First Nations peoples. Relocate them onto marginal lands, attempting to convert them from hunting and gathering to settled agriculture with domesticated animals. Promote low cost settlement by Japanese (squatting on the land and cheap pricing for squatted land that was purchased was allowed beginning in the late 1880s). Once the development of a quick-maturing rice strain around 1900 occurred, the fate of the Ainu was sealed. They were swamped by the tide of immigration of Japanese moving into the region from all over Japan. Most of these immigrants came from the Japan Sea and northern Honshū districts where the climate was harsh, relatively similar to that in Hokkaidō.

Between 1873 and 1936 the population of Hokkaidō jumped. Setting the population in 1883 at 100, it was 753 in 1913, over 1270 in 1936. Despite this, the population of Ainu actually declined. It was decimated by diseases brought in by the Japanese settlers, drained by out-migration to the major urban districts of Japan where they could find work as unskilled and semiskilled laborers mainly taking up positions in the construction sub sector. The proportion of Ainu declined from about 15 percent of the population in 1873 to around 0.5 percent in 1936. The percentage of arable land in Japan that was located in Hokkaidō gradually marched upward as more and more fields were converted to paddy – by 1931 about 24 percent of the arable was in paddy – reaching a figure of 16 percent in 1936. The "inner empire", the internal frontier colony of Japan, was being aggressively settled.

Thus a combination of diffusing best practice techniques from the southwest to the northeast and settling frontier zones, especially Hokkaidō, raised the output of the Japanese agricultural sector over the period 1870 to 1915. At the same time – even as the number of farm households in Japan remained relatively constant (increasing ever so slightly in the northeast and in more dramatically in Hokkaidō) – the number of persons per farm household declined as family members, particularly young girls, made their way from rural villages to silk filatures and cotton textile mills to work in the nascent textiles industry.

The massive internal migration of young women back and forth, going from farming to textiles and from textiles back to farming, was crucial to the early industrialization of Japan. From Table 3.1 it is evident that wages for girls recruited in the cotton textile mills and the silk filatures were approximately equal to those that a girl could garner in a farming village.Or rather, the farming wage was higher than the factory wage but because the farming wage was typically seasonal and the industrial wage year around it is fair to say that wages in the two sectors – farming and light manufacturing – were approximately equal. Moreover, real wages, measured either in terms of their general purchasing power (i.e. when deflated by the consumer price index as shown in Panel A of the table) or by their cost to employers (i.e. when deflated by the output prices for the agricultural and manufacturing sectors as shown in Panel B of the table) did not rise appreciably between the late 1880s and 1910–14.

It is this fact that serves as the empirical backbone of the surplus labor interpretation of early Japanese industrialization. The idea is captured in Figure 3.1 that is based on the so-called Fei-Ranis – see Fei and Ranis (1964) – version of the surplus labor model. Agriculture in the surplus labor model.

At an early phase labor is in absolute surplus in villages, redundant. Agricultural workers can be removed from farming, moving to manufacturing, without disturbing the level of agricultural production. Reducing the labor supply in farming from the point L_{0A} to L_{1A} as indicated on the graph (see the lower panel of the diagram) does nothing to change agricultural production (in the technical jargon of neo-classical economics, the marginal product of labor is zero in this range).

Wages in farming are paid in terms of average productivity of labor. On the graph this wage – characterized as the culturally defined subsistence wage w_S – is the ratio of agricultural output Q_{0A} produced by the labor force L_{0A} that is $Q_{0A}/L_{0A} = W_S$. Q_{0A} is the level of agricultural output that is indicated at the top of Panel A in Figure 3.1. At the initial point the economy starts out with L_{0A} workers employed in agriculture – the total output Q_{0A} is divided up equally amongst everyone employed L_{0A} in agriculture yielding an average "subsistence wage" Ws that is the ratio of Q_{0A} divided by L0A namely Q_{0A}/L_{0A} (on the diagram this ratio is the angle created in the triangle that has one leg running from the origin to L_{0A}; one leg running from the origin out to the ordered pair of points (L_{0A}, Q_{0A}); and one leg running from the ordered pair (L_{0A}, 0) up to the ordered pair (L_{0A}, Q_{0A}). As long as labor is in absolute surplus in agriculture, wages there will be low reflecting the surplus of people on the land.

Note that removing workers from agriculture reduces the number of mouths to be fed, the number of persons among whom agricultural production must be shared, thereby generating a surplus that can be tapped by government taxing it,

Table 3.1 Real daily wages in agriculture and manufacturing deflated by price indices: wage differentials (manufacturing/agriculture with agricultural wage = 1); and nominal wages, average labor productivity and labor's share in cotton spinning and cotton weaving, 1885–1914

Panel A *Real daily wages (yen) deflated by the consumer price index, CPI (1934–36 = 1)*

Period	Real daily wages deflated by CPI				Wage differential	
	Agriculture		Manufacturing			
	Males	Females	Males	Females	Males	Females
1885–1889	0.73	0.48	0.86	0.39	1.18	0.81
1890–1894	0.87	0.59	0.80	0.40	0.92	0.68
1895–1899	0.96	0.71	0.82	0.40	0.85	0.56
1900–1904	0.91	0.70	0.91	0.42	1.00	0.60
1905–1909	0.82	0.66	0.89	0.41	1.09	0.62
1910–1914	0.88	0.67	0.90	0.44	1.02	0.66

Panel B *Nominal daily wages (yen) deflated by price index for the sector (1934–36 = 1)*

Period	Agriculture		Manufacturing	
	Males	Females	Males	Females
1885–1889	0.65	0.42	0.51	0.23
1890–1894	0.67	0.45	0.50	0.25
1895–1899	0.75	0.55	0.54	0.26
1900–1904	0.77	0.59	0.62	0.28
1905–1909	0.72	0.58	0.60	0.33
1910–1914	0.77	0.59	0.67	0.32

Panel C *Nominal wages (W), nominal labor productivity (q), and labor's share in value added (S): cotton spinning, Cotton weaving*

Period	Cotton spinning				Cotton weaving			
	Wages (W)		q	S (%)	Wages (W)		q	S (%)
	Males	Females			Males	Females		
1895–1899	0.22	0.14	0.63	25.7	0.24	0.13	1.53	9.8
1900–1904	0.34	0.21	0.51	46.6	0.37	0.22	1.32	18.2
1905–1909	0.43	0.26	0.92	32.1	0.44	0.27	1.06	27.6
1910–1914	0.49	0.31	0.88	39.8	0.53	0.34	1.90	19.2

Sources: Mosk (1995) Table 2.4, pp. 65–6 and Table 2.6, p. 74.

or by rural dwellers accumulating capital that they can invest in proto-industry or manufacturing. This surplus is shown in the shaded area in the upper panel of Figure 3.1. Note that the surplus begins to increase until the point L_{1A} is reached. From this point on it falls.

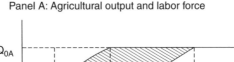

Panel A: Agricultural output and labor force

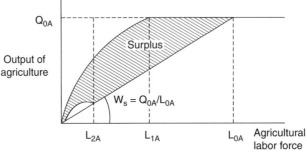

Panel B: Marginal product of labor in agriculture

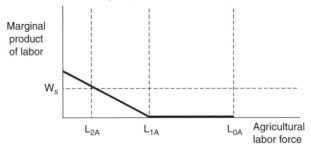

Figure 3.1 Agriculture in the surplus labor model.

Manufacturers can secure workers at approximately similar wages, namely at w_S. Why pay more than you need to? If one person won't work at this low level of remuneration, someone else will. That is the force of competition in the labor market. Manufacturers will go on absorbing these cheap wage workers until the extra amount of output is equated to the subsistence wage, that is until the extra unit of output produced by the worker equates to the extra unit cost of hiring that worker. This is the situation envisioned in Figure 3.2. For a given initial amount of capital equipment this is point L_{1M}. Note that the rectangle formed by going up w_S units on the vertical axis and L_{1M} units on the horizontal axis is the total wages paid out by the manufacturing sector. The rest of the area underneath the marginal productivity curve is profits. It accrues to the owners of capital. Thus if wages are low profits are substantial. Assuming the owners of capital plough back their profits into accumulating more capital, they can absorb more labor in the next period as they increase their capital stock. Thus in the next period they end up absorbing more workers, employing L_{2M} in the next period, and so forth.

At some point – at L_{2A} in Figure 3.1 – enough labor is drained out of rural villages to drive up marginal productivity of labor past the w_S subsistence wage

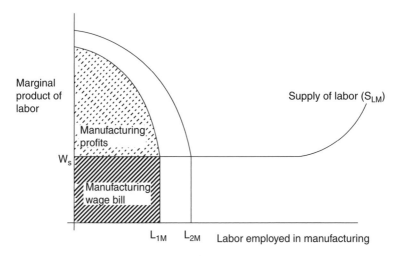

Figure 3.2 Manufacturing in the surplus labor model.

floor level. After this point is reached both agriculture and manufacturing pay competitive wages, real wages equally marginal productivities in the two sectors. The point **L₂ₐ** is called the commercialization, or second turning point.

The figures appearing in Panel C of Table 3.1 support the view that a low wage floor for cotton textiles suppressed labor costs as a share of value added, thereby bolstering profits, creating an engine of growth for manufacturing.

As long as marginal productivity of labor in agriculture falls below the subsistence wage level, wages in both agriculture and manufacturing will not rise. Only when enough workers are removed from farming does the marginal productivity of labor rise above the subsistence wage level, forcing farmers and manufacturers hiring workers to pay above subsistence level wages.

In the upper panel of Figure 3.1 two "turning points" can be seen. The first is at **L₁ₐ**. This is the first point at which labor is no longer in absolute surplus. Reducing the labor force beyond this point reduces the total level of agricultural output. Therefore the marginal productivity of labor rises. The second turning point occurs where the rising level of marginal labor productivity in farming equals the subsistence wage **wₛ**. On the graph this point is denoted by **L₂ₐ**. Once the labor force in farming is drained out below this level, a farmer hiring a worker (or electing to retain a family member in farming rather than dispatching the person to a factory) must pay a wage that exceeds the subsistence wage (or believe that the contribution of the person to the farm output exceeds or equals the income forgone by not working in a factory). This is called the commercialization point. Once enough labor is taken from farming, workers are paid competitive wages equal to their marginal contributions to output everywhere. As can be seen in the upper panel in Figure 3.1 after the commercialization point is reached any surplus that can be secured from agriculture is squeezed by the rise in real wages in that sector.

The simplest way to think about this argument is to envision a huge reservoir of labor sloshing around in villages. There are too many people there so they are effectively redundant. You can do without them and not lose output. To live in such an environment they must be sharing output since the incremental contribution of an extra person is basically zero, zilch, there. Thus the subsistence wage is the average product of a worker in farming activities. Manufacturers can drain away this labor, paying low wages, garnering hefty profits. The process of drawing off labor from villages at these low wages goes on until enough people are transferred from farming to manufacturing to eliminate the redundancy in the villages and to push up the value of an incremental worker past the subsistence wage. The existence of surplus labor promotes accumulation of capital in the manufacturing sector.

Documenting that female workers in the textile mills received low wages, and wages that did not rise in real terms appreciably for a very long time even when their productivity in manufacturing increased – see Table 3.1 – has led many Marxist historians to conclude that the workers were being exploited. Maybe they were. But the labor surplus story offers another convincing story about why wages remained low and profits were high in the textile sector: the force of competition for employment in a labor surplus environment.

Advocates of this labor surplus interpretation must explain several things that are puzzling. One problem is why would someone work, exerting energy, expending the precious food resources that they have stored up from the meals that they consumed, if they are not contributing to output? Does this make sense? Is it reasonable to assume that the marginal product of labor is zero?

An interpretation that is consistent with people not working unless they are productive and yet having redundant labor in the countryside goes like this: rural households give over their daughters (or sons in some cases) to the textile mill without forgoing agricultural output. If each person works harder when they give up a daughter or son they can accomplish this. For instance suppose there are four adults in the farm generating thirty hours of work a day in farming (on average each works 7.5 hours). One adult leaves to work in a factory, leaving three adults on the farm. If each remaining member of the household increases his or her hours of work – up to ten hours a day on average in this example – farm output may be unchanged. Moreover, if the departing member of the household sends back remittances to the farm (a portion of earnings) the farm household may actually be better off when it is able to dispatch one of its own to a factory. Rather than be exploited it is actually improving its lot, taking advantage of the new opportunity offered by industrial employment.[5]

Another puzzle concerns how Japan managed to successfully develop its silk and cotton textile industries, even captured markets throughout East India, seizing them from already well established manufacturers in India and China. Presumably cheap surplus labor existed in these countries as well. As Clark and Feenstra

(2003) point out Japan's success does not stem from cheap labor *per se*, but rather from the fact that labor productivity in export oriented industries like cotton textiles and silk rose rapidly in Japan but not in India and China. Indeed if Japan's silk sector labor productivity was one twentieth of that in France and Japanese wages – expressed in francs – one tenth, France would actually have a tremendous advantage over Japan in silk, presumably having the capacity to export to Japan.

Reasons for Japan's dramatic surge in output per worker in light industries are contained in the various chapters in a volume edited by Tanimoto (2006). Motivating worker loyalty was one. By exercising tremendous flexibility in the way labor was managed – for instance accommodating the needs of workers called away from manufacturing employ by their farmer parents during periods of peak agricultural demand for labor – the owners of silk filatures and rural cotton mills created a sense of worker commitment, a feeling of obligation toward their benevolent employer. A second factor involved giving workers incentives to produce a potent combination of high-quality output wedded to substantial throughput for instance by tying wage payments to individual worker performance rated in terms of both quality and quantity. By maintaining account books listing the characteristics and volume of daily output for each individual employee – for instance luster and strength of thread, number of reels of thread produced, etc. – managers in the factories (and in silk re-reeling companies in the case of silk production) held each worker accountable for his or her contribution to the enterprise's output.

A third factor was scale economies. A prominent example is the forming of community level associations under the aegis of the Trade Association for Strategic Export Commodities and Trade Association for Strategic Commodities laws promulgated in the late nineteenth century. Especially in rural districts that had specialized in a particular proto-industrial sector during the Tokugawa era, manufacturers, merchants and farmers producing raw materials for particular indigenous products like cotton textiles, silk thread, and pottery coordinated their activities in a cooperative fashion under a common umbrella. Under these umbrellas suppliers and users of specific raw materials devised strategies for capturing markets abroad – like those in the United States for resilient silk thread used in the silk-stocking industry – that mutually benefited all parties involved. These community level activities are described as "social capital" in the economics literature. One could argue that the social capital that contributed to scale economies in early Meiji Japan was derived from the Tokugawa legacy of community-level proto-industrial development.

In concluding the discussion of surplus labor I would like to note that the debate between those who argue that surplus labor existed in rural Japan setting a low wage floor for industry and those who argue that industrial workers were exploited along Marxist lines raises the same issues that we confronted in the previous chapter where we contrasted passive and active peasant interpretations of Tokugawa rural behavior. Are households basically doing as well as they can in a highly competitive world? Or are they being exploited?

Early industrialization and the *zaibatsu*

One of the corollaries of *fukoku kyōhei* was *shokusan kōgyō* ("encourage manufacture and promote industry"). It implied a close interaction between government and manufacturing, between economic policy and industrial development. Arguably it was a Meiji version of the Tokugawa view that government at all levels should assist industry by coordinating it, by taking a long view of development rather than the short-run emphasis on making annual profits characteristic of decentralized "invisible hand" capitalism, that can appreciate the input–output connections between different sub-sectors of manufacturing.

To Marxist historians the *shokusan kōgyō* creed suggests that the government is operating hand in glove with business, especially big business. They see in the emergence of the *zaibatsu*, the financial cliques who controlled diversified economic empires – ranging from banking to insurance to international trade to textiles to iron and steel to shipbuilding to iron and steel manufacture – evidence that Japan jumped rapidly into the phase of monopoly capitalism through the connivance of the Meiji oligarchs. Alternatively one can view the rise of the *zaibatsu* as an efficient solution to a dearth of entrepreneurship in early Meiji Japan. Only a few towering figures were really innovative in business. They served as a catalyst, picking out talented subordinates to manage their businesses on a daily basis, jumping from field of endeavor to field of endeavor in a restless effort to get industry going. That these dynamic figures had close connections with the political elite is not surprising. After all, the number of great innovators in political and economic affairs in any given period of history is usually small.

Of all of the Meiji industries extensively utilizing Western technology the most important was cotton textiles employing British mules, power looms, ring frames and steam engines. Mainly centered in Osaka where the ecological conditions were attractive (raw cotton was produced in the hinterland, damp breezes wafting from the Pacific Ocean brought in moisture), the steam powered industry continued to coexist with the old proto-industrial sector organized along putting-out lines. The Western technology using firms used wide looms favored by Western firms operating in India from which many of the textile imports into Japan came, while the proto-industrial sector employed narrow looms suitable for making *kimono*, garb worn during the Tokugawa era and before. The sector using Western technology competed directly with imports. The proto-industrial sector did not.

Instrumental in pushing steam powered cotton textiles in Osaka was the multifaceted dynamo Shibusawa Eiichi.[6] Shibusawa was an ex-samurai who became involved in the restoration movement. Recruited in the Ministry of Finance he helped work up proposals for promoting industry, for substituting domestic manufactures for imports, a kind of neo-mercantilism if you will. Moving on to assume the presidency of the First National Bank he attempted to cajole his banking colleagues into devising lending methods that would foster long-run economic growth, as opposed to methods revolving around maximizing the short-run bottom line of borrowers.

Determined to get his hands dirty in actual business, Shibusawa decided to establish the Osaka Spinning Factory (*Osaka boseki kaisha*) in the early 1880s, during the somewhat chaotic and troubled Matsukata Deflation. Arranging loans from the First National Bank Shibusawa raised enough capital through his efforts to purchase over ten thousand spindles and a steam engine that could be run night and day. Moreover, he reached out across the seas to recruit an engineer adept in management, hiring Yamanobe Takeo who was abroad studying economics in London. Through Yamanobe's brilliance and Shibusawa's capacity to generate funding, the Osaka Spinning Factory emerged as a model for private enterprise, profitable even during the deflationary period caused by Matsukata's policy of debt reduction and retrenchment.

During the period that the Osaka Spinning Factory spearheaded a dynamic cotton textile industry in the Osaka region, the national government tried to step in with its *shokusan kōgyō* agenda, attempting to form a guild structure for the industry. The government officials reasoned that any one of the enterprises was too small to send research teams to Western countries to study the latest techniques, to learn the ins and outs of the most advanced equipment. By exploiting the economies of scale in an industry wide guild, pooling resources to mount a study abroad effort, a guild could accomplish what a single company could not.

The government's efforts to reorganize the industry met with a firm rebuff. Merchants who continued to operate in a putting-out mode were numerous. Many were hostile to joining a large guild. At the same time the large Western technology using integrated spinning and weaving companies did band together, on their own, not through the agency of government officialdom. They formed a cartel known as the *boseki rengōkai*, their own private guild. Pooling their resources, they sent out a fact-finding mission abroad to ferret out new production methods. They also made arrangements to jointly curtail production in times of glut.

Association in the cotton textile industry

During the 1880s, the national government, bent on encouraging the spread of scale economies facilitating the importation of Western technology – large organizations could afford to send missions abroad to study foreign practices systematically, something far beyond the capacity of small enterprises – tried to get the cotton textiles industry to form an industry wide guild.

The government's plan failed. Against it was deep division within the industry. On the one hand, decentralized putting-out production facilitated by the activities of myriads of merchants, prevailed in many districts of the country, especially in rural areas. This sector tended to rely on labor intensive techniques, employed narrow handlooms and focused on producing traditional Japanese garb for the domestic market. On the other hand in Osaka a modern Western technology employing, steam power using, integrated spinning and weaving sector using the wide looms common to the West was emerging. Cajoling these two very different types of firms proved to beyond the capacity of officialdom.

Rather the large steam-using enterprises decided to forge cooperative agreements among themselves. They banded together to form their own guild, the boseki rengōkai. Basically this operated like a cartel. Because most of the associated companies were located in the Osaka area, it was easy for their executives to hold meetings. They set up study groups and dispatched fact-finding missions abroad. They were innovative in other arenas. They established rules for jointly curtailing production when gluts emerged in their product markets.

In short the government's initial effort to organize the entire industry fell flat. Where a cartel-like structure did come into being, it emerged because the firms participating in it felt it was in their interests to cooperate.

Widespread electrification after the 1910s and 1920s transformed the situation on the ground. Small proto-industrial producers who had operated under the putting out system mechanized, driving out handloom production and leading to the consolidation of domestically oriented production in small factories, often managed by the merchants who in earlier decades had organized putting-out networks. The interests and practices of the owners of these shops were quite consistent with the interests and practices of larger integrated spinning and weaving enterprises.

The government, seeing an opportunity to promote rationalization of manufacturing during the slow growth period of the 1920s in the changing face of the industry, reopened its campaign to create guilds in textiles. The resulting guilds, whose numbers proliferated during the era between the two world wars, took the form of industrial associations authorized by the Ministry of Commerce and Industry. These associations ensured minimum quality standards, secured equipment and machinery for common use by affiliated companies, and purchased raw material in bulk for distribution to member firms. In short, this cartel was able to exploit scale economies in marketing and the acquisition of capital that individual companies could not hope to exercise. Cooperation and competition in textiles were now operating under the watchful eye of government.

In short, in the cotton textile industry one cannot make a convincing case for government coordination. Indeed, some authorities go further, arguing that government had virtually nothing to do with early Meiji manufacturing expansion, whether in textiles, railroads, shipping or mining. Advocates of this point of view emphasize the investment activity of the *meibōka* in rural villages, and the acquisition of stocks and bonds issued by private railroads by a tiny clique of wealthy urban investors.

However, a case can be made for government coordination in creating and supporting the emerging *zaibatsu*. The managers of the *zaibatsu* typically started out as *seishō*, "merchants by the grace of political connections". Some like the Mitsui were old merchant houses that had helped bankroll the restoration. Many benefited from government contracts, supplying clothing, blankets and foodstuffs during the Western war that suppressed the Satsuma Rebellion. Some were able to buy factories and mines on favorable terms when the government elected to privatize its state-owned enterprises. For instance Mitsubishi picked up a shipyard in Nagasaki; Mitsui secured the Miike mines from the government.

Iwasaki Yatorō, Mitsubishi and the N.Y.K.

During the 1880s the distinctive structure of the zaibatsu – massive combines diversifying into a variety of industries and sectors, textiles, railroad construction, international trade, banking – began to emerge. Symbolic of the movement to create massive corporations that could grapple with competition from Western firms in shipping and trade was the N.Y.K., the great steamship company that was financed by capital secured from the imperial household ministry, the Mitsui Bank, and Mitsubishi, the dynamic company founded by Iwasaki Yatorō, a former samurai from Tosa fief.

His interest in developing shipping fueled by advice from Tosa domain officials in charge of trade and industry, Iwasaki plunged into the politically sensitive field of shipping during the early 1870s. Famous for his "one-man rule" approach to business, Iwasaki built his fledgling company by becoming the monopoly supplier for naval munitions transport. During the Western War in 1877, Mitsubishi transported over sixty thousand soldiers for Yamagata's conscript army, allowing thirty-two of his forty ships to be requisitioned for the war effort. Suppressing Saigō's Satsuma rebellion became very profitable business for the shipping firm.

By the late 1880s when the N.Y.K. brought together zaibatsu capital marshaled by rival Mitsui and Mitsubishi, Mitsubishi was already diversifying away from shipping, moving into manufacturing and mining. Without doubt, the government's encouragement of the merger from which the N.Y.K. sprang, signaled to the business community a commitment to make the N.Y.K. the favorite upon which subsidies and lucrative government contracts were to be lavished, supplanting Mitsubishi as the monopoly supplier of shipping services to the state.

The lesson is clear: the Meiji oligarchs understood the importance of competition amongst the few. Concerned about Mitsubishi's initial monopoly in naval munitions transport, the oligarchs moved to forge competition in the domestic shipping sector, cleverly spinning off a fearsome rival to Mitsubishi's shipping business with the aid of Mitsubishi capital. At the same time the oligarchs helped to launch a company larger than Mitsubishi, the N.Y.K., able to exploit scale economies in going head to head with Western shipping companies, first in the domestic oceanic shipping business, later on along trans-Pacific shipping lanes.

Note: This discussion draws heavily from various pages in Wray (1984).

What were the chief economic implications of the *zaibatsu* structure? Advocates of the monopolistic competition model on international trade (see for instance the Feenstra, Huang and Hamilton (2003) article) argue that multi-industry combines like the *zaibatsu* were not only able to reduce transactions costs and benefit from scale economies – consider intermediate goods like glass or rubber both produced and outsourced by companies operating under the common group umbrella – but also to exploit market power, the affiliated companies squeezing higher profit rates out of activities coordinated through planning and negotiation taking place between the affiliated enterprises. While intra-firm scale economies were surely important within the *zaibatsu* combines, geographic scale economies external to individual firms also played a crucial role in driving down production costs in Meiji Japan.

As manufacturing grew it tended to concentrate in the Tōkaidō region where the costs of importing and exporting were relatively low, Yokohama near Tokyo and Kobe near Osaka being natural deep water ports. The clustering of factories stretched from the Kantō plain in the north – from Tokyo and Yokohama – through Nagoya on the Nobi plain down to Osaka, Kobe and Kyoto in the south. The major conurbations linked together through the Tōkaidō steam railroad line and by steamship, shippers coming in and out of Japan could move up or down the coast picking up cotton textiles or silk thread bound for Europe or America, depositing raw cotton imported from China and India, carrying tourists and persons traveling on business alike.

Exercising a particularly strong magnetic attraction to the new mechanized factories was Osaka that became known as the "Manchester of the Far East". Lining the Yodo River within the city, stretching out along the river banks in the suburbs of the great metropolis were textile mills, shipbuilding yards, iron and steel companies, spewing out dark smoke as they generated power from coal. By 1900 Osaka had emerged as the most important industrial metropolis in all of Asia, the Tōkaidō taking on the trappings of a mighty industrial belt to be reckoned with across the oceans in England, the European continent and the United States.

Trade and international relations

Trade and international geopolitical relations are intertwined. A good example of this principle is the nature of the treaties that the *bakufu* signed with the Western powers in 1858. Under the terms of these treaties Japan's ability to impose tariffs on imports was severely limited. These constraints did not completely vanish until 1911, a full half century after they were acceded to by a government severely pressed by the United States, England, France and Russia.

In analyzing the expansion, character and structural change of Japan's trade during the Meiji era five points should be highlighted. Trade expanded rapidly because of growth in the capacity of Japan's ports to handle steamship traffic and because of growth in the railroad infrastructure that drove down domestic transportation costs, permitting remote silk producing villages in the Alps to export into far flung markets abroad. Trade expanded because giant trading companies like Mitsui Bussan, C. Itoh, and Iwai emerged, exploiting economies of scale and scope in importing raw materials, especially raw cotton, and exporting finished products, tea, silk thread, and cotton textiles particularly.[7] Trade expanded because the Japanese government was able to successfully switch the precious metal base backing up its currency from the silver standard to the gold standard. Trade expanded because Japan began to build an empire in Asia and the Pacific, securing Taiwan and later Korea as colonies, obtaining special rights in northern China and Manchuria. Trade expanded because Japan's textile industry – especially cotton textiles – rapidly moved through the product cycle, proceeding from import substitution to export promotion.

Rapid expansion of trade depends upon transportation costs, both domestic and international. If a region is geographically isolated it cannot compete in global markets, let alone in domestic markets. The fact that there was already in place a relatively good internal transportation system – consisting of roads, canalized rivers that could readily support traffic in shallow wooden boats – prior to the Meiji Restoration meant that there were relatively few completely isolated communities in Japan. As harbors were dredged, breakwaters built, steam railroad lines laid down, transport costs fell even further, both the costs of shipping goods in and out of Japan, and within Japan itself.

In Table 3.2 there is evidence consistent with this interpretation. As the reader can see, silk (mainly silk thread) was a major export item during the Meiji period. The main silk producing villages – recall the discussion on Hida Takayama in Chapter 2 – were located in the Japanese Alps and in northeastern Japan. They could not have aggressively moved into exporting had the costs of getting the silk out to the major seaports been substantial. They could not have competed on international markets if a major portion of their export price represented high internal costs of transportation. To be sure that Japan is an island archipelago helped keep depress the costs of shipping goods in and out of the country. Most international commodity transport moves across the water. But getting goods at low cost is important as well.

The creation and rapid growth of Japan's trading companies is one of the most interesting features of Meiji economic development. Some of these trading companies emerged as key components of the *zaibatsu*. Mitsui Bussan is a good example of this type (the trading companies developed by Mitsubishi and Sumitomo are fairly similar to Mitsui Bussan). Some emerged because they specialized in a particular type of business: C. Itoh and Iwai are examples of this type.

The sheer size of the trading companies and their association with the *zaibatsu* has made them a target for Marxist historians who view the rapid expansion of the companies as symptoms of monopoly capitalism in early industrializing Japan. Neo-classical mainstream economists take a different view. They argue that trading companies emerged because of transactions costs. Few Japanese had a mastery of foreign languages. Few Japanese had been abroad and knew much about market conditions abroad, where to secure raw materials, where to see finished goods. Massive enterprises that specialized in transoceanic trade reaped

Table 3.2 Major exports and the pace of the product cycle, 1870–1920

Panel A   *Percentage of total yen value of Japan's exports in selected products, 1870–1920*

Year	Semi-processed raw materials				Manufactures	
	Green tea	*Lumber*	*Coal*	*Silk*	*Cotton textiles*	*Silk textiles*
1870	30.5	0.2	2.1	29.4	0.03	0.01
1880	20.2	0.4	3.9	30.8	0.1	0.1
1890	10.9	0.3	8.6	24.8	0.3	2.1
1900	4.1	0.8	10.0	22.3	2.9	9.3
1910	3.0	1.6	3.6	28.6	4.5	7.2
1920	0.9	1.5	2.4	20.0	17.5	8.3

Panel B   *The pace of the product cycle, 1887–1919; net exports/domestic product = 100 ratios for three sub-sectors of manufacturing and for manufacturing as a whole*

Period	Textiles	Chemicals	Machinery	Manufacturing
1887–1897	0.04	0.5	−21.2	−0.4
1897–1904	1.3	0.3	−18.6	−0.4
1904–1911	2.1	0.2	−8.8	−0.1
1911–1919	3.0	0.1	−3.2	0.6

Sources: Japan Statistical Association Volume 3 (1987) Table 10–3-a, pp. 22–37 and Mosk (2001) Table 6.1, p. 184.

huge economies of scale and scope in distribution. Japan's geographic and linguistic isolation from its major markets in Europe and North America rendered the large trading company all the more attractive.

Paradoxically, the large trading company smacks of neo-mercantilism. Indeed, the fact that pre-Tokugawa Japan had come in contact with the great mercantile houses of Europe – the Dutch V.O.C., the British East India Company – probably served as a model for Japanese entrepreneurs. In any event the growth of trading companies depended on the growth of particular sectors in the domestic economy. Mitsui Bussan's business exploded because it specialized in cotton textiles. It purchased raw cotton in China, India and the Middle East. It purchased spindles, mules and power looms in England and brought them into Japan. It exported finished cotton textiles. The rapid growth of the cotton textile industry – see Table 3.2 – translated into a huge growth in demand for Mitsui's services. Nor was Mitsui alone in responding to growing demand for cotton textiles related services. C. Itoh emerged out of the activities of Japanese cotton textile wholesalers. Iwai also expanded because of its connection with wholesalers, in its case wholesalers in iron and steel.

Finding an effective way to manage international exchange was also crucial to Japanese exporting and importing capacity. During most of the Meiji period Japan ran trade deficits, importing more than it exported. It was able to pay for these net imports of goods, machines and services by exporting gold and silver reserves that had been built up by the *bakufu*. The Matsukata Deflation policy also helped the Japanese government manage its foreign exchange. Had domestic prices continued to rise as they did during the late 1870s in the wake of the Satsuma Rebellion, Japan's export prices would have soared, forcing the government to find some way of devaluing its currency. Moreover, as long as Japan's currency was inconvertible, foreign traders operating in the Japanese market would shy away from using it, impeding the growth of international transactions taking place on Japanese soil. The fact that the Bank of Japan was able to establish a fully convertible currency in the second half of the 1880s definitely contributed to the ability of Japanese companies to carry on international business dealings.

For most of the period prior to 1897 Japan operated on a silver standard. This presented a problem since most of the advanced industrial countries were operating on the gold standard, following the lead of the United Kingdom. Indeed, in the latter half of the nineteenth century London had become the global center for much of the world's international finance and international oceanic insurance, and the British pound, tied directly to gold at a fixed exchange rate became the international clearing currency, countries settling their international accounts in London using either gold or pounds. As the price of silver relative to gold fluctuated so did the price of Japan's imports and exports. Thus there was a strong argument for going onto gold, especially strong given the demands of the Japanese army and navy for weapons, ships and war-making material produced in the advanced industrial economies and marketed in currencies tied directly to gold.

How to get onto the gold standard posed a problem for the Japanese government. To do so meant that Japan's central banks, either the Bank of Japan or the Yokohama Specie Bank, had to amass a major quantity of gold. Victory over China in the Sino-Japanese War came at an opportune time. Japan secured a 362 million yen indemnity from China as a result of the war, also taking on Taiwan as a colonial possession. The Japanese government negotiated that the indemnity be paid in gold. This huge influx of gold in 1896 allowed the government to credibly go onto the gold standard in 1897, setting a fixed exchange rate between the yen and gold.

The subject of the product cycle and changing comparative advantage exercised a particular fascination for Japanese economists. Indeed, drawing upon Confucian concepts of the heroism of geese in flight, the Japanese economist Akamatsu Kaname developed the "flying geese" paradigm for trade. The idea is this. In the first stage of industrialization a country imports manufactures and exports raw materials. As is evident from Table 3.1 this is what Japan did in the early Meiji period. Then one sector, the leading sector, the first goose, breaks through, substituting domestic production for imports, eventually moving onto exports. The other geese follow, drafting off the lead goose. As can be seen from Panel B of Table 3.2, the textiles sector was the first sector to make this transition. But machinery was rapidly moving through the product cycle, following the lead goose, textiles.

We shall return to the "flying geese" model in subsequent chapters, developing further its interrelationship with the *zaibatsu* structure and pre-1945 Japanese empire building and colonialism. At this point we shall simply point out that it provides a compelling and colorful description of Japan's international trade product cycle.

Between 1868 when the restoration oligarchy took over the reins of power and the early twentieth century Japan made a wrenching political and economic transition, establishing the groundwork for constitutional government, commencing industrialization, revolutionizing its infrastructure and starting down the road of empire building. This set the stage for the massive infrastructure boom of the early twentieth century that is the subject of our next chapter.

Key terms and concepts in Chapter 3

Path dependence
Fukoku kyōhei
Satsuma Rebellion
Dajokan
People's Rights Movement
Meibōka
Liberty Party
Oligarchy
Land Tax Reform
Matsukata Deflation
State owned enterprises
Banking Act of 1872
National banks
Mujin

Imperial Rescript on Education
"Veteran farmer" seed varieties
Surplus labor model
First and second turning points
Trade Association for Strategic Export
Commodities
Shokusan kōgyō
Osaka Spinning Factory
Boseki rengōkai
Zaibatsu
Tōkaidō industrial belt
Trading companies
Gold standard
"Flying geese" paradigm for trade

4 Infrastructure and heavy industry

Fissuring fukoku kyōhei

Crowding into the big tent of *fukoku kyōhei* ("enrich the country, strengthen the military") were elites with wildly divergent agendas. Among the ranks of former samurai was a significant group primarily interested in bolstering Japan's military capacity. Seduced by the promise of *kyōhei*, some appreciated the importance of building up a manufacturing sector that could spew out the battleships, field guns and transport vehicles required by modern warfare. In this sense they saw *fukoku* as an important, albeit less pressing, priority. This group tended to be pragmatic and rational, calculating the costs and benefits of going to war with a sophisticated appreciation of geopolitical realities. Others were less convinced, joining the ranks of mystical ultra-nationalist societies that were prepared to jettison the economy in order to convince other countries and peoples of the superiority of Japan through the force of Japanese fighting spirit.

Among the ranks of the rapidly growing business community were former samurai, merchants and peasants, *meibōka* entrepreneurs whose main interest was *fukoku*. To this group *fukoku* trumped *kyōhei*. They wanted a government that allocated resources to infrastructure reducing transportation and communication costs, that worked to make energy relatively cheap, that facilitated trade and the import of foreign technology, that were "market conforming", that carried out stabilization monetary and fiscal policies in a responsible matter.

This is not to say that the *fukoku* group rejected aggrandizing Japan's military capacity. Military activity could be good for business: it could translate into lucrative contracts for ships, rifles and uniforms; it might deepen the skill level of the engineering community, government funded armories training engineers in the use and manufacture of the latest American, German and British machines. Raising national prestige through military successes could pay off as well. It might yield indemnities freeing up reserves for acquiring goods and services from abroad. It might enhance the status accorded to Japanese traveling abroad. Finally in so far as territory was acquired abroad through warfare, the horizon for investing in plant and equipment outside of the homeland protected from nationalization or sabotage by Japan's military forces broadened. Still, many in the business community were leery of Japan being, or even appearing to be, militaristic. It could alienate potential customers. It could drain the coffers of the central bank of precious foreign reserves. It could drain away the ranks of young engineers and technically trained blue-collar workers from the private sector.

During the early Meiji period, the *fukoku kyōhei* ideology accommodated the interests of enough members of the elite to provide a big tent within which consensus prevailed. By the end of the Meiji period, by the early twentieth century, this consensus was breaking down. New realities were causing the ideological umbrella to develop fissures, to collapse along seams opened up by the winds of political friction.

One reality was the change in Japan's status on the international political stage. The flexing of Japan's burgeoning military muscle serving as backdrop, arguing that their government was being forced into adopting civil and commercial codes consistent with those prevailing in Western Europe and North America but not with Japanese tradition, Japanese diplomats undid the humiliating legacy of extraterritoriality imposed on their country during the 1850s. Beginning with a treaty with the United Kingdom, Japanese negotiators worked steadfastly to become a normal nation-state, freeing up Japanese policy makers to freely set tariffs on imported commodities.[1] For those members of the business community that did not do extensive business with the government and did not make use of armory trained engineers, establishing national independence may have been the most positive fruit borne by *kyōhei*.

Treaty revision and the Anglo-Japanese alliance

Two treaties negotiated between the British and Japanese governments paved the way for Japan to break free of the unequal treaty and extraterritorial system it was forced to accede to the 1850s and to emerge as a contender for regional hegemony in the Asia-Pacific.

The first treaty, signed in London in 1894, the Anglo-Japanese treaty of commerce and navigation, brought to an end the system of extraterritoriality for British citizens. From the date of the signing of the accord, British citizens in Japan were subject to Japanese laws and could be tried in Japanese courts. Other countries that had negotiated unequal treaties with Japan followed the British lead. By 1900 the Japanese government had freed itself from the humiliations imposed upon it by the Western powers in the wake of Perry's voyages to Japan that forced the bakufu to abandon its isolationist policy.

Signing the first treaty was an important prerequisite for negotiating the second treaty, the Anglo-Japanese alliance of 1902. This is because the second treaty was predicated on equality between the two "High Contracting parties."

From a geopolitical viewpoint, the cementing of the Anglo-Japanese alliance was a de facto acknowledgement of Japan's growing power in East Asia. One clause made it clear that the United Kingdom was going to give Japan a free hand in pursuing its (Japan's) "special interests" in Korea.

Another clause guaranteed that if either party went to war with a third party – as Japan did when it fought Russia in 1904–05 – the other would remain neutral.

The Anglo-Japanese alliance treaty was to hold for five years, but was actually renegotiated in 1905. The renewed treaty guaranteed British neutrality in the Russo-Japanese war, and acknowledged Japan's "paramount political, military and economic interests in Korea".

In the aftermath of World War I, opposition to British renewal of the Anglo-Japanese alliance developed in a variety of quarters, both inside and outside of the British Empire. Within the Empire, Canada and Australia, somewhat reluctant co-signatories to the original treaty, voiced their opposition to unrestricted immigration of Japanese citizens to their dominion territories, a right implicit in the treaty that encouraged commercial intercourse between the British Empire and Japan. The United States also expressed its concerted opposition, partly motivated by Washington's opposition to immigration from Japan, partly by the buildup of the American navy in the Pacific that followed upon American takeover of the Philippines and Hawaii after the Spanish-American war in 1898. As a result the treaty was allowed to lapse, being replaced by the Washington Treaty of 1922 that limited the sizes of the navies of Japan, the United States and the United Kingdom.

A second reality was that the conditions imposed by Japan upon a power it defeated militarily did not necessarily stick diplomatically. One example is the triple intervention following the Sino-Japanese War. After signing the Treaty of Shimonoseki concluding the conflict – according to which Japan secured Taiwan, gained status as a treaty power in China, wrenched Korea away from Chinese control, and took over Chinese territory on the Liaotung peninsula – representatives of Russia, France and Germany appeared in Tokyo, advising the Japanese government of their collective alarm over Japan obtaining Liaotung territory, cajoling Japan in no uncertain terms to return it to China. The willingness of Russia, France and Germany to threaten Japan militarily was hardly rooted in altruism toward China. Russia had an interest in expanding into the Liaotung region in the future. France expected to secure Russian support for French ambitions in the southern zone of Asia; and Germany was hoping to draw Russian ambitions into the Far East, thereby diverting it away from meddling in the power politics of Western Europe.

Japan acceding to this intervention – it withdrew from Liaotung in exchange for an additional indemnity – made many informed Japanese cynical about the benefits that could be reaped through military activity, costly in terms of lives lost, costly in terms of fiscal resources that could be otherwise channeled into economically productive endeavors – building railroads and coal burning electricity generating plants, aggrandizing reserves in the central bank that could be used to pay for the imports of machinery or the licensing of foreign patents – instead of into acquiring battleships, machine guns and uniforms.

Japan's military activity even fanned the flames of unrest among industrial workers. Deep strains in Japan's relations with Russia precipitated by Russian reluctance to withdraw from Manchuria where the Russian railroad project was floundering, led to Japan's surprise attack on the Russian fleet at Port Arthur just as Russia was transferring troops to the far east on the Trans-Siberian railroad in 1904. Decimating a Russian fleet dispatched from the Baltic in the Straits of Tsushima in May 1905, Japan emerged again as victor. Intervening to bring hostilities to a peaceful conclusion, President Theodore Roosevelt convened a peace conference at Portsmouth, New Hampshire, that recognized Japan's paramount interests in Korea, restored sovereignty over Manchuria to China, awarded the southern half of Sakhalin Island and part of the railroad Russia built in Manchuria to Japan. The demand for military procurement falling off in the aftermath of the conflict, overtime work in mines and military arsenals vanished. Protest against the boom and bust nature of employment in the war industries amongst blue-collar workers propelled forward the drive to organize the industrial labor force. The law of unintended consequences harassed Japan's leadership despite its success in raising Japan's status as an emergent great power within the international community of nation-states.

A third reality is that the successful *zaibatsu* were becoming larger, increasingly capable of standing on their own feet, able to diversify into new endeavors – the manufacture of electrical motors and synthetic materials – without necessarily having to rely upon contracts drawn up by the army or navy. This does not mean that individual *zaibatsu* eschewed military procurement opportunities. To the contrary, Mitsubishi thrived on such contracts. What it does mean is that slowly but steadily the main *zaibatsu* were becoming states within a state.

In short *fukoku* and *kyōhei* had splintered apart. From mutually supporting one another, from advances in one domain positively supporting advances in the other, the two had moved towards an increasingly antagonistic relationship or at least one perceived as antagonistic in political circles. Public consciousness that there were tradeoffs – a budgetary increase for the navy coming at the expense of a budgetary increase for imperial universities or steam railroads – loomed larger and larger during the late Meiji period.

It must be acknowledged that many Japanese Marxist scholars reject this view. Believing Japan's pro-military elite never surrendered control over Japan's political agenda, this school of thought argues that the business community remained firmly committed to following the military as it became increasingly aggressive abroad. Arguing that the Meiji Restoration was an incomplete bourgeois revolution in which a military-bureaucratic class emerged triumphant, monopoly capital in the form of the *zaibatsu* operating hand in glove with the authorities, advocates of this approach maintain that the Japanese state between 1868 and 1945 was absolutist. The nation was hijacked by a tiny elite consisting of powerful militarists and monopoly capitalists reaping the fruits of absolutism in terms of power and profits.

Whether one accepts or rejects the view that the *fukoku kyōhei* consensus was coming apart as the nineteenth century wound down to a close – business, labor and government taking up contrary positions about the wisdom of allocating resources to future military adventures on foreign soil – there were a cluster of domestic investment activities around which policy makers and businesses large and small coalesced, forging a common front. Fired up by enthusiasm to participate in profit oriented activity coordinated and facilitated by government, the private sector jumped into a new cluster of infrastructure opportunities. At the dawn of the twentieth century this cluster involved simultaneously constructing railroads in tandem with harnessing and distributing electrical power.

Electrification and the railroads

During the first decade of the twentieth century electrification and railroads spread, intercity and intra-city electrical railroad companies spearheading the drive to simultaneously sell power and move freight and passengers. Serving as a spur to this wave of private sector infrastructure investment was passage by the Diet of a bill nationalizing the steam railroad lines. Motivated partly by military concerns – controlling the trunk lines around the four main islands of Japan was a goal of a government intent of minimizing the time required to mobilize and move armed forces – partly by economic concerns, partly by pork barrel political pressures, the Diet authorized the government to buy up most of the steam railroad lines already constructed, creating a network of trunk lines girding the nation, encouraging the private sector to construct shorter lines linking together key hub cities already serviced by the trunk lines with nearby cities and villages not yet brought into the network.

Nationalizing the steam railroads

In 1906 a Diet under the domination of the Seiyukai, that had built its political base heavily in rural districts, passed a bill that nationalized most of the steam railroad lines in Japan, especially the main trunk lines that ran around each of the major islands of the Japanese archipelago (further nationalization occurred in 1907 and 1908, when the Railroad Department was set up, the Ministry of Railroads gaining full ministry status in 1920).

This was not the first Diet to consider nationalization of the steam railroads. Throughout the period between the 1870s and the 1890s, political leaders had discussed the economic, political and military logic of creating a national railroad company in Japan.

The economic logic was clear. Creating a huge company that could exploit scale economies in research and development for the manufacture of rolling stock was an obvious allure. By 1912, Japan National Railroads was delivering on this portion of the agenda. It imported four steam engines from four different suppliers in three different countries – the USA, the UK, and Germany – directing its technicians to painstakingly study each and every component in the engines purchased. Working with the knowledge gained, Japan National Railroads was able to draw in a small number of manufacturing firms in a massive reverse engineering project that involved using various components from each of the engines it obtained to create a totally new product, a uniquely Japanese steam engine. The government company was acting as a facilitating and coordinating agent, promoting innovation in the transport sector.

The military logic was also clear. In the event of war, troops could be rapidly dispatched from bases to harbors and staging areas throughout the land on government owned rails and in government owned rolling stock.

The political logic was also clear. Pork barrel politics – exemplified in the post-1970 period by the ability of the Liberal Democratic Party's master of pork, Tanaka Kakuei, to get a line of the shinkansen bullet train built out to his remote rural prefecture, Niigata – underlay the nationalization drive. Under Seiyūkai dominated cabinets, new construction of national lines was heavily weighted toward rural areas that the Seiyūkai politicians represented. Moreover, under the scheme of buyout payments devised by the Diet, the lines that the Mitsui owned garnered prices relative to earnings far in excess of the prices commanded by the Mitsubishi lines. Mitsui had backed the Seiyūkai, making generous payments to the election war chest of the party. Mitsubishi had backed the Seiyūkai's rival, the Kenseikai. Not surprisingly, the nationalization bill of 1906 favored Mitsui's interests over Mitsubishi's. The local nature of politics – in terms of districts, in terms of the financial fortunes of the companies bankrolling the major parties – is strikingly evident in the political logic of railroad nationalization.

Largely built after the technology for generating and transmitting hydroelectric power had been developed in North America and Europe – after many intra-city tram lines in the United States had switched from horse drawn power to electrical power, pioneering the use of electricity as an alternative to steam in the railroad sector – private Japanese companies and municipally managed corporations jumped into the business of creating a sprawling network of electrical railroads and trams between 1904 and 1911. Connecting cities in the hinterland of great metropolitan conurbations to stations feeding passengers into local transit networks, companies raising capital through aggressive placing of new stock on equity markets joined hands with freshly created corporations managed by the governments of the great metropolitan centers to move passengers from suburban bedroom cities springing up along the intercity rail lines. Local governments functioned as facilitators of a process largely driven by market forces, coordinating the plans of private companies through their regulatory control over allocating rights of way for laying track, ensuring that lines radiating out from major station hubs to the suburbs were serviced by tram lines laid down within the confines of the city.

Consider the two key great metropolitan centers of the Tōkaidō, Tokyo anchoring the burgeoning industrial belt in the north, Osaka anchoring it in the south. Both became major electrical railroad and tram hubs beginning with the first decade of the twentieth century. As is apparent from Table 4.1, Tokyo enjoyed an initial advantage in track laid out. Why? Crisscrossed with vast boulevards along which horse drawn streetcars dunging the center of the streets could be run without creating unbearably noxious smells and health hazards for the residences and shops lining the thoroughfares, Tokyo embraced horse drawn tramlines in the mid-1880s. The costs of conversion to electricity falling far short of laying wholly new lines, Tokyo's within-city electrified quickly making it a pioneer in the laying down of an extensive railroad infrastructure. For instance

Table 4.1 Electricity and the railroads, 1900–1930 (indices with 1920–1921 = 100)

Panel A   *National figures (indices with 1920–1921 = 100)*

Period	Railroads – operation kilometers			Electricity		
	National	*Regional*	*Street*	*Years*	*Generated*	*Electrified cars*
1900–1909	35.6	104.4	–	1910–1914	30.4	46.1
1910–1919	85.1	66.7	92.5	1915–1919	93.8	75.0
1920–1929	115.9	141.8	113.2	1920–1924	103.3	126.1
				1925–1929	143.3	179.9

Panel B   *Electricity in Japan and in the Tōkaidō (indices with 1920–1921 = 100)*

Period	Number of electrical lights			Electricity generated and supplied		
	Japan	*Tōkaidō*	*% in Tōkaidō*	*Japan*	*Tōkaidō*	*% in Tōkaidō*
1900–1909	2.4	3.8	65.2	70.4	74.7	45.3
1910–1919	41.7	51.4	54.5	164.6	182.7	47.6
1920–1929	127.2	119.7	38.6	339.6	386.7	48.6

Panel C   *Electric street cars in Osaka and Tokyo (indices with 1920–1921 = 100)*

Osaka: Track and passenger-kilometers			Tokyo: Track and passengers		
Period	*Track*	*Passenger-kilometers*	*Period*	*Track*	*Passengers*
1903–1910	14.3	8.7	1905–1909	52.8	40.8
1911–1915	57.6	57.4	1910–1914	77.5	53.0
1916–1920	84.3	82.9	1915–1919	91.7	72.5
1921–1924	113.1	107.0	1920–1924	103.4	98.4
1925–1930	132.3	110.2	1925–1929	112.4	104.3

Source: Mosk (2001) Table 5.1, pp. 142–3 and Table 5.2, pp. 154–5.

Tokyo Railway began electrifying its lines in 1903. By contrast Osaka, a checkerboard of narrow streets and canals, eschewed the horse drawn tram, throwing up electrical lines mostly after 1910. Gradually Osaka emerged as the major transport hub of the Kinai region: the Hanshin company developing a line between the great natural deepwater port city of Kobe and Osaka; two companies (Hankyū and Keihin) connecting Kyoto to Osaka, one line following the Yodo River on its eastern banks, the other on the west; the Hankai company connecting Sakai lying upon Osaka's eastern reaches along Osaka Bay to the great commercial and industrial heart of the Kinai.

Following the logic of internalizing, realizing, the economic benefits of externalities that they spawned, these electrical railroads followed the model staked out by combines like Mitsui and Sumitomo, diversifying into a host of new businesses, becoming local *zaibatsu*. At first they focused on selling electrical power in the cities and villages dotting the countryside near their rights of way, eventually buying up land in locales where they anticipated building stations. Expecting a real estate boom to follow upon the heels of the company opening up a new station, companies like Hanshin and Keihin set up real estate companies to develop residences for future sale or rent. Or consider running a line to a hot spring resort. Would it not be attractive to create a tourism division of the railroad company that managed hotels and entertainment outlets, offered fresh profit-making opportunities spun off of the transport business? Especially enticing was constructing department stores near or above the stations serving as transit hubs within great conurbations like Tokyo and Osaka, taking advantage of the vast flows of commuters making connections.

In short, the first decade of the twentieth century witnessed a massive invest-ment boom in infrastructure, intercity railroads and intra-city tramlines spawning a wave of suburban expansion closely linked to the buildup of electrical power generation and distribution. At first the surge in use of electricity was heavily concentrated in the Tōkaidō industrial belt (see Panel B of Table 4.1), not surprisingly given the economies of scale implicit in electrical transmission, the unit cost of stepping down electricity flowing along high voltage lines and dis-tributing it to users decreasing in proportion to the density of population. However as is apparent from Table 4.1, by the 1920s power was being supplied to many locales outside the industrial belt. Within a few short decades Japan was becoming a major global center for electrical power generation and consumption. Testimony to the force of this wave of infrastructure expansion was a major overhaul of land use. Notably in the great metropolises of the industrial belt, land in the vicinity of the great railroad station hubs increasingly became home to

Electrification

Japan is famous for its lack of raw materials. Yet it has one in abundance: rainfall due to the monsoons that sweep across in the late spring/early

summer. For this reason hydroelectric power generation has played a crucial role in Japanese economic development.

Even before the technology for generating and transmitting high voltage across hydroelectric power grids had been developed, Japanese companies were experimenting with electricity. For instance in 1887, a mere half decade after New York became the world's innovator in providing electrical lighting, Tokyo Dentō (Tokyo Electric Light) began selling power for lighting. Typical of the Japanese electrical industry before the drift toward a total war economy in the late 1930s brought on nationalization, this company was private. Developing the industry along private lines entailed some problems that plagued Japanese producers of electrical machinery and electrical consumer durables before and after World War II: lack of standardization. For instance, Osaka Dentō brought in alternating current in 1889; but Nagoya Dentō and Yokohama Dentō opted for direct current. Osaka and western Japan ended up employing a current with sixty cycles; Tokyo and eastern Japan settled on a current with fifty cycles.

In any case, it was the harnessing of the hydroelectric power secured from great power stations located in the Japanese Alps where waterpower was abundant that gave a strong push to electrification. For instance, setting the number of kilowatts generated in 1920–21 at 100, the index for the years 1940–41 was 1,494.

The intercity and intra-city railroad and tramlines gave a strong push to electrification. Running between and within the burgeoning cities of Japan's industrial belt, and primarily focused on transporting passengers and not freight, the intercity and intra-city lines that flourished in the aftermath of the 1906–08 nationalization of the steam railroad network, ran on electricity that they also sold to towns along their rail lines. A city like Osaka became a massive hub for intercity lines radiating out to Kyoto, Kobe, and Nagoya: the Hanshin electric railroad company serviced the Kobe/Osaka traffic; and the Hankyū line the Kyoto/Osaka passenger flow.

Machinery production and mechanization were also revolutionized by electrification. Unlike steam engines that are best utilized in a large factory where a myriad of machines are linked to its motion through straps kept in motion by the central power source of the engine, electric power can be delivered on a unit drive basis. Turn the switch on and you have power; turn it off and you don't. For this reason the smallest factory could mechanize with electricity. Not so with steam.

By the 1930s Japan was one of the most electrified countries in the world. Despite falling far short of the United States, the United Kingdom, France and Germany in terms of per capita income, its per capita supply and consumption of electricity made it a leader in the field of power generation. This was a point that Japanese engineers often emphasized when they spoke to foreign audiences in the period between the world wars.

Table 4.2 Land use and relative land prices, Osaka and Tokyo, 1900–1938

Panel A *Paddy, dry field and takuchi (indices for land area with 1920–1921 = 100)* [a]

Period	Osaka prefecture			Tokyo prefecture		
	Paddy	Dry field	takuchi	Paddy	Dry field	takuchi
1900–1904	97.6	122.5	77.7	114.2	98.3	79.9
1905–1909	99.1	114.9	81.0	111.9	98.9	85.1
1910–1914	101.0	105.8	88.0	106.2	97.7	91.1
1915–1919	100.1	80.2	94.4	101.8	97.3	95.8
1920–1924	99.4	104.4	89.1	106.5	98.0	91.2
1925–1929	98.4	96.7	120.8	93.1	95.8	110.5
1930–1934	95.3	89.4	147.4	84.6	90.9	143.1
1935–1939	91.8	83.6	164.7	77.2	86.8	166.0

Panel B *Ratio of land prices, Osaka prefecture/Tokyo prefecture (base of ratio = 100)* [b]

Year	Paddy	Dry field	takucihi
1911	122.8	206.4	121.1
1918	122.2	192.6	97.5
1924	122.8	188.1	99.1
1929	123.1	170.7	100.0
1938	120.5	94.9	87.5

Source: Mosk (2001) Table 5.3, pp. 158–9.

Notes
a The term *takuchi* refers to land used for commercial, residential and industrial purposes. Typically the term excludes wasteland and land used for agricultural cultivation.
b Ratio of Osaka land prices to Tokyo land prices with the Tokyo value = 100.

department stores, entertainment arcades, banks and office buildings for professionals, for lawyers, insurance agents, and the like commuting into their workplaces from freshly minted suburbs. As can be seen from Table 4.2, a combination of industrial and commercial buildup in the prefectures of Osaka and Tokyo went hand in hand with the conversion of land, agricultural fields giving way to *takuchi* (industrial, commercial or residential uses) land use, developers like the intercity railroad companies spearheading the drive.

Directing this process of land conversion was the guiding hand of the market. Land prices soared in the centers of metropolises such as Osaka, encouraging merchant houses and small retail outlets to sell, using the proceeds culled from their selling off real estate (formerly cheap, now expensive) to set up business further away from the core zones of the city. By 1910 the growth rate of the price of *takuchi* land relative to paddy land was around 30 percent per annum. This growth rate was sustained throughout most of the next decade, especially during the World War I industrial boom. But even during the relatively anemic growth of the early 1920s the price of Osaka's *takuchi* land relative to paddy grew at annual rates of over 25 per cent, during the late 1920s rising to over 30 percent. Indeed it is not farfetched to refer to this escalation in *takuchi* land in the major conurbations of the Tōkaidō like Osaka, as Japan's first pronounced speculative land price boom, foreshadowing the mighty urban land price booms of the post-World War II (for instance during the 1960s and 1980s): expectation of future surges in land prices fueling the feverish purchase of land.

The World War I boom

Between 1910 and 1920 the Japanese economy went through a wrenching structural transformation. Industrialization – the diversion of labor, capital and land resources from agricultural to industrial purposes – was rapid and unrelenting. In particular the heavy industries (iron and steel manufacture, shipbuilding, chemicals, machinery making) expanded vigorously. The industrial labor force – heavily female in the first phase of Japanese industrialization, girls from rural villages swelling the ranks of the recruits to cotton textile mills – became increasingly male as the heavy industries grew by leaps and bounds. Table 4.3 captures some of the highlights of this transformation – note the surge in the number of companies, the rapid expansion in the non-agricultural labor force, the transformation of Japan's trade balance from negative to positive – setting it off from the previous and subsequent decades.

There are two distinct views about why the decade from 1910 to 1920 took on its distinctive trappings: that emphasizing exogenous circumstances, namely the fact that World War I occurred during the period, disrupting most of Europe's capacity to carry on international trade between 1914 and 1918; and that grounded in domestic considerations, arguing that the infrastructure buildup of the previous decade provided the foundation upon which rapid industrialization could and did take place. It should be apparent that the two arguments are potentially complementary: the World War I disruption of international trade promoting import substitution in Japan exercising its magic on Japan's economy primarily because an infrastructure base that drove down the costs of transporting goods and people and supplying energy had been put into place during the previous decade.

Turning to the direction impact of World War I on Japan's economy, one must begin with the observation that Japan was brought into the war through its alliance with the United Kingdom. Because World War I was mainly fought on European soil, however, Japan's military played almost no role in the conflict. Indeed, the Japanese government exploited the fact that diplomats in Europe were almost completely absorbed in managing the two alliance systems that confronted one another in the mighty conflict, to secretly press its infamous twenty-one demands on the Chinese government, delivering them in the form of five carefully crafted groups. The fifth group was especially onerous, giving effective control of China's policy making over to Japanese advisors who would exercise direct control over the police and arms acquisition. After Chinese officials leaked the demands to the press and eventually made them a matter of international diplomacy at the Paris Peace Conference of 1919 that negotiated the end of

Table 4.3 Structural change, capital accumulation, price movements, trade and expansion of factory production, 1904–1930

Panel A Structural change, 1904–1930

Period	Percentage of GDP in:		Average annual growth rate of labor force in:		Average annual growth rate of labor productivity in:		Number of companies[a]
	Agriculture	Manufacturing	Agriculture	Non-agriculture	Agriculture	Manufacturing	
1904–1911	31.9	13.6	−0.1	1.5	2.3	3.4	9,006
1911–1919	28.7	17.9	−1.4	3.5	3.0	2.6	17,149
1919–1930	22.3	19.8	−0.2	1.8	0.8	3.9	34,345

Panel B Composition of capital formation, 1904–1930

Period	Percentage of capital formation in:					Percent of government capital formation military
	Private primary industry	Private non-primary industry	Private residential construction	Government	Total	
1904–1911	8.6	13.9	30.6	46.9	100	11.3
1911–1919	6.1	18.4	31.4	44.1	100	8.4
1919–1930	5.3	18.1	28.5	48.2	100	6.8

Panel C *Trade and prices: ratio of net exports to total trade (NX/T), percentage of primary commodities in trade, and growth rate of consumer price index, 1904–1930*

Period	Net exports to total trade (%)	Percentage of primary commodities in:		Average annual growth rate of consumer price index (%)
		Exports	Imports	
1904–1911	7.0	21.8	49.8	2.9
1911–1919	5.2	16.3	59.0	8.2
1919–1930	–2.6	9.9	56.7	–0.6

Panel D *Factories in Osaka, 1905–1924*

Period	Index of average number of factories (1900–1901 = 100)	Average number of workers per factory	Percentage of factory employment in:		
			Textiles	Machinery	Chemicals
1905–1909	146	6.7	44.5	17.3	25.9
1910–1914	232	5.7	44.0	19.3	22.7
1915–1919	400	7.4	28.2	32.1	15.9
1920–1924	431	6.0	23.9	33.7	12.0

Source: Mosk (2001) Table 4.3, pp. 120–4 and Table 6.3, p. 193.

Notes

a Figure for 1904–1911 is for 1905; figure for 1911–1919 is for 1915; and figure for 1919–1930 is for 1925.

World War I, a nationalist movement emerged in China that viewed Japan as China's major adversary, organizing boycotts of Japanese goods as part of its political strategy.

Invited to the Paris Peace Conference as one of the five great victorious powers by dint of its alliance with the United Kingdom, Japan picked up some German colonial possessions in the North Pacific and East Asia, forcing a number of European powers to accede to Japan's drive to secure more territory in China in secret backroom deals. This angered the United States, providing grist for the mill of those in the Congress of the United States opposed to ratifying the Treaty of Versailles negotiated at Paris, thereby keeping the United States out of the League of Nations set up to guarantee collective security against future military threats posed by aggressive powers bent on aggrandizing their regional hegemonic power.

In short, Japan's leaders saw its international prestige rise to widely acknowledged great power status, garnering a seat on the council set up to direct the newly created League of Nations, in the aftermath of a major war in which it managed to avoid expending its military resources. Testimony to this lack of military involvement is the low level of military related spending as a proportion of government spending on capital formation during the decade 1911–19 (see Panel B of Table 4.3). Indeed, from an economic point of view the main impact of World War I was to cut off imports of machinery and technology from the European powers, the United States serving as the only major supplier prior to its entry into the conflict. Blockades and trade embargoes tying up the trade of the European powers had two implications for Japan. Japanese companies began aggressively selling their products in the colonial possessions of the European powers, in India, in the Dutch East Indies, in French and British possessions throughout South East Asia, in Africa. At the same time it became difficult, and increasingly costly, for Japanese companies to secure machinery and capital equipment from foreign sources, giving a fillip to import substitution. Panel C in Table 4.3 documents this fact.

The expansion of heavy industry during the decade of the 1910s created tremendous opportunities for the *zaibatsu* to grow. With their voracious demand for immense amounts of capital, a typical shipyard or iron and steel complex or chemical plant sought out large banks with which they could deal, negotiating long-term loans that they could and did roll over for further investing. This put pressure on a heavily fragmented banking sector, many banks established during the early Meiji period between unit banks with only one branch serving as the headquarters of the bank, mainly serving as extensions of local *meibōka* investment activity. This structure generally satisfied the demands for financing typical of light industrial firms – an integrated spinning and weaving mill for instance – but not the needs of the new capital-intensive heavy industrial firms. Thus the banking sector became increasingly concentrated, unit banks being absorbed into larger banks as branches. The share of the big five (*zaibatsu*-affiliated) banks grew as a share of the total paid in capital of the banking sector. By the 1911–19, this share had grown to around 15 percent. Relatively decentralized capitalism was gradually giving way to concentrated capitalism.

A dualistic economy emerges

As heavy manufacturing industry grew relative to the rest of the Japanese economy, the economy became dualistic. The dualism emerged simultaneously in labor and capital markets. Capital market dualism refers to segmentation of markets according to the type of firm seeking funds. Consider bank financing. If one company is asked to pay back the loans it negotiates at a high interest rate – say, for instance, 10 percent – while another company is asked to repay at a relatively low interest rate – say, 4 percent – we say that the capital market is segmented, evidencing dualism. Similar logic applies to labor markets. When one firm pays its typical employee twice or three times what another firm pays we say that the labor market is segmented, is dualistic.

In the Japanese case, capital market and labor market dualism overlap. Reasoning from capital markets to labor markets suggests why this might be so. As a rule large firms hold substantial assets, in land, in equipment and machinery, in transport vehicles. Using this as collateral for bank loans gives them a credibility advantage over small firms. Large firms are less likely to go bankrupt because they can cash in assets in times of financial duress. In the event that their borrowing does not yield profits, they have assets that they can use to satisfy the demands of their creditors. Better equipped to shop around for funds amongst banks, large firms are better able to drive a better bargain with their financiers. Thus the relative cost of capital compared to labor (the ratio of the cost of borrowing a unit of capital over the wage at which a worker was hired) tended to be lower for large firms than for small firms. Responding to these relative prices, large firms are more likely to be capital intensive, the ratio of capital to labor being high. By contrast, small firms are more likely to be labor intensive, combining copious inputs of labor services with scant amounts of machinery and structures.

We can also reason our way from labor market dualism to capital market dualism. Suppose the supply of hard working, diligent workers is small relative to the entire labor force. Staying competitive in industries where the latest technologies are well known and fully incorporated into production, where much work is fairly routine, the extra effort of employees required to master esoteric machinery not being sought after by employers, is managed fairly readily in such an environment. Standards expected of a rank and file worker can be readily set. It is even possible to set up regularly scheduled tests to see how well workers perform. The Japanese textile industry around World War I is a good example of such an industry. Japanese manufacturers had mastered most of the details used in the most advanced textile manufacturing concerns by the early twentieth century. They had learned how to bring workers up to minimum work standards relatively quickly, even introducing weekly tests of worker proficiency in some cases. This was the state of affairs governing most employment of females in late nineteenth-century and early twentieth-century Japan. A typical girl recruited into the mills stayed a few years, returning to her home village to marry.

Industrious workers?

Between 1987 and the mid-1990s the Ministry of Labor compensated almost two hundred families for the loss of their primary breadwinner due to death from overwork (karōshi). International labor surveys consistently show Japanese employees putting in longer hours of work than workers in other advanced industrial economies. For instance in 1990 it is estimated that the typical Japanese worker clocked in around 350 hours more per year than the typical French employee. And this is based upon official data. In point of fact the official figures almost certainly understate Japanese labor inputs. Some estimates point to Japanese working almost twice as many hours as employed persons in Germany and Sweden. Was this true of Japanese during the early period of economic development?

There is substantial evidence that Japanese workers were not especially prone to work hard and diligently until the late 1930s and especially during World War II. Concerned about regularizing work inputs across social classes – the samurai were considered to be especially lazy – the Meiji government established the "1–6 holiday" system that set all dates ending in a one or a six as holidays. In addition, the government established ten holidays a year for carrying out rituals related to the imperial family. When the Western calendar was introduced, the rest days were set at half of Saturday and all day Sunday; but holidays related to the imperial family continued. Moreover, during the blistering summer, it was customary to avoid work. Only in 1938, when Japan was on the brink of plunging into total war, did government employees lose the right to take off substantial stretches during the heat of summer.

Consistent with this picture are complaints of Meiji industrial workers failing to show up for work, and drinking up their wages as soon as they were paid. It was not uncommon for wives to ambush their husbands as their spouses exited the factory on payday, the wife anxious to secure the wages before her husband consumed it in liquor. Western observers traveling in Japan during the Meiji period commented on the apparent indolence and lack of discipline of many Japanese workers. This suggests that the Japanese work ethic changed dramatically during World War II and during the miracle growth era, 1955–70, when workers, especially shop floor managers and participants in quality control (QC) circles, put in substantial overtime in an economy whose growth was nothing short of phenomenal.

Consistent with this is the view that employees in the 1955 environment tended to log long hours because they were afraid of what their colleagues, and especially their supervisors,would think of them. If the supervisor stays at the helm and does not go home until the evening, is it wise for the subordinate concerned with garnering a promotion or getting an especially generous bonus to leave work at the time legally stipulated by labor law?

Alternative speculations are plausible. Japan is densely populated, especially in the great cities. As a result finding true leisure spots, out of doors locales that are free of noise and congestion, is difficult. Another argument rests on the trends in health and physical well being documented in Appendix Table A.7. According to the logic spelled out in that table, Japanese used to be less robust, less capable of carrying out long hours of physical work. As their net nutritional intake improved so did their ability to labor long and hard.

Toyoda Sakichi, the Toyoda automatic loom, and the Toyota Motor Corporation

One of the most famous stories in Japanese industrial history involves Toyoda Sakichi's invention of Type G automatic loom with non-stop shuttle changeover, the sale of the patent for his loom to Platt Brothers and Co. of Britain, and the use of the proceeds from the patent's sale for an initial investment in the Toyota Motor Corporation.

The story neatly illustrates a number of propositions: that Japanese were not mere slavish imitators of Western technology, making important breakthroughs on their own; and that diversification from an already established industry to another newer field of endeavor was not restricted to the zaibatsu.

Unfortunately, the simple version of the story is untrue. The proceeds from the sale of the patent were insufficient to fund the investment of Toyoda Kiichiro, son of Toyoda Sakichi, in the fledgling automobile company; rather it was shared amongst the employees of Toyoda Automatic Loom Works who had suffered wage cuts in the struggling company. What was the relationship between the automatic loom invention and the start up of Toyota Motors? How important was the innovation made by Toyoda Sakichi?

The Type G automatic loom was a real breakthrough: it was sufficiently sophisticated to build in feedback, the loom sensing that a warp or weft thread had snapped, or a shuttle had run out of thread, stopping operation until a new shuttle was thrust into its place, all of this occurring automatically. Toyoda Sakichi developed a prototype for this loom in 1924, securing *a patent in that year. Actually building looms that could effectively make use of the shuttle changer was a protracted process, however, one that tied up Toyoda Kiichiro in manifold trial and error experiments during 1925. On the basis of the trials, a new company dedicated to manufacturing the looms was established in 1926, Kiichiro assuming the role of managing director, plunging into the fray with other companies that were attempting to build and market similar looms.*

It was at this juncture that Platt Brothers entered the picture, hoping to arrange a tie up with Toyoda Automatic Loom Workers. Out of these negotiations came the offer of Platt Brothers to sign a contract with Toyoda Automatic Loom Works, securing the patent rights in 1929. Under the terms of the agreement Platt Brothers gained the exclusive right to manufacture and sell the Toyoda automatic loom in all countries except Japan, China and the United States.

In fact Platt Brothers was unable to effectively make use of the patent, encountering numerous difficulties in harnessing the new loom to actual production. Why had Platt Brothers, once a world leader in the field of textiles, been unable to invent something the Toyodas had achieved? Why was it encountering difficulty in making the numerous adjustments to put the loom to work in textile manufacturing, something Toyoda Automatic Loom Works was managing to accomplish in Japan?

The inference from the version of the story related here (based on the research of Wada Kazuo) is that Toyoda Kiichiro gained confidence from his interaction with Platt Brothers, realizing his company could accomplish what Platt couldn't. On the basis of this burst of confidence he set up in 1930 a research room within the confines of Toyoda Automatic Loom Works in which he and his colleagues could study the feasibility of manufacturing automobiles.

Note: This discussion draws heavily on the manuscript written by Wada (undated).

By contrast in the new heavy industries foreign technologies manufacturers were eager to ferret out, license and perfect the use of foreign technologies. Training periods for many shop floor workers were protracted. Hard working, focused workers able and willing to experiment with innovative techniques were at a premium. Firms were willing to pay a premium to hire such workers.

The nature of this premium wage level can be readily analyzed in terms of two labor market models, the efficiency wage model and the human capital model. According to the efficiency wage model a firm is prepared to pay a wage above the market-clearing wage in order to motivate the worker to give extra effort, to not shirk, to take his or her employment seriously. According to the human capital model the firm attempts to bind the worker to itself, encouraging the worker to invest in human capital specific to the particular firm (human capital that he or she can not necessarily take with them to another employer) by setting up a wage profile in which wages rise with accumulated years of seniority on the job. Suppose the contribution to firm net revenue of a typical worker exceeds the level of the wage paid to the worker after several years of training, only falling short of the worker's remuneration towards the end of his or her employment career in the company. If we set the discounted present value of the wages to be earned equal to the discounted present value of the employee's contributions to firm net revenue the worker is still paid his or her marginal revenue product. At the same time the payment scheme binds the worker to the firm, rewarding the worker for loyalty with generous wages toward the end of his or her career in the enterprise.

Following the logic of the efficiency wage or human capital arguments, the fact that large firms in the heavy industries began paying premium wages to male workers who were much more likely to remain with the firm for a protracted period is explicable in terms of the technological imperative that they faced. To be competitive in the new fields of endeavor required hiring the most able, technically competent, highly motivated workers, especially engineers tooled up in the latest methods. Prior to 1910 the number of such workers was relatively small. After the World War I boom, the demand for this type of employee soared.

Note that this line of argument in which labor market segmentation is crucial can be used to explain why large firms in the heavy industries were more likely to be capital intensive than small firms in these industries. Facing relatively high costs to attract and hold onto premium workers, these firms faced markets in which the relative cost of capital was low relative to the cost of labor. Naturally they were inclined to substitute relatively cheap capital for relatively expensive labor everywhere they could.

At a general level these arguments are consistent with the diverging paths in relative levels of wages paid to males and to females in agriculture and in manufacturing. As Table 4.4 shows wage differentials between agriculture and manufacturing – the agricultural wage falling substantially below the industrial wage – opened up for males in the aftermath of the World War I boom but not for females. Indeed, while real wages for males in manufacturing tended to rise substantially between the World War I boom and the mid-1930s (almost doubling between 1915–19 and 1930–34), real wages for females in manufacturing rose only modestly, falling back in the early 1930s. These arguments are also consistent with the estimates for growth in the demand and supply of engineers displayed in Panel C of Table 4.4. With the exception of the early 1920s – when the manufacturing firms that had flourished in the hothouse conditions of World War I, largely protected from foreign competition, once again faced harsh competition from abroad, many slipping into bankruptcy – growth in demand for engineers outstripped growth in the supply of engineers. Thus the premium above market wages, above the wage set in agriculture from which many of the new recruits to manufacturing came, should have remained strong throughout the post-1916 period.

Table 4.4 Real daily wages in agriculture and manufacturing (deflated by the consumer price index), wage differentials by gender and sector, and estimates of the demand and supply of engineers, 1915–1940

Panel A   *Real wages in agriculture and manufacturing (deflated by the CPI with 1934–1936 = 1)*

Period	Agriculture		Manufacturing	
	Males	*Females*	*Males*	*Females*
1915–1919	0.99	0.73	1.09	0.51
1920–1924	1.23	0.94	1.65	0.74
1925–1929	1.20	0.96	1.85	0.75
1930–1934	0.95	0.71	2.14	0.69
1935–1939	0.97	0.77	1.84	0.60

Panel B   *Wage differentials (denominator = 1)*

Period	Female/male		Agriculture/manufacturing	
	Agriculture	*Manufacturing*	*Males*	*Females*
1915–1919	0.73	0.47	0.92	1.42
1920–1924	0.76	0.45	0.75	1.26
1925–1929	0.80	0.41	0.65	1.27
1930–1934	0.75	0.32	0.45	1.03
1935–1939	0.79	0.33	0.53	1.30

Panel C   *Estimated demand for, and supply of, engineers, 1916–1940*

Period	Supply: students of higher education in science and engineering		Estimated demand growth[a] (%)	Estimated demand growth minus supply growth (%)
	Percentage of all higher education students	*Estimated growth rate of graduates in science & engineering (%)*		
1916–1920	13.1	10.1	16.1	+6.0
1921–1925	14.2	17.3	11.4	−5.9
1926–1930	15.7	2.1	7.1	+5.0
1931–1935	11.8	8.3	6.1	+2.2
1936–1940	14.3	3.7	13.9	+10.3

Source: Mosk (1995) Table 2.1, p. 37; Table 2.4, p. 65; Table 2.8, p. 83.

Notes

a Estimated by adding growth rate of employees in railroads and public utilities to growth rate of prime mover horsepower in manufacturing.

Wage levels are one thing. Employment contracts are something else. Both efficiency wage and human capital arguments do link them up in the sense that they appeal to the firm's desire to bind workers to itself. The fact that corporate paternalism becomes an increasingly visible feature of the industrial landscape after World War I is sometimes taken as evidence that companies were actively experimenting with programs designed to retain and motivate workers.

Paternalism versus Taylorism

During the interwar period, a substantial number of Japanese industrial enterprises introduced paternalistic practices – company housing for the families of workers, side payments to cover commuting costs, special financial payments to aid workers who were taking care of aged parents – collectively referred to by the Japanese term "onjōshugi". Many Japanese writers argue that the movement on the part of Japanese firms embracing these "beautiful traditional" practices was rooted in culture, namely in "groupism, feelings of dependency, and a demand for harmony in the work place". They maintain that adopting these practices was tantamount to rejecting the scientific management approach known as Taylorism that characterized the trend toward corporate paternalism evident especially in the United States, to a lesser extent in Western Europe.

Taylorism in the United States was intimately tied up with the spread of the assembly line in manufacturing. Time and motion studies grounded in systematic observation of the shop floor practices of rank and file blue-collar employees by engineers and managers, stopwatch in hand, were used to determine time ratings for specific tasks, these ratings being used to evaluate the productivity of individual workers, these ratings then used to set job requirements for particular work assignments. As a philosophical approach to management, Taylorism was decidedly rational, rooted in quantitative measurement, objective in ignoring the personal needs and travails affecting individual workers in their domestic lives outside the factory.

By contrast onjōshugi was supposedly grounded in a respect for the individuality of particular workers, their need to respect and assist their fellow employees when their colleagues were struggling, to work peacefully and productively in a corporate family dedicated to the mutual interests of shareholders and employees alike. Detailed research on interwar corporate practice explodes as a myth the idea that Taylorism was rejected in Japanese industry. Rather it suggests that onjōshugi and Taylorism made their way into the industrial sector hand in hand, perhaps progress in introducing the scientific and engineering approach being sugar coated by wrapping it up with the more emotional and particularistic trappings of paternalism.

To understand the context in which onjōshugi and/or Taylorism spread throughout the industrial landscape of Japan, it is important to appreciate that the movement to bring it into manufacturing was largely limited to the new heavy industries that concentrated on hiring male workers who embodied substantial skills garnered through years of experience. Its progress in the older light industries like cotton textiles that relied on female workers whose skills were acquired rapidly was far more circumscribed.

During the early Meiji period the small island of heavy industrial firms – arms manufactures, iron and steel concerns – relied on a system of indirect management, contracting with labor bosses who brought their work gangs into the shop floor, who allocated work assignments and wages, who trained their subordinates. Relying on these bosses was problematic. If the labor bosses bringing in their work groups banded together, deciding to go out on strike together in a coordinated fashion, they could shut down the operation, disabling production. Moreover, the labor bosses were frequently unaware of technological developments in the West, developments that a university trained engineer hired by the company might have studied. Japanese manufacturers intent on securing the rights to utilize foreign patented technologies naturally wanted their university recruited managers and engineers to organize training programs for blue-collar workers. Continuing to rely on labor bosses presented them with major headaches.

The movement to co-opt the labor bosses, bringing them into the ranks of company management, giving them status comparable to, or not markedly inferior to that enjoyed by a university graduate manager, was part and parcel of the drift toward paternalism and Taylorism that gripped Japanese industrial circles during and in the wake of the World War I boom.

Arguments based upon path dependence can be used to explain why Japanese firms might have favored combining the holistic and warm appeal of onjōshugi with the cool hard Western rationality of Taylorism. During the Tokugawa period merchant houses operated with internal promotion systems – promoting from detchi to tedai to bantō – housing their young recruits on the premises before their promotion to tedai status engineered marriage and a move out away from the lodgings owned by the house. Again, a samurai was effectively an employee of a relatively large corporate entity, expected to provide loyal service, the psychological feeling of loyal obedience to a master who rewarded his subservient partner with a stipend being fundamental to the relationship of samurai and daimyō. Perhaps the ideology of reciprocal obligation inherent in the implicit contract between samurai and daimyō, and the blurring of boundaries between the personal and the corporate inherent in the merchant house model, retained sufficient strength in the minds and hearts of industrialists, many born and raised under Tokugawa rule, to foster a commingling of Taylorism and paternalism during the period between the world wars.

A term that is often used to describe and analyze those labor markets in which labor mobility is low – workers staying with their main employer throughout the vast majority of years that they spend in the labor market – is the internalization of labor. Practices introduced by many Japanese companies after the World War I boom governing the recruitment and promotion of white-collar professional workers is consistent with the internalization of labor concept.

A limited internalization of labor

During the American occupation of Japan and its immediate aftermath, Japanese labor markets became famous for their three "jewels": age-seniority based wage payments (known as "nenkō"); lifetime employment from entry into the firm until the compulsory age of retirement (set at age 55 during the 1950s and 1960s); and enterprise unionism, unions largely being organized along company as opposed to industry or craft lines. Collectively, these characteristics of Japan's labor market – workers being bound to companies for the bulk of their careers, unions being formed within companies, wages being determined within companies through promotion and seniority rather than by the movement of workers between firms – are known in the economics literature as symptoms of an extreme internalization of labor. Extreme in the sense that many functions of Western labor markets – collective bargaining, wage setting partially set through competition for mid-career workers – are blunted in the Japanese case, the internal labor market within the enterprise taking precedence over the external labor market.

To some degree this description of the Japanese labor market as heavily balkanized is a myth. Still it contains an important modicum of truth. Thus the question naturally arises: to what extent was the internalization of labor peculiar to post-1945 Japan and to the institutional environment brought on by the American occupation?

The view that the internalization of labor in Japan is tied up with the spread of paternalism and Taylorism during the interwar period, as opposed to the view that something totally new sprang up during the American occupation, rests on the observation that white-collar, but not blue-collar workers, were being internalized during the World War I boom and the subsequent decades leading up to the total war regime of the late 1930s.

As the indirect style of management employing independent labor bosses was giving way to the system in which professionally trained managers were largely recruited out of universities, high schools and vocational schools, larger Japanese enterprises introduced a two-track system of employment. An elite consisting of former labor bosses and graduates of institutions of higher learning were accorded "shain" ("shain" literally means "company member" or "company person") status. They were paid according to age and performance ("nenkō"), were granted job security until they reached the age of compulsory retirement (using pre-1940 life tables this was set at age 55) at which point receiving generous pensions, and the opportunity to compete for promotion to the highest ranks of the enterprise. The remainder of the company's employees – rank and file blue-collar workers – were known as "kōin" (literally an "employed person"), were paid on an hourly basis rather than on the salaried basis common for "shain", and were denied the benefits accorded to their white collar colleagues.

In this discriminatory environment, two avenues seemed most open and appealing to blue-collar workers seeking improvement to their earnings and their status: pushing to remove the distinction between "shain" and "kōin", in effect extending the internalization of labor down to the rank and file laboring on the shop floor; or organizing unions that had a base outside of their enterprises, thereby gaining the muscle to strike against a wide range of companies at a single time, improving their wages and the conditions of their employment through friction creating collective bargaining.

As it turned out, pursing the second option, organizing, proved difficult prior to the American occupation. The reasons are two-fold: legal suppression and political fragmentation, factionalism, in the nascent labor movement.

From a legal standpoint, the ability to hold union rallies and to call for strikes was seriously hampered and hemmed in by the way the Peace Preservation Law was interpreted by the authorities. The police tended to break up union meetings.

Moreover, factionalism was rampant in the interwar left-wing labor movement. Three wings contested for the allegiance of the working class created by industrialization: a right wing represented by the Grand Federation of Labor Unions Fraternity Association; a left wing organized under the banner of the Japanese Council of Labor Unions; and a centrist federation, the Japan Labor-Farmer Party. Divisions on the left made it that much easier for a conservative government to suppress unionization and the drive to establish a system of collective bargaining, "divide and rule" being an age-old form of governance and control well known to the Tokugawa bakufu.

To summarize: the wage floor set by agricultural productivity that governed wages in manufacturing prior to the early 1910s continued to characterize the market for females who were largely concentrated in light industry after 1920; for males, a widening gap between the agricultural and manufacturing sectors grew up after World War II. On the male side of the labor market, but not on the female side, the economy became decidedly dualistic by the mid-1920s, dualism in the relative level of wages being paralleled by dualism in capital intensity. Developments in both labor markets and capital markets underlay this emergent dualism so that it is difficult to disentangle the influences flowing from one market from the influences flowing from the other market. Dualism became a new reality after World War I, and with it paternalism and the gradual internalization of labor.

The drive to empire

In 1910 Japan officially incorporated Korea into its growing empire that already included Taiwan and the southern half of Sakhalin Island. In addition it exercised informal control over an unofficial empire including assets and territory in Manchuria and Northern China. To an important degree, the drive to empire was driven by military and strategic considerations, being part and parcel of the agenda of those elites ardently committed to the *kyōhei* doctrine.

Most of the elites committed to military aggrandizement were not interested in completely eschewing, downplaying the importance of *fukoku* both on the domestic and on the colonial fronts. Integrating the colonies into an empire wide economy was a tantalizing goal. For some economic considerations dominated. For others economic issues were secondary but still not to be ignored. Emerging to the forefront as an economic issue at the close of the World War I boom was the state of the domestic agricultural sector.

Prior to 1910, agricultural productivity growth – growth in farm output per hectare farmed – was substantial. This was the largely the result of diffusing best practice from the southwest to the northeast. But it also stemmed from improving rural roads, irrigation and drainage ditches, from the penetration of railroads into remote areas, encouraging farmers to diversify into crops like silk that they could ship to distant markets. In this process involving improving planting techniques, selecting the most appropriate rice seedlings, lobbying for roads and railroads, the rural elite consisting of literate landowners that often put out part of their fields to tenant farmers who paid them rent typically on a fixed rent basis played a crucial role. Because a large percentage of those renting land also owned land – and even leased it out on occasion – sharecropping which in many ways is more suitable to motivating both land owner and tenant (any gains in the productivity of land accruing immediately to both parties) did not gain a strong foothold in most rural communities.

During the early Meiji period the literate rural elite tended to send at least one son to an agricultural vocational school where he learned about new farming techniques. Appreciating the importance of marketing quality rice – rice that would not be distrusted and avoided by consumers – the rural elite took a proactive stance, promoting the establishment of organizations that tested rice, ensuring that all that was sold met minimum standards. While the landlord renting out land on a fixed rent basis did not have direct short-run interest in improving the output of the fields farmed by their tenants, elites in the countryside worked hand in hand with those subordinate to them in improving output per hectare. They did so because by so doing they showed their benevolence;

they did so because they expected to raise rents in the future. Eventually the pace of agricultural productivity gain waned. It waned because squeezing additional gains from the diffusion of best practice Tokugawa techniques had largely been exhausted; it waned because the payoff from additional improvements in transportation infrastructure were falling; and it waned because the rural elite was shifting their interest toward the industrial sector. As a dualism within the economy grew, investing in new rural activities paled, being decisively trumped by the rewards offered by the manufacturing sector. Rather than train a son at an agricultural vocational school would it not be better to send him to an industrial vocational school where he could master the skills required to operate the newest electrical motors?

As a result the growth in domestic agriculture slowed. But growth in demand did not slow down. Prices of rice rose. In 1918 rice riots broke out, spreading from rural districts into the great cities of the industrial belt like Osaka. Those with an interest in integrating the colonies into the imperial economy saw an opportunity to address the problem of how to increase the supply of rice through the promotion of agricultural exports from the colonies. By encouraging the spread of Japanese techniques in rice farming to the empire, especially to Korea where the natural soil and climatic conditions were unusually favorable, colonial output levels would soar, exports to the home country increasing in tandem with colonial production. One of the consequences of stepping up imports of rice, however, was the depressing of rice prices in Japan (as long as supply increased faster than demand), eroding the incentives of Japanese farmers to concentrate on expanding rice yields as opposed to shifting towards fruits, vegetables, animal husbandry and raw silk production. Using the empire to solve domestic rural problems was a two-edged sword.

All of the factors that we have mentioned – the growing disinterest of the rural elite from taking an active role in rural affairs, the slowdown in the growth of yields per hectare, the growth in imports from the empire that kept domestic prices for rice from rising – dismembered the social fabric of many rural communities in the aftermath of World War I. Disputes between rural tenant unions demanding rent reductions and landlords became increasingly bitter throughout the 1920s. How this outbreak in discontent in village Japan is interpreted depends upon one's viewpoint about pre-World War II Japanese society. Scholars, especially those Marxists who view exploitation and repression by the rural landlord elite as endemic, view the outbreak of violent disputes in rural Japan as symptomatic of the backward social conditions of imperial Japan, an oppressed tenant class acting out of desperation. Others view the tenants who took the initiative in pushing for rent reductions as motivated by a desire to seize opportunities for increasing their incomes, for getting a larger slice of the pie, for taking the lead in promoting further productivity growth away from the landlords.

Regardless of which view one subscribes to one thing is clear. After 1918 theories about Japan's foreign policy were either implicitly or explicitly linked to theories about how to reduce tensions between landlords and tenants, how to stabilize rural prices, how to ensure that industrial workers could afford to eat an acceptable diet with the wages they were garnering in the cities.

Between 1904 and 1919 the Japan experienced strong discontinuities in its international affairs. At the conclusion of World War I it was accorded the status of a great power, a power with a growing colonial empire off the coasts of China and Russia and on the Chinese mainland. From a situation in which they struggled to undo Japan's semi-colonial status under the unequal treaties it had been forced to sign in the 1850s, Japan's political and military elites had managed to rapidly and decisively cast off these humiliating conditions, in the process becoming a major imperial power. In doing so they brought Japan into the rough world of geopolitics in which national leaders cynically operated through the logic of deception, seeking to ward off war through the calculus of the balance of power. In this world military victory did not automatically translate into political and economic aggrandizement.

As a result a national consensus operating under the umbrella of *fukoku kyōhei* strategy, rooted in the idea that improvements in the economy automatically meant improvements in military prowess and vice versa, broke down. For a Japanese farmer in the early 1920s, answering the question of whether Japan should maintain a colony on the Korean peninsula from which it imported growing volumes of rice and other foodstuffs was not easy and obvious. To *zaibatsu* doing extensive trade and commercial dealings with the companies in the United States and Europe was the potential souring of diplomatic relations due to military action too hefty a price to be paid for continuing with a policy approach rooted in the *kyōhei* ideology?

Paralleling the discontinuities in Japan's international position were the economic transformations associated with rapid industrialization, the growth of heavy industry, the buildup of transportation and energy supplying infrastructure, the remaking of the great metropolises in the Tōkaidō industrial belt, the slowdown in productivity growth in the agricultural sector, and the emergence of pronounced labor and capital market dualism. Most of these changes worked to create differentials in income, wealth, and status within the body politic. A relatively high-income industrial belt that was surging ahead was leaving behind a rural agricultural sector struggling with growing tension between landlords and tenant farmers.

Was it realistic to suppose that the divisions and debates opened up by Japan's military and economic successes between the 1890s and the early 1920s would not spawn deep seated domestic political divisions? This is the issue that we shall take up in the beginning of our next chapter.

Key terms and concepts in Chapter 4

Sino-Japanese War	*Takuchi* land
Liaotung territory	Twenty-one demands
Electric railroad companies acting as local *zaibatsu*	Dualism in labor and capital markets

5 Reform and renewal

Taishō democracy

The splintering apart of the *fukoku kyōhei* consensus spawned political fragmentation in post-World War I Japan. Right, left and moderate middle persuasions broke apart the mold of *fukoku kyōhei*, combating each other in the public arena, sometimes resorting to physical violence and intimidation tactics, even worse assassination to terrify their political rivals.

In the moderate middle were advocates of democracy. Riding a wave of popular demonstrations, their arguments bolstered by the growth of literacy and expansion in the ranks of eligible voters successfully hurdling the annual earnings qualification bar, using as a selling point their ability to deliver on a growing chorus of demand for pork barrel infrastructure projects, promoters of government responsible to the voters, not to the good will of the emperor, made substantial headway during the 1920s. Erecting the foundations for cabinets formed from the dominant parties in the Diet, they pioneered an alternating two-party system that vigorously debated many of the key decisions facing the nation during the decade.

Basing their case for democracy on the notion that there was an indivisible bond between the Japanese people and the imperial will, Seiyūkai party leaders like Hara Takashi (Kei) argued that the spirit of the Meiji Restoration and the Meiji Constitution was consistent with the twin principles of party cabinets and parliamentary government. It should be emphasized that Hara and his supporters were not claiming that the emperor could not continue to appoint cabinets and prime ministers populated by the *genrō*; what they were asserting is that the emperor had the option of not relying upon a *genrō* oligarchy, rather choosing to appoint party cabinets along British lines if he so chose. In making this argument they embraced rather than rejected the ambiguity symbolized in the phrase "indivisible bond between people and the imperial will".

Basing his ascendancy to power on Seiyūkai success in securing a strong base in the bureaucracy, drawing upon the coffers of Mitsui to mount effective campaigns, its political credibility bolstered by its staunch advocacy for infrastructure buildup – notably railroads and harbors – Seiyūkai's leader Hara dominated the Diet of 1917 after his party became the largest in the parliament. When the Terauchi cabinet resigned in the wake of the Rice Riots of 1918, Hara became prime minister, the first heading up a party cabinet. Although Hara was a former samurai and was definitely more than willing to play the game of political infighting and manipulation amongst a small coterie of elites, he was committed to extending the franchise, despite harboring reservations about seeing government by elites fall to the wayside.

The fact is that until the mid-1920s Japanese democracy was elite democracy. Only those paying substantial taxes – hence mainly the *meibōka* elite and a small handful of industrialists and professionals who became wealthy as a result of manufacturing expansion especially during the World War I boom – could vote. That Japan restricted the franchise during its early experimentation with democracy is hardly unusual. So did the United States and Canada during the early nineteenth century; also the Latin American republics throughout the nineteenth century.

The ambiguity in attitudes held by Taisho period political elites like Hara is nicely encapsulated by the Diet's passage of a universal male suffrage bill. At the same time the legislation was passed, a "thought control" Peace Preservation Bill aimed at cracking down on controversial expressions of free speech, including demonstrations and meetings in the incipient labor movement, was passed by the Diet.

Because elections to the Diet were based on a simple-plurality, single-ballot "first past the post" system of voting adopted by the United States and Great Britain, rather than on the proportional representation system prevailing in France, there was strong momentum for a two-party system to emerge once party cabinets and full-fledged parliamentary government were established. The reason is simple. Under "first past the post" voting, voters have a strong incentive to eschew support for a small startup party or a single issue party, feeling that they will be throwing away their contribution to determining which party secures a majority and the mandate to form a cabinet.

Aggrandizing voter support by absorbing smaller parties, a contender to the Seiyūkai emerged, the Kenseikai, later becoming the Minseitō. Committed to British liberalism, favoring balanced budgets, drawing up the Mitsubishi *zaibatsu* for financial support, the Minseitō became a worthy opponent to the Mitsui backed Seiyūkai, the two parties alternating in the forming of cabinets throughout the 1920s. The priorities of government spending – the relative sizes of the pie going to national educational institutions, to roads, to harbors and railroads – and its volume became the subject of vigorous debate in the Diet, and the grist for successive election campaigns.

Despite the success of the two parties in pushing through an interpretation of the "indivisible bond between emperor and people" rationalizing parliamentary government, harsh critics of democracy on both right and left gained traction as the Meiji consensus broke down. On the right circles promoting various brands of nationalistic militarism typically advocating the untrammeled power of the emperor became increasingly vocal. Extremist, ultra-nationalist, societies proliferated. Some of these – the Black Ocean Society originating in the early 1880s with former samurai; the Rōninkai, representing samurai who banded together under the rubric of coming from fiefs that had been disbanded – had initiated their activities during the early Meiji period. Throughout the 1920s, both the ranks of the ultra-nationalists in terms of members and the number of ultra-nationalist secret societies swelled reaching a crescendo in the early 1930s when hundreds of new groups emerged. The right-wing revolutionary fanatic and author Kita Ikki joined Okawa Shumei in founding the Society for the Preservation of the National Essence in 1921, publishing a book entitled *An Outline Plan for the Reconstruction of Japan* that advocated a thoroughgoing revision of the social fabric so that Japan could become the leader of a general revolution throughout Asia. Under his plan major industries would be nationalized, the fortunes of the wealthy confiscated and private landholdings above a certain cutoff level would be seized and redistributed. He argued that a military *coup d'état* was the proper vehicle for ushering in the new order.

Supporting the notion that the emperor should make foreign policy decisions in consultation with those individuals he personally decided to listen to (as opposed to those individuals who held powerful positions in the dominant party or parties in the Diet), often contemptuous of other Asian cultures, organizations like the Society for Life in the East, the League of East Asia, and the League for Development of the Orient carried out nefarious activities on occasion, gathering intelligence for the army and navy, operating in secret on the fringes of the official military. As disputes over the rectitude of treaties negotiated by the party cabinets and signed by the emperor caused both officers in both the army and navy to form opposing factions (pro-treaty and anti-treaty), links between right-wing societies and factions within the military strengthened, the views and doctrines of the societies and the military factions sometimes becoming virtually overlapping, even identical.

On the left, inroads made by Marxist scholars in universities spread cynicism about parliamentary democracy among students many of whom went on to careers in the national bureaucracy. Arguing that the two major parties were tools of the *zaibatsu*, the monopoly capitalists, Marxists expressed contempt for party cabinets, arguing that they were corrupt, that they carried on intrigues working hand in glove with the old *genrō* factions, that their policies were heavily influenced by the organizations bankrolling their political campaigns. While the left was as cynical about parliamentary democracy as the right, right and left were divided in their views on the emperor (many of the left were opposed to the religious aura claimed by the emperor), in their enthusiasm over the growth of the labor movement, and in their views on foreign policy.

Indeed, divisions over foreign policy were crucial in breaking up the Meiji political consensus. They were always in the background. The most important of the foreign policy disputes involved Japan's status in the League of Nations organization that emerged from the Peace of Paris ending World War I, the military expedition to Siberia in the wake of the Communist revolution in Russia, whether to stay on the gold standard or abandon it, and whether Japan should cooperate with or challenge the United States and the United Kingdom. In each case decisions were being made about how to engage foreign powers and the international economic order. Was it better to embrace the collective security doctrine crucial to the League of Nations or continue to play the geopolitical balance of power game? Was it better to continue the military intervention in Russia's civil war between Soviet forces and pro-Tsarist forces originally designed to provide a cover for the retreat of the Czech army fighting its way out of Russia in 1918 by the United States, Britain, France, Canada and Japan after 1920 when the United States decided to call off the intervention? Should Japan remain on the gold standard at the pre-World War I par, effectively making the yen overvalued on international markets? Should Japan cooperate with a United States that was promoting the Open Door doctrine in China and a treaty limiting the sizes of the navies of the United Kingdom, the United States and Japan?

The Washington naval treaty

In the aftermath of World War I, the three great naval powers – the United Kingdom, the United States, and Japan – agreed to meet in Washington to head off a major naval arms race. Negotiations occurred in Washington in 1922.

Lurking in the background of the negotiations were the breakdown of the Anglo-Japanese alliance; the rapid buildup of the American navy; the Japanese navy's policy of maintaining a fleet strength of 70 percent of the American fleet strength and its belief that the United States was its greatest potential enemy in the Pacific; and the perception on the part of some figures in the Japanese navy that military power was increasingly linked to industrial capacity, rendering the thought of protracted war with the United States with its behemoth industrial output pure folly.

After extensive negotiations, the Japanese accepted a compromise that angered many in the navy, ultimately dividing the naval command into two diametrically opposed factions, a pro-Washington treaty and an anti-Washington treaty faction. Total tonnages were set for the naval tonnages of the five powers attending the conference as follows: 525,000 tons each for the United States and the United Kingdom; 315,000 tons for Japan; and 175,000 tons for France and Italy. As can be seen, in agreeing to the treaty, the Imperial Japanese Navy abandoned its demand to possess 70 percent of the American naval tonnage.

In 1930, the parties to the Washington naval treaty met in London, agreeing to modifications in the force levels accorded to the various parties. Under the revised quotas, the Japanese navy was granted parity with the United States in submarines. Hardliners in the navy opposed to ratifying the treaty appealed to the emperor to reject the agreement, but it was forced through a Minseitō dominated Diet headed up by Hamaguchi Osachi, subsequently shot by a right-wing extremist opposed to the treaty.

Adherence to the treaty was becoming an increasingly contentious political issue within Japan.

As preparations for the renegotiating of the treaty were being made throughout the early 1930s, support for continued Japanese participation in the Washington naval treaty system both within and outside the navy continued to wither. The minister in charge of the navy had purged it of the key pro-treaty faction. Beginning in 1931 the Kwangtung army began pursuing an increasingly aggressive military campaign in Manchuria, creating the puppet state of Manchuko in 1933, putting Japan on a potential collision course with the Soviet Union, and also with the United States and the United Kingdom.

When negotiations between the powers signing the revised Washington agreement of 1930 met in London in 1934, the stance of the Japanese delegation was completely shaped by the anti-treaty hardliners. After making demands unacceptable to the American and British delegations, the Japanese delegation withdrew from the negotiations in 1936, and the treaty, set to expire in 1937, became a dead letter. Japan's navy was well on the road to attacking the United States, an act that it took in 1941 when squadrons from its air force, well drilled in dive bomb maneuvers, swarmed down from above on that portion of the Pacific fleet of the United States anchored at Pearl Harbor.

Those on the pro-militarist right were more than willing to take on Russia, especially a Soviet Russia experimenting with implementing central planning under the aegis of communism. Preferring to see a Japan armed to the hilt than one agreeing to limit armaments in the name of cooperation, ultra-nationalist groups distrusted the Washington naval treaty and the idea of beating weapons into ploughshares in the hope of preventing wars through collective League of Nations intervention aimed at stopping the aggressive moves of particular national regimes. By contrast, the Marxist left saw great hope and potential in the Soviet experiments with central planning, the collective ownership of the means of production, the crushing of "bourgeois democracy".

Operating in an environment of domestic political fragmentation intensified by deep seated differences over foreign policy, the party governments of the 1920s struggled with revamping and revitalizing the nation's infrastructure, responding to the demands placed on it by the massive industrial expansion of the World War boom. Surging demand for engineers and graduates of industrial vocational schools equipped to manufacture and repair electrical machinery was an issue that cried out for new policy making. Shoring up a fragmented banking sector that aggressively financed startup companies during the World War I boom, many proving to be unprofitable once imports from Europe and America were resumed, and managing trade distorted by an overvalued official exchange rate called for financial reform. Promoting rapid development of roads, sewers, and transport systems in the burgeoning metropolises of the Tōkaidō industrial belt posed challenges especially at the municipal level. Meeting these demands for infrastructure renewal and reform required resources, resources that might otherwise go to the military, resources that might otherwise be ploughed into building up the colonies. Mitigating demand on governmental resources was the fact that the government increasingly decided to operate in a facilitating/coordinating role, bringing the private sector in as a coequal contributor on many of the freshly conceived projects being undertaken. The utility of a strategy that first saw the light of day in the 1880s was now being pressed upon more than ever, becoming integral to economic policy making, during the troubled and divisive 1920s.

Reform of the educational system

First some general considerations concerning the demand for education: the demand for schooling is shaped by the average level of household income per capita (the capacity to pay), the length of life expectancy (the longer the payoff period to investments in education in children and young adults, the more attractive to making the investment), the fewer children a couple has the greater the willingness of the couple to expend resources on each child, and the composition of employment opportunities. In the aftermath of the World War I boom the composition of the labor market – especially for males – shifted sharply away from agriculture towards infrastructure and manufacturing, especially heavy manufacturing. This raised the expected payoff to investing in training that could be readily applied in the burgeoning new fields of electricity, machinery manufacturing, and shipbuilding. Rising income per capita – according to Table A.1 rising at a rate of 3.95% between 1911 and 1915 and 2.87% between 1916 and 1920 – put more resources into the hands of parents, increasing their capacity to support their children for longer periods of schooling. From Table A.2 it is apparent that death rates began to decline during the 1920s, and from Table 9.2 (in Chapter 9) it is apparent that birth rates had reached relatively low levels in regions of the country by 1930. This is a proposition to be taken up in more detail at the end of this chapter. The point is that there was a sharp expansion in the demand for schooling due to economic and demographic changes. To this list of factors we can add two others: demand for schooling as a consumption, status-enhancing, good; demand for schooling because it increases the probability of securing employment in a prestigious *zaibatsu* affiliated company.

In theories that emphasize the impact of Confucian culture on Japan, Confucian priority on academic achievement is deemed crucial to the diffusion of credentialism, according to which excellent performance in examinations contributes to the social status enjoyed by an individual. In a theory like that espoused by Nakane that stresses the overriding importance of frame – for instance securing employment in a Mitsui or Mitsubishi affiliated company trumps entering a prestigious occupation – the fact that the *zaibatsu* were becoming increasingly active in the labor market increases the demand for securing a credential from an institution of higher learning, simply to signal to putative employers the diligence and intelligence of the graduate.

For an increase in the demand for education to translate into an expansion in education achieved the supply of slots provided by the educational system must grow. This requires buildings, classrooms and teachers. For this to happen the authorities regulating the educational system – the Ministry of Education – must make decisions accrediting new institutions or increasing the number of slots allocated to existing institutions. As we can see from Table 5.1 the growth in the supply of teachers very closely mimics the growth in the demand for teachers. Resources were being pulled into the sector through a process involving new public and private funding for school facilities and employment of teachers under the guidance of the Ministry of Education in Tokyo.

One of the interesting features of the data reported in Table 5.1 is that the growth rates tend to decline over time for elementary, middle and vocational school but not for higher (non-vocational) education. This makes sense. Graduates from the elementary school either leave the educational system entering the labor market or continue in the school system; graduates from the secondary level have a similar choice to make. An expansion at the lower levels usually yields an expansion at the upper levels. The demand for tertiary schooling can only expand in step with the number of graduates from prior increases in the supply of secondary schooling graduates and so forth. With this in mind convince yourself from a perusal of Table 5.1 that the subsectors of the educational system expanding the most vigorously during the 1920s were higher schools for females, vocational schools, *senmongakkō* (technologically oriented schools accommodating students who could not or did not want to gain entrance to a university) and universities. During the 1920s demand pressure was being felt at the apex of the educational system, and at the middle level component most directly connected to industrial needs, the vocational school component. How did the Ministry of Education interact with the private and public sectors in meeting this pressure?

To appreciate the nature of the strategy the Ministry developed to meet this challenge it is useful to contrast its strategy regarding higher education and vocational schooling with the one it developed to meet the demand for primary schooling during the period 1872–1900. The Fundamental Code of Education of 1872, subsequently modified and developed into the Imperial Rescript on Education of 1890, required that local areas fund a program whose main features – hour by hour – were dictated by bureaucrats in Tokyo, bureaucrats committed to insuring that every child became literate and numerate at a basic level, receiving a strong dose of indoctrination in the virtues of the emperor system, embracing nationalism through dedication to the cult of the emperor. By estimating the number of school age children expected to enter primary schooling each year, the Ministry calculated the number of additional teachers needed to meet demand (taking into account expected retirement of teachers), creating and staffing normal schools in accordance with these estimates. Indeed during the period 1873–85 the number of teachers actually increased faster than the number of students at the primary school level.

Table 5.1 Expansion of the educational system, 1873–1940[a]

Panel A *Average annual growth rate in number of students (%)*

Period	Elementary School	Middle level: non-vocational		Higher education: non-vocational				Vocational	
		Middle school (males)	Higher school (females)	High school (males)	senmongakkō	University	Normal school	Regular	Continuation
1873–1885	7.1	50.7	n.e.	n.e.	2.5	n.e.	6.2	597.0	n.e.
1886–1900	2.4	17.5	40.7	18.1	4.1	6.9	6.0	31.0	n.e.
1901–1920	3.6	5.8	21.1	2.2	8.5	9.0	5.4	15.0	59.9
1921–1940	2.0	5.3	8.9	6.2	4.9	15.0	2.2	9.2	6.3

Panel B *Average annual growth rate in number of teachers (%)*

Period	Elementary School	Middle level: non-vocational		Higher education: non-vocational				Vocational	
		Middle school (males)	Higher school (females)	High school (males)	senmongakkō	University	Normal school	Regular	Continuation
1873–1885	11.8	45.8	n.e.	n.e.	3.4	n.e.	13.9	584.1	n.e.
1886–1900	0.1	12.7	19.4	28.7	5.4	2.9	2.2	23.3	n.e.
1901–1920	4.0	6.0	20.2	1.3	8.1	9.9	4.4	13.4	24.5
1921–1940	2.4	4.3	7.3	8.7	5.7	13.5	2.2	8.0	24.5

Sources: Mosk (1995) Table 2.2, pp. 46–7.

Note
a n.e.= not estimated

The strategy developed around expanding the elementary school system involved central control of the curriculum, each child expected to study from a textbook identical to that used by every other child throughout the land, and it involved funding the system by local tax sources. The idea was to make the compulsory component of the educational system completely standardized and publicly funded, to exercise complete control over the number of student slots allocated to each school in terms of the number of teachers and the facilities commanded by the school. Using demographic projections of the number of children in the age groups six to twelve gave the Ministry of Education the information it needed to allocate slots in future years, increasing the number of teachers and resources required of particular schools in accordance with these projections. At higher levels of the system the Ministry also retained control over the number of slots allocated to each school, at least in principle. Its mandate was to collect information on the number of teachers, classrooms and library books possessed by a school, allocating its students slots in accordance with these numbers. In theory it aimed at keeping a steady balance between demand and supply for slots throughout the system. This is known as the bureaucratic supply of slots. However above the primary school level, schooling was not compulsory. Thus adjusting the number of slots to be allocated was not straightforward. Moreover, above the primary level education was highly specialized and differentiated and the private sector played a major role in meeting demand. This complicated the task of the Ministry of Education in carrying out its mandate to regulate and direct the system.

For women from "better" families with funds to expend on a daughter's schooling, there were normal schools to attend. Graduates of these schools formed the backbone of the elementary school teaching labor force. An increase in the capacity to pay for the schooling of female normal school graduates, driven by the rise in per capita income, accounts for much of the increase in the supply of elementary school teachers.

For men, the situation was more complicated. Private companies established vocational schools to train workers, securing accreditation from the Ministry for institutions they funded, sending workers to these schools at company expense. Prefectures and local governments also established vocational schools, subsidizing them at least partially. Military schools received special governmental subsidies. Household income was certainly an important factor, but opportunities in the labor market were more important in shaping the demand for schooling for males than for females.

What about the demand and supply of slots in the highest echelon of the system (open to males only for a long time): universities and technical colleges (*senmongakkō*)? During the early Meiji period, the government ensured the imperial university would be at the peak of the educational pyramid, focusing on funding science and engineering and on training future bureaucrats in law faculties that melded social science with legal studies. The University of Tokyo was designated as the first imperial university in 1886. By 1906 there were two imperial universities and by 1916 four. Growth in the imperial university system was slow since only graduates from the most prestigious high schools could apply for admission.

At first most of the graduates went into national ministries. But as demand for technically trained personnel in heavy industries boomed, more and more staked out careers in the industrial sector, especially in *zaibatsu* controlled enterprises. However, as important as the imperial university system was as growth in the demand for higher education graduates picked up, the bulk of the graduates came out of the lower prestige *senmongakkō*. In 1915 there were 29 imperial *senmongakkō*, 7 additional public – but not imperial – *senmongakkō*, and 56 private *senmongakkō*. The private sector was playing a pivotal role in supplying higher education graduates to companies in the infrastructure and manufacturing fields. To regulate the higher educational system more systematically, and to oversee its expansion in response to the surge in demand coming from the industrial sector in the wake of the World War I boom, the government sponsored an extraordinary conference on education whose recommendations became the basis for the University Ordinance of 1918. In order to increase the number of public and private single and multiple-faculty universities to supplement the imperial university system, the government upgraded a number of the *senmongakkō*, according them university (*daigaku*) status.

It is important to appreciate the hierarchical nature of the system above the compulsory school level. Entrance examinations at each level of the system above primary school produced a ranking system that was extremely hierarchical. To gain admission to a prestigious university – an imperial university, especially the University of Tokyo, or Keio or Waseda in the private sector – one had to pass highly competitive entrance examinations. To successfully navigate through this battery of tests, gaining admission to a prestigious high school where students were drilled in mastering the material asked on the prestigious university tests was essential. Gaining admission to a highly ranked high school required passing a rigorous test for entry. And so forth down to the middle school level. The rank of a school ultimately became identical to the rate at which it rejected applicants to its faculties, a high rejection rate translating into great prestige earned within the pecking order for schools at each level of the system.

The status of a company was directly linked to the status of the educational institutions from which it recruited its new entry-level employees. *Zaibatsu*-affiliated firms could pick from the cream of the crop, preferring students who graduated from the imperial universities or the most highly ranked private universities. By hiring someone who managed to pass the entrance tests for a prestigious school, the employer was fairly sure of taking on a worker who was dedicated, willing to work long hours (after all he had crammed immense amounts of information into his brain in order to pass the entry tests), and/or highly intelligent, hence able to master new material quickly. Rather than devoting considerable resources to investigating the putative ability of a potential new hire, how much easier – and cheaper – to rely on the "signal" sent forth from his or her achievement in the school system. In this interpretation the most important contribution of education, at least higher education, is providing signals about ability to prospective employers. An alternative interpretation invokes human capital as embodied in individual students. On average a student reaching the highest echelons of the school system embodies more human capital, has received more training at every stage moving up the educational ladder, than a student who performs less well. Perhaps a little bit of both is involved: a typical student masters skills, including the skill of efficiently learning more information and comprehending freshly developed theories.

A good indicator of the hierarchical nature of the system as it evolved between World War I and World War II is the number of *rōnin* students, those enrolled in cram schools waiting to once again take the entrance tests for the school they ardently wished to enter (the term "*rōnin*" literally indicates a "masterless samurai", jokingly referring to the fact that the student has not yet gained admission to the school to which he or she aspires, having already failed on the entrance test at least once, perhaps twice). Using information on the number of *rōnin* in the system, the Ministry of Education was able to gauge the degree of excess demand for particular schools in the system. Using the *rōnin* figures, it allocated additional slots. Schools for which the number of *rōnin* were unusually large typically received permission to increase the number of slots on condition that they increased the size of their teaching staffs and made sure they had sufficient classroom space and books in their library to meet the anticipated demand for their services.

Above the level of primary schooling, the demand for education pulled by the labor market was crucial in shaping the nature of Ministry of Education regulatory policy. While the Ministry of Education exercised nominal control over the system, allocating slots on the basis of standards it set for each school throughout the land, in practice it responded to market forces by relieving pressure on the system as evidenced by the existence of *rōnin* and changes in the acceptance rates of each school. The market and policy makers interacted. The Ministry of Education actively engaged in coordinating and facilitating activity, regulating and at the same time cajoling private and public schools to expand or contract their facilities and their teaching staffs. Policy was market conforming in the sense that it was designed to meet the needs of employers whose demand for workers was an ever present consideration in the minds of students trying to advance successfully in the school system and the needs of households whose willingness to pay and whose income levels constrained the ability of students to move up through the stages of the system.

In marked contrast to the early Meiji period when the chief concern of the Ministry of Education was setting up a standardized system, virtually operating in a command and control mode – mandating local districts to adjust their schools to the demographically projected demand for slots and to adopt textbooks stipulated by the Ministry – the Ministry of the 1920s was operating in a coordinating/facilitating mode, relying heavily upon market oriented private educational institutions to realize its goals.

Reform of banking and finance

After World War I Japan's political leadership faced two major challenges in the financial field. One was international, managing the exchange rate between the yen and the currencies of foreign nations as the gold standard disintegrated. The other was primarily domestic. The policy challenge was how to keep a domestic banking sector from collapsing as the threat of widespread bankruptcy loomed. This sector was destabilized by the fact that a myriad of small banks had advanced funds to shaky firms, companies flourishing in the hothouse conditions of World War I when foreign competition was virtually completely cut off, only to see orders for their products vanish when cheaper and higher-quality imports from Europe and North America reappeared in the market. The fear was that public panic set off by the failure of a few banks could lead to massive withdrawing of deposits from the remaining banks, general financial collapse resulting.

While one problem was primarily domestic and the other mainly international, the two policy problems were intertwined in the sense that they both involved trade and the credibility of the yen both on domestic and international markets. Indeed under the logic of the gold standard, there was a direct linkage between the trade balance and the domestic money supply. The collapse of the gold standard was part and parcel of the general collapse of the international economic order. During the period 1870–1914 international trade flourished under British leadership. The Bank of England managed the British pound to meet both international and domestic needs. It fixed the value of the pound in terms of gold only (and not in terms of other precious metals like silver), accommodating the desire of many of its trade partners to follow its leadership by fixing their currencies relative to gold by letting the pound serve as the international clearing currency. Under this system countries settled their trade balances through banks based in London, operating either with gold bullion or with pound notes (primarily with gold bullion). Crucial to the British pound based gold standard was the fact that Great Britain practiced free trade, eschewing tariffs on imports. Equally important was the fact that Great Britain's trade volumes were dominant in international markets, stimulating a strong demand in countries far and wide for the pound, willingness to operate in pounds being widespread among commercial circles in the Americas, Europe and Asia.

How does the trade balance influence the domestic money supply?

The extent to which exports exceed or fall short of imports – the trade balance – impacts the domestic money supply of a country, the reserves of foreign currencies and gold being depleted when the trade balance is negative, being bolstered when the trade balance is positive.

Under the classical gold standard system of the late nineteenth century the relationship between trade and money supply was sharp. Assume that the gold standard applies in both domestic and international affairs. The central bank or the finance ministry maintains a fixed ratio between the gold it holds in government reserves and the domestic money supply, only expanding the currency it issues when its gold holdings grow. The same fixed ratio of gold to currency determines its exchange rate with respect to other national currencies. Under this assumption suppose that the gold standard exchange rate overvalues the currency of the country on international markets, the country's exports being too expensive to be competitive abroad, its import prices low, thereby cutting into the sales of domestic competitors. A negative trade balance results. Paying for the excess of imports over exports depletes national gold reserves, as gold or foreign currency inflows are not matched by the outflows used to purchase goods and services abroad. As the metallic base for the money supply is eroded, the central bank must act to cut back on the money supply. In a classical world where wages and prices are totally flexible, the curtailment in the money supply translates into lower prices, deflation.

We can interpret this story in terms of the aggregate demand/aggregate supply model (the IS/LM model with variable prices), the LM curve being vertical, demand for money being solely shaped by the level of transactions in the economy. Suppose the currency is overvalued, leading to a trade deficit, in an economy that is initially at full employment. Money supply shrinks. Output falls, creating unemployment. In the classical world, wages fall so that the labor market clears, dragging down prices because of competition between producers whose unit output costs are plummeting. The economy returns to full employment at lower prices, the lower domestic prices counteracting the overvalued exchange that precipitated the adjustment. The trade balance moves back to equilibrium, imports equaling exports. By the same reasoning, an undervalued exchange rate that produces an export surplus generates an increase in money supply, ultimately inflation, leading the economy back to equilibrium in its balance of payments.

This was the theory behind the classical gold standard: a country's trade would tend to equilibrium, its domestic prices adjusting whenever its fixed exchange rate to gold was either too high or too low to keep imports in balance with exports.

In practice, the classical gold standard did not operate in such a simple manner. Central banks intervened to a greater or lesser extent to "sterilize" or counteract upward surges in unemployment when their currency was overvalued, conducting open market operations involving the purchase of bonds in an attempt to stave off the contraction in money stock due to outflow of precious metal. Still, under the classical gold standard system central banks did try to coordinate their interventions with one another aiming to avoid destabilizing the fixed exchange rate regime through rash unilateral interventions, and they did try to encourage return to full employment and a zero trade balance through domestic inflation or deflation.

In a Keynesian world in which the demand for money depends both on the volume of transactions (the key assumption of the classical, vertical LM curve), real national income or output, and on the demand for liquid assets that compete with stocks and bonds, the story of how countries adjust to overvalued or undervalued exchange rates is more complex than in a pure classical world with flexible wages and prices. For instance in the most perverse case – a liquidity trap (a horizontal LM curve) – outflows or inflows of gold and the associated fluctuation in money supply has no impact on domestic output or the domestic price level.

Suffice it to say that if the LM curve is neither vertical nor horizontal, trade imbalances that impinge upon the domestic money supply can generate unemployment that is sustained, intractable in the short run and politically worrisome to a government. In this kind of world, countries are far less willing to sit on the sidelines while the ranks of the unemployed soar and domestic peace and tranquility is undermined, waiting for domestic price movements to bail them out from the unemployment that adherence to the fixed exchange rate regime spawned.

Between 1870 and 1920 the conditions on which this system was erected changed dramatically. Two new industrial giants emerged challenging British leadership, Germany and the United States. American growth was particularly dramatic: in 1850 the ratio of American gross domestic product to British was 70.2 (setting the British base at 100). By 1913 the ratio was 241.5, the national income of the United States more than double the size of the British. As the German and American economies surged, their share of international trade advanced inexorably. England's share of international export trade dropped from 22 percent in 1870 to 17 percent in 1913; between the same two dates Germany's share increased from 12 percent to approximately 17 percent. The United States, more isolated and more capable of operating in autarky conditions (the American economy built upon tremendous regional diversity in its domestic sector, internal trade between its various regions equaling that of trade between most of the independent nation-states within Europe) also saw its share of international trade increase, from around 4 percent in 1870 to around 8 percent in 1913. This trend threatened the ability of Great Britain to manage the gold standard system.

World War I further complicated the viability of an international economic order dependent on the British pound as international reserve currency and British commitment to free trade. The British economy suffered as the war sapped its labor force, and disrupted its ability to trade abroad. Moreover most of the major belligerents during the conflict had drawn upon American financial circles in financing their war related expenditures. How were they to pay off their war debt? Was it not tempting to let their currencies depreciate relative to gold, thereby reducing the value in gold of their international obligations?

Another reality emerging out of the Paris Peace Conference, the Treaty of Versailles, and associated treaties posing an ominous threat to the viability of the international trade regime was the breakup of old empires, the Austro-Hungarian, Russian and Ottoman. As nation-states proliferated, so did national boundaries. As old and new nations erected tariffs to protect their domestic employment in the aftermath of the conflict, international commitment to an open trade dissipated. Protectionism spread, even the English growing restive with free trade, considering adopting an imperial preference policy with lower tariffs imposed on goods imported from the empire, higher tariffs imposed on countries outside the empire, a policy it eventually adopted in concert with its empire at the Ottawa Conference of 1932.

Had the United States agreed, or at least attempted, to assume leadership of the international economic order, it might have been possible to work out a political solution to the interlocking problems of shoring up the gold standard and staving off a drift towards "beggar-thy-neighbor" trade wars. But this was not to be. After the Paris Peace Conference the United States began to veer towards isolation and autarky. The United States Senate, concerned about the legitimacy of the Monroe Doctrine under the terms of the League of Nations charter, angered by the accommodating attitude of many of the European powers toward Japan's aggressive policy towards China, and moving toward adopting an immigration law that would sharply limit immigration from most countries outside the British isles and Germany, refused to ratify American entry into the League. Traditionally a high tariff country, the demand for restrictions on imports being driven in part by political pressure from the labor movement, the United States was also reluctant to lead a campaign for dismantling tariffs. True, as its share of world trade increased, the American government's interest in negotiating lower tariffs on a bilateral reciprocating basis so that American exporters faced lower barriers to their products abroad loomed larger and larger. Still, in the late 1920s, the Congress of the United States held hearings that would eventually serve as the basis for the most protectionist tariff schedule it had ever had, the Smoot-Hawley tariff.

In the unstable international economic environment of the 1920s, the party cabinets negotiating agreements and making policy on behalf of the nation had to make difficult choices about their commitment to internationalism, to the gold standard and to the League of Nations. In the new League of Nations Japan secured a permanent seat on the council and membership of many of the organs of the League. That said, Japan was rebuffed on the racial equality clause. Moreover the delegation for the United States made it clear to Japan that it opposed Japan's China policy, working to stymie it at the Washington Conference of 1921–22 that negotiated the naval treaty. Still from the point of view of the main political parties Japan had much to lose by rejecting the gold standard system on the grounds that if it returned to the gold standard at the prewar exchange rate, the yen would be overvalued on international markets. During World War I, Japan's domestic inflation rate had been substantial, a fact that the reader should check by examining Table A.4 in the Appendix. To return to the gold standard at the prewar par with an inflated price level would force the monetary authorities to deflate the price level, thereby moving the real exchange rate back towards its pre-World War I level.

Under pressure from their *zaibatsu* benefactors who favored internationalism and a relatively open international trade regime in order to stave off barriers to their exports – and believing that internationalism would be the best check to wholesale militarism – the party cabinets decided to accept the harsh medicine of deflation. They committed Japan to keep the yen/ United States dollar exchange rate relatively constant – around two yen to a dollar – motivated by a standing commitment to return to the gold standard. Japan eventually did accomplish this, returning to the gold standard in January 1930. As can be seen from Table A.4, prices fell throughout the 1920s. Internal price adjustments were used to correct the fact that a yen pegged at its pre-1914 par meant the real Japanese export prices were too high, real import prices too low. Reflecting this, Japan's net export position worsened especially during the early 1920s before deflation had helped correct the situation (see Table A.6 in the Appendix). The party cabinets worked hard to keep Japan in the camp of those countries striving to keep the international economic order afloat.

Deflation hurts debtors more than creditors. This is true since loans negotiated in nominal terms (repayable in so many yen) have to be extinguished in terms of the number of yen stipulated in the loan contract regardless of what happens to the debtor's nominal income. Poorer farmers – tenants and small landowners without much land that they could sell off so that they might pay off their debts – suffered under these circumstances just as they did during the Matsukata Deflation of the early 1880s. Not surprisingly, the deflation of the 1920s exacerbated tensions between landlords and tenants that broke out in the aftermath of the 1918 Rice Riots and the stepping up in imports from the colonies of the empire. Exporters also suffered under the commitment on the part of the cabinet to stay with the gold standard.

The pressures felt by poorer farmers, exporters and companies who had taken advantage of the World War I embargo on imports to start new ventures whose viability became tenuous in the 1920s, were transmitted to banks that extended loans to farmers and exporters during the previous decade especially during the World War I boom. During 1920 and 1922 banking crises broke out, followed by a 1923 crisis triggered by the Kantō earthquake. In 1927 when the Bank of Taiwan collapsed, the government decided that enough was enough. Realizing that the fragmented character of the financial infrastructure, the existence of a myriad of tiny financial institutions, was no longer able to handle the demands of a rapidly growing heavy industrial sector requiring massive inputs of capital for major investment projects, realizing that the bank runs of the early 1920s spelled trouble for the credibility of the entire system, the Diet abolished the old Banking Law, bringing in a new law effective in January 1928. Under the terms of the new legislation, a bank had to have a minimum amount of capital to remain in business. As a result of the law about 1,400 banks were disqualified, ultimately being absorbed by larger financial institutions or amalgamating so that they met the requirement. Concentration – ongoing during the 1910s as the *zaibatsu* affiliated banks grew vigorously – accelerated. By 1931 there were less than 700 banks; by 1936 only slightly more than 400 had their doors open for business.

One of the byproducts of the 1928 reorganization of the banking system was elaboration of the convoy system. Under a pure convoy system approach the lender of last resort – the Bank of Japan – is not called upon to bail out banks that are in trouble. Rather banks are placed into groups, the larger banks becoming the centerpiece of a convoy group. In the event that a member of the group finds itself in distress, it is supposed to call upon the better off members of the convoy to bail it out. Under the convoy system the banking system is expected to insure itself, the convoy acting under the administrative guidance of the Ministry of Finance and the Bank of Japan. This is another example of government acting as facilitating/coordinating agent, its financial arm acting in concert with the private sector that it regulates. The relevant ministry works under the assumption that private enterprises can muddle through, managing many of their own problems, provided they operate under the ministry's guidance, acting with the knowledge and approval of the bureaucracy that theoretically enjoys a general vantage over the actions of all actors in the system.

City planning and physical infrastructure expansion

An example involving local government can help us nail down the point concerning government interaction with the private sector. Consider municipal activity. One of the most striking aspects of Japanese municipal activity is its focus on infrastructure construction and its reliance on coordination as opposed to regulation.

At the outset it must be acknowledged that part of the reason for the focus on infrastructure lies in fiscal constraints. Under the system created in early Meiji, fiscal power, the purse strings, were heavily concentrated in the hands of the powerful ministries located in Tokyo. Vesting most tax collection in the hand of the national government meant that prefecture and city governments had to rely either on special surtaxes, bond issues for which they were obligated to pay interest, user fees or upon subsidies underwritten by the national government in generating revenue. Because infrastructure buildup was a priority for the national government, it is not surprising that most of the subsidies accruing to local governments were for infrastructure improvement and enhancement projects and that these projects became the hallmark of city planning in Japan.

Beginning with the passage of the Tokyo Municipal Ordinance in 1889 that placed planning for the national capital under its aegis, the Ministry of Home Affairs began to study Western developments in city planning, absorbing plans for New Towns and Garden Cities in England, and the planning done under the direction of Baron Haussmann for Paris that resulted in demolishing many of the tiny alleyways and winding narrow streets, replacing them with bold wide boulevards radiating out from central hubs in a star pattern. Influenced particularly by the Haussmann scheme that imparted a sense of imperial grandeur to Paris, they used many of his ideas in modifying the streets in Tokyo, creating grand boulevards out of the wide streets that had crisscrossed Edo even during the Tokugawa period.

In the same year that the national government decided to revamp the educational infrastructure – 1918 – it decided to extend city planning to the six big cities in the Tōkaidō. In doing so they were acknowledging the pressure on the transportation infrastructure of big metropolitan centers of the industrial belt from the growing use of trucks, buses and cars. The World War I boom had stretched to the limit the capacity of cities to supply relatively wide paved roads to the rapidly growing phalanx of transport vehicles. The Ministry of Home Affairs retained its advisory control over the activities undertaken by the big city cities, adding an additional twenty-five cities in 1923 under its umbrella. Pushing its agenda of building the road networks in the industrial belt in order to reduce transport costs, the prefecture governments that contained within their boundaries the six big cities – Tokyo prefecture in the case of Tokyo, Osaka prefecture in the case of Osaka – were encouraged to reorganize their sub-districts, incorporating the counties known as *gun* on the outskirts of the big six cities into the cities, turning them into new wards (in Japanese called *ku*) of the big six cities. Following this logic, the larger cities in Japan took on more and more responsibility for managing the infrastructure, particularly the road networks, of the prefectures in which they were located. After World War II, this process accelerated, city boundaries expanding throughout the country.

We can see evidence for this process of incorporation for Osaka and for Tokyo prior to 1938 in Table 5.2. Note the massive increase in Osaka due to its gobbling up hinterland in 1925 (while the table does not give land area estimates for officially defined Tokyo in 1932, the figures in Panel C indicate that a dramatic increase in the road network took place within legally constituted Tokyo between the period 1925–31 and 1932–38, testifying to the expansion in the city's boundaries). Note also the buildup in cars, trucks and buses registered in the two cities, a buildup that was foremost in the minds of the ministry officials when they began working with city officials on strategies for planning. Apparent from the figures is the fact that former rural roads threading their way through farm fields and villages now incorporated in the great metropolises were narrow. Incorporating hinterland put considerable pressure on city governments to come up with solutions to the problem of how to secure land from farmers so that they could improve – pave and widen – the roads that they were now inheriting.

Given its interest in emulating European innovations in city planning we might expect that Garden City beautification projects might have been high on the agenda of the Ministry of Home Affairs. In fact this was definitely not the case. The main thrust was not on building grand parks and playgrounds. Rather it was on widening, lengthening and paving roads. Employing a law originally devised for improving agricultural productivity by encouraging the consolidation of small farming plots into large plots, the Ministry of Home Affairs hit upon a policy – known as land reorganization (*kukaku seiri*) – to smoothen the process by which

Table 5.2 Roads in Osaka and Tokyo, 1900–1938[a]

Panel A *Population and roads in the cities of Osaka and Tokyo, 1900–1938*

City/date	Population (1,000's)	Roads		
		Area (1,000 sq. meters)	Length (1,000 (meters)	Average width (meters)
Osaka, *c.* 1900	695.3	2,220.4	406.0	5.5
Osaka, 1930	2,453.6	10,496.5	2,533.9	4.1
Tokyo, *c.* 1900	1,339.7	6,515.0	894.0	7.3
Tokyo, 1930	2,070.9	14,598.0	1,362.8	10.7

Panel B *Demand for, and supply of, roads in city of Osaka, 1910–1937*

Period	Average growth rate of buses, trucks and cars combined (%)	Roads			
		Index of area (1920-1921 = 100)	Percentage in city-managed roads	Percentage in narrow roads	Percentage paved
Pre-1925					
1910–1914	79.9	60.9	87.7	4.3	n.e.
1915–1919	52.9	76.8	87.7	9.0	n.e.
1920–1924	27.8	106.1	81.9	6.5	n.e.
Post-1925					
1925–1929	20.7	182.1	82.4	57.2	5.1
1930–1934	n.e.	205.2	81.7	56.3	8.7
1935–1939	n.e.	246.6	85.3	n.e.	13.9

Panel C *Demand for, and supply of, roads in city of Tokyo, 1910–1938*

Period	Average growth rate of buses, trucks and cars combined[b] %	Roads		
		Index of area (1920–1921 = 100)	Average width (meters)	Percentage of city roads that are wide
Pre-1932				
1910–1914	45.5	92.8	8.6	95.5
1915–1919	38.5	94.1	8.7	95.6
1920–1924	20.6	101.2	9.1	91.2
1925–1931	17.8	128.4	9.8	n.e.
Post-1932				
1932–1938	n.e.	500.4	5.7	n.e.

Source: Mosk (2001) Table 5.5, pp. 170–2.

Notes
a n.e. = not estimated.
b Growth rate for 1925–1931 is actually for 1925–1929.

cities under their guidance could secure the land required for the improving and extending the road infrastructure. Under *kukaku seiri*, local Land Reorganization Associations form within neighborhoods communities with the blessing and encouragement of municipal authorities. They are encouraged to apply for grants-in-aid from the national government – from the Ministry of Home Affairs during the period of interest to us here – coming up with their own plan for how to improve the streets, create pocket parks, and obtain proper sewer lines and clean water delivery.

The incentives for the household within an association are obvious. Improve the infrastructure by giving up a little bit of property to a project expecting to see the value of the property left to you, the portion not surrendered to the project, escalate in value. In effect the local community holds the city planners hostage in this approach. They dictate the conditions of infrastructure improvement. Not surprisingly, households driven by a desire to give up as little land as possible, hoping that the value of what remains in their hands will increase in value as much as possible, tend to put a priority on those things most likely to increase the price that they can secure for their land on the market. To build a grand park is not realistic: too much land must be surrendered. What is most likely to pay off is improving roads, sewer systems and potable water delivery so that a buyer can access the transport system at relatively low cost and enjoy minimum health standards.

While this strategy minimized opposition to infrastructure expansion within local neighborhoods, it did put municipal officials in a weak position when they were attempting to work with powerful local *zaibatsu* in developing zones surrounding train stations, department stores and grand hotels. Only one player in a complex game of give and take, planning departments within municipal governments had to use all of their ingenuity to coordinate the potentially conflicting interests of major private market players. This was government operating in the coordinating/facilitating mode in the extreme.

During the 1920s, national ministries and local governments expanded, improved upon and reformed the infrastructure that had been put into place prior to the World War I boom only to be found wanting in the aftermath of the boom. Working within relatively tight fiscal constraints they relied heavily upon the coordinating/facilitating functions of government. As a result government policy making during this period was centered on meeting the needs of the private market, of private companies, of households, especially within the industrial belt. Its main focus was domestic although plans were being laid and put into place for building infrastructure in Korea and Taiwan. Because policy was mainly aimed at reducing transportation energy costs; shoring up banking; and meeting the needs for technically trained labor who were most likely to work in public utilities and heavy manufacturing, it had a strong bias in favor of the business community and of those households living in urban areas. Left out of these priorities to a significant degree was the majority of the population residing in rural villages. What policies could effectively resolve the tension between landlords and tenants that was threatening to rend the social fabric of rural Japan?

Population pressure as the demographic transition begins

During the 1920s expansion of the industrial sector, having pressed up against the limits of the infrastructure that supported its massive explosion during the previous decade, shaken by the ending trade embargoes that spurred on the World War I boom and the overvalued exchange rate for the yen once Japan's commitment to the gold standard was revived, slowed to a crawl. This is reflected in the anemic growth in per capita income recorded for the 1920s evident in Appendix Table A.1. Growth was especially desultory in the light industries like textiles during the latter half of the decade in great metropolises of the industrial belt such as Osaka. In heavy industry recovery seems to have been underway during the second half of the decade. The main successes in the 1920s are in the infrastructure field, in reforming education, in revitalizing banking, in expanding road networks and hydroelectric systems. As we have seen one consequence of the infrastructure buildup in the metropolitan centers was a surge in the prices for land in the hinterland of these centers.

This slowdown in light industrial growth and the expansion of infrastructure during the decade impacted rural Japan. In the vicinity of great metropolitan centers such as Osaka, Kobe and Kyoto in the Kinai zone, owners of farmland were naturally tempted to sell off redundant land to real estate developers. This was especially tempting given the slowdown in agricultural productivity that seemed to spell the end of increases in yield per hectare especially for paddy rice at least in the medium term. The fact the Japanese government was intent on developing rice production in Korea, and sugar and fruit production in Taiwan, added weight to these concerns. The slowdown in textiles production diminished the demand for raw silk thereby putting special pressure on the Chubu district that includes prefectures replete with mountainous silk producing villages like Yamanashi, Gifu and Nagano. Thus it is not surprising that tension between landlords and tenant farmers should have been especially acrimonious during the 1920s in the Chubu and Kinki regions (on the map Chubu is the amalgamation of the Hokuriku, Tōsan and Tōkai districts; the terms Kinai and Kinki are used interchangeably to delineate the same region of Japan). This is apparent in the regional figures on the percentage of landlord/tenant disputes taking place in the regions of Japan presented in Table 5.3.

During the 1930s the industrial sector resumed rapid growth. As a result the number of farm households concentrated in the Kinki district with its great industrial centers in Osaka, Kobe and Kyoto declined sharply. Table 5.3 testifies to this. As a result economically besieged farm households found alternative opportunities, abandoning agriculture altogether as they took up industrial jobs in the industrial zones of the Kinki region. Pressure on the land being relaxed as households abandoned rural villages, the percentage of nationwide landlord/tenant disputes taking place in this region dropped sharply. Unfortunately the industrial resurgence of the 1930s did not help out farm households within the Chubu silk producing district to anything like the same degree. Depending to a significant degree on exporting silk thread to the United States that slipped into a deep depression after the stock market crash of 1929, and lacking a strong industrial base to absorb labor, the number of farm households in the region did not change

Table 5.3 Pressure on arable land and incidence of landlord/tenancy disputes, 1925–1940

Prefecture/ region	Arable land per farm household (hectares)			Percentage change in number of farm households	Percentage of landlord/ tenant disputes in region		
	1925	1940	Percentage change 1925/1940		1917–1931	1932–1941	Change in percentage (absolute)
Japan	1.08	1.09	+1.4	−1.2	100.0	100.0	0
Hokkaido	4.6	5.3	+17.0	+5.8	2.0	5.6	+3.6
Tōhoku					8.0	25.8	+17.8
Aomori	1.5	1.5	−5.0	+16.8			
Iwate	1.4	1.3	−8.4	+12.8			
Miyagi	1.4	1.4	+1.5	+10.3			
Akita	1.5	1.5	−4.4	+9.9			
Yamagata	1.4	1.4	−4.7	+11.8			
Fukushima	1.4	1.4	−2.6	+4.5			
Kantō					10.3	12.8	+2.5
Ibaraki	1.2	1.2	−0.6	+2.2			
Tochigi	1.3	1.3	−2.7	+9.4			
Gumma	1.0	1.0	+2.5	+4.4			
Saitama	1.0	1.0	+3.5	−4.2			
Chiba	1.2	1.2	+1.7	+0.4			
Tokyo	0.9	0.8	−10.3	−10.4			
Kanagawa	0.9	0.9	−4.5	−5.2			
Chubu[a]					23.1	18.2	−4.9
Niigata	1.3	1.2	−5.1	+2.0			
Toyama	1.2	1.2	−1.1	−3.7			
Ishikawa	1.0	0.9	−1.0	−8.6			
Fukui	0.9	0.9	+8.2	−8.2			
Yamanashi	0.7	0.7	−10.3	+2.0			
Nagano	0.8	0.8	−0.5	−0.1			
Gifu	0.8	0.8	−3.6	−3.6			
Shizuoka	0.8	0.8	−0.8	+0.2			
Aichi	0.8	0.9	+9.2	−9.4			
Mie	0.9	0.8	−2.0	+1.0			
Kinki					34.9	13.6	−21.3
Shiga	0.8	0.9	+11.0	−8.1			
Kyoto	0.8	0.8	−0.2	−6.8			
Osaka	0.7	0.7	−3.7	−12.0			
Hyogo	0.7	0.7	+0.02	−6.5			
Nara	0.7	0.7	−1.9	−30.7			
Wakayama	0.6	0.7	+4.5	−2.5			
Chūgoku					8.0	7.5	−0.5
Tottori	0.9	0.9	+4.9	−3.7			
Shimane	0.8	0.8	−1.2	−9.7			
Okayama	0.8	0.8	+5.4	−6.0			
Hiroshima	0.6	0.6	+9.6	−10.7			
Yamaguchi	0.9	0.9	+4.2	−11.2			
Shikoku					5.7	6.8	+1.1
Tokushima	0.7	0.7	−3.0	+1.7			
Kagawa	0.6	0.6	+6.4	−3.6			
Ehime	0.9	0.7	−15.5	−1.1			

(*Table 5.3 continued*)

Table 5.3 Continued

Prefecture/ region	Arable land per farm household (hectares)			Percentage change in number of farm households	Percentage of landlord/ tenant disputes in region		
	1925	1940	Percentage change 1925/1940		1917– 1931	1932– 1941	Change in percentage (absolute)
Kochi	1.5	0.9	−37.2	−10.5			
Kyūshū					8.0	9.7	+1.7
Fukuoka	1.0	1.0	−0.7	−4.5			
Saga	1.1	1.1	+4.3	−5.7			
Nagasaki	0.8	0.8	+1.2	−4.1			
Kumamoto	1.2	1.1	−4.1	−3.0			
Oita	0.8	0.8	−0.3	−5.6			
Miyazaki	1.3	1.1	−13.5	+13.0			
Kagoshima	1.1	0.8	−25.9	+6.1			
Okinawa	0.7	0.7	−8.8	+4.4			

Sources: Japan Statistical Association (1987), *Historical Statistics of Japan. Volume 2*: Tables 4–7, pp. 70–7 and Waswo (1977) pp. 96–7.

Notes
The Chubu region consists of three sub-regions, the Hokuriku, Tōsan and Tōkai regions.

to an appreciable degree. As Table 5.3 demonstrates the district remained mired in conflict between landlords and tenants.

More generally Table 5.3 suggests that the growth in the number of farm households – whether it was negative, positive or approximately zero – was crucial to the perpetuation of landlord/disputes from the 1920s when tenants were pushing for rent reductions to the 1930s when landlords were on a counter-offensive, terminating tenancy relationships, bringing in replacements for the tenants they were determined to remove from their lands. Using this criterion it is apparent that the region with the fastest growth rate for farm households was the Tohoku region in northeastern Honshū. As Table 5.3 shows this is the district with the most substantial positive growth rate for farm households between 1925 and 1940. Why was population pressure being felt with such a vengeance in this region of the country?

The answer lies in the geography of population increase in interwar Japan.

Consider the basic equation of the growth of a population (**gp**) expressed in terms of the crude birth rate (**b**), the crude death rate (**d**) and the rate of net immigration (**nimr**). The variable **b** is calculated by estimating births per 1,000 persons; the variable **d** is calculated by estimating deaths per 1,000 persons; and net immigration is calculated by taking the difference between the flow of immigrants and flow of emigrants, dividing the difference by population, putting the net immigration rate on a per 1,000 person basis. With these definitions we have the basic balance equation:

$$\mathbf{gp = (b - d) + nimr} \tag{5.1}$$

The difference between the crude birth and crude death rate is the rate of natural increase (**nri**). Estimates for the **b**, **d**, **nri** and **gp** appear in Table A.2 in the Appendix.

Although demographers do use the crude rates they realize these can be misleading, mainly because they reflect the age structure of population. A population in which the proportion of females in the main reproductive ages lying between age 15 and age 50 is large tends to have a high crude birth regardless of how many live births a typical female has over her reproductive life span. A population in which the proportion of persons over age 60 is large tends to have a high crude death rate because mortality rates for the elderly tend be substantial, running far above those in the age range between 5 and 59. For instance between the period 1976–80 and 1996–2000 the proportion of the Japanese population in the age range 60 and over grew substantially. For this reason the computed rise in the crude death rate is misleading. Age specific death rates for the Japanese populace continued to fall during this period.

There are two main approaches to handling the problem of age structure distortion: (1) directly standardizing age specific birth and death rates on an arbitrary standard age structure – following a procedure similar to that used to compute real income by adjusting for changes in commodity prices – or indirectly standardizing by indexing the value of births or deaths against a theoretical maximum; and (2) creating age structure independent measures that only reflect the age specific hazards – of giving birth, of dying – to which a specific population is subject. For instance standardizing on a specific unchanging age structure yields a declining, not an increasing, crude death rate for Japan between the mid-1970s and 2000. Specific examples of age- standardized death rates appear in Table 9.2 and are discussed in Chapter 9. In the case of mortality the principal age structure independent rates are those generated through the calculation of life tables. The value of life expectancy at age zero or at age fifty for instance – is an example of an age structure independent measure.

In the case of fertility, indexing – indirectly standardizing – has yielded very useful measures of fertility, the Hutterite indices, discussed in Chapter 9. Age structure independent measures include the gross reproduction rate (a measure approximating the number of female births a woman has over her lifespan ignoring the force of mortality), and the net reproduction rate (a measure adjusting the estimate of the number of female births a woman has over her life span for mortality). Estimates of the age structure independent rates appear in Panel B of Table A.2 in the Appendix to this volume. It should be noted that if the net reproduction rate is below one, as is the case for Japan after 1975, the long-run growth potential of the population, the intrinsic population growth rate, is negative.

Returning to the basic crude rate computation equation 5.1 we can restate the proposition concerning regional population pressure with the assertion that the natural rate of increase was greater in the rural areas of Japan, especially in the extreme northeast of Honshū. Why this was the case lies in the geography of the demographic transition, the fact that fertility tended to fall first in the urban districts of Japan, especially in the industrial belt, despite mortality risks remaining relatively high – though falling off – in intensity within these districts until after World War II.

Demographic transition theory contested?

In the classical theory of demographic transition developed by social scientists such as Frank Notestein during the period between the 1920s and late 1940s, fertility and mortality rates were initially high and approximately equal to one another. A combination of rising income per capita and the diffusion of the germ theory of disease changed this, driving down death rates, enhancing life expectancy and the number of healthy years lived by individuals.

The impact of the improved standard of living on health was not a matter of public policy, the warmer clothing enjoyed during the cold of winter, the enhanced diet of proteins and calories, and housing protecting inhabitants from the fluctuating ravages of the elements working through the expansion in household demand for marketed goods and services occasioned by the rise in household resources. Moreover scientific progress linked to the accumulated knowledge about germs promoted a better understanding of how and why vaccination and treatment with antibiotics like penicillin actually work, giving a strong fillip to research and development in the pharmaceutical industry, ultimately coming up with mass production techniques for the manufacturing the low cost "magic bullets" that have kept many – airborne, food and water borne – infections at bay, preventing sustained bouts of debilitating fever and physical wastage. The market was crucial to rise in life expectancy.

In the public arena understanding how and why micro-organisms impaired healthfulness stimulated governmental public health initiatives such as the chlorination of water; regulation of the sale of meat, fish and poultry, rejecting rancid and putrid foodstuffs, Pasteurization of milk, and the like.

In short, according to Notestein, scientific advance and improvement in living standards working through the market and public policy, but largely operating independently from fundamental changes in norms or values, caused mortality to decline. By contrast, fertility was strongly shaped by norms, by laws, and by religious values. Because mortality was initially high, high fertility norms were essential for social survival. Populations unable to muster the required fertility enhancing norms disappeared, killed off by a mortality far exceeding procreation.

In populations that did survive, the pro-procreation norms being deeply rooted in social behavior, fertility did not initially respond to falling death rates. As a result the natural rate of increase – initially close to zero – climbed, successive generations of family sizes growing. Parents observed that the number of offspring in their households, once held in check by the cruel ravages of infant mortality, was far larger than it had been in their parent's or grandparent's generations.

Ultimately, household competition for economic resources that favored the fortunes of smaller families, urbanization spawning individualism and the growing demand for costly education essential for success in an industrial economy, undercut the old norms and values. Couples became more rational in their decision making, relating ends to means in the most intimate areas, including child bearing and child rearing. Fertility fell, a growing demand for contraceptive technologies reducing the costs of preventing unwanted births. Industrializing and urbanizing societies moved toward the ideal of a perfect contraceptive society, ultimately achieving zero or even negative natural increase.

What is clear from this account is that Japan's long-run trajectories for fertility and mortality do not fit the classical theory of demographic transition. From Chapter 2 we know that fertility was relatively low in most of the villages in Tokugawa Japan, at least in the period 1720–1850. Life expectancy was relatively good in these populations, and infant mortality risks comparatively muted. Moreover, the trends for fertility and mortality rates over the period 1886–1920 documented in Panel A of Table A.2 are upward.

To some extent this apparent rejection of the classical theory of demographic transition is a statistical artifact, created by the registration system. As we argued in Chapter 2, under the Tokugawa system of religious registration of household vital events, some of the births ended in infant demise that occurred prior to the new years date on which the birth would have been registered. Replacing the religious registers with a national system of official household registers – known as "koseki" – in the early Meiji period, government officials attempted to generate a completely accurate account of households and their vital events. Unfortunately compliance with the system was uneven: it is unlikely that births soon turning into infant deaths were completely registered in the 1880s and 1890s. By the early 1920s, perhaps yes, both births and infant deaths were recorded. Some of the rise in recorded fertility and mortality may be attributed to changes in the degree of accuracy of the data.

But not the entirety of the trends: as we know from Chapter 2, villagers in many districts of late Tokugawa Japan seem to have used infanticide and/or the stretching out of intervals between live births to protect the health of the surviving offspring and to shape the sex ratio. Underlying these practices was a lack of household resources, a dearth of opportunities for placing children in sustainable social positions in the village, and concern over maintaining domestic tranquility under a system of single child inheritance that tended to favor the first-born male over other children.

Release of these harsh constraints may have encouraged a rise in fertility. As best practice technique in rice farming diffused throughout rural Japan after the demise of the fief system, incomes of the farming population rose, particularly in northeastern Japan where famine and hardship had been the dismal lot for many peasants. Land, once considered useless for paddy rice cultivation, was converted for use in producing rice, or was harnessed for raising tealeaves, silk cocoons or cotton plants. As land was converted the opportunity to settle non-inheriting sons or daughters on newly created paddy blossomed, as did the demand for child labor services on freshly created fields. To this argument one can add the fact that the opening of the country to international trade in the late nineteenth century created a strong export market for silk, which was produced by family labor especially in the northeast and the Japanese Alps.

Does this mean we have to reject the concept of the demographic transition for Japan? Not necessarily: we need to distinguish between controlling reproduction by selective use of infanticide or by drawing out intervals between life births – three years between births seeming to be an ideal sought after – and stopping behavior. Stopping behavior, sometimes known as parity specific control, refers to a family planning regimen. Once the couple reaches a desired surviving family size, they cease to have additional children. There is precious little evidence of stopping behavior in Japan prior to the 1920s. Thus it is likely that stopping behavior was relatively new to the Japan of the interwar period, and was not a refashioned version of the type of control used to shape family size and outcomes during the late Tokugawa period. Using the idea of stopping behavior we can rephrase the theory of fertility decline during demographic transition as follows: modern fertility decline is characterized by stopping behavior. The diffusion of stopping behavior occurred in Japan only after it had experienced decades of sustained industrialization and urbanization. In this way, we can salvage the idea of demographic transition for Japan.

What is harder to accept for Japan is Notestein's emphasis on individualism. Whether the individualism and individual based rationality believed characteristic of Western societies during the nineteenth century and after was widespread in interwar Japan is questionable. In this sense we can say that Notestein's formulation of demographic transition doctrine is too heavily influenced by the pattern of demographic transition occurring in Western Europe, North America, and Australia. Like many other examples of Western social science, the classical theory of demographic transition is an imperfectly realized bit of induction, rather than a universally valid set of propositions derived from deductive logic.

As can be seen from Table A.2 during the 1920s birth and death rates began to decline. As is shown in Table 9.2 in Chapter 9 this decline was initiated in the economically advanced districts on the country, in the great metropolises of the Tōkaidō, in the hinterland of these metropolises, and even in the smaller cities within the most agricultural prefectures. This was most strikingly evident for the birth rate. For instance in central Honshū – in the Kinai (Kinki) region for instance – both the proportion of females in the reproductive ages married (weighted by potential reproductive capacity) and fertility within marriage had fallen to quite low levels (less than 50 percent of maximum potential) by 1930. By contrast in northeastern Japan – especially in the Tohoku district – female proportions married and the level of reproduction within marriage were considerably higher than they were in central Japan. The number of births per household was far higher in Tohoku than it was in both rural and urban districts of central Japan.

What about mortality levels? Analysis of age standardized death rates shows that age standardized death rates in the most urbanized districts of Japan in 1908 – for instance in the Tōkaidō industrial belt – were higher than age standardized death rates in rural districts. The reason lies in case rates (**cr**) – the number of cases per age standardized population – and death rates per case (**dpc**) – for the major diseases caused by micro-organisms.

Analysis of mortality transitions worldwide suggests that the main reason life expectancies rise from the 1930s to the 1970s lies in decline in the number of deaths per capita due to diseases attributable to micro-organisms. The major food and water borne diseases caused by micro-organisms are cholera, diarrhea, dysentery, non-respiratory tuberculosis, typhoid and typhus; the major airborne diseases caused by micro-organisms are respiratory tuberculosis, bronchitis, pneumonia, influenza, whooping cough, measles, scarlet fever and diphtheria, smallpox, and infections of the ear and larynx. For life expectancy, for the age standardized death rate to reach low levels, the age standardized death rate for every – or at least most – causes attributable to micro-organisms (d_i) must reach low levels. The level d_i depends on the incidence of cases in the population and deaths per case:

$$d_i = (cr_i) * (dpc_i) \tag{5.2}$$

The incidence of new cases of a particular micro-organism caused disease in a population and the number of deaths per case of that disease.

Throughout the world – including Western Europe and North America – prior to the twentieth century there was an urban graveyard effect. Most infectious diseases did not take on an endemic character in remote rural isolates. Epidemics might sweep through small villages, killing the weak and infirm, sparing some who typically gained lifetime immunity from the ravages of the particular micro-organism causing the epidemic by producing antibodies. The micro-organism would disappear. In cities it was different. As new micro-organisms were introduced into large crowded conurbations some would die, some would survive and become immune, but the micro-organism would not necessarily vanish. Case rates tended to be high in cities, in part because epidemic diseases became endemic there, in part because city populations could only be sustained by absorbing in-migrants from outside. As individuals swarmed into cities – many not enjoying that immunity from the diseases that those born and raised in densely inhabited environs possessed – they fell victim to infectious conditions. The result was that urban populations tended to die at higher rates than rural populations.

The typical urban population did have one advantage in combating mortality: income and food consumption. An individual's resistance to an infection – to the debilitating fever that comes when the body is under the siege by a micro-organism – depends on the reserves of energy stored up in the individual's body. The wealthy merchant family living in Osaka was likely to eat better than most farmers. This helped. But it was not likely to tip the balance in favor of the urban area. Many city dwellers were poor, not rich; and exposure to new infections was so much more common in the city that in rural isolates. Before the twentieth century the high case rates in cities rendered them mortality sinkholes, staving off decline through the force of in-migration alone.

After the late nineteenth century the disadvantage of cities began to disappear as case rates were driven down through public health measures – treatment of water, construction of sewers, campaigns to insure that meat and dairy products were free of micro-organisms, vaccination and immunization – and through medical advances that brought down the rates of death per case. While some of the advances in Europe were made by innovators who rejected the germ theory of disease that was gaining force in the scientific community – Florence Nightingale promoted antiseptic practices in hospitals despite clinging to a theory of infection of infection based upon vapors – the painstakingly slow investigation of micro-organism properties did yield results eventually. Vaccination against smallpox was well advanced in Europe and North America by the mid-1800s; the tubercule bacillus was identified in the 1880s; pasteurization of milk reduced the incidence of a number of food borne infections conditions. For this reason applications of the germ theory of disease in the West – mainly in the period after the mid-1800s when postulates for the scientific investigation of effects that specific micro-organisms made on the healthfulness of organisms had been advanced and accepted in the many parts of the scientific community – eventually proved crucial in the reduction of incidence of cases and of deaths per case especially in cities. To be sure intellectual advance was inseparable from industrial developments in Europe and North America. The effective implementation of the germ theory was facilitated by the growth of the precision machinery industry producing low cost microscopes and other laboratory equipment and by the chemical industry that experimented with the consequences of heating liquids (Pasteur was working on fermentation when he made his major breakthroughs that led to the purification of milk). What implications did these advances made in the West have for Japan?

As early as the late Tokugawa period the Japanese elite began absorbing Western medical ideas, at first studying the medical treatises of Dutch scholars. By the mid-1850s, over fifty fiefs had set up schools where Western physiological and medical principles were taught. Though the *bakufu* continued to cling to Chinese medical principles (known as *kanpo*) the battle between the two schools was already underway at the time of the Meiji Restoration. Based upon systematic comparison between the Chinese and Western approaches the Meiji oligarchs and the bureaucracy following their direction, decided to promote Westernization of medicine in Japan, giving preference to Western trained doctors in granting new medical licenses. Eventually a Sanitary Bureau was set up under the aegis of the Ministry of Interior.

In the period prior to the late 1940s public health work to limit exposure dominated the conscious efforts to combat micro-organism induced mortality in Europe, in North America, and in Japan that borrowed heavily from technology from the West in the public health and medical fields. Efforts to improve resistance, lowering the death rate per case, were less effective, hence less utilized. Resistance was improved somewhat through gains in per capita food intake pushing up energy levels for the typical child; inoculation and vaccination campaigns (e.g. for smallpox); by natural evolution in the human population, persons with a pronounced genetic propensity to contract respiratory tuberculosis often dying before they reproduced for instance; and by the use of drugs spun off from experiments in the chemical industry and in dye-making. However effective medical therapy for most micro-organism related conditions was limited prior to the discovery and mass production of antibiotics like penicillin was achieved (not until the 1940s). To reiterate: during the period between the wars the main determinant of risks of death in the different geographical districts of Japan was exposure to micro-organisms, that is the number of cases of micro-organism related illnesses per person.

With this in mind consider the situation in 1908. In the great metropolises of the Tōkaidō municipal authorities were struggling with the implications of huge influxes of in-migrants from rural districts mainly in their hinterlands. There was tremendous pressure on infrastructure, slum housing being thrown up on the edges of many cities, water for cooking and cleaning being drawn from nearby rivers through ditches made fetid with industrial waste. Airborne infection often ran rampant. The crowding together of persons migrating in from rural isolates who lacked natural immunity to diseases like tuberculosis, bronchitis, influenza, scarlet fever and measles contributed to the spread of micro-organisms. Not surprisingly mortality levels were elevated in the large cities prior to 1910. Statistical evidence bearing on this point is reviewed later, in Chapter 9.

Gradually both national government and local government responded to the threat to health. Local authorities, working in a coordinating/facilitating mode, marshaled the assistance of health cooperatives (*eisei kumiai*) that sprang up spontaneously in figuring out ways to remove fecal material from cities, selling it as night soil to nearby farmers. At the national level, the Diet took up bills modeled on the progressive health and worker disability laws of countries like Germany, passing a Factory Act in 1911, not implemented until 1916 banning child labor and setting minimum sanitary conditions for industrial work. This law became the landmark piece of social legislation in interwar Japan, testimony to the importance of the Diet's role prior to the era of party cabinets. In 1922 the Diet passed a health and disability law covering industrial workers, extending it to rural communities in 1938 with the National Health Insurance Law establishing health insurance societies in local communities, especially in farming communities.

Because the political pressure to intervene in the public health conditions of urban areas was greater than it was in rural districts, because the per person costs of providing clean water and sewers was lower in densely populated zones, by the 1930s age standardized mortality rates were pretty much the same in large cities and in remote rural villages. Through public health intervention, the case rates for the infectious diseases, the risks of exposure to micro-organisms, had been brought down sufficiently in industrialized urban areas to match those in rural Japan. Thus by the 1930s the main difference between areas with high rates of natural increase and those with low rates of natural increase lay in fertility, not mortality. By the late 1920s and early 1930s the pressure of natural population increase was greater in northeastern Japan than it was elsewhere. Living in communities remote from the burgeoning industrial belt, the excess of births over deaths was fueling relentless tension between landlords and tenants, landlords taking advantage of the competition between farm families to terminate the leases of malcontents, selecting competitors who were more amenable to the landlord's demands.

Why was fertility higher in northeastern Japan than it was in most of the rest of Japan, than in most of the rural zones throughout central Japan? We can call upon three distinct hypotheses to explain this phenomenon: human capital theory emphasizing income per capita driven demand for child quality versus child quality; the demand for child labor; and the diffusion of innovations.

According to the per capita income hypothesis the income elasticity of demand (the percentage increase in demand due to a 1 percent increase in per capita income) for child quality (as evidenced by the educational attainment and health of the average child in a household) exceeds the income elasticity of demand for quantity (the number of children). Higher income per capita families – for instance those residing in the industrial belt – invest more per child in each child they raise to adulthood, substituting quality for quantity by having fewer children than those in lower income per capita communities. Farm families in northeastern Japan were probably the poorest community in interwar Japan, hence the least likely to restrict quantity in order to invest more in quality.

In Chapter 9 we shall investigate the logic of the human capital argument in greater detail, discussing some of the key assumptions about how decision making takes place within households and how employment opportunities for women – or alternatively pressure to work – for women might have contributed to depressing fertility in the great cities of the industrial belt.

A second argument, also economic, appeals to the fact that children were an important source of labor services in Tokugawa Japan, remaining so in regions where secondary education had not made substantial inroads. During the Meiji period, the demand for child labor grew especially in northeastern Japan: the harnessing of seed varieties and the irrigation techniques and fertilizers of southwestern Japan promoted land reclamation in northeastern Japan; as opportunities for marketing silk thread expanded, farm households in northeastern Japan diversified in this booming business; and farmers in the region discovered that much revenue could be generated from producing fruit, especially apples, and grasses for raising horses. An outward shift in the demand for child labor may have encouraged couples to raise an increasing numbers of offspring, perhaps shortening the intervals between live births in order to achieve this.

A third argument rests on the idea that the idea to systematically limit the number of children – to set a definite target for family size, modifying behavior once that target is reached – was new, arising first in urban Japan, then diffusing throughout the rest of the country. Flying in the face of pro-fertility government policies, city dweller households began averting births in growing numbers, embracing family planning, perhaps using contraceptives to achieve these goals. Located in a remote region of the land, northeastern rural Japan was one of the last to absorb the attitudes and concepts associated with family limitation. Social norms may have been crucial.

In any event, population pressure on farmland was most strongly felt in northeastern Japan. Not surprisingly this was the district in which landlord/tenant acrimony became most pronounced during the late 1920s and early 1930s.

Conclusion

The strong growth of the Japanese economy during the decade of the 1910s slowed down during the 1920s. This is not surprising. The main focus of the 1910s was industrial expansion, its fruits being relatively immediate, showing up in terms of so much shipping tonnage, so many yards of cotton cloth, so many electrical machines produced. During the 1920s the emphasis was on infrastructure reform and expansion whose payoff was stretched out over a much longer period. The World War I boom had exhausted the limits of the infrastructure put into place before 1911. Reform and renewal of infrastructure during the 1920s was a natural response to the pressures placed upon it. In its absence the industrial surge of the 1930s would have not occurred. To their credit, the party cabinets of the 1920s oversaw this process of infrastructure reform and renewal in part by keeping military costs down throughout the decade by negotiating agreements with the Anglo-American powers and by active participation in the League of Nations.

This was not the way matters were seen by the critics of democracy in Japan. They pinned the blame for slow economic growth on the policies of the parties dominating the Diet, on the *zaibatsu* financing the parties, on the emphasis of government on promoting infrastructure reform and renewal through coordinating/facilitating approaches grounded in appealing to the profit oriented interests of private corporations. On the left Communist inspired thinkers expressed admiration for central planning, jettisoning reliance on market prices for allocating goods and the factors of production, equalizing incomes and assets through nationalization of industry. On the right, ultra-nationalistic militarists also wanted to limit sharply the role of the market in the interests of restoring a hypothesized national virtue mystically rooted in the emperor, a beacon that the rest of Asia should follow.

Friction between landlords and peasants, friction that the Diet could not defuse because landlords constituted a significant bloc within its own ranks, exacerbated tensions between the extreme right, the extreme left and the moderate middle. The slow growth of the industrial sector fed the rural tension because the expansion of opportunity for poor farm families in industry was lethargic. The rural conflict between landlord and tenant was a domestic powder keg, fueling and fueled by political divisiveness. Whether domestic events alone would have produced the swing toward militarism experienced during the next decade remains an open question. Deterioration in the international economic order, brought on by the United States slipping into the great depression and the growing ideological confrontation of Communist, Fascist and liberal democratic governments in Europe, further poisoned the divisive political brew of early 1930s Japan. The powder keg was about to explode.

Key terms and concepts in Chapter 5

Seiyūkai

"First past the post" system of voting

Minseitō

An Outline Plan for the Reconstruction of Japan

Credentialism

Senmongakkō

University Ordinance of 1918

Rōnin students

Smoot-Hawley tariff

Washington Conference of 1921–1922

The yen/dollar exchange rate during the 1920s

Kantō earthquake

Bank of Taiwan

Convoy system

Kukaku seiri

Demographic transition

Sanitary Bureau

Eisei kumiai

Factory Act

National Health Insurance Law

6   Under the shadow of militarism

Out of the crucible of domestic and international turmoil

As the decade of the 1930s opened, the future of Japanese economic policy emerged as an increasingly contentious political issue.

For the major political parties continuing along the path of employing a mix of policies honed over the period after 1870 – stabilization, modest transfer, regulatory and especially facilitating/coordination – was the proper thing to do. This mix had worked in the past; it should perform well in the future.

The stabilization approach developed so far was not aimed at manipulating aggregate demand in order to reduce unemployment. Unemployment was not a crucial issue given the realities of how most workers responded to industrial ups and downs, returning to their villages of origin, often being reabsorbed into the agricultural labor from which they came in the face of cutbacks in manufacturing. Rather the twin foci of fiscal stabilization policy were beefing up domestic infrastructure and funding the army and navy. Monetary policy was designed to meet international commitments – bolstering the international economic order by remaining on the gold standard – and the domestic needs of a growth in real gross domestic product requiring expansion in liquidity to meet an expanding volume of transactions. True, the deflation needed to keep Japan on the gold standard at the pre-World War I par was an unpleasant medicine to swallow. Still, manufacturing growth seemed to be picking up in the latter half of the 1920s.

As for the other policies there seemed little ground for complaint. Regulatory policy, employed to keep the private banking system viable had stabilized the financial sector in the late 1920s; the educational reforms seemed to be meeting the growth in demand for engineers and vocational school graduates in a system in which both private and public schools were held to standards by the Ministry of Education; and the medical profession was being properly certified to promote the diffusion of germ theory of disease. True, transfer policies – welfare, social insurance – were just getting off the ground. Most important, the facilitating/coordination approach appeared to efficiently accommodate the needs of market oriented firms and government, generating expansion of physical infrastructure – intercity electric railroad and tramway networks, hydroelectricity transmission and delivery systems, wide paved roads and sewer lines – that would and could accommodate massive industrial expansion anticipated to occur during the coming decades.

Dissatisfied with this policy mixture were the extreme right and left, both of which advocated subjecting the economy to command and control by the national government. To the Marxist-Leninist left this meant adopting five year central plans for nationalized industries, civilian bureaucrats setting targets and quotas for particular sectors and specific factories. For the ultra-nationalist right, this meant control of the economy by the military, directing the allocation of resources in order to achieve both foreign policy goals through armed intervention abroad and domestic political objectives that could be piggybacked onto the military objectives. For instance settling "surplus" Japanese farm families in the empire was one proposal that tied together domestic and foreign policies in a neat package. Mindful of rural discontent as an unresolved festering domestic problem, both right and left pointed to it, illustrating their argument that the mainstream political parties had failed to develop effective economic and social policies because of the narrow range of modes of governmental interaction with the economy with which they chose to operate. However it was disruptive developments in the international arena coupled with a series of assassinations of Prime Ministers by right-wing fanatics, not rural discontent, that finally convinced the last of the *genrō*, Saionji Kimmochi to appoint a "national unity cabinet" headed up by Admiral Saito Makoto in mid-1932, the first of a long line of military cabinets that succeeded each other until the surrender of Japan to the United States and its allies in 1945.

Some of the disruptions were purely economic. On the heels of the stock market crash of 1929, the United States, the largest and most powerful economy in the world, slipped into a sustained depression. Setting the level of real American gross domestic product at 100 in 1929, its level in 1930 was 91.1, in 1931 it was 84.1, in 1932 it was 73, and in 1933 it finally bottomed out at a level of 71.5. From this low it slowly crept up – although not steadily – finally reaching a value above its 1929 value only in 1938 after a lost decade. Unemployment soared, reaching levels of over 20 percent in some years. The wholesale collapse of the American economy had two major ramifications. It provided grist to the arguments made by those on both the extreme right and left in Japan that reliance on markets and mainstream economic policies could be disastrous; it pulled down global income as American demand for imports from other nations floundered, including raw silk from Japan.

Partly in response to the economic collapse of the American behemoth, partly in response to the signing by the American presidency of the extremely protectionist Smoot-Hawley tariff, more and more countries moved into trade blocs abandoning the gold standard once and for all. The decision of the United Kingdom to go down this path by negotiating an imperial preference system within its own empire was a decisive step along this road. There was a general drift toward autarky – either taking the form of economic nationalism restricted to a single country or operating under the guise of a trade bloc like the partial customs union adopted by the British empire in 1932 – encouraging militaristic strategic thinkers in Japan to consider carving out its own empire in Asia, relying on the yen to be the monetary linchpin of a trade bloc centered around Japan as its industrial heartland.

Another set of disruptions was rooted in politics. Some were rooted in geopolitical conflicts stemming from drives for regional hegemony in Europe. Some emerged from ideological division. On the ideological front, the threat that the leaders of the Soviet Union could export their Marxist-Leninist ideology either by political means – undermining "bourgeois democracies" through the subsidizing of Communist parties in other countries – or through the force of their military arms shook faith in liberal parliamentary democracy in many European countries.

Fascism emerged in Italy and Germany partly as a response to the Marxist-Leninist threat. In Italy, the Fascism that grew up was a form of nationalist corporatism. Bringing together labor, business and government syndicates structuring specific industries under single umbrellas, the Fascist doctrine tried to curtail the activities of independent unions – though collective bargaining between business and government syndicates was allowed and a restive peasantry, suppressing the vitriolic class struggle crucial to Marxism-Leninism. Collectivism, a variant of socialism, was integral to the Italian model. In Germany, the emphasis of one wing of the Nationalist Socialist (Nazi) party had been collectivist, the emphasis in the other main wing more racist in thinking, emphasizing the reunification of the German people living in Austria, the Rhineland, and Czechoslovakia and the suppression of non-German peoples, Jews and Gypsies for instance. The Nazi model of collectivism, put forward in the 1934 law for the organization of national labor, brought together employees and employers at the enterprise level, in the name of forging a classless society abolishing contracts negotiated through collective bargaining, socialist unions, prohibiting strikes and lockouts.

Despite their ideological differences the Fascist states shared two important characteristics with the Soviet Union: totalitarianism, dictatorial rule; and a drive for regional hegemony. Mussolini was in charge in Italy, Hitler in Germany; Stalin in the Soviet Union. While German and Italian Fascism differed in their emphasis on how collectivism was to be achieved through Fascist institutions, they shared a common interest in expansionism abroad, Italy in the Balkans and northern Africa (in addition to supporting Franco in the Spanish civil war), Germany in the Rhineland, Austria, Czechoslovakia, and Poland to the east. Equally interested in expansionism was most of the leadership of the Soviet Union, wishing to create a buffer zone between Germany and itself by bringing under the Russian heel Finland; the Baltic states of Estonia, Lithuania, and Latvia; and Poland. Inevitably, these drives to regional hegemony within Europe had to clash: there was tension between Italy and Germany over Germany's absorbing of Austria; and between Germany and the Soviet Union over the fate of Scandinavia and the Baltic states.

Reflecting deep divisions within the leaderships of the major European powers – especially England and France – on how to hem in the pushes to hegemony of the three totalitarian powers, the liberal democracies veered between relying on the collective security doctrine of the League of Nations and building a geopolitical alliance that might stymie aggression through the balance of power, an approach that had dominated European diplomacy for centuries. Key to the balance of power approach was cooperation between England and France. But this alliance failed to stop Hitler from sending in military forces to the Rhineland in 1936, and absorbing Austria and parts of Czechoslovakia in 1938. It also failed to stop Italy from waging a vicious campaign in the horn of Africa. Watching the liberal democracies cave in to German and Italian aggression, Stalin kept his options open, courting the British and the French with the aim of containing the German drive to hegemony on the one hand, feeling out the Germans on the other. However one major impediment stood in the way of intervention by the Soviet Union in forging an alliance with the liberal democracies: the refusal of Poland to allow Russian troops on its soil.

The deteriorating geopolitics of Europe played into the hands of those factions in the Japanese military with aggressive designs on the Pacific and the Asian mainland. During World War I when the focus of the European powers had been almost exclusively directed upon Europe itself, the Japanese government felt it had a virtual free hand to bully China with its infamous twenty-one demands. As a combination of ideological friction and geopolitical instability poisoned the European theater, the fortunes of the factions in the navy and the army opposed to continuing cooperation with the powers and institutions favored by the party cabinets – with the European powers, the United States and the League of Nations – blossomed.

Consider the navy that had divided into a fleet faction and a pro-Washington naval treaty after the Japanese government had ratified the Washington conference treaties during the early 1920s. Attending the London conference organized to confirm and extend the agreements made in Washington, the Japanese delegation and in particular the navy minister agreed to approve the London naval treaty despite the objections of the naval chief of staff who argued in the Privy Council that Japan should not ratify the treaty. Ultimately the civilian cabinet headed up by Hamaguchi Yuko prevailed in the Privy Council, securing confirmation of the treaty despite the argument of the fleet faction that the navy minister was obligated to support the views of the naval chief of staff. The upshot of this incident was the resignation of the naval chief of staff and reflecting the political turmoil set off the shooting of Hamaguchi by a right wing fanatic. By 1934 the views of the fleet faction had become so dominant – partly because it had managed to secure the purging of the pro-treaty faction – that Japan moved to abrogate the treaty altogether, contributing to its isolation from the Anglo-American powers.

Even more disruptive of Japan's international posture were the actions taken by the army in Manchuria. Achieving at Mukden in 1931 what it was unable to accomplish during the late 1920s, the faction of the army active in defending the Manchurian railway fomented a military incident that it could hypocritically blame on the forces of the Chinese warlord controlling Manchuria, eventually conquering the entire region. Taking over control, the army moved to create the puppet state of Manchuko, inviting the former Emperor of China, deposed by the Chinese nationalist movement, to become the nominal head of the new country. Completing the pacification of Manchuko in 1933, the army managed to create a second puppet regime –Jehol–on the southeast of Manchuko through its aggressive moves. Censured by the Lytton report tabled at the League of Nations – the report argued that Manchuko was not a legitimate state, recommending that the Japanese army withdraw so that China could make it an autonomous region under its sovereignty – and pressured by the army high command, the Japanese government withdrew from the League, thereby isolating it from the one organization committed to collective security as opposed to the balance of power.

The road leading to the appointment of military cabinets in place of the civilian party cabinets that had prevailed between 1918 and 1932 was extremely lengthy. Countless international and domestic crises played a role in the abandonment of civilian rule. That there were no constitutional safeguards against it occurring however was a byproduct of the way compromises were made by the Meiji oligarchs. Under these compromises, the army and navy enjoyed direct access to the emperor in securing support for their activities. They did not have to go through the Diet. This opened the door to factions in the army and the navy making their own policies, operating under the fiction that they were the truest interpreters of the imperial will.

Did the military cabinets of the mid-1930s attempt to substitute the command and control mode for managing the economy, abandoning the package of modes relied on by the party cabinets, namely stabilization, transfer, regulation, and facilitating/coordination? Most of the evidence suggests "no". The most important revision of policy carried out by the post-1931 cabinets involved stabilization. Acting under the direction of the minister of finance, Takahashi Korekiyo, who had already been appointed to the post under civilian cabinets, the government expanded its level of spending, mostly on military equipment and empire building in Manchuria, paying for the beefing up of expenditure by issuing bonds, not by increasing taxes. This bold "deficit-financed" expansion of government expenditure (the Bank of Japan absorbing most of the bonds issued by the government) is consistent with Keynesian policy prescriptions, although the motivation for it – funding military buildup – was not a key element in the thinking of Keynes. Further contributing to expansion was a surge in exports brought on by Japan's abandonment of the gold standard in late 1931, its currency sharply depreciating, driving down the international prices of its exports and up the yen denominated prices of its imports.

It is apparent that Takahashi's thinking about economic policy making during the 1930s was profoundly shaped by the breakdown in the international economic order during the 1920s. He felt that economic liberalism was dead, economic nationalism taking its place; that the gold standard was moribund, being replaced by a system of managed national and regional currencies; and that the drift toward regional trade blocs would accelerate, making war more likely in the future. This view of the world was consistent with the goals of most members of the military cabinets who were prepared to work constructively with politician-bureaucrats like

Takahashi who had served during the 1920s, even those who had attempted to shore up the international economic order with their policy recommendations.

Not only did monetary and fiscal stabilization methods continue to have considerable traction during the 1930s, so did facilitating/coordination approaches. Notable are the efforts made by the Ministry of Commerce and Industry to promote rationalization, especially in major export industries like cotton textiles that had suffered under the overvalued yen policies of the early 1920s. Rebuffed early during the 1880s when it attempted to form an industry wide guild in textiles due to fragmentation in the industry – large integrating/spinning concerns coexisting with proto-industrial activity organized along putting-out lines in which countless numbers of merchants mediated between household producers – the government tried again to organize the industry with the aim of pushing down costs beginning in the early 1920s. This time it was successful, mainly because electrification had reshaped textiles, drastically reducing the role of small proto-industrial units in the field.

Electrification transformed the industry because of the unit-drive principle embodied in electric machines. With electric motors available on the market, even the smallest establishments could contemplate mechanization. Merchants versed in textiles once active in putting-out now turned to setting up their own factories, albeit tiny in scale, often becoming sub-contractors for larger firms in the field. Increasingly these small enterprises abandoned traditional Japanese clothing, switching to Western style clothing that could be marketed both domestically and abroad. As a result of these trends the number of enterprises active in textiles dropped significantly. In addition hostility between large integrated spinning/weaving firms and smaller firms abated. Taking advantage of these circumstances the Ministry of Commerce and Industry moved to create powerful economies of scale and scope in the purchasing of raw materials and the marketing of output. It began regulating output, ensuring minimum quality standards; it purchased equipment and machines at discount, purchasing in quantity, making it available for affiliated companies; and it purchased raw cotton in bulk, distributing it amongst the firms affiliated with it. It carried out facilitating/coordination on a grand scale, helping the industry get through the downturns of the 1920s and early 1930s, buffeted as it was by the overvalued exchange for the yen and the deep depression of the United States.

In short, the military cabinets that set economic policy over the period between 1932 and the beginning of widespread warfare in China in 1937 tended to rely on modes other than command and control, modes refined between the 1880s and the early 1930s. The one striking exception is Manchuko. Reorganizing administration for the puppet regime in 1934, the army began experimenting with a two-pronged policy: encouraging immigration of farm households from Japan, and putting together plans for industrial development. The first prong was designed to relieve population pressure in rural districts of Japan especially where landlord/tenant disputes had become particularly acrimonious; the second prong was designed to promote the rapid buildup of production of coal, iron and steel, even automobile and aircraft parts through the systematic elaboration of plans, some inspired by those being developed in the Soviet Union. Settling farmers was a priority because it satisfied another policy objection: building up Japanese communities on the border region of Manchuko that separated Outer Mongolia, a client state of the Soviet Union from Manchuko, a client state of Japan.

The consensus view is that the efforts of Japanese advisors directing the Manchuko economy did not reap great rewards, the economic payoffs small, the expenses required to improve infrastructure and subsidize Japanese companies active in the region skyrocketing. If the army's experiments in Manchuko were designed to showcase the virtues of command and control modes of directing economies, if it was to serve to intensify the drumbeat for the use of similar modes of governance in the homeland, it does not appear they were successful. Not that this stopped ultra-nationalist militarist factions and secret societies from giving up on command and control modes. A major faction in the army, the Imperial Way faction, sympathizing with the radical ultra-nationalist views of Kita Ikki, gained increasing prominence in the early 1930s. Converts to this cause even included former university students, once adherents to Marxist-Leninism, now becoming ardent opponents of Communism with its emphasis on materialism. Now convinced that ethics rooted in revering the emperor should serve as the basis for a New Order in which greedy profit oriented capitalists and selfish market oriented incentives would wither away, the converts to the Imperial Way included bureaucrats employed in the ministries of the 1930s. Imperial Way thinking was hardly limited to the military and radical extremists like Kita Ikki.

Opposing the Imperial Way faction was the Control faction organized within the ranks of the armed forces, more rational in its thinking, more willing to work with bureaucrats adhering to modes of governance other than command and control, more willing to accommodate the profit oriented thinking of the business community.

Intensifying the conflict between the two factions were differences over foreign policy. Hostile to international communism, the Imperial Way faction believed that the future enemy of Japan, against which its high command should devise a military strategy, was the Soviet Union. Believing that the military should follow its tried and true approach of fighting one enemy at a time, the Imperial Way faction argued against intensifying a war against China, using Manchuko as a base from which to fight Russia rather than China. By contrast, the Control faction believed that Manchuko and Jehol should serve as a staging area from which Japan should strike south. In the mid-1930s struggle between the two factions intensified. Assassinations and political infighting stemming from the factional fighting poisoned the domestic political scene. In mid-February 1936 the Imperial Way faction struck, seizing the center of the capital, attempting to pave the way for a general revolution. Having assassinated the finance minister Takahashi and the Privy Seal, the revolt was contained by the forces of the Command faction, a surrender of the rebels being negotiated during the latter half of February. Swiftly putting on trial and executing the leaders, and a year later Kita Ikki, the Control faction came out of the 1936 confrontation in charge of the policy making agenda.

For many Japanese political thinkers the defeat of the Imperial Way faction represented the defeat of revolutionary Japanese Fascism by a conservative military elite that was prepared to rely on modes of governance harking back to the heyday of *fukoku kyōhei*. Was the defeat of Imperial Way complete? There is some evidence that it was not, that bridge building compromise between the two powerful factions continued despite the *coup* debacle. In 1936 the Japanese government negotiated with Germany, signing the Anti-Comintern Pact publicly committing the two governments to combat international communism, secretly laying the groundwork for an anti-Russian alliance.

The economics of trend acceleration and the long swing

As is apparent from Table A.1 and Table A.6 in the Appendix the growth of per capita income and gross domestic expenditure was substantial during the 1930s. Indeed the pre-1950 Japanese economy achieved its most dynamic advance during the 1930s. Nor can this be simply written off as the result of surging government spending, either on beefing up rural infrastructure or on the army and navy. As Table A.6 shows, the growth of private investment was far more important than the growth of government expenditure during the 1930s. Why was investment demand so buoyant during this period? For many economists there is very strong continuity to the process of economic development of Japan over the period from the mid-1880s until 1938 when the command and control mode of managing the economy gained force in a country girding for total warfare. These economists – including this author it should be said – adhere to the idea that there are long swings in Japanese economic history, upswings being followed by down-swings within designated swing periods or downswings followed by upswings depending on how one goes about doing the measurement.

The long swing

Between 1930 and 1938 the growth rate of Japan's gross domestic product was almost 5 percent using seven year moving averages for annual growth rates yields an average figure of 4.6 percent for the decade. Given the rapid buildup of Japan's military spending during this period it is appropriate to ask whether the growth of the 1930s – the highest growth rates prior to the miracle growth period rates, levels of approximately 10 percent clocked in for the period between 1956 and 1962 – were directly linked to the militarism of the era. Long swing analysis suggests that militarism had relatively little to do with the growth of the 1930s. Rather the surge of the 1930s was part and parcel of a long-run growth process extending back to the mid-1880s.

The idea of the long swing originated with the research that Simon Kuznets did on the national income estimates of a variety of Western countries covering the period from the mid nineteenth century until the

World War I. Kuznets observed that for variety of countries studied – the United Kingdom, Germany, Sweden, Australia and the United States – there was a regular pattern to income growth. Rapid spurts (upswings) were followed by periods of slower growth (downswings). Measuring the average growth rate over a period extending from the inception of the rapid growth period to the close of the slow growth period yielded a trend period rate of growth intermediate between the spurt and the slow growth sub-periods. Kuznets dubbed the wave-like movements "long swings".

Based upon the national income estimates prepared by the Long Term Economic Statistics (LTES) project organized by the Institute for Economic Research at Hitotsubashi University, Ohkawa and Rosovsky (1973) offered the first systematic interpretation of long swings in the Japanese economy for the period 1897–1969. In their interpretation there is strong continuity in the long swing process. Upswings (1901–17, 1931–37, 1956–62) were periods of exceptionally high rates of capital formation, of investment. Capital formation not only drove aggregate demand expansion; it was also a vehicle for the absorption of foreign (mostly Western) technology, the absorbing of technology generating unusually high rates of total factor productivity growth. In effect the long swing trajectory captures an investment led growth process, upswings involving strong capital accumulation, downswings weak capital formation.

Ohkawa and Rosovsky argue that wage growth lagged behind productivity growth during the upswings, giving a strong impetus to growth in profits per unit of capital installed, thereby sustaining the upswing for a considerable length of time. They also argue that Japan became increasingly capable of absorbing foreign technology over time – households increased their savings as income per capita grew, household investment in the educational levels of children was highly response to income increase, firms learned how to better motivate their workers through the internalization of labor, government gradually groped toward an effective industrial policy minimizing the costs of securing foreign technology patent rights – thereby generating trend acceleration. By trend acceleration is meant growth in the trend rate of growth calculated for successive long swings (upswing followed by downswing) eras.

In Chapter 8 you will learn more about the Ohkawa-Rosovsky model, exploring its utility for understanding the dynamics of the miracle growth era. For now what you should take away from this discussion of the Ohkawa-Rosovsky interpretation of the long swing is the notion that the 1930s are not unique. Their growth simply represents the upswing of the third long swing, a period when fixed capital formation growth was very brisk. A slightly different characterization of Japan's long swing growth process, more eclectic, appears in Minami (1994). Minami accepts the trend acceleration principle and the importance of investment for surges in income growth but relies more on the changes in the trade regime, domestic price movements and financial crises, for his explanation of why downswings inevitably followed upswings.

In Minami's chronological account, the first long swing occurred during the period 1885–1903, the upswing associated with the establishing of the steam driven integrated spinning and weaving cotton textiles industry, the downswing with deterioration in the terms of trade (export prices relative to import prices) following Japan's adoption of a fixed exchange rate between the yen and gold. He dates the second long swing period 1904–28, the upswing highlighted by the World War I boom when imports were sharply curtailed due to trade embargoes, the downswing characterized by a banking crisis in the late 1920s and balance of payments woes brought on by Japan's attempt to go back on the gold standard at the pre-World War I par. His third long swing extends from 1929 to 1956, the upswing process assisted by the decision of the cabinet to take Japan off the gold standard (to embargo the shipment of gold abroad), the downswing between 1937 and 1956 including the period when the war in China intensified, the Pacific war took place, followed by the American occupation and the Korean war.

Minami follows Ohkawa and Rosovsky in interpreting the miracle growth era between 1959 and 1969 as the upswing of a fourth long swing, heavily driven by technology import and exceptionally high rates of capital formation. He argues that the downswing of the fourth long swing occurred between 1970 and 1975, being brought on by the collapse of the Bretton Woods system, yen appreciation, the first oil crises and the associated upward spike in domestic prices. He sees the fifth long swing – slower than the fourth because trend de-acceleration set in after miracle growth brought levels of Japanese technology up close to Western levels – involving an upswing between 1976 and 1987 brought on by a favorable trade balance and an accumulation of foreign reserves, and the downswing between 1987 and the early 1990s by the wild running up of land and stock market asset prices known as the bubble economy.

A third interpretation of Japan's long swings appears in Mosk (2001). Mosk interprets the long swings between 1887 and 1938 as innovation waves (akin to Schumpeter's Kondratieff waves only shorter), arguing that each successive upswing involved major changes in the technology of energy production. Harnessing steam power was crucial to the upswing of the first wave that occurred between 1887 and 1897; harnessing hydro-electric power to the upswing of the second long swing (1904–19); and thoroughly exploiting the internal combustion engine in ground and air transport for the upswing of the third long swing (1930–38).

Mosk views downswing phases (1897–1904, 1919–30) as periods of retrenchment, infrastructure being built up to cope with the demands put upon it by the massive industrial expansion occurring during upswing surges. For instance he sees the 1920s as focusing on the reform of human capital formation enhancing infrastructure (e.g. the reform of the educational system), the reform of financial infrastructure (banking) during the late 1920s, and the expansion of physical infrastructure (hydroelectric power grids and paved roads). Ultimately each downswing period, by shoring up and expanding upon the infrastructure of the country, paves the way for another industrial expansion wave. From this point of view the upswing of the 1930s is not due to militarism but rather represents an industrial expansion surge whose groundwork was laid in the infrastructure renewal and expansion era of the 1920s. In short in Mosk's interpretation of long swings, downswing periods is focused upon intense infrastructure reform and growth, preparing the groundwork for industrial expansion that in turn puts pressure upon infrastructure, generating further progress in the infrastructure sphere.

While the three interpretations of long swings discussed here differ, they share one common theme: the relatively rapid growth of the 1930s is not primarily tied up with militarism, but rather represents an upturn in an ongoing rhythmic process of economic development extending back to the 1880s.

For those who work with the long swing concept, there is a consensus that trend acceleration characterizes the long swing process of Japan's economic development between the mid-1880s and the early 1970s. By trend acceleration is meant the fact that the growth rate for a swing period (a swing period consisting of an upswing followed by a downswing or of a downswing followed by an upswing) is greater than the growth rate for the previous swing period and slower than the growth rate for the swing period that follows. The growth process accelerates from period to period. Dating of the swing period differs somewhat depending on who is doing the dating. Moreover, interpretation of the exact meaning of the swing periods differs from investigator to investigator. Still, there is general agreement on when growth was relatively slow and relatively rapid. Using the five-year periods appearing in most of the tables in the Appendix and relying on the estimates of the increments to real gross domestic expenditure assembled in Panel B of Table A.6 it is apparent that the sub-periods 1886–90, 1891–95, 1906–10, 1916–20, 1931–35 and 1936–40 were periods of relatively rapid expansion. It is also apparent from a comparison of the absolute magnitudes of the increments to gross domestic expenditure that the increments increase in magnitude over time. They reach their pre-1940 apex in 1936–40, the final five year period prior to 1940.

The dating of the rhythm of growth rates secured from the growth rates estimates in Table A.1 paints a slightly different picture but not one appreciably

Table 6.1 Three interpretations of Japan's long swings

Panel A *Ohkawa and Rosovsky periodization (1880s through 1960s)*

Period	Long swing phase	Features
1887–1917	First long swing	Peak in 1917; trough in 1901. Private sector investment is crucial to growth of national output, higher rates of capital formation generating higher rates of growth. "Cheap" labor swing.
1917–1937	Second long swing	Peak in 1937, trough in 1931. Investment rate drives income growth rate over swing. The social capability for importing foreign technology improves due to rise in savings, improvements in educational characteristics of labor force relative to the first long swing.
1937–1962	Third long swing	Peak in 1962. Investment rate drives growth rate over swing. Massive improvements in social capability for importing foreign technology in post-1945 period fuels miracle growth.

Panel B *Minami periodization (1880s through 1980s)*

Period	Long swing phase	Features
1885–1896	First long swing upswing	Modern industries expand; electrical use begins.
1897–1903	First long swing downswing	Adoption of gold standard causes financial crises.
1904–1918	Second long swing upswing	Russo-Japanese War (1904–1905) and foreign loans stimulate modern industrial growth.
1919–1928	Second long swing downswing	Balance of payments problems exacerbated by Great Kantō Earthquake in 1923 and bank runs in 1927 impede growth.
1929–1936	Third long swing upswing	Impact of Depression in the United States counteracted by expansionary fiscal policy in Japan.

Table 6.1 Continued

Period	Long swing phase	Features
1937–1956	Third long swing downswing	War with China commencing in 1937 and Pacific War commencing in 1941 lead to command economy. By 1943 Japan had lost command of seas, followed by surrender and occupation by the United States and other allied powers.
1957–1969	Fourth long swing upswing	Sharp rise in investment accompanied by introduction of new technology fuels high speed growth.
1970–1975	Fourth long swing downswing	Yen/dollar exchange rate appreciation coupled with "oil shock" generates inflation, the Japanese government reacting with tight money policy slowing growth. Trend de-acceleration commences.
1967–1987	Fifth long swing upswing	Trade balance moves into surplus, generating friction in Japan's bilateral trade especially with the United States. Government expansionary policy takes place of exports as growth engine.

Panel C *Mosk periodization (1880s through 1930s)*

Period	Long swing phase	Features
1887–1897	Upswing of first (balanced growth) long swing	Agriculture, Western technology using light manufacturing and infrastructure expand simultaneously.
1897–1904	Downswing of first long swing	Shift from silver to gold standard.
1904–1911	First upswing of second (transitional growth) long swing	Focus on infrastructure buildup: railroad network expands; electric intercity and intra-city railroads pioneer widespread electrification.
1911–1919	Second upswing of second long swing	Heavy industry expands. Electrification promotes

(*Table 6.1 continued*)

Table 6.1 Continued

Panel C *Mosk periodization (1880s through 1930s)*		
Period	*Long swing phase*	*Features*
		unit drive system and widespread mechanization of manufacturing. Embargoes on imports from Europe stimulate import substitution.
1919–1930	Downswing of second long swing	Focus on infrastructure reform (education, banking) and renewed expansion of physical infrastructure (roads and electrical power grids).
1930–1938	Upswing of third (unbalanced) long swing	Heavy industry expansion tied to military buildup, machinery sector growing rapidly.

Sources: Minami (1994), Mosk (2001) and Ohkawa and Rosovsky (1973).

at variance with the one we have seen for increments to gross domestic expenditure. According to Table A.1 growth is fairly rapid at the end of the nineteenth century, during the 1910s, and again during the 1930s.

There are those who argue that we can best understand the surges and slowdowns in growth in terms of exogenous military and political events: in terms of the Sino-Japanese war, World War I and the military buildup of Japan on the Asian continent. While it is impossible to prove that this is not the case, it is possible to point out that the Russo-Japanese War and the Siberian expedition did not seem to impart a strong push to Japanese economic advance. The fact is that the Japanese military was active abroad during most of the years between the mid-1890s and 1940 (and during 1940–45). So it is not obvious that the rhythm of growth of the pre-1940 economy can be tied to military activity in any kind of neat and tidy manner.

Rejecting the exogenous military activity view suggests that we need to look for an explanation of the swing growth process and the trend acceleration phenomenon within the logic of economic growth itself, focusing specifically on aggregate economic variables. As a first pass, let us consider one obvious variable namely the level of capital formation, investment in plant and equipment and infrastructure especially investment by firms in the private sector responding to expected rates of return on their investments. As can be seen from Panel B of Table A.6 in the Appendix, a combination of government spending and private investment expansion tends to be particularly vigorous during the late nineteenth century, during the World War I boom and during the 1930s.

Using the models we have discussed earlier in this volume, there are three ways to think about the influence of investment on the economic development of a country. In a Keynesian framework, investment increases expand aggregate economic activity, raising demand for goods and services that gets multiplied throughout the economy. In the Schumpeterian framework an investment boom, especially a private sector boom, is symptomatic of innovation that drives up productivity growth. In a Swann-Solow framework, an increase in investment per worker – in excess of the demands put on it by population growth and the fact that the capital is always depreciating – bolsters the capital/labor ratio, raising labor productivity and per capita income.

Modifying the Schumpeterian and Swann-Solow models to accommodate the idea that a later developing country has the opportunity to borrow technology from more advanced country – lifting the level of output per worker at each level of the capital/labor ratio in the case of the Swann-Solow model, contributing to innovation within the country importing the technology in the Schumpeterian framework – we can see that there is a fourth mechanism through which capital accumulation raises the level of per worker productivity and per capita income; by serving as a carrier of foreign technology. The idea is that technology can only be imported through some form of investment in new private plant and equipment or in new infrastructure. During Meiji, steam power was harnessed by putting down railroad track and by building integrating spinning/weaving mills in the cotton textile industry. The capital invested in intercity railroads served as a carrier for the adaptation of Western technology in the electrical field. Capital invested in trucks and buses was indispensable for the initial harnessing of the internal combustion engine in Japan.

Two of the models developed to explain long swing dynamics and the relationship of these dynamics to trend acceleration – the framework developed by Ohkawa and Rosovsky and the framework developed by Minami – work with the assumption that capital formation spurts are related to the pace of importation of foreign technology. We restrict our discussion here to the model developed by Ohkawa and Rosovsky (1973). The central idea in their model of the swing mechanism is that output per unit of capital (Y/K) surges during an upswing in investment – the productivity of capital bolstered by the input of foreign technology that makes both labor and capital more productive – while the wage bill per unit of capital (wL/K) does not. They assume that the wage does not rise appreciably during the upswing phase because of the internalization of labor: workers enjoying implicit long-run contracts with management do not push for wage increases in the immediate aftermath of the productivity boom. Only later on, as the productivity expansion runs its course and slows down, the wave of foreign technology being fully absorbed and its potential for further expansion largely exhausted, does labor demand wage increases, thereby cutting into the profits earned by firms during the upswing in investment.

In Figure 6.1 we illustrate the cyclical process. Because total output equals the sum of profits earned by capital (the rate of profit per unit of capital times the capital stock) and the total wage bill:

$$Y = rK + wL \tag{6.1}$$

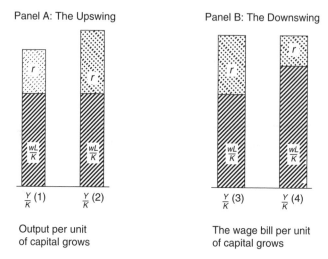

Panel A: The Upswing

$\frac{Y}{K}$ (1) $\frac{Y}{K}$ (2)

Output per unit
of capital grows

Panel B: The Downswing

$\frac{Y}{K}$ (3) $\frac{Y}{K}$ (4)

The wage bill per unit
of capital grows

Figure 6.1 Profits and wages in the long swing: the Ohkawa-Rosovsky model.

the rate of profit per unit of capital is the difference between the level of output per unit of capital (Y/K) and the wage bill per unit of capital (wL/K). Thus the profit rate rises in the first phase for two reasons: output per unit of capital increases due to the infusion of foreign technology; and the wage bill per unit of capital does not change. This state of affairs is illustrated in Panel A, the left hand panel, of Figure 6.1. The right hand panel of Figure 6.1, Panel B, illustrates what happens when output per unit of capital no longer grows, but the wage bill per unit of capital does. In this case the profit rate is squeezed. Making the reasonable assumption that private companies accumulate capital in order to generate profits, it is apparent that the investment rate (gross domestic capital formation as a percentage of national output) remains high as long as the profit rate remains strong. Downward pressure on the profit rate – due to rising wages and a drying up of technological progress – dampens investment. In short during the long swing investment booms during the upswing driven by high and rising profit rates, and slackens during the downswing.

Ohkawa and Rosovsky add some empirical bite to their long swing framework by incorporating dualism into the model through their argument about distribution of output per unit of capital between profits and wages. They argue that two hundred and fifty years of autarky during the Tokugawa period fostered strong allegiance of the consumer to domestic industries almost exclusively oriented to producing goods for the Japanese market by relatively timeworn labor intensive techniques. Examples of such consumer goods are *kimono*, *tatami* mats, *geta* (elevated wooden "sandals"), and the plethora of foods that are considered "Japanese" (*sushi*, *sashimi*, *shabu-shabu*, etc.). During the investment upswing the focus of acquisition of capital equipment and structures is on Western technology using industries aimed at both import and export (e.g. Western style cotton textiles and clothing, chemical fertilizers, steel plate, steamships, trucks, airplanes); as wages rise, however, cutting into profit rates, demand shifts from capital accumulation of Western style equipment producing goods for both domestic and international markets to consumption demand for traditional Japanese goods. The capital flowing into these traditional sectors does not benefit from productivity enhancement stemming from the importation of foreign technology. Thus technological progress slows down as the shift in income distribution from owners of capital to wage earners swings aggregate demand towards goods primarily aimed at the domestic market.

One of the important features of this argument is that imports do not rise appreciably during downswing phases of the long swing. The reason is simple. During the downswing demand shifts toward traditional Japanese goods that can be – are only – efficiently produced by domestic suppliers. In general, the Ohkawa-Rosovsky model downplays the role of trade in shaping long swings: investment demand is the driving force, determining what periods will enjoy rapid growth in income, what periods will experience sluggish growth in output. Trade is less important. During an investment boom, the import of foreign manufactures – machines, transport vehicles – typically increases (the World War I boom being an exception), import substitution in the capital goods industry taking time. Securing foreign patents requires funds as well. All of this puts pressure on the balance of payments, hence on the financial sector since central bank reserves – gold when Japan was adhering to the gold standard – tend to be depleted during the investment boom driven upswing. Working through central bank policy this pressure brakes the momentum of the boom, government policy swinging heavily towards export promotion during the downswing.

Onto this argument about the dynamics of the long swing, Ohkawa and Rosovsky graft a theory of the social capability for importing and adapting foreign technology. They argue that improvements in the social capacity are the cause of trend acceleration, raising the average rate of growth of the economy over successive long swing episodes. Implicit in their model of the social capability for importing and adapting foreign technology is positive feedback working through the domestic savings rate; positive feedback working through the market for post-primary schooling; positive feedback in the way firms develop implicit contracts binding workers to firms; positive feedback in terms of learning by doing at the shop floor level; and positive feedback in terms of government management of the economy, as exemplified by the pioneering of industrial policy, initiated during the interwar period by the Ministry of Commerce and Industry.

As for the savings rate(s), Ohkawa and Rosovsky assume that it responds both to the level of national income and the growth rate of national income, namely:

$$S/Y = s = a_0 + a_1 Y + a_2 G(Y) \qquad (6.2)$$

where $G(Y)$ is the growth rate of national income. What are the sources of this feedback, in particular the feedback of growth of income on the savings rate?

Several suggest themselves: at the household level a rise in household incomes, households increasing their savings propensity in order to fund future purchases and the education of their children; again at the household level, a delayed reaction of consumption demand to household income growth, consumer tastes being heavily oriented towards traditional Japanese goods; and at the corporate level a rise in corporate savings as profit rates surge during upswings. The rise in savings is important because domestic investment is almost totally financed by domestic savings, foreign savings playing only a modest role in Japan's capital accumulation. To accommodate acceleration in successive long-swing phases, the average investment rate increasing from the preceding to the next long swing phase, the savings rate must increase.

A second source of positive feedback making its way through the household sector involves the demand for education. The idea here is that a strong elasticity of demand for education of children by households increases the demand for schooling, thereby raising the capacity of the labor force to learn about, absorb, adapt and improve upon, foreign techniques.

A third mechanism of positive feedback works its way through the corporate sector, firms becoming more efficient in motivating workers, in training workers to handle foreign technology. The internalization of white-collar professionals – especially engineers – is a good example of a set of institutional innovations designed to accomplish the twin goals of motivating and training employees. To this one can add the fact that workers often learn by doing something. Give them the opportunity to work with new machines and time to practice on the machines and they learn how to use them, the efficiency of their use improving over time. Binding workers to firms through the writing of implicit contracts adds to the capacity to marshal learning by doing tendencies.

A fourth source of positive feedback involves government, a good example being the Ministry of Commerce and Industry rationalization policies of the 1920s and 1930s that built on the coordination/facilitating approach of the Meiji government.

An alternative interpretation for the social capability of importing and adapting foreign technology is in Mosk (2001) which advances an approach that has been incorporated into this text to a degree. In this interpretation the emphasis is on infrastructure driven growth: physical, human capital enhancing and financial infrastructure. Infrastructure expansion and renewal paves the way for industrial booms that in turn put pressure on infrastructure. Periods of intense infrastructure buildup and reform generate slower growth in income than are generated during periods of industrial expansion because the payoff to infrastructure expansion is only fully realized during the succeeding industrial boom. In this interpretation the role of the government as coordinating/facilitating agent is paramount.

Zaibatsu and *shinzaibatsu* at home and abroad

During the Meiji period, the *zaibatsu* were at the forefront in securing and adapting foreign technology. During the 1930s, their contribution in being technological pioneers was overshadowed by the new industrial groups known as *shinzaibatsu* (literally "new" *zaibatsu*). Why?

Part of the reason lies in the drift towards ultra-nationalism and militarism during the 1930s, the gradual taking over of the political agenda by those factions most interested in promoting national prestige through aggressive action abroad. By the standards of the ultra-nationalists, the *zaibatsu* were too greedy, too interested in profits at the expense of Japan's national interests, too rich and too committed to internationalism. When Mitsui managed to reap a windfall gain by speculating against the yen in 1931, popular demonstrations against the company broke out. Inflamed by the outrage against Mitsui, a member of the Blood Brotherhood, a group mostly composed of students committed to a leader who they believed would deliver Japan through his connections with cosmic forces to a greatness from which it could reconstruct the world, assassinated Dan Takuma, the chief executive of Mitsui, in early 1932. Dan's successor, Ikeda Seihin, took to wearing a bulletproof vest and to riding in an automobile equipped with bulletproof glass. He also jettisoned a number of long standing Mitsui policies, including refusal to sell stock to the public and to avoid donating to public causes. He saw to it that Mitsui created a charitable foundation, denoted funds for the relied of the unemployed, and issued stock to the public. He also oversaw a systematic weeding out of older employees – those over age fifty – so that it could fill a number of its offices with new faces, with young people committed to the nationalist and militaristic sentiments awash in political circles. Following Mitsui's lead, Sumitomo and Mitsubishi also established relief funds for the indigent.

The military cabinets, though willing to work with the *zaibatsu* just as they were willing to work with the bureaucracy, also took steps to rein in the dominance of the *zaibatsu* in the marketplace. Most important, the cabinets promoted competitors to the old-line *zaibatsu*, new industrial groups eager to cooperate with the plans of the army in Manchuria, Korea and China, eager to meet the needs of the navy in Taiwan and on the Pacific. Known as *shinzaibatsu*, many of the freshly established industrial groups rise to prominence by building their holding company empires around the new heavy industries that were key to the military effort: truck and automobile manufacture; airplane fabrication; chemicals for munitions. An excellent example of this new type of *zaibatsu* is Nissan.[1]

Brought into the growing industrial empire headed up by Aikawa Yoshisuke, in 1931, Dat Motors had begun manufacturing the Datsun (a name meant to convey "son" of Dat in English), a small automobile designed to build a niche in an automobile market heavily dominated by Japanese subsidiaries of Ford and General Motors who often built their cars from knock-down packs brought over from the United States. Interested in automobiles since his visit to the United States in 1908 when he saw the Model T manufactured by Ford, Aikawa brought Dat Motors under his umbrella through a stock buyout, already well versed in using the stock market to build his capital base. In relying heavily on equity markets, he explicitly rejected the approaches of the *zaibatsu* that refused to issue stock for public purchase prior to the 1930s. By the 1930s his holding company "Nippon Sangyō" (Japan Industries) issued stock under the abbreviation "Nissan."

Typical of the *shinzaibatsu*, Nissan's interests were diversified through the new high growth industries of the 1920s and 1930s – metals, machinery, chemicals, automobiles and trucks. Equally typically the growth of his empire was extremely rapid – by 1945 there were 74 companies operating under the Nissan umbrella, by 1941 the yen values of its investments exceeded those of Mitsui and those of Mitsubishi – and it was heavily involved in carrying on business in Japan's burgeoning empire. Indeed, in 1937 Aikawa transferred the Nissan holding company to Manchuria.

Nissan's automobile and truck divisions relied heavily on American knowledge during the 1930s. It brought in American engineers to work on machinery, vehicle and engine designs; it reached out to General Motors with the aim of setting up a joint venture, a plan that fell through after the Diet passed the Automobile Manufacturing Business Act of 1936. Designed to establish a domestic automobile industry that could contribute to Japan's national defense and its industrial expansion, the new law gave preferential treatment to Japanese carmakers in financing and taxation and imposed tariffs and quotas on imports. This legislation was pointedly aimed at driving Ford and General Motors out of the Japanese market and at building up Toyota and Nissan.

By the mid-1930s Aikawa's relationship with the militarists grew deeper. In 1935 he decided to diversify out of Datsun cars, adding standard-size trucks ordered by the army to the product line. This proved to be a mixed blessing. After 1938, the army interfered directly with the management of automotive production in Aikawa's company, ordering it to abandon cars and focus exclusively on trucks. This proved to be an expensive proposition: shifting to trucks reduced earnings drastically during the later 1930s. As the military moved increasingly to a command and control mode in its interaction with the private sector, it was prepared to bully its suppliers into following exactly military requisition targets set by the military.

The geopolitics and economics of the new order

By the mid-1930s, the official positions taken by the Japanese governments took on the mystical trappings of *kokutai* ("national essence"). To ultra-nationalists fervently committed to the emperor, the national essence of Japan was unique, rooted in the fact that Japan's Emperor was a god descended from the goddess of the sun. Protected by its gods and goddesses, Japan was superior to all other nations, having a divine mission to bring all nations under a single political roof headed by the emperor. While these theories rationalizing *kokutai* were extreme, a more common version emerged to gained currency during the 1930s amongst both elites and the general populace. Known as *nihonjinron* (the "theory of the Japanese"), this theory mixed scientific racist (eugenics) doctrines developed in the West that argued that some racial groups were inferior to others because of their lower genetically transmitted intelligence and physical abilities with mystical ideas about the uniqueness of the Japanese people. In one version or another, *kokutai* became the new umbrella concept of the 1930s, bringing under its shade ultra-nationalists, militarists, business, and, by 1940, labor.

Emerging from under the *kokutai* umbrella was the ideology of the New Order, a theory of how to organize economic life so that Japan could achieve its geopolitical, military, and ideological goals. To a greater extent than had been true in any period after the Meiji Restoration, under the New Order the command and control mode began to take on prominence in setting government policy for the economy. Still, under the apparent harmony of *kokutai* and New Order flourished fierce infighting and debate, between and among factions trying to have their way in a world of deteriorating international relations. Ideological principles, geopolitical calculations and hardnosed economic considerations involving access to oil, minerals and rubber pulled factions off into different directions. Out of this welter of infighting grew compromises patched together to yield something to each powerful faction. Saving face was crucial. The problem was that in the geopolitical and ideological environment of the late 1930s, compromise meant overreaching, attempting to achieve goals that were unreachable due to the constraints of resources, both military and economic, and the constraints of geographic distance.

One of the hallmarks of Japan's military successes between the 1890s and the mid-1930s was its taking on one enemy at a time, forming alliances with third parties in order to keep Japan's military out of wars that pitted it against massive alliances. Even during World War I and the Siberian Intervention, deciding who was the one enemy was reasonably clear: Germany during World War I, the revolutionary Red army during the Siberian Intervention. Beginning in 1937 this strategy was slowly but inexorably abandoned. First the Japanese army became increasingly embroiled in the quagmire of a protracted China conflict, only to find itself fighting on two fronts in 1938 and 1939, pitting troops against Soviet tank divisions on the Manchuria/Outer Mongolia border at the same time as it continued to fight in China where it was engaged against both Chinese Nationalist and Chinese Communist troops. While it was able to reach an accord with the Soviets, negotiating a ceasefire agreement in 1939 and a neutrality pact in April 1941, the period when Japan had only one enemy to concentrate its firepower upon was short lived. By 1942 it was fighting China, the United States and the United Kingdom. In early August 1945 it was fighting all four of its former enemies at once, the Soviet Union declaring war against Japan on August 8. What complex of international circumstances could see Japan drawn into such an overreaching military strategy, fighting throughout the Eurasian landmass while simultaneously taking on the two great Anglo-American maritime powers on the waters of the Pacific?

At the heart of the fateful decisions taken by Japan's leadership was the outbreak of total war in Europe. In September 1939, drawing a line in the sand with their commitment to defend Polish independence at all costs, the United Kingdom and France declared war on Germany. Behind the decision of Hitler to subject Poland to blitzkrieg was an alliance between Germany and the Soviet Union signed earlier in 1939 that agreed to the division of Poland, giving both the Communist and the Fascist power buffer zones separating the two potential adversaries. After a "phony war" in which little military activity took place, full-scale conflict broke out in mid-1940, the German blitzkrieg rolling through the Netherlands, Belgium and into France. Most of the British troops committed to the defense of France and Belgium and some French forces escaping from France at Dunkirk, England watched as its former ally surrendered to the triumphant Germans. Now England stood alone.

Unsuccessful in invading England – the Royal Air Force beating back the German air force in the Battle of Britain – Hitler now recoiled eastward, putting into his sights the huge Russian empire that was committed to a Communist doctrine that his Fascist principles despised. In June 1941, German troops moved against their supposed Russian ally, opening up a vast contested war zone in Russia. Germany was now fighting the United Kingdom and the Soviet Union simultaneously.

With Germany's attack on the Soviet Union, the Japanese military faced a critical strategic decision. Should it take advantage of the fact that German troops were tying up countless Russian divisions in the life and death struggles of Leningrad and Stalingrad to break its neutrality pact with the Soviets, striking northward? If so should it abandon its plans to carve up China and promote Japan's New Order throughout Southeast Asia? After all with the European powers caught up in the European military theater, would it not be better for Japan's military to take advantage of the European situation by striking south, taking Hong Kong and Singapore from the British, the Philippines from the United States, and the Dutch East Indies from the Netherlands? In Southeast Asia lay great rubber plantations, oil fields, deposits of tin and bauxite which the combined forces of the Japanese army and navy could exploit for resources, at the same time consolidating a sprawling Japanese empire under the aegis of the New Order. Pulled in different directions – some wanting to take on Russian Communism, following the logic of Imperial Way and anti-Cominterm doctrines, some wanting to push the New Order in the Southeast – Japan's militarists finally decided to focus on Southeast Asia and China. In doing so they realized that that might push the United States into declaring war against Japan.

Long committed to the Open Door principle in China, the executive and legislative branches of the United States made their displeasure with Japanese aggression in China evident to Japan with a number of specific gestures, some involving economic sanctions, some involving military decisions. In 1940 the US-Japan Treaty of Commerce and Navigation was abrogated and an embargo was placed on American exports of oil to Japan; in 1941 Japanese assets were frozen in the United States (and in the United Kingdom and the Netherlands). The Pacific headquarters of the American navy were moved from the West Coast to Pearl Harbor in Hawaii; a bill passed by the American Congress set the country on a huge program of naval buildup. In the face of these American actions, the Japanese military realized that the time frame – the window of opportunity – within which they could effectively operate was limited. If they were going to exploit the war raging throughout Europe in order to take over Southeast Asia, they had to move quickly before the American Pacific fleet was sufficiently powerful to check Japan's ambitions in Asia and the Pacific. With this in mind the

Japanese military began planning for a devastating attack on the American Pacific fleet in the fall of 1941, convinced that an American declaration of war against Japan would precipitate a German declaration of war against the United States, embroiling the United States in a two-front conflict, on the Pacific and on the Atlantic. After all in 1940 Japan had signed the Tripartite Pact with Germany and Italy, the Axis powers jettisoning the vague Anti-Comintern Pact for a military alliance.

Would the United States not be compelled to sue for peace with Japan, cutting a deal that would allow Japan to consolidate a vast empire in Asia and the Pacific, so that the Americans could concentrate on fighting the Nazis? After all, most Americans had descended from immigrants arriving in the new world from the various lands of Europe. Would not the German surge to hegemony in Europe be perceived as a more dangerous threat to the interests of the United States than Japan's surge to hegemony in the Asia-Pacific? Following this line of wishful thinking Japanese naval ships bristling with airplanes and pilots well versed in dive bombing, moved out towards Hawaii to attack Pearl Harbor in early December. Sinking or damaging eight battleships anchored in the harbor on December 7, the Japanese naval command felt it had done its job, giving diplomats on both sides of the Pacific the incentives and the opportunities to hammer out an agreement allowing Japan to consolidate its empire on the Eurasian mainland and in the island archipelagos to its south.

During December 1941 and early 1942, everything went as the Japanese high command wished: British Hong Kong fell on Christmas Day; Manila falling in January 1942, the American territory of the Philippines fell into Japanese hands soon after; and British Singapore, supposedly impregnable, fell to Japanese attack in mid-February. Soon thereafter Japanese forces moved into most of Southeast Asia and the Dutch East Indies, thereby assuring access to oil, rubber, tin, and other strategic materials required by an army and navy tasked to defend the perimeters and interior of the burgeoning Japanese empire, warding off attacks by the forces of its three enemies, the United States, the United Kingdom and China.

Even as the Japanese high command exulted in its bold moves – reminiscent of Hitler's blitzkrieg campaigns that led to the takeover of the Netherlands, Belgium and France – it realized it faced three major threats to its continued success: its vulnerability to aerial and submarine attacks that could create havoc with its supply lines; the fact that it faced three great foes; and most important the sheer size of the American economy, over five times the Japanese in terms of gross domestic product. It was understood that in a protracted war, the capacity of a belligerent country to spew out battleships, fighter planes, tanks, submarines, bombers, could be decisive. From Japan's point of view prior to December 1941 the United States was a sleeping giant. Would an awakened economic giant prove to be an implacable foe?

Indeed amongst the leaderships of all of the belligerents in World War II, there was a deeply ingrained belief that effective management of the economy – including the economies of the home country and of territories conquered through force of arms – was a key component of success in a protracted military campaign. Armed with this knowledge Japan's military cabinets and military planners began developing an economic model for achieving their diverse goals during the 1930s. The economic model of the New Order naturally stood on two legs: domestic and international. How rooted was this model in the command and control mode basic to hierarchical organizational structures epitomized by military organizations? To what extent did it rely on the modes of government interaction with the economy that had evolved out of years of experimentation under the *fukoku kyōhei* rubric? How crucial were stabilization, welfare, regulation and facilitating/coordinating modes in the political economy of the New Order?

In the domestic arena, the military cabinets brought forward legislation approved by the Diet that smacked of the command and control mode. In 1936 planning began for an Industrial Patriotic Movement modeled on that created under the Nazi law of 1934 setting up national labor organizations at the enterprise level. Under this plan labor unions and labor federations were to be dissolved. In 1940 most were; by 1943 there were only three tiny unions left in Japan. It should be emphasized that the Industrial Patriotic Movement was building on something that the private market had already been fashioning: the internalization of labor that was pioneered for white-collar workers during the 1920s. Nationalization of key sectors was another goal of the military. In 1938 two major laws nationalized the electric power industry within Japan, creating nine government controlled regional power companies. In 1938 under the aegis of the Materials Mobilization Plan, the government moved to create a linkage system wedding imports directly to exports. At first introduced for raw cotton – later extended to leather and rubber – the only imports of raw cotton allowed were those that would be used to produce exports. As these three examples illustrate, the military cabinets were not opposed to experimenting with command and control type policies.

At the same time it is clear that the military cabinets relied heavily on the other modes of government-economy interaction. After all the Control faction that had been willing to work within the traditional modes of managing the economy had defeated the Imperial Way faction in 1936. The military cabinets of the late 1930s attempted to regulate prices, setting up a Central Price Committee, developing a program for government purchase of all of the rice generated by Japanese farmers with the aim of setting prices on both the supply and demand side. They bolstered the regulatory environment governing the stock market, limiting dividends to be paid on stock issued in the market. They attempted to further consolidate the banking sector, reducing the number of banks from 186 in 1941 to 61 in 1945. They shifted the burden of taxation from income and taxation originally based on land, sales of luxuries, and imports to the taxation of household incomes and corporate profits. They began experimenting with a program of transferring government revenues from industrial districts to rural areas.

In short, the military cabinets relied heavily on fiscal, regulatory and welfare modes to bolster the coffers of the government; to stabilize financial and commodity markets; and to transfer income to a rural sector smarting from protracted decline in income relative to urban districts, that had directly felt the social harmony of its centuries old villages dissolve in bitter, often violent, dissension between landlords and tenants. Noguchi (1998) refers to the package of fiscal, regulatory, welfare and Industrial Patriotic Movement policies as the 1940 system, arguing that adoption of the system under the aegis of New Order ideology set the stage for the institutions and policies basic to the miracle growth period from the mid-1950s to the early 1970s. He argues that wholesale internalization of labor within larger firms in the postwar period – enterprise level unionism, wages based on age and seniority, guaranteed employment until mandatory retirement – was rooted in the 1940 legislation promoting enterprise level integration of management and labor. He argues that the shift to a system of financing investment through a relatively small number of banks rather than through the stock market emerged in the late 1930s as a result of bureaucratic pressure and cabinet approved legislation. And he argues that a system for shoring up the rural sector at the expense of the urban sector through transfer programs and a revamping of taxation was also a byproduct of the New Order.

Noguchi's argument has its merits, but there are some reasons to be skeptical about its overarching validity. First, the command and control mode experiments of the New Order were abandoned in the aftermath of the war; second, many of the developments that he sees as appearing under military rule actually began much earlier: labor markets were being internalized in the 1920s; and banking was being restructured during the late 1920s. As for equity financing it should be noted that ultra-nationalist political pressure on the old-line *zaibatsu* actually encouraged them to enter the stock market. As for shoring up the rural sector, the failure of the bureaucracy and cabinets to get a major land reform bill through the Diet inevitably put pressure on the government to redistribute income to rural areas. Rural discontent could not be ignored indefinitely. Encouraging emigration to the empire did not seem to be solving the problem. Moreover, as we shall see in the next chapter, many of the most important changes that set the stage for miracle growth – the expansion of education, collective bargaining, dissolution of the *zaibatsu*, land reform, dramatic reduction in military spending, the setting of a fixed exchange rate between the yen and the United States dollar, a drastic shift in exports toward the United States and away from Asia – came during the late 1940s and the early 1950s. Arguing that the 1940 system left traces on the economy of the 1950s and 1960s is plausible; arguing that it was fundamental to miracle growth is not.

While the military architects of the New Order were most active in drafting plans for the domestic economy they did not ignore the economic development of Japan's colonial possessions. Indeed, the army was active in developing the idea of the Greater East Asia Co-Prosperity Sphere, believing that Japan would promote economic development for all of East Asia including Southeast Asia through its promotion of the "flying geese" model of development. Developed by Akamatsu Kaname for the army during the 1930s, the "flying geese" paradigm had three major components: the product cycle for particular sectors within a nation or regional economy, the image of a sector moving from import substitution through exports and back to imports captured in the picture of a goose crossing the horizon; the shifting comparative advantage of nations or regional economies as the geese fly across the horizon in a wedge-shaped pattern, the lead goose cutting the horizon first, breaking the air for the successor geese; and the geographic realignment of nations or groups within a trade zone, labor intensive industries in the industrial heartland moving out into the periphery zones under the pressure of rising real wages in the heartland. In the third proposition – the one involving geographic realignment – it is evident that the lead goose is the industrial heartland, namely Japan in the Greater East-Asia Co-Prosperity Sphere.

As applied to Japan's empire in early 1942 the implications of the model are clear enough: Japan is the lead goose; the newly industrial zones of Korea, Northern China and Manchuria are the geese immediately behind Japan; and Southeast Asia follows behind the Korean, Chinese and Manchurian geese. As the lead goose advances steadily forward, more and more industries flow to the geese immediately behind it through the principle of geographic realignment. In turn the older labor intensive industries in the geese of the second rank – in Korea for instance – move to the geese of the third rank. In this way all zones with the empire benefit from belonging to it.

The economic advantages of being within the Japanese empire were certainly designed to encourage pro-Japanese sentiments in the areas conquered by the Japanese army and the Japanese navy during the 1930s and 1940s. Another selling point was political. Asia for Asians was preferable to Asia run by European powers, by the British, Dutch, and French. The Europeans had been arrogant towards Asians, contemptuous of them, racist in their thinking. Japanese colonialism might be colonialism, but at least it was not colonialism directed by Europeans or Americans.

The problem, indeed the inherent contradiction, with the political argument in favor of the Greater East-Asia Co-Prosperity Sphere is not hard to see. Japanese ultra-nationalism as expressed in racist ideas like *nihonjinron* and *kokutai* served as the ideological umbrella underpinning the militarism of the 1930s and 1940s. Most of the Japanese who went abroad – either as soldiers or sailors in the armed forces or as settlers or as bureaucrats implementing the polices of the Greater East-Asia Co-Prosperity Sphere – felt far superior to the peoples that were being incorporated in the empire. After all they were part and parcel of the national essence, the mystical *kokutai*. Not surprisingly, these Japanese were often cruel, brutal and vicious in their treatment of the peoples whom the Japanese army and navy

The Kwangtung Army

Infamous for its unit 731 that carried out biological warfare experiments during World War II – including vivisection on prisoners of war, injecting individuals with gruesome infectious diseases – the Kwangtung Army (also known as the Kantōgun) played a pivotal role in shaping Japan's military and political posture on the Eurasian mainland. Its behavior during the late 1920s and 1930s, operating independently of the civilian political leadership and even of the Imperial Japanese Army high command that controlled its actions in name only, is a dramatic indicator of the factionalism that divided the Japanese military during the fifteen years after 1930.

Originally established as the Kwangtung Garrison to defend the Kwangtung Leased Territory, its ranks including troops stationed along the South Manchurian Railway that had been wrested away from Russia after the Russo-Japanese war of 1904–05. The Imperial Japanese Army's interest in moving northward and eastward from its northern Chinese base in the Kwangtung Leased Territory was signaled early on by its occupation of significant portions of Siberian Russian territory in 1918–22 during the chaos of the civil war that broke out in Russia in the aftermath of the Russian Revolution. After the Japanese army left Russia in 1922, signing a peace treaty with the Soviet Union in 1924, the Kwangtung Army focused on bringing all of Manchuria under its heel. In 1927 and again in 1928 officers of the Kwangtung Army carried out provocations designed to trigger conflict between their units and the troops of the Chinese warlord ruling Manchuria, failing to ignite a full-fledged war in both years. Finally, in the Mukden Incident of 1931, the Kwangtung Army, having blown up a portion of the South Manchurian Railroad, blamed the Chinese for the attack, thereby garnering the excuse they had long sought for taking over Mukden and eventually conquering all of Manchuria. Presented with the problem of setting up a puppet government under nominal Chinese rule as a cover for Kwangtung Army rule, the Japanese authorities approached the former emperor of China, Pi-Yu – who had sought protection in the Japanese Embassy in 1924 after the agreement of abdication he and his advisors had negotiated in 1912 was called into question by Chinese warlords and by Chiang Kai-shek – with an offer to make him regent, and ultimately emperor, over the state of Manchuria. In 1934 Pi-Yu became the emperor of Manchuko, ruler in name only as his advisors were gradually purged from his government, being replaced by Japanese officials loyal to the Kwangtung Army.

From its base in Manchuko, the Kwangtung Army now pushed eastward, into Chinese territory to the south, and into Soviet dominated Mongolia to the north. In 1933 it secured control over the former Chinese province of Jehol, forcing China to recognize it as an independent country, one that the Kwangtung Army quickly turned into a second puppet state.

Penetrating Inner Mongolia at the same time, the Kwangtung Army began probing territory that the Soviets were intent on keeping as a buffer zone between themselves and Japanese dominated Manchuko. In 1938 at Zhanggufeng, and at Nomonham in 1939, the Kwangtung Army fought the Soviet Union's Red Army, going down to bloody defeat. Securing a ceasefire in 1939, Japan and the Soviet Union negotiated a neutrality pact, freeing up the Red Army to move its troops back to the west and freeing up the Imperial

Japanese Army to focus on its ongoing invasion of China. An alliance of convenience, the pact actually remained in effect until 8 August 1945, when the Soviets joined the United States and the United Kingdom in their war against Japan. At this point the Red Army swept into Manchuria, decimating a Kwangtung Army whose reserves of weapons, ammunition and fighting force had already been depleted by the Imperial Japanese Army's decision to deploy most of the army's units in the Pacific islands, pitting them against American military units that were working their way up towards Japan through a campaign of island hopping.

Testimony to the Kwangtung Army's prestige, many of its leaders secured important positions in the Imperial Japanese Army and in the military cabinets of the 1930s and early 1940s. In particular Tōjō Hideki rose from the Kwangtung Army to become Prime Minister of Japan, occupying the post from October of 1941 through July of 1944. In a number of dimensions – political, strategic and military – the leadership of the Kwangtung Army was the very embodiment of the Japanese militarism that intensified after World War I, only to perish in the ashes of defeat that ended World War II.

subjugated. Pointing out that the Europeans and Americans could be supercilious did not make the Japanese any less reprehensible in the eyes of Malays, Chinese, Koreans and Filipinos. Overextended militarily and hated by many of the peoples whom they conquered during the 1930s and 1940s, Japan faced mounting difficulties in defending the perimeters and territorial possessions of its vast empire by the late 1940s. American submarine attacks harassed Japanese shipping; in the spring of 1942 Japanese naval losses in the battles of Coral Sea and Midway blunted Japan's thrust towards Australia and New Zealand. By early 1945 Japan was in retreat on all fronts, losing islands in the Pacific and territory it had taken in Southeast Asia. To add to Japan's woes, the war in Europe was gradually coming to an end as Germany collapsed, squeezed between advancing British and American armies coming from the west and south and Russian armies sweeping in from the east.

Under the doctrine of unconditional surrender, the brainchild of President Franklin D. Roosevelt of the United States and Prime Minister Winston Churchill of the United Kingdom, the enemies of the three major allied powers – the United States, the United Kingdom and the Soviet Union – were ordered to surrender without conditions. Heavily criticized within the allied camp because of its vagueness and its rigidity, the unconditional surrender doctrine had one great virtue: it prevented any one of the allied powers from signing a separate ceasefire agreement with an enemy about to go down in defeat. It did hold the allied alliance – unstable at best given that it welded together communist totalitarian Russia with the two great Anglo-American powers committed to liberal democracy – together in bringing the war in Europe to an end. The problem in the late spring and summer of 1945 was whether the doctrine would impede Japanese surrender. Fighting for the *kokutai* as embodied in the emperor was crucial to the Japanese war effort. If Japan surrendered unconditionally, would it see its emperor system abolished?

Meeting at Potsdam in late July and early August, the leaders of the allied powers (Harry Truman now President of the United States taking office upon Roosevelt's death) drew up plans for the reconstruction of Germany and the final conquest and reconstruction of Japan. Stalin, having already given his word in earlier conferences held by the big three powers that he would soon enter the war against Japan, stood by in the sidelines as Truman, Attlee (taking Churchill's place) and Chiang Kai-shek representing China hammered out a statement that they hoped would convince the Japanese leadership to surrender. This declaration – the Potsdam Declaration – was to serve as a blueprint for the allied occupation of

The Potsdam Declaration

On 2 May 1945, Premier Josef Stalin announced the fall of Berlin as seventy thousand German troops laid down their arms in a defeat that Adolf Hitler declared would never come. Five days later, the leaders of Germany formally surrendered to the nations united in their onslaught upon the dismal remainder of its greatly depleted armed forces. Between July 17 and 2 August, 1945, the leaders of the Soviet Union, the United States and the United Kingdom met at Potsdam, near the very Berlin their forces had just conquered, dictating the terms and conditions governing the planned occupation of German territory. On August 2, Harry Truman signing for the United States, Clement Attlee for the United Kingdom, and Josef Stalin for the Soviet Union, issued a declaration that covered a number of points pertaining to the occupation of Germany and the establishment of a council (eventually known as the Security Council) for the United Nations.

Under the terms of the declaration Germany was to be divided into four zones of occupation – American, British, French and Russian – from which each of the victorious powers could secure reparations. The National Socialist Party (Nazi) was ordered dissolved; provisions for the arrest of war criminals and important Nazi officials were set forth; German disarmament and demilitarization was demanded; and justification for an occupation period long enough to establish democratic institutions in the defeated nation was laid out.

Meeting separately at Potsdam, Harry Truman, Winston Churchill (soon to lose the British election thereby being replaced by Clement Attlee for the final negotiating of the August 2 declaration) and Chiang Kai-shek laid out

the conditions for Japan's surrender. This declaration was issued on 26 July 1945, and to the Japanese is known as the Potsdam Declaration. Boasting that " the prodigious land, sea and air forces of the United States, the British Empire, and of China" are "poised to strike the final blows upon Japan," the declaration called for Japan's leaders, their nation tottering on "the threshold of annihilation" to "follow the path of reason", acknowledging the defeat that the powers allied against it were determined to impose upon it through their combined military muscle. In line with the terms being negotiated for the German occupation, the allies indicated that they intended to occupy Japan "until their basic objectives" were met, those objectives including the stamping out of militarism within Japan, and the meting out of "stern justice" against war criminals and "those who have visited cruelties upon our prisoners". In addition, the declaration made it clear that strengthening democratic institutions and ensuring the establishment of "freedom of speech, of religion, and of thought, as well as respect for the fundamental human rights" was a goal of the planned occupation.

Japan.In the wake of the issuing of the Potsdam Declaration events moved swiftly. On August 6, the United States dropped an atomic bomb on Hiroshima; on August 8, the Soviet Union declared war on Japan, its troops swarming into Manchuria and taking the Kurile islands north of Hokkaidō; on August 9 the United States dropped a second atomic bomb, this time on Nagasaki, the original target in northern Kyūshū being too covered in clouds to be bombed.

Noguchi Jun, Nitchitsu, and the atomic bomb

From a military viewpoint, the chemicals industry is of immense strategic value, well worth subsidizing especially in time of war or in preparation for war. The industry produces many things – fertilizers, plastics, vinyl, carbide – including gunpowder and other explosives that are used in manufacturing bombs and munitions of all types. The emergence of the Nitchitsu (Japan Nitrogen Fertilizer Company) under the leadership of Noguchi Jun as a new zaibatsu (shinzaibatsu) during the 1930s and its intimate connection with the last ditch effort on the part of the Japanese military to fashion an atomic bomb during the closing months of the Pacific war amply illustrates the intertwining of military demand and industrial progress that intensified during the 1930s in the key strategic sectors of Japanese manufacturing.

Noguchi Jun was a college graduate engineer who began his career in the fields of hydroelectric power generation and chemicals during the early twentieth century. Induced by the inhabitants of the village of Minamata, on the west coast of southern Kyūshū to set up a carbide production plant using the electrical power from a power plant he had helped build nearby, Noguchi established Nitchitsu and struggled to make a go of it in the carbide business, branching off into the creation of metamorphic ammonium based chemical fertilizers in an attempt to diversify out of carbide alone, the market largely limited to making lights for night fishing. Even in this new fertilizer business, however, Nitchitsu's survival and prosperity were hardly guaranteed. Low cost imports of chemical fertilizers threatened to undercut its business. Bailed out from potential insolvency by the curtailing of imports during World War I, Nitchitsu managed to establish a virtual monopoly in the domestic supply of chemical fertilizers. After World War I, Noguchi visited Europe, securing the rights to the new Casale ammonia synthesis technology that was still in an experimental stage. Searching for ever cheaper sources of hydroelectric power to fuel his fertilizer business, Noguchi moved outside of Japan proper, setting up production in Korea with the construction of a massive electric power plant at Hungnum, the largest in Asia.

With the growth in military demand for explosives during the early 1930s, Nitchitsu secured lucrative contracts, ultimately setting up its own zaibatsu structure in 1934, an example of the new zaibatsu spun off by militarism. Not only did Nitchitsu supply explosives and synthetics to the military; it also developed hydroelectric power plants and manufactured dam making machinery at various facilities throughout Korea. It was its base in Korean hydroelectric power generation and its expertise in manufacturing chemicals useful in munitions production that brought Noguchi Jun into the race to produce an atomic bomb, developing it at a plant in Konan.

Nitchitsu's massive Konan complex tapped into the greatest hydroelectric power grid in the Japanese empire. Moreover, Korea was a source of uranium ores. Not surprisingly, one of Noguchi's Korean companies – the Korean Nitrogen Fertilizer Company – began to mine uranium during the early 1940s, presumably working under contract from the Japanese military. Although many of the documents and machines relating to Nitchitsu's activities in processing uranium-bearing ores and the construction of an atomic bomb were destroyed in August 1945 – blown up with dynamite by Nitchitsu scientists only hours before the Soviet Union's troops, already advancing through Manchuria, reached Korea – there is ample evidence that Nitchitsu's effort in atomic bomb manufacture was nearing success, perhaps had been successful, in the closing days and months of the Pacific war.

> In the aftermath of the war, Japan lost its empire, and Nitchitsu lost its affiliated companies and facilities in Korea. Renaming his company Shin Nitchitsu (New Nitchitsu), Noguchi returned to his Minamata roots, producing chemical fertilizers and branching off into the manufacture of polyvinyl chloride that was used in making the polyvinyl chloride plastics employed in wrapping electric wires.
>
> One of the byproducts of the Shin Nitchitsu plant at Minamata was organic mercury that it dumped into Minamata Bay as wastewater. In 1955 the first signs of Minamata disease appeared – mercury poisoning due to eating fish that had been caught in and around Minamata Bay. Some individuals, primarily fishing families, began to display signs of mercury poisoning, including dizziness and an inability to see clearly. It is said that cats fed the fish did wild dances before perishing.
>
> After researchers at the national university in Kumamoto prefecture where Minamata is located documented the connection between Nitchitsu wastewater and the terrifying neurological disease, Shin Nitchitsu responded to the public outcry by first attacking the credentials of the researchers, ultimately providing modest compensation to the victims and building a water purification system that it claimed would remove any mercury byproducts in its wastewater. By 1960 the company and the Japanese government claimed that the disease was vanquished. However, new cases have continued to crop up not only in Minamata but also in nearby communities. Shin Nitchitsu's intimate connection with the Japanese government, forged during the 1930s in the Korea based hydroelectric and atomic bomb projects of Noguchi Jun, continued to shelter it for a while. But not forever. Ultimately a media campaign predicated on documenting the horrors of Minamata disease in photographs and literature created a public environment hostile to the chemical company, inducing the courts to award compensation for damages far in excess of that originally provided by Shin Nitchitsu.

At Japan's Supreme War council meeting on August 9 the question of whether Japan should accept the conditions laid down in the Potsdam Declaration was bitterly debated, the chiefs of staff of the army and navy arguing that holding out longer might yield more favorable surrender conditions. Even in Japan's darkest hour, fierce factionalism continued to impede decision making at the highest level. The emperor coming down on the side of surrender, the Japanese leadership finally agreed to send telegrams to the allied powers indicating that they would accept the terms of the Potsdam Declaration. Six days later, on August 15, the Emperor of Japan delivered a radio address beamed into the remotest corners of the land, announcing that Japan would end its participation in the war, enduring the unendurable.

A great historical arc begun in 1868 was completed in the late summer and early fall of 1945.

Fukoku kyōhei had emerged as an umbrella ideology uniting Westernizers supporting liberal values of democracy and individualism, ultra-nationalists and militarists bent on beefing up Japan's military prowess, and a nascent business community in the common cause of promoting Japanese industrialization through the import and adaptation of foreign technology. By the early 1920s the *fukoku kyōhei* consensus had broken down completely. Groups bent on military aggrandizement were as often as not at loggerheads with those advocating market oriented economic growth and democracy. Throughout most of the 1920s those committed to markets, democracy and international cooperation – with the Anglo-American powers, with the League of Nations – were in the ascendancy, though threatened by opposition from within the military and from threats issuing out of the growing ultra-nationalist community. During the 1930s the military and the ultra-nationalists gradually managed to seize control over the political agenda, pushing Japan into military adventures on the Eurasian mainland, promoting the ideology of the *kokutai* as a rationale for their actions that placed a far greater weight on *kyōhei* than on *fukoku*, developing the New Order as the blueprint for the political economy of Japan's burgeoning empire in Asia.

Pushed and pulled by a bewildering sequence of political and military realignments in Europe in the aftermath of England's declaration of war against Germany – awash with geopolitical and ideological conflicts – factions in Japan's leadership argued and debated over how Japan should align itself in the global conflict that seemed on the near horizon. Some wanted to fight the Soviets; some wanted to strike south, taking over British and Dutch colonial territories, absorbing China along the way; some wanted to take on the United States that threatened to stymie Japan's advances to the south. It is likely that no faction wanted to fight the Soviets, the Americans, the British and the Chinese simultaneously. Yet this is what happened in early August 1945.

The fruits, the yield, of *kyōhei* seemed hollow at best, poisonous, bringing on humiliating defeat, undermining *fukoku* through the drastic reduction in Japanese per capita income suffered during the isolation of a protracted Pacific war and the destruction of much of Japan's capital stock in the American aerial bombing campaign that laid to ruins much of the real estate in the great metropolises of the Tōkaidō industrial belt.

On 2 September 1945, as the formal surrender of Japan took place on the decks of the USS Missouri, it seemed that the *fukoku kyōhei* itself was being laid to rest. Certainly what was to take its place was unclear, not at all obvious to Japan's elite, not at all obvious to its non-elite masses, shocked and shaken as they were by the enormity of accepting the conditions of unendurable defeat. One thing was clear: a new day was about to dawn.

Key terms and concepts in Chapter 6

Fascism

Totalitarianism

London naval treaty

Manchuko

Imperial Way and Control factions

New Order

Long swings

Trend acceleration

Wage bill per unit of capital

Social capability for importing and adapting foreign technology

Implicit contracts in the labor market

Ministry of Commerce and Industry rationalization policies

Infrastructure-driven growth

Shinzaibatsu

Kokutai

Anti-Cominterm and Tripartite Pacts

Industrial Patriotic Movement

Greater East-Asia Co-Prosperity Sphere

Potsdam Declaration

Part III
Convergence

7   Japan in the new international economic order

The cold war and the golden age of convergence

The two decades after 1950 were truly a golden age. Per capita income growth rates were substantial and sweeping. A wide range of countries came to enjoy historically unprecedented levels of prosperity by 1970: the United States and Canada in North America; most of Western European excluding the Iberian region, and Japan in East Asia. Moreover, while the Soviet Union and the eastern European communist regions positioned between Russia and Western Europe did not reach Western European levels of wellbeing per person by the early 1970s, they did achieve rapid per capita income growth averaged over the two decades between 1950 and 1970.

The era is sometimes known as the golden age of convergence. Convergence refers to the fact that countries tend to look more and more alike over time, notably in terms of per capita income. One particular version of the hypothesis asserts that countries starting out with a relatively low initial per capita income level grow faster than countries starting out with a higher initial standard of living. This is sometimes called the "catch-up" growth hypothesis. One story about convergence consistent with this is that there is a leader, the highest income, technologically most advanced economy, and a host of followers that "catch-up" with the leader. The "catch-up" growth hypothesis rests on two assertions about the logic of economic growth in lower income countries, one involving accumulation of capital and the other involving absorbing technology from the leading country. As for capital accumulation, lower per capita income countries enjoy less capital per worker than high-income countries. Being capital poor – lacking factories, roads, hydroelectric generating plants – each increment to their capital stock, each new factory, yields a larger increment to output than would occur in a capital abundant economy. Technological progress, one of the key elements of total factor productivity growth, is another matter. Firms in lower income per capita countries can and do secure technologies and organizational practices – license it, carry out reverse engineering – from firms in more advanced high income countries, thereby promoting growth in output per unit of combined (capital and labor combined) input.

The convergence hypothesis is easily captured in the following equation that can be estimated by regression analysis (see the Appendix to this volume, "Japanese Economic Development: A Statistical Portrait," for a brief discussion of regression analysis):

$$G(y) = a_0(yin) + \varepsilon \tag{7.1}$$

the left hand term being the growth rate of income per capita over a given period; the variable "yin" is the level of income per capita at the beginning of the period; and the coefficient a_0 representing the influence of initial income per capita levels on growth. For the convergence hypothesis to hold the estimate for a_0 should be negative.

Evidence that "leader/follower" convergence has occurred between 1950 and 1973 appears in Panel A of Table 7.1.

Table 7.1 The calculus of convergence, the cold war, and crossover, 1950–1973

Panel A   *Convergence for seventeen advanced industrial economies*

Country	Real income per capita, 1950	Growth rates, 1950–1973% for:		Real income per capita, 1973
		Real income	Population	
Japan	1,873	8.0	0.7	11,017
Italy	3,425	5.0	0.7	10,409
Austria	3,731	4.9	0.4	11,308
Finland	4,131	4.3	0.7	10,768
Germany	4,281	5.0	0.9	13,152
Norway	4,969	3.2	0.8	10,229
France	5,221	4.0	1.0	12,940
Belgium	5,346	3.5	0.5	11,905
Netherlands	5,850	3.4	1.2	12,763
Denmark	6,683	3.1	0.7	13,416
Sweden	6,738	3.1	0.6	13,494
United Kingdom	6,847	2.5	0.5	11,992
Canada	7,047	2.9	1.1	13,644
Australia	7,218	2.4	1.4	12,485
New Zealand	8,495	1.7	0.7	12,575
Switzerland	8,939	3.1	1.4	17,953
United States	9,573	2.4	1.0	16,607
Average	5,904	3.7	0.8	12,745
Gap (highest minus lowest): absolute	7,700			7,724
Gap: relative to average income per capita in group	1.30			0.61

Table 7.1 Continued

Panel B *Growth and income per capita in seven eastern bloc countries and China, 1950–1973%*

Country	Real income per capita, 1950	Growth rates, 1950–1973% for:		Real income per capita, 1973
		Real income per capita,	Population	
China	614	2.9	1.5	1,186
Romania	1,182	4.8	1.1	3,447
Yugoslavia	1,516	4.4	1.1	4,738
Bulgaria	1,651	5.2	0.8	5,284
Poland	2,447	3.4	1.3	5,334
Hungary	2,480	3.6	0.5	5,596
Soviet Union	2,834	3.4	1.4	6,058
Czechoslovakia	3,501	3.1	0.7	7,036
Average	2,032	3.9	1.1	4,835
Gap (highest minus lowest): absolute	2,887			5,580
Gap: relative to average income per capita in group	1.42			1.21
Seven eastern bloc (European) countries only				
Gap (highest minus lowest): absolute	2,319			3,589
Gap: relative to average income per capita in group	1.04			0.67

Panel C *Calculus of the cold war: indices with denominator the average or total value of the variable for eastern bloc countries including China = 100, numerator the average or total value of the variable for the seventeen advanced industrial economies*

Variable	1950	1973
Population (total)	61.2	51.9
Income per capita (average)	205.0	355.0
Income (total)	126.0	184.0

(*Table 7.1 continued*)

Table 7.1 Continued

Panel D   *Crossover comparison, seven Latin American countries*

Country	Real income per capita, 1950	Growth rates, 1950–1973% for:		Real income per capita, 1973
		Real income per capita,	Population	
Brazil	1,673	3.8	2.9	3,913
Mexico	2,085	3.1	3.2	4,189
Columbia	2,089	2.3	2.9	3,539
Peru	2,263	2.5	2.8	3,953
Chile	3,827	1.2	2.2	5,028
Argentina	4,987	2.2	1.7	7,970
Venezuela	7,424	1.6	3.8	10,717
Average	3,478	2.4	2.8	5,616
Gap (highest minus lowest): absolute	5,751			7,178
Gap: relative to average income per capita in group	1.65			1.28

Source: Various tables in Maddison (2000).

In this panel the countries are ranked in inverse order to their initial (1950) level of per capita income. As can be seen the growth rate of income per capita tends to be larger the lower the initial level of income per capita. Taking the United States as the leader in 1950, we can see that the other sixteen advanced industrial economies converged towards American standard of living by 1973; indeed Switzerland even surpassed the American level. Thus at the proximate level – at the level of the nuts and bolts of an economy – convergence is tied up with accumulation and technological progress. But what larger picture lies behind these nuts and bolts? Why did the golden age occur at this particular historical watershed?

One theory emphasizes the expansion of trade and the ending of wars between major industrial nations (wars continued to occur including civil conflicts and regional conflicts involving one great power pitted against a less economically advanced adversary but not wars sucking at least two industrial giants into the vortex of armed conflict), attributing this salutary state of affairs to the hegemonic power wielded by the United States in the aftermath of World War II. This argument is based upon the theory of hegemonic cycles. In the aftermath of a major conflict, only one contender for global hegemony emerges, economically and politically dominant. In order to promote its trade it creates public goods that other countries benefit from. Free riding off the public goods supplied by the hegemonic giant, the other countries expand their economies, eventually challenging the leader.

For instance according to estimates appearing in Maddison (1995), the national income of the United States was about 27 percent of world income in 1950, and about 56 percent of the combined incomes of the seventeen advanced industrial powers listed in Panel A of Table 7.1. A colossus striding across the world stage, its private industrial capital stock largely untouched by the great conflict engulfing the world between 1939 and 1945, the United States promoted international multilateral agencies – the United Nations, the International Labor Organization, the World Bank, the International Monetary Fund, the General Agreement on Tariffs and Trade (the G.A.T.T.) – with the aim of encouraging a reduction in trade barriers and the avoidance armed conflicts between major industrial countries. At the regional level it was happy to serve as midwife for movements toward regional economic cooperation – the establishment of the European Iron and Steel Community that eventually laid the groundwork for the European Economic Community and later the European Union – that reduced the possibility of tensions between traditional adversaries like Germany and France.

A second line of argument attributes American support for multilateral organizations to the outbreak of the Cold War, a protracted geopolitical and ideological struggle between the alliance of the United States with other major capitalist powers (e.g. the United Kingdom, Western Germany, France, Italy in Western Europe and Japan in East Asia) and the alliance of the Soviet Union with its major Eastern European Iron Curtain allies (East Germany, Czechoslovakia, Hungary, Poland, Bulgaria and Romania) and with mainland China that fell under Communist rule after protracted civil war in 1949. According to this analysis, Stalin sought a buffer zone between Russia and Western Europe, therefore he encouraged Communist takeovers of the so-called Iron Curtain countries in the aftermath of World War II. The United States was far more powerful and its economy far larger than that of the Soviet Union. However Russia had the advantage of geography: to get to the core of Europe it could move its troops across the land while the United States had to move them across the vast waters of the Atlantic Ocean. The "stopping power of water" worked against the military prowess of the United States in the European political theater.

Adding to the Communist threat was sheer size of the total population of the Soviet Union and its Communist allies. From the power equation, the military power of a country or an alliance of countries is:

$$M = mY = m(yP) \tag{7.2}$$

where "m" is the rate at which a country converts its national income to military purposes, and Y is national income, equaling per capita income (y) times population (P). From Panels B and C of Table 7.1 it is apparent that while the Soviet Union and its allies had far lower per capita incomes than the Western European allies of the United States, growth in the Communist bloc was not shabby, and the population size of the Communist powers combined was formidable. Indeed, the estimates in Panel C suggest that the Communist advantage in terms of human numbers actually increased between 1950 and 1973 because population growth rates were lower amongst the allies of the United States than they were amongst the allies of the Soviet Union (compare the population growth rates in Panel A with those in Panel B). This said, because the average income per capita of the capitalist country alliance was far greater than that of the Communist country alliance, the overall income advantage that the capitalist countries had over their Communist adversaries actually increased between 1950 and 1970 (from a relative indexed level of 126 to a level of 184). To equal the military potential of the capitalist countries, the Communist countries had to convert their income to military purposes at higher rates than did the capitalist countries, thereby pressuring downward the standard of living of their peoples.

In setting out the logic of the Cold War competition argument, I do not want to imply that all seventeen of the advanced industrial countries were allied politically with the United States. Sweden, Ireland, Austria, Switzerland remained neutral; Finland, although a member of the Nordic Council, was under heavy – and heavy handed – Soviet influence. Still, most of the neutral countries tended to gravitate more toward the Western European allies of the United States than toward the Soviet Bloc, at least in their trade and commercial dealings. However limits on the extent of this gravitation towards the West should never be forgotten. For instance international capital markets were not particularly open during the golden age of convergence. Investors in countries converging towards American levels of per capita income had to rely mainly on domestic savings for capital accumulation. As Obstfeld and Taylor (2004) show in detail the volume of international capital movements was extensive during the heyday of the first gold standard between 1880 and 1914, investors throughout the world drawing upon capital markets in London, Paris and New York. However this period of international capital mobility came to a dismal end with the onset of World War I which ushered in a long period of international capital immobility that did not really come to an end until the 1980s. Political alignment with the United States did not guarantee an inflow of capital from the United States or from its major allies in Europe like the United Kingdom and France.

In sum, from the perspective of the United States the political calculus of the Cold War involved containing the spread of Communism in Eurasia, bottling it up, not letting it spread across a line in the sand drawn around the southern borders of China in East Asia and along the Pacific coastline of Eurasia, keeping Japan and Taiwan (to which the Chinese nationalist opponents of the Communists had fled after 1949) free from the Communist menace. It was to contain Asian Communism that the United States and its allies fought the North Koreans and Chinese in the Korean War that raged between 1950 and 1953, leaving the Korean peninsula divided approximately along the 38th parallel that has become a demilitarized zone, no permanent peace treaty ending the conflict having been signed. It was also in this context that the United States and Japan signed a series of mutual security treaties during the 1950s leading up the treaty of mutual cooperation and security initialed in 1960. Containment also served as the backdrop for the Vietnam War that the United States fought during the 1960s and early 1970s. Containment in Asia involved more active hot wars than did containment in the European theater.

One important background feature that is a backdrop to the "leader/follower" convergence interpretation of the experience of the seventeen advanced industrial countries is the relatively steady growth of the leader, the United States. Recall that during the Great Depression the American economy faltered, a major factor precipitating the geopolitical crises of the 1930s. Several reasons have been

The US–Japan treaty of mutual security

Twice before its capitulation to the United States and its allies ending the Pacific war, Japan had entered into alliances with the world's dominant naval powers: the Anglo–Japanese alliance of 1902 and the Washington naval treaty of 1922. In signing these agreements the government of Japan embraced alliance systems acknowledging the global prowess of the Anglo-American powers.

The Japanese government's decision to abandon the second alliance system during the 1930s was not only a capitulation to Japanese militarism and to opposition within the Imperial Japanese Navy to the conditions imposed on it by the Washington naval treaty. It also signaled a clear intent on the part of Japan to confront, rather than cooperate with, a geopolitical order hinged upon the military prowess of the Anglo-American powers. Japan's defeat at the end of the World War II and its occupation by the United States underlined the folly of this strategy.

In 1960 representatives of the governments of the United States and Japan put their signatures to a third treaty – formally known as the "Treaty of Mutual Cooperation and Security between Japan and the United States of America" – that built upon earlier mutual security agreements between Japan and the United States that were signed in 1949, 1951 and in 1954. Negotiations over the 1960 agreement became a major domestic political issue in Japan, precipitating massive left-wing demonstrations against the United States. Left-leaning Japanese felt that signing onto the alliance with the United States was de facto acknowledgement of Japan's status as a client state of the great North American power.

According to the articles of the treaty Japan agreed to work together with the United States towards the strengthening of the United Nations; it affirmed a commitment to free institutions; and it agreed to allow the United States to maintain bases on Japanese soil. In exchange the United States agreed to use its military force to deter armed attack directed at any of the territories under the administrative control of the Japanese government. The governments agreed to ongoing consultation concerning security issues of mutual interest to the two powers.

> *The political rationale underlying the treaty has been the subject of much debate. Did it allow Japan to "free ride" on American military might, focusing almost all of its resources to private sector economic advance? Was it an acknowledgement that domestic Japanese revulsion against the militarism of the 1930s was so deep seated that nothing short of an agreement that foreclosed on a return to confrontation with the Anglo-American powers would satisfy the majority of the electorate? Was American interest in negotiating the agreement designed to send a signal to other Asian powers, especially to the two Koreas and to China, the United States was committing itself to reining in any return to militarism on the part of the Japanese government? Was the American military primarily concerned with obtaining continued use of Japanese territory for the possible launch of military action against the Communist powers on the Eurasian mainland, Communist China, the Soviet Union and North Korea?*

advanced as why the United States enjoyed relatively stable post-1945 growth conditions: pent-up technological progress, federal government commitment to Keynesian demand management policies from the early 1960s onward, the development of automatic stabilizers associated with the welfare state, Cold War military spending and the expansion of global trade and commerce fueled in part by the activities of American multinational corporations. The pent-up technology thesis emphasizes the backlog of technologies – in communications, in the bulk shipping of goods, in airplane travel, in computation, in the manufacture of precision instruments – that were developed during the Great Depression and World War II and not put into commercial usage until the early 1950s. The welfare state policies referred to include unemployment insurance that transfers purchasing power to the unemployed during downturns in the economy, thereby promoting expansion. The argument around Cold War military spending rests on the idea that the federal government bolstered aggregate demand through its military spending, implicitly – not explicitly – inflating demand through the demand for military equipment.

A second background feature of the convergence process that should be mentioned is crossover. Crossover occurs when a country starting at a level of income per capita lower than that of another country surpasses that country later on, its income soaring past the country that started off in a more prosperous state. Crossover does not necessarily work against convergence, particularly in the case of convergence conceived in terms of countries looking more and more alike over time. A good example of crossover is Japan's crossover with the Latin American countries (see Panel D of Table 7.1). This is of particular interest because a number of Japanese nationals migrated to Latin America in the aftermath of World War II, settling in countries like Brazil, Chile and Paraguay. Many of these emigrants – or their children or grandchildren – returned to Japan during the 1980s and 1990s, attracted by the higher standard of living that Japan had managed to achieve compared to the Latin American nation states. In understanding this crossover phenomenon it is useful to highlight the potential importance of population growth. As is shown in Panel D of Table 7.1 population growth tended to be especially rapid in Latin America during the period when the seventeen advanced industrial economies were converging towards a fairly common income per capita level.

Convergence, crossover and the Cold War are the backdrop for the story of Japan's high speed – miracle – growth between 1955 and the early 1970s. Japan was hardly unique among the post-1950 period allies of the United States – linked to the political and economic giant through trade, diplomacy and transfer of technology – generating growth rates that exceeded those of its former enemy, now friend, lying across the waters of the Pacific Ocean. In laying the groundwork for a subsequent discussion of the interaction of the two economic powers that is a major theme in Japan's post-1950 economic performance, we need to consider albeit briefly the era of the Occupation of Japan (1945–52), when the fates of the two nations were more deeply intertwined than they were before the Occupation or subsequent to it.

The political economy of the American Occupation

The political economy of the allied powers' occupation of Japan – basically led and largely shaped by the United States – must be understood in terms of the stated goals of the allied powers as set forth in the Potsdam Declaration and the realities on the ground. The resources that the United States and its allies could devote to the effort were limited, forcing the three main non-Japanese bodies making occupation policy decisions – the Supreme Commander of the Allied Powers; the Far Eastern Commission meeting in Washington that represented all eleven countries having a direct role in the occupation; and the Allied Council for Japan that included the Supreme Commander, his/her deputy, representatives for the Soviet Union, for China plus one other delegate – to rely heavily upon the Japanese bureaucracy and Japan's political leadership for the actual drafting of legislation and a new constitution and for the implementation of fiscal and monetary policy.

An additional reality of the Occupation is that most of the occupying authorities had very limited knowledge about Japan. They operated with theories about why Japan had become so aggressive during the 1930s: the country had been hijacked by feudalistic militarists ideologically committed to nationalism who drew political sustenance from the cult of the emperor, supported in their endeavors by a repressive landlord system in the countryside and the *zaibatsu* in industrial circles. This was a view that was probably not shared by most Japanese – it was a view espoused by the Communist Party of Japan revitalized after its suppression under military rule especially after Japan signed the Anti-Comintern Pact – but it was a view that opportunists amongst the Japanese population seized upon in attempted to avoid being purged by the Occupation authorities. This said, there is no doubt that most Japanese felt a quiet revulsion towards militarism. In Germany the program of occupation centered about stamping out Nazi thought, purging the political leadership of former Nazi elements. In the case of Japan the program of occupation revolved around stamping out militarism, remodeling the emperor system to bring it in line with Western ideas about constitutional monarchy, solidifying democracy through the introduction of the universal franchise and the elimination of confusion about how the cabinet in the Diet was to be selected, and reform of education, eliminating emperor worship from the curriculum.

An additional reality shaping the direction that the Occupation took was geopolitical. Cold War tensions intensified during the late 1940s, the Iron Curtain coming down on Eastern Europe after 1946, civil war between Communists and Nationalists raging in China. After 1949 the Cold War conflict in Asia intensified, the Communists taking over the reins of power in Beijing, North Korea's army crossing the 38th parallel in June of 1950.

In humdrum hard practical day-to-day operation the Occupation of Japan from 1945 through mid-1952 involved so much give and take between occupiers and occupied that it is difficult to separate the agendas of the foreigners from the agendas of Japan's political and bureaucratic leadership, including the agendas of bureaucrats and politicians who had either spearheaded legislation, or had been stymied in achieving reforms, during the era of military rule from 1932 to 1945. Given the interaction of Japanese leaders and Occupation authorities widely different interpretations are possible. With this in mind it is not surprising that some schools of thought maintain that the bureaucracy that dominated Japan during the period of total war (1937–45) continued to call the shots, shaping the legislative and regulatory agenda of the Occupation while other schools of thought argue that many key themes in occupation policy were spun off the agendas of the occupiers, especially of the Americans.[1]

On some points there is consensus. Most writers accept the fact that promulgation of a new constitution for Japan was the most important contribution made by the Occupation. This was certainly the view of General Douglas MacArthur, the Supreme Commander of the Allied Powers from 1945 until he was removed from the post by President Harry Truman in April 1951.[2] For many Japanese, during the period the new constitution was drafted and ratified by the Diet at the behest of the Emperor, the new constitution was "made in America", it was something very different from what Japanese authors drafted. Proof that this was the case is indicated by the fact that the early drafts of the revised constitution, commencing with those coming out the Constitution Problem Investigation Committee set up under the cabinet in late 1945, hardly made any changes to the original Imperial Constitution of 1899: most important, the doctrine imperial sovereignty was retained.

What finally emerged from the government for approval by the emperor and the Diet in the summer of 1946 strongly reflected the views of MacArthur and his advisors. The concept of *kokutai*, national polity, was downplayed; political and civil liberties – including equality for women in voting and education – were guaranteed; checks and balances were built in to the law writing process (the Supreme Court was given the power to declare unconstitutional laws passed by the Diet); and in the famous Clause 9, Japan renounced militarism, hewing to a "no-war" clause. It is the last clause that makes Japan unique among nation-states, stripping it of the "normal" right to participate in conflicts other than those strictly undertaken for purely defensive purposes. Still many Japanese worked on the draft that was submitted to the Diet, arguing strongly for certain points including the renunciation of war, and the Diet did deliberate long and hard before approving the document.

While the revamped constitution lies takes center stage in the Occupation reforms, the Occupation carried out other far-reaching reforms: it revamped the institutions governing the supply and demand for labor; the way assets, both land and industrial capital, were held and managed; and it reshaped the way fiscal and monetary policy operated. Occupation policy impacted labor supply through its reform of the educational system. Given the dominance of Americans in the ranks of non-Japanese charged with carrying out reform, it is not surprising that there was pressure to adopt the decentralized, unspecialized and democratic model characteristic of the United States.

In the American model a pivotal function of education is creating a well-informed, literate, populace capable of participating in the democratic process. The comprehensive local school drawing on a specified catchment district for both primary and secondary students; the important role played by state and local administrations in specifying curriculum; the parent–teacher advisory board; the emphasis on general schooling prior to enrolment in tertiary educa-tion developed out of the common school movement of frontier America. Building on these principles, the 6-3-3-4 system – six years of elementary school; three years of junior high school; three years of high school; four years of college – emerged as the main template for American schooling in the twentieth century. By contrast the prewar Japanese system was centralized under the aegis of the Ministry of Education; highly specialized, vocational and academic streams being sharply differentiated for those students advancing on within the system after graduation from compulsory elementary school; hierarchical in the sense that advancement was tied to performance on competitive entrance tests; and differentiated, girls and boys entering separate institutions after elementary school.

Under the main reforms of 1947, 1948 and 1949 – the Fundamental Law of Education, the School Education Law, the School Board Law, and the Private School Law – Japan did adopt many features of the American system. A 6-3-3-4 system was put in place; completion of middle (junior high) school was made compulsory and co-educational; and school boards were established. The national university system was expanded, each of Japan's prefectures granting at least one national university (Tokyo had several).

How long lasting were these reforms? Since the Occupation ended, many features of the prewar system have reemerged: the Ministry of Education's control over curriculum and textbook content has largely returned; a steep hierarchy, a pecking order, was quickly reestablished in tertiary schooling, the former imper-ial universities of Tokyo, Kyoto and Osaka ranking at the apex of the expanded nationally funded system; competitive entrance examinations rearing their head in allocating admission to elite public schools (i.e. those schools with a reputation for getting their graduates into prestigious universities) within large catchment districts. To be sure there are forces arrayed against an across the board return to prewar principles in education: the Japan Socialist Party, backing the left-leaning Japan Teachers Union, has strongly resisted elitism and the reintroduction of nationalistic tendencies in the curriculum; some left-leaning prefectures governed by socialists have experimented with highly restrictive catchment, the districts being narrowly drawn, striking a blow against hierarchy.

The Occupation's attempt at revamping education included script reform. The Japanese language can be written with at least four writing systems: Chinese characters, *kanji*; *hiragana* and *katagana*, phonetic writing systems ultimately derived from *kanji*; and the Roman alphabet. Mastering thousands and thousands of *kanji* is a daunting task: relying on the full set of Chinese characters creates a strong barrier to universal literacy. Recognizing this those committed to universal democracy – as opposed to those elites clinging to their superior knowledge of the full character set in classical Chinese and Japanese – advocated for script reform as early as 1900. In that year Hara Takashi (the first prime minister owing his appointment to the party system) then editor of the *Mainichi Shinbun* newspaper published a series of articles recommending reduction in the number of *kanji*. Encouraged by Hara's ascension to the Prime Minister's post a number of major newspapers announced that they would replace difficult *kanji* with *katagana* in the early 1920s. Soon thereafter a list of everyday characters – 1,963 *kanji* – was being discussed. Even the military, its officer class an elite capable of writing the most difficult *kanji*, began experimenting with a reduced character set during the Pacific War.

There were those in the Occupation who wanted to jettison all of the scripts excepting the Roman. This was the most radical idea being discussed in the late 1940s: indeed selective experimentation with such a system was even carried out in the early 1950s, only to meet concerted opposition from Japanese political and bureaucratic elites. The compromise reached did simplify Japanese considerably – a list of 1,850 general use *kanji* was created – but this outcome was really a meager advance over the ideas being discussed by political leaders like Hara a full half century earlier.

The educational reforms definitely improved the quality of school graduates entering the labor market in search of jobs. The average literacy ability of new job recruits improved considerably in comparison to the prewar period. So did their general grasp of geometry, algebra, and fundamental principles of statistics and science. Managers in companies working with new school graduates remarked on this fact. To an important extent pressure by Japanese bureaucrats who had wished to reform Japanese education during the interwar period played a role the success of reforms during the Occupation.

Legal changes also impacted the demand side of the labor market. Three pieces of legislation were passed by the Diet during 1945–47: the Trade Union Law; the Labor Adjustment Law; and the Labor Standards Law. Each of these laws was influenced by American precedent and by principles laid down by the International Labor Organization. The Trade Union Law guaranteed the right of workers to form unions and ensured that collective bargaining outcomes are binding on both management and labor. Mediation, conciliation and arbitration – to be handled by labor relations commissions – were provided for in the Labor Adjustment Law. Finally the Labor Standards Law built upon the Factory Law of 1911, prohibiting indentured servant contracts, ruling out discrimination based upon gender, providing for paid vacations, prohibiting the employment of children under the age of fifteen. Progressive bureaucrats in the Home Ministry had toyed with these ideas prior to the 1930s, encountering stiff opposition from a business community preaching the virtues of Japan's "beautiful" traditions governing the relationships between employers and employees arrived at independently of bureaucratic interference. Under Occupation pressure they were finally able to push them through the Diet.

According to the principal theory of Japan's aggressiveness held by the Americans and their allies, the social and economic roots of its militarism were two-fold: in the rural sector, landlordism; in the industrial sector dominance of manufacturing by mighty oligopolies, the *zaibatsu* and the *shinzaibatsu*. In developing a program to reconfigure village Japan and the industrial organization of urban Japan, the Occupation program redistributed assets, effectively wiping out the wealth of landlords, less effectively undermining prewar industrial organization. As with the reforms carried out in the labor market, the legacy of prewar reforms or stymied attempts at reform echoed through the legislation enacted during the late 1940s and early 1950s.

Tension between landlords and tenants had poisoned village life in interwar Japan. Depending on which theory one accepts – the pessimistic thesis that the increasing misery of tenants was driving them to the brink of desperation or the optimistic view that tenants' successful management of rented fields filled them with growing confidence that they would make highly productive owner-farmers – the tension either stemmed from parasitic landlordism or tenant ambition. This is a matter of debate. What is not debatable is the sheer magnitude of tenancy. For instance in 1926, less than one third of farm households were owner-farmers. The remaining two-thirds was divided between part-tenant/part-owner households and tenants, the former being considerably more numerous than the latter (the proportion of farm households in the part-tenant group was about 42 percent, the proportion pure tenants was about 27 percent). Neither bureaucrats nor the main parties in the Diet could ignore rural unrest, especially as the scope of divisive clashes between landlords and tenants intensified during the 1920s.

Indeed the two major prewar parties – both Seiyūkai and Minseitō – supported some kind of reform, the former advocating a program to increase the proportion of owner-farmers, the latter a tenancy law protecting and advancing the interests of renters. In the aftermath of the 1925 reform of the franchise – all adult males acquiring the right to vote, automatically granting tenant-farmers political voice – the pressure for reform intensified by leaps and bounds. Not surprisingly, a program of subsidizing buyouts of landlord held land was enacted in 1926. More important the lower house of the Diet actually passed a tenancy law in 1931 that was blocked from enactment by a vote of the upper house where landlord interests were strongly entrenched. It is estimated that about 5 percent of land was purchased by tenants under the 1926 program, about 7% of farm households benefiting from the attempt at reform.[3]

Under the logic of the command and control management of the economy introduced on a wide scale in the late 1930s – the military bent on stabilizing village Japan in order to cement domestic political unity in anticipation of total war – a decidedly more radical law emanated from the Diet. The Agricultural Adjustment Law of 1938 restricted the right of landlords to terminate leases – the only exception being when tenants violated the spirit of tenancy by withholding rent – and gave the government the right to unilaterally acquire lands held by landlords for resale to tenants provided the landlord refused the government's invitation to voluntarily sell off holdings.

Despite these attempts to carry out land reform, the burden of tenancy remained largely unchanged throughout the years of total war. In 1946, approximately a third of the farm households were owner-farmers, the proportion hardly changing from the 1926 ratio. Indeed the proportion of pure tenants – as opposed to part-tenants – actually increased very slightly between 1926 and 1941. This was the reality confronting the Occupation authorities, the Japanese bureaucracy and the Japanese political establishment in the aftermath of Japan's surrender.

Recognizing that some kind of land reform was necessary – the fears of all political parties that rural unrest could jeopardize any hope of economic recovery intensified by the fact that soldiers were being repatriated to rural Japan in droves – the cabinet, in 1945, drafted a bill designed to transfer sizable chunks of rural real estate to tenants, all tenant land owned by absentee landlords and all tenant land owned by farmer-landlords above and beyond a designated landlord average maximum retained area (LAMRA) of three *chō* (one *chō* equals 2.45 acres) to be subject to compulsory purchase either by tenants directly or by Agricultural Associations operating under government aegis and financial backing. A modified version of the original cabinet draft passed the Diet in December 1945. This version established a LAMRA of 5 *chō*. It is estimated that the percentage of agricultural land to be transferred under this level of the LAMRA would be around a third (the lower the LAMRA established, the more land would be transferred to tenants). This version was unacceptable to the Supreme Commander of the Allied Powers and to the Allied Council. After much political maneuvering two bills emerged from the cabinet and passed the Diet in October 1946 (the land reform program came into effect in December 1946 and was to be completed by the end of 1948). These bills set a LAMRA of 1 *chō*; set up Agricultural Land Commissions to facilitate the sales and purchases of land; and established prices for upland and paddy fields that were to be adhered to in the transfers. They also provided for government loans to tenant farmers, the payoff period to be thirty years at a fixed interest rate of 3.2 percent.

As it turned out the real value of the buyout price – relative to the prices that farmers were getting for their produce on the market – plummeted due to the inflation of the late 1940s (see Table A.4 in the Appendix). Thus the wealth of the landlords was effectively wiped out. Landlordism was destroyed. By 1950 less than 12 percent of farmers were tenants. A rural sector of owner-farmers had been established. The reform was radical. Given the fact that a relatively anemic Diet bill of late 1945 was transformed into the sweeping reform of a year later through the intervention of the allied powers occupying Japan it is one wonders about the validity of the assertions advanced by some commentators that the Occupation was a failure, or foreigners working for the Occupation government accomplished little, most of the agenda being dictated by domestic Japanese reformers who had contemplated the changes long before Japan's surrender.

The dissolution of the *zaibatsu* was less far-reaching, less long lasting in its impact, than the land reform. Under legislation passed by the Diet in 1947 – the Law for the Elimination of Excessive Concentration of Economic Power – a Holding Company Liquidation Commission (HCLC) was established to dissolve the assets held by the most important *zaibatsu* and *shinzaibatsu* active during the period of militarism. The original list of companies ordered for dissolution ran in the hundreds; political give and take reduced the list to around 100 and excluded all banks; by late 1948 the list was reduced to nine companies. The most famous of the prewar *zaibatsu* – Mitsui, Sumitomo, Mitsubishi, and Yasuda – were broken up, a number of the high ranking managers in the companies being purged as well. But even in these cases, the groups of companies held together under the *zaibatsu* umbrellas ultimately came back together to form *keiretsu* groups, no longer operating under holding companies, now linking through cross-shareholding of stock and regular meetings of company presidents.

Did the Occupation authorities back off on the *zaibatsu* dissolution program and on the degree to which they went in purging politicians, bureaucrats and businesspeople who played a prominent role in the militarism of 1931–45 out of fear of communism? Under the logic of the so-called "reverse course", the Supreme Commander of the Allied Powers did water down some of the proposals for reform and – beginning in 1950 – began to purge leadership of the Japan Communist Party.

The final piece of the Occupation program of reform that we consider here is the Dodge line. Joseph Dodge was a Detroit banker appointed by Washington in 1949 to implement a nine-point program of stabilization for the Japanese economy. The program had various aims: to reduce the dependence of the Japanese government on aid and subsidies granted by the United States; to stabilize the price level, inflation running rampant; to bring under control the activities of the Reconstruction Bank that had been issuing bonds, hidden from proper scrutiny by independent auditors because they were treated as off the general government's fiscal account; and to establish a fixed exchange rate between the yen and the United States dollar.

The Dodge Line established a number of principles crucial to Japanese fiscal and monetary management during the miracle growth period that followed upon the heels of the Occupation.[4] The exchange rate for the yen was set at a level of 360 yen to the American dollar. Dodge felt that at this exchange rate Japan could run a modest trade surplus. He pushed through a "super"-balanced budget that produced a surplus that could be used to amortize Reconstruction Bank bonds. In addition the Reconstruction Bank was instructed to not make any new loans. In order to generate a surplus in the government's budget, Dodge pushed for higher user fees on public infrastructure. Responding to Dodge's urging ticket prices on the Japan National Railway and postal rates were pushed up. Ironically the Dodge Line program echoes the one carried out under Matsukata in the aftermath of the Satsuma Rebellion. Both programs were designed to fight inflation generated by war; both programs involved bringing the government's fiscal and monetary house in order; both programs involved running a surplus. There is one striking difference however. The Matsukata Deflation of the 1880s increased tenancy in the countryside, serving the interests of wealthy rural landlord-merchants. Taking place in the wake of the land reform, the Dodge Line had no impact on the tenancy problem that plagued Japan from the Meiji Restoration until Japan's acceptance of the Potsdam Declaration.

The emergence of the Liberal Democratic Party

Testimony to the thirst for political democracy – for the give and take competition for voters by political parties – four new parties emerged in the wake of Japan's surrender. Suppressed under the total war regime, politicians regrouped under the guarantee of civil and political liberties announced by MacArthur in October 1945. The first party to be formed was the Japan Socialist Party; quickly following were the formations of the conservative Liberal Party, the Democratic Party. The fourth party that came into the open was the Japan Communist Party. With the four parties a spectrum of legally recognized political organizations, running from right to left, took the place of the two parties shaping the Diet's activities during the 1920s prior to military rule when the parties began to atrophy.

In the first election held under the new constitution in April 1947 the Socialists, then the most popular party in Japan, managed to secure a plurality of seats in the 466 lower house to form a coalition cabinet with the Democratic Party. This election, notable not only for producing a Socialist Prime Minister, Katayama Tetsu, also established rules for voting that continued in place with minor modifications for decades. Under the system of medium-sized multimember districts each voter was given a single ballot – a single vote – that he or she could assign to one candidate. However the number of candidates elected in the district was variable, ranging from three to five in number depending on the size of the election district. Thus a party aiming at garnering up to five of the seats for a given district had to mount a slate of candidates who were forced to run against each other. This is one reason why Japanese political parties tend to form factions, each faction running a candidate in a particular district. Still what is the chicken and what is the egg is not totally clear. If parties are faction ridden anyway, the single ballot/multimember district system only accentuates something that is already there.[5]

Even in victory the Socialists were deeply divided. Two factions fought over the policies that should govern proposed legislation: a Marxist faction opposed to accommodation with capitalists, committed to a class warfare theory, and a wing of social moderates who advocated gradualist change through compromise with pro-business political parties. After the factional fighting led to the collapse of the Socialist government in 1948, a rupture occurred in the party itself. The party split apart in 1951, the more conservative social moderate faction forming the Rightist Socialist Party of Japan, the Marxist faction the Leftist Socialist Party of Japan.

The fragmentation of the left oriented party reflected fragmentation of the union movement. By the early 1950s most viable unions were being established along enterprise lines. To improve their clout in collective bargaining the unions banded together into larger federations. Just as ideological factionalism weakened the prewar union movement so did it the postwar movement. In the center was the Sōdōmei federation; on the left, more committed to class warfare, were the Sanbetsu and Sōhyō federations. Each federation lined up behind a left–leaning party, chiefly one or other wing of the Socialists, bankrolling candidates in elections for the Diet. Ideological disputes in the union federations spilled over into ideological disputes within the ranks of the Socialists.

Desperate to improve their vote getting prowess, the two factions of the Socialist Party reunited in 1955 to form the Japan Socialist Party. How successful this patching together of two ideological opposites was is questionable. The combined party was never able to break past the "one-third barrier", garnering at most a third of the popular vote. Eventually the party began to experience a decline in voter support. This said, the party continued to collect more seats than more left-wing parties like the Communists.

Reacting to the reestablishment of the Japan Socialist Party in 1955, the Liberal Party and the Democratic Party combined to form the Liberal Democratic Party, also in 1955. The merger was to put together to present a united opposition to the Socialist Party. Ironically what started out as an alliance of convenience ended up forging an almost unbeatable vote getting machine. From the election of 1955 that the Liberal Democratic Party won (garnering about 58 percent of the popular vote and securing about 62 percent of the seats in the lower house) until 1993 the only party able to form a government in the Diet was the Liberal Democratic Party. In place of the prewar two-party system of alternating party cabinets initiated with the Hara Takashi cabinet of 1918, the election of 1955 ushered in a protracted period of one party rule.

Why was the Liberal Democratic Party able to retain its dominance for so long? One factor is the opposition: the left has been splintered along ideological lines, fragmentation weakening the position of each left–wing party, earning the contempt of some voters more interested in practical results than in ideological purity. A second factor is the coalition of interests that the Liberal Democratic Party represents: farmers, rural dwellers more generally, small businesses, large businesses, and bureaucrats. A third factor is the policy agenda of the party: pro-American, pro-economic growth, pro-export promotion. Whether the policies of the Liberal Democratic Party actually promoted miracle growth is a question open to debate. Indeed, some scholars go so far as to argue that the main role of the Liberal Democratic Party has been to provide cover for the bureaucracy, especially for the Ministry of International Trade and Industry and the Ministry of Finance during the era of miracle growth. However, the party governed during the period of miracle growth without cessation, winning election after election – lower house elections occurring on average every 2.8 years during the period 1955–87 – thus was able to take credit for the growth.

That maintaining good relations with the United States was not unimportant is indicated by the huge growth in Japan's trade with the United States, and by the ability of the Japanese government to keep a tight lid on self-defense force military spending (allowed under the new constitution and held under 1 percent of national income for many decades). Testimony to the importance of the Liberal Democratic Party to strategic interests of the United States is the fact that the Central Intelligence Agency of the United States covertly plowed funds into the coffers of the party during the 1950s and 1960s.

The dominance of the Liberal Democratic Party is usually cited in theories of the so-called iron triangle. The iron triangle theory asserts that there is a coalition of political, bureaucratic and business elites that has ruled postwar Japan from the mid-1950s until the early 1990s: highly placed bureaucrats in powerful ministries; the heads of major business federations like Nikkeiren or Keidanren; and the Liberal Democratic Party politicians with an ability to get reelected in election after election, thereby moving up the ladder of power within the party, perhaps able to secure a position in the cabinet, becoming the minister in charge of a key ministry like the Ministry of Finance. A crucial facet of the Japanese iron triangle is that it excludes labor. In many European countries with strong left–leaning social democratic movements, organized labor was able to gain a seat at the pinnacle of national power. Not so Japan.

It should be noted that the iron triangle theory does not assign pride of place to any one member of the triangle. Some scholars argue that the business community is in charge; some the bureaucrats; some the politicians; some a mixture. This is an issue that will occupy us in subsequent chapters of this volume. Suffice it to say here that it is crucial to interpretations of long-run economic development in Japan. Does the market – that is business interests – rule the roost? Or is it an independent bureaucracy protected by the Liberal Democratic Party? How important is the voter in this story?

In the wake of World War II Japan was occupied by the allied powers that defeated it for over six years. During the Occupation due in part to the reforms carried out under the watchful eye of the Supreme Commander of the Allied Powers, Japanese agriculture and Japanese manufacturing began to recover (see the 1936–40 and 1951–55 figures for per capita income appearing in Table A.1 in the Appendix). Soon after the Occupation concluded – 1955 – Japan was poised for the remarkable growth in per capita known as miracle growth. Much of the story of that growth is specific to Japan. However it is important to keep in mind that it is only one – perhaps the most dramatic – of the stories of convergence whereby countries allied with the United States (or neutral but located within a region largely allied with the United States) experienced unusually rapid growth in living standards over a period of two decades.

It is important never to forget that miracle growth in Japan occurred during an era when the United States supported trade and diffusion of technology within the non-Communist world through its support for multilateral institutions, global and regional. The end of World War II and the onset of the Cold War marked a major watershed in global history. The international economic order that had deteriorated into beggar thy neighbor protectionism, autarky, empire building and drives to regional hegemony during the 1920s and 1930s gave way to a new international economic order predicated on rejecting the mistakes of the 1919–45 past. Hallmarks of this new international order were convergence and crossover. Japan's miracle growth – as remarkable as it was – was just one chapter in that mighty convergence story.

Key terms and concepts in chapter 7

"Catch-up" growth
Golden age of convergence
Theory of hegemonic cycles
Cold War
Pent-up technology thesis
Crossover
Clause 9 of the revised Japanese Constitution
Reforms of the Japanese educational system between 1947 and 1949
Trade Union Law, Labor Adjustment Law and Labor Standards Law
Land reform
Landlord average maximum retained area (LAMRA)
Agricultural Land Commissions
Dodge Line
Medium-sized multimember single ballot voting system
Liberal Democratic Party
Iron triangle thesis

8 Miracle growth

Trend acceleration with a vengeance

The number of countries converging towards the income per capita of the United States between 1950 and 1973 is considerable. Its membership includes most of the nations of Western Europe. Within the European club the two former Axis powers – Italy and Germany, ravaged by the destruction of war during the last two years of World War II – grew at a particularly brisk pace in terms of income per capita. However neither of these countries achieved the phenomenal record of Japan, their Asian Axis partner. Japan's remarkable record of growth achieved by no other country before the early 1970s – Taiwan, South Korea and Hong Kong were to match it subsequently – is known as miracle growth.

As you have learned in Chapter 6 trend acceleration was one of the most intriguing features of Japan's pre-1938 long swings. The average rate of growth over long swings increased over time: the first long swing had the slowest average rate of growth; the third – albeit truncated by the embracing of the total war economy – the most brisk. If we connect the growth experience of the 1955–73 period to the prewar record – ignoring the period 1938–55 marred by war, massive aerial bombing of its industrial belt bringing the agonizing conflict to a close, and allied Occupation – we can say that the miracle growth experience is a continuation of the acceleration experience, the leap in average growth rates above those achieved during the previous swing (the upswing of the 1930s) being especially dramatic.

Two of the factors driving pre-1938 trend acceleration were capital formation and industrialization, shifting the economy away from agriculture towards manufacturing enterprise. Over successive long swings the rates of industrialization and capital accumulation crept upward (see Table 4.3 in Chapter 4 and Appendix Table A.5). To some extent the two phenomena are interrelated: in densely populated countries like Japan manufacturing tends to be more capital intensive than agriculture. For manufacturing to grow capital has to be ploughed into the sector. Accumulation and structural change are intertwined.

Because manufacturing uses a mixture of imported Western technologies and traditional Japanese methods developed for the proto-industrial economy while agriculture relies almost exclusively upon an updating of traditional techniques, and because manufacturing has higher capital/labor ratios than farming, the average productivity of labor in agriculture is low compared to that achieved in mining, construction and manufacturing. Table A.3 in the Appendix confirms this for the post-1950 period. Moving workers out of agriculture tends to raise labor productivity. As for savings, Appendix Table A.5 reveals that miracle growth savings grew from modest levels during 1956–60 to substantial levels by the early 1970s. More important annual capital formation rates in manufacturing soared during miracle growth: around 14 percent in 1956–62; and slightly above that in 1962–64.

According to the hypotheses elaborated in Chapter 6, the third factor driving trend acceleration is improvements in the social capability for importing and adopting foreign technology, especially in manufacturing. That earlier discussion suggests four sources of positive feedback enhancing the social capability in Japan: at the household level savings and the demand for health and education; at the enterprise level, the internalization of labor in industrial enterprises creating incentives to invest in training and skill formation; and at the government level, the perfecting of coordinating/facilitating policies and investments in infrastructure.

Putting together this list of factors – structural change, accumulation of capital in manufacturing, borrowing and adapting foreign technology, internalizing labor and mobilizing capital within firms, and government intervention in the economy – yields a roadmap for this chapter. As we traverse the various roads we shall see that most of the hypotheses are controversial, in some cases bitterly debated in the literature. So we should be prepared for differences of opinion, differences of emphasis. Before we proceed down the first road – structural changes in agriculture that freed up workers to move into manufacturing – we consider two classical exercises in growth accounting, that due to Kuznets (1971) and that due to Denison and Chung (1976). We do so to garner a full overview of the landscape spread out before us before traversing particular roads. Perspective is required lest we bog down focusing on debates over specific points whose overall relevance for the entirety of miracle growth may be more limited, less overarching, than partisans in the various debates are prepared to acknowledge.

As can be seen from Panel A.1 of Table 8.1, extrapolating over a century the growth rate of the Japanese economy over the period from the 1870s to the mid-1960s is remarkable, especially when we focus on the metric of income per capita. From Panel A.2 it is apparent that growth rates for labor and capital combined play less of a role in the growth of income for a number of advanced industrial economies than growth in income per unit of input. Fitting the two observations together suggests that a decomposition of miracle growth rates for Japan will reveal that growth in inputs combined pales next to growth in income per unit of input. Evidence supporting the view that growth in inputs played less of a role than growth in output per unit of input for Japan during its miracle growth phase appears in Panels B.1 and B.2 of Table 8.1. These figures, worked up by Denison and Chung (1976), are solidly grounded in a technique pioneered by Edward Denison that explicitly takes into account improvements in the quality of labor and capital inputs when doing sources of growth accounting decompositions.

Table 8.1 Sources of growth accounting for Japan and selected advanced industrial economies

Panel A.1 *Long run growth estimates (coefficients of multiplication in a century) by Kuznets*

Country/time period covered	Total income	Population	Income per capita
Canada, 1870–1874 to 1963–1967	31.8	5.7	5.6
England & Wales, 1765/85 to 1963–1967	8.4	2.6	3.2
France, 1831–1840 to 1963–1966	7.2	1.4	5.3
Norway, 1865–1869 to 1963–1967	15.3	2.2	6.9
Japan, 1874–1879 to 1963–1967	51.4	3.1	16.4
United States, 1834–1843 to 1963–1967	34.4	6.9	5.0

Panel A.2 *Growth accounting estimates by Kuznets*

Country, Period	Income (1)	Input growth			Income per unit of input (5)	Population (6)	Income per capita (7)	Ratio of column 5 to column 7 (8)
		Labor (2)	Capital (3)	Combined input (4)				
Canada, 1926 to 1956	3.89	0.77	2.86	1.18	2.68	1.70	2.15	1.25
France, 1913 to 1966	2.33	−0.50	1.95	0.18	2.15	0.40	1.92	1.12
Norway, 1899 to 1956	2.80	0.25	2.47	0.72	2.07	0.79	1.99	1.04
United States, 1929 to 1957	2.95	0.53	1.01	0.64	2.30	1.24	1.69	1.36

Panel B.1 *Sources of growth accounting estimates by Denison, total factor input*

Country, period	Total factor input	Labor					Capital	Land
		Employment	Hours of work	Age-sex Composition	Education	Total		
Japan, 1953–1971	3.95	1.14	0.21	0.14	0.34	1.85	2.10	0.00
France, 1950–1962	1.24	0.08	−0.02	0.10	0.29	0.45	0.79	0.00
United States, 1948–1969	2.09	1.17	−0.21	−0.10	0.41	1.30	0.79	0.00

Table 8.1 Continued

Panel B.2 *Sources of growth accounting estimates by Denison, output per unit of input and standardized growth rate for total income*[a]

Country	Output per unit of input							Income growth rate
	Advances in knowledge	Improved resource allocation[b]				Economies of scale	Total	
		A decline	SE decline	Less trade barriers	Total			
Japan	1.97	0.64	0.30	0.01	0.95	1.94	4.86	8.81
France	1.51	0.65	0.23	0.07	0.95	1.00	3.46	4.70
United States	1.19	0.23	0.07	0.00	0.30	0.42	1.91	4.00

Sources: Tables 2–13 in Denison and Chung (1976) and Tables 1 and 9 in Kuznets (1971).

Notes
a The period covered is identical to that given in Panel C.
b The term "A decline" stands for "contraction in agricultural inputs;" the term "SE decline" stands for "contraction of nonagricultural self employment;" the term "less trade barriers" stands for "reduction in trade barriers".

By taking into account improvements in labor input stemming from improvements in the educational attainment of the labor force and the like; by taking into account types of capital stock growth – inventories, dwellings, plants and equipment – Denison's methodology is a refined version of the decomposition technique used by Kuznets (1971). To be sure one can quibble about the precise estimates; about how accurately improvements to the skill and knowledge level of the labor force are measured. Other assumptions about how to carry out these types of decomposition can and do yield different results in estimation. In any event the Denison and Chung (1976) decomposition supports the hypothesis that growth in output per unit of input exceeds growth in the contribution of inputs. To be sure, growth in inputs stemming from extremely high rates of accumulation of capital in the Japanese case – far exceeding rates of accumulation for the United States and France over the comparable period – was extremely important during miracle growth. In comparison to France, growth in Japan's employment and hours of work was also impressive. But these contributions are exceeded by growth in output per unit of input. Why did output per unit of input grow so fast in the Japanese case, exceeding the comparable growth rate for France, another country converging towards American levels during 1950–73?

The figures in Panel B.2 of Table 8.1 offer important clues. One clue is that economies of scale were particularly important in the Japanese case. The sheer growth of the size of the economy – the scale of operation of its interrelated subsectors – fostered improvements in the efficiency with which capital and labor combined were being used. Slightly less important was improved resource allocation: moving workers out of a relatively low productivity activity like agriculture into a higher productivity activity like manufacturing helped raise the efficiency with which labor and capital were combined to generate output. Finally advances in knowledge, mainly but not exclusively attributable to "catch-up" through the importing and adapting of foreign technology, played a crucial role in miracle growth.

Decompositions like those carried out by Kuznets (1971) or Denison and Chung (1976) are helpful, albeit only scratching the surface of things: they offer up clues about what matters. The decomposition by Denison and Chung points to the importance of the agricultural sector in freeing up labor for use elsewhere in the economy; of the possible impact of specialization and division of labor due to the proliferation of relatively new high growth subsectors in manufacturing, boosting economies of scale; of "catch-up" technological progress; of advances in the average educational attainment of the labor force; and of steadfast gains in the efficiency with which labor and capital are combined to generate output. What they do not tell us is how much of these efficiency improvements stem from innovating private sector competition in unregulated markets, how much is due to the increasing diligence and attention to detail of the labor force spurred on by institutional changes like the internalization of blue-collar labor in large firms, and how much to public policy making up for market failures through coordinating/ facilitating policies, especially industrial policy.

Agriculture

In the wake of the land reform, the small-scale owner-farmer became the norm in Japanese agriculture. These farmers responded to changes in changes in relative prices – for labor, machinery and fertilizer – in determining inputs; and to relative prices for outputs – for rice, for sericulture, for livestock – in determining what type of farming they diversified into.

On the output side prices were not completely determined by impersonal forces of supply and demand. The domestic rice market was protected, largely closed to imports. Domestic rice prices were not simply set by impersonal forces of supply and demand. Abandoning a quota system that had been put into effect during the Occupation, the government moved towards a dual price system. Under this system there were two main prices, the supplier's price and the consumer's price. The government purchased rice at one, relatively high price, selling it through designated distributors at a lower price. How was the supplier's price determined? Several schemes were tried out: for some time a price parity formula was used, the supplier price being linked to prices for goods purchased by farm households; later on, an income parity approach was used, the price for rice purchased by the government being set high enough to at least partially equalize rural and urban household per capita incomes. Using figures on consumption patterns of urban and rural households, the government's purchase price for rice was set sufficiently high to ensure an income for the typical farming household comparable to that of an industrial worker living in a city. Considerations of income distribution trumped reliance on pure market forces.

Keeping foreign rice out was crucial: in California Japanese style glutinous rice could be grown at far lower prices than in Japan. Letting in imports would create havoc in the government managed system because an urban sector free to consume California rice would shift out of domestic rice, leaving a government aggrandizing larger and larger stocks of rice it could not sell on the market. So markets were constrained by politics and policies. The vote-gathering machine of the Liberal Democratic Party of the 1950s and 1960s being strongly entrenched in rural districts, especially amongst the farming populace, the party saw to it that legislation was passed by the Diet benefiting rural districts, farmers in particular.

That said, farm families did respond to market signals. The most prominent signal was the rising wage in manufacturing driven by supply shifts: by the massive expansion of industry and the rising productivity of labor therein. Factories sprang up in the vicinity of rice fields or within a day's commute from farming villages: more and more men in particular became part-time farmers and part-time factory workers, putting in five or six days of toil in manufacturing, working the farm together with the women in the household who increasingly became the backbone of the village labor force. So the relatively elevated level of factory wages – representing the hourly or daily opportunity cost of staying in farming fulltime – shaped the decisions of farmers. So did other relative prices. Evidence that a wide range of relative prices faced by farm households mattered is given in Table 8.2. From Panel C of the table it is evident that there was steady fall in the relative price of fertilizers beginning as early as the 1920s, the decline outstripping the drop in the relative price of machinery – especially power tillers but small tractors as well – during the 1955–65 decade. As can be seen from Panel B the use of fertilizers soared during the 1945–55 era, augmenting the inherent productivity of land. During the 1945–55 era land productivity grew extremely rapidly reflecting these massive increments of fertilizer.

However, during the 1960s the ongoing surge of wages in agriculture – drawn upward by the pull of demand for workers in manufacturing, especially in factory jobs fairly close to rural villages – encouraged farm families to sub-stitute machines for labor, machine prices falling as factories spewed out cheaper and more versatile power tillers, mowers, and small-scale tractors. For this reason labor productivity growth as opposed to land productivity growth became the driving force behind agricultural productivity expansion during the 1960s.

In terms of the labor surplus model discussed in Chapter 3 we can say that the period when there was overabundance of labor in village Japan definitely ended by the late 1950s if not earlier. During the 1960s the draining of workers from rural Japan into the burgeoning manufacturing sector forced farming to become completely competitive with non-agriculture. Farm families now found it increas-ingly difficult to entice any of their sons – eldest or younger – to remain true to family traditions, to remain tied to the villages of their birth.

That agriculture was largely able to meet the demands for food from the entire population is testimony to the great gains in productivity. These gains are

Table 8.2 Annual growth rates for the agricultural sector, 1920–1970

Panel A   *Percentage growth rates for agricultural production*

Period	Crops		Sericulture	Livestock
	Rice	Total		
1935–1945	−0.4	−0.8	−10.3	−7.6
1945–1955	1.4	2.5	−0.5	16.3
1955–1965	2.2	2.0	−0.3	11.0

Panel B.1   *Percentage growth rates for inputs (labor)*

Period	Number of workers			Workdays	
	Male	Female	Male equivalents	Total	Per worker
1935–1945	−1.7	2.0	−0.2	−0.9	−1.0
1945–1955	1.5	0.3	1.0	1.3	0.4
1955–1965	−3.5	−2.5	−3.0	−2.7	0.3

Panel B.2   *Percentage growth rates of inputs (land)*

Period	Cultivated land area			Crop area	
	Paddy fields	Upland fields	Paddy-field equivalents	Rice	Total
1935–1945	−0.3	−0.6	−0.4	−0.8	−1.1
1945–1955	0.3	0.1	0.2	0.8	1.0
1955–1965	0.2	−0.2	0.2	0.3	−0.7

Panel B.3   *Percentage growth rates of inputs (variable and fixed capital)*

Period	Fixed capital		Variable capital (current inputs)	
	Machinery & implements	Total	Fertilizers	Total
1935–1945	−0.2	−1.4	−5.0	−6.6
1945–1955	3.1	2.0	13.5	15.0
1955–1965	11.5	7.8	3.6	8.5

Panel C   *Percentage growth rates of relative prices of inputs relative to agricultural output price*

Period	Labor and land		Fixed capital		Variable capital (current inputs)	
	Labor wages	Cultivated land prices	Machinery & implements	Total	Fertilizers	Total
1920–1930	1.9	2.9	0.3	1.3	−1.7	−1.2
1955–1965	6.1	4.3	−3.2	−0.9	−5.0	−4.5
1960–1970	7.2	−1.1	−7.1	−1.1	−5.4	−5.0

Table 8.2 Continued

Panel D   *Percentage growth rates of productivities of labor and land*

Period	Labor productivity		Land productivity		Relative contribution to labor productivity of land productivity growth	
	Per male equivalent (1)	Per workday (2)	Per paddy-field equivalent (3)	Per hectare of crop area (4)	(3)/(1)	(4)/(2)
1935–1945	−1.7	−0.9	−1.5	−0.7	88	78
1945–1955	2.2	1.9	2.9	2.1	132	111
1955–1965	6.9	6.5	3.4	4.3	49	66

Source: Various tables in Hayami, Akino, Shintani and Yamada (1975).

clear from Panel D of Table 8.2. Had agriculture not responded with massive improvements in productivity as it did the transfer of workers to manufacturing could not have occurred as rapidly as it did. How important was policy – land reform and the establishment of a dual price system for rice – to these improvements in productivity? There are compelling reasons for believing that land reform stimulated mechanization of agriculture. Former tenants no longer worried about having their leases unilaterally terminated by a landlord. This uncertainty removed, the typical farming household was inclined to invest in capital equipment that it knew would yield benefits for many years. The same can be said of the rice price support system. By guaranteeing a price for the main staple that would make farming reasonably competitive with employment in a typical factory – one suspects a fairly small operation, not a massive plant bristling with machines – the dual price system also contributed to stabilizing the pursuit of agriculture. Stability encouraged investment in land improvements and mechanical equipment, hence productivity gain.

To be sure, one can imagine a counterfactual world in which farming acreage was consolidated into larger production units. For instance if the land reform legislation of the late 1940s had established a landlord average maximum retained area (LAMRA) greater than one *chō*, average farm sizes during the miracle growth period might have been larger than they actually were. Perhaps this state of affairs would have stimulated reliance of tractors at an earlier date than actually occurred – at least on larger farms with sons abandoning farming for factory employment mechanization might have caught on fairly quickly – but who knows? If the LAMRA had been set higher, the proportion of tenanted land would have been greater. Playing out counterfactual exercises depends heavily on assumptions that might be legitimately questioned, for instance on the basis of political realism.

Manufacturing

While yields of rice and livestock expanded briskly during miracle growth, agriculture played second fiddle to manufacturing. At the core of miracle growth was factory production. To some extent this was true of the upswing of the 1930s. However in comparison with the massive surge in manufacturing output that took place during 1955–1975, the 1930s experience pales.

This is apparent from the figures assembled in Table 8.3. From Panel A of the table it is apparent that the volume of manufacturing output for the first five years of miracle growth (1956–1960) – especially in capital goods and construction materials but also in consumption goods – far exceeded the levels recorded in the last five years of the 1930s. More dramatic though is the pace of growth in sheer volume of output between the early 1960s and the mid-1970s. While the pace of increase in the sectors that had been key to Japan's pre-1940 industrialization – light industries such as textiles and food processing – was fairly modest, the heavy industries exemplified by iron and steel, non-ferrous metals and chemicals recorded breathtakingly high growth rates.

The chief lesson of input–output analysis (see Chapter 1 for a discussion) is that inter-industry flows are crucial, especially in an economy that is relatively self-sufficient in manufactures – not in raw materials – sectors supplying the industrial products used as intermediate inputs or as capital equipment for other sectors. Demand cascades. Consider the figures on weaving machinery snapped up by the cotton textile sector displayed in Panel B of Table 8.3. As can be seen from a comparison of the column on volumes of cotton textiles and the column on weaving machinery demand from the textiles sector pulls demand for weaving machines. When textile output volumes decline, volumes of weaving machinery produced follow suit. Inter-industry flows of this sort buttress the contribution of scale economies to growth in output per unit of input highlighted in our earlier discussion of the Denison and Chung (1976) on decomposition of income growth.

A second illustration of this process of scale expansion stemming from inter-industry flows is apparent in the figures on automobiles, non-electrical machinery and crude steel appearing in Panels A.3 and B of Table 8.3. Automotive and truck assembly requires inputs of steel, of glass, of rubber, of electrical wiring. As growth of the automobile and truck sector soared so did the demand for crude steel. Similar logic applies to the relationship between machinery and steel: most machinery construction involves parts manufactured by the metal working sector, either steel or non-ferrous metals. In an environment in which most Japanese manufacturing industries relied upon outputs from other domestic sectors for supplying inputs, had iron and steel sector's output failed to grow as it did, the outputs of the machinery and automobile/truck sectors could not have grown as they did.

In Western Europe national economies integrated with one another in the aftermath of World War II, sectors like iron and steel being concentrated in some nations, sectors using their outputs as inputs being located in other nations. For this reason scale economies were less important in the national convergence experience of individual European convergence than they were in the Japanese case.

Table 8.3 Manufacturing expansion in the era of miracle growth

Panel A.1 *Indices of industrial production, value added weights, 1980 = 100, investment goods, consumer goods and mining*

Period	Investment goods			Consumption goods			Mining
	Total	Capital goods	Construction materials	Total	Durable goods	Non-durable goods	
1931–1935	2.4	1.5	5.4	6.5	0.5	14.1	69.9
1936–1940	4.7	3.2	7.9	8.2	0.8	17.2	105.1
1956–1960	11.3	8.6	20.0	15.4	4.7	26.9	118.7
1961–1965	24.4	20.3	35.8	28.2	13.3	42.3	138.2
1966–1970	50.3	44.4	64.9	47.9	30.6	62.9	144.1
1971–1975	77.8	71.5	92.2	67.5	51.4	78.8	116.4

Panel A.2 *Indices of industrial production, value added weights, 1980 = 100, sub-sectors of manufacturing other than machinery*

Period	Manufacturing total	Heavy industry sub-sectors			Light industry sub-sectors	
		Iron & steel	Non-ferrous metals	Chemicals	Textiles	Food & tobacco
1931–1935	4.3	2.5	3.7	2.6	26.2	18.9
1936–1940	7.1	5.1	6.2	5.2	32.2	21.7
1956–1960	13.4	12.4	13.4	12.1	36.5	31.6
1961–1965	27.0	27.1	27.5	22.9	55.2	48.9
1966–1970	51.0	56.5	52.2	45.1	83.1	70.9
1971–1975	75.8	84.0	77.6	71.4	100.5	86.1

Panel A.3 *Indices of industrial production, value added weights, 1980 = 100, machinery sub-sector of manufacturing and the main sub-sectors of machinery production*

Period	Total	Non-electric machinery	Electric machinery	Transportation Equipment	Precision machinery
1931–1935	0.8	2.1	0.2	0.6	0.8
1936–1940	1.8	3.4	0.4	2.3	1.3
1956–1960	6.7	9.1	4.0	7.6	5.7
1961–1965	16.5	21.9	11.7	18.0	13.2
1966–1970	37.5	46.3	29.1	42.9	22.0
1971–1975	62.7	70.8	52.2	73.7	34.6

Panel B *Indices for production volumes (volume or number produced) for selected sub-sectors of manufacturing, 1974–1975 = 100*

Period	Cotton textiles	Weaving machinery (spun yarn)	Truck chassis	Passenger motorcar	Crude steel	Radio receivers
1956–1960	137.6	158.5	6.7	1.8	13.6	42.5
1961–1965	143.5	160.1	35.8	10.4	30.7	114.7

(*Table 8.3 continued*)

Table 8.3 Continued

Period	Cotton textiles	Weaving machinery (spun yarn)	Truck chassis	Passenger motorcar	Crude steel	Radio receivers
1966–1970	129.5	164.1	75.0	47.5	64.2	186.2
1971–1975	109.8	140.0	95.9	97.5	95.6	138.3

Panel C   *Total factor productivity and rate of increase in money wages in selected sub-sectors of manufacturing, 1952 to 1961(percentage growth rates)*

Variable	Chemicals	Transportation machinery	Machinery	Rubber products	Metals & metal products	Textiles	Food & tobacco
Total factor productivity growth	18.8	11.8	8.7	7.5	5.1	4.4	1.4
Wage growth	8.3	7.0	7.3	5.8	7.4	7.8	7.1

Panel D   *Percentage growth of physical labor productivity and product price, selected sub-sectors of manufacturing for various sub-periods of the 1960–1973 period*[a]

Subsector	1960–1965		1965–1970		1970–1973	
	Labor productivity	Price growth	Labor productivity	Price growth	Labor productivity	Price growth
Food	3.3	6.6	3.7	5.0	6.5	8.2
Textiles	6.9	2.4	9.8	6.1	10.5	15.2
Paper & pulp	7.7	4.8	13.8	0.2	11.6	11.7
Chemicals	10.2	1.0	15.6	−2.8	11.5	8.6
Ceramics	7.8	2.1	11.0	3.2	10.2	10.0
Steel	10.8	−2.1	17.5	−0.7	13.4	6.9
Non-ferrous metal	8.9	0.5	13.5	0.2	12.9	11.4
Metal products	n.a.	n.a.	14.9	0.3	11.9	5.0
General machinery	3.7	5.9	15.7	2.6	12.5	2.0
Electric machinery	6.2	−1.6	20.6	−4.7	17.6	−3.3
Transportation machinery	n.a.	n.a.	13.6	1.2	12.0	2.1

Sources: Japan Statistical Association (1987), *Historical Statistics of Japan. Volume 4:* various tables; Ohkawa and Rosovsky (1973), p. 183; and Teranishi (2005), p. 255.

Note
a n.a. = not available.

However at the level of Western Europe as an entire integrated region scale economies played a role similar to those experienced by Japanese manufacturing. Had other economies located nearby Japan developed their industrial sectors during the period Japan was going through miracle growth, it is likely Japanese firms would not have relied so exclusively upon domestic manufactures for inputs. The tyranny of distance should not be forgotten. The Pacific Ocean is a vast ocean.

Shipping costs were not inconsiderable, although they were falling steadily as bulk shippers made cost-saving advances, placing orders for larger and larger oil tankers, for grain, for pulp, for coal, for machinery, for automobiles. Iron and steel firms on the west coast of the United States were at a considerable disadvantage in establishing a strong foothold in the Japanese market, partly due to distance. Iron and steel firms in the United States had another disadvantage relative to fledging Japanese competitors: the vintage of their capital stock. In the early 1950s there were two major advances in steel manufacturing: employing basic oxygen furnaces and massive plants generating output with continuous slab or billet casting procedures. Prior to these innovations, state of the art production involved steel mills generating ingots that were rolled out into slabs or billets in separate mills.

Integration into larger and larger plants was crucial to seizing the cost-reducing advantages of the new processes. Because the Japanese steel industry was just getting back onto its feet during the 1950s it was logical for manufactures to build plant and equipment embodying the new technology. Much of its capital stock had been wiped out during the aerial bombing campaign carried out by the United States in 1945. By contrast the United States steel sector enjoyed a well built up capital stock embodying an earlier technology – relying upon open-hearth furnaces and separate rolling mills – that saddled it with a cost structure that was relatively high compared to their Japanese competitors. Theoretically the American industry could have scrapped its plant and equipment, thereby staying competitive with the rapidly expanding industry on the other side of the Pacific. Indeed mainstream neo-classical economic theory emphasizes variable costs, denigrating fixed costs. But this theory offers cold comfort to real world businesses. Scrapping plant and equipment involves substantial costs: direct costs involved in purchasing new equipment, building new structures, tearing down old buildings; indirect costs involving labor, workers being required to jettison old skills compatible with open-hearth furnaces and ingot production and master new ones.

This argument emphasizes accumulation of capital, the vintage of plant and equipment actually implying – embodying – techniques, requiring particular skills amongst the pool of workers employed. While it is compelling in the case of steel, it is not a story that is readily ported over to other subsectors of manufacturing. In automobile and truck assembly advances in knowledge played a greater role than sheer accumulation, surges in capital formation driving down the average vintage of plant and equipment. In Japan's automobile industry growth in output per unit of input is tied up with the diffusion of quality control and just-in-time inventory practices. The unrelenting pursuit of the principles of zero-defects, of building quality into every component of an automobile is usually credited to the Toyota Motor Corporation.

Ōno Taiichi and kanban

During the miracle growth era, Japanese industrial circles became obsessed with quality control and just-in time-inventory (JIT) management.

The concern with quality was undoubtedly related to the desire on the part of Japanese exporters to focus their attention on the high income per capita markets in North America and Europe, away from the low income markets in Asia that had become their main targets during the heyday of Japanese imperialism in the 1930s and during World War II.

Interest in JIT amongst manufacturers of automobiles and consumer durables probably stemmed from producing small lot sizes for a relatively limited domestic market during the 1950s and early 1960s. Perhaps it reflected the relatively high costs of warehousing components stemming from dearth of non-mountainous land and concentration of population in relatively few major metropolitan clusters, those located along the burgeoning Tōkaidō industrial belt, in the Kantō and Nobi plains and within the Kinai region centered around the Yodo river and Osaka.

Market conditions aside, the drive to build quality into every component of an automobile, every facet of a refrigerator or a camera – the desire to produce, or acquire from a sub-contractor, every single component just before they were needed in the assembly process – reflected a conscious intellectual commitment to the supermarket principle.

A cost/benefit oriented manager of a supermarket is presumably concerned about maximizing the net revenue for the operation from every single bit of counter space, from every square foot of floor space. Relying on the principle that consumer demand should determine how space is to be allocated – stock what sells well, do not stock what nobody is buying – managers responsible for making purchasing decisions follow the flow of sales, using inventories run up or run down as a triggering device. Key to a supermarket's long-run viability is flexibility. The consumer can be fickle. Fads come and go. Management has to adjust constantly to these changes in demand, be alert to innovations. Keeping down inventories is one of the most cost-effective strategies of achieving this flexibility, reordering an item just before its inventory is exhausted, the shelf space allocated to it going empty.

The most famous example of JIT in the Japan of the miracle growth era is Toyota Motor Corporation's "kanban" system. The system involves organizing the flow of production on the shop floor through the constant movement of small vehicles that pick up empty boxes from the pallets in front of each division on the shop floor, dropping them off in front of other divisions where the boxes are to be filled up, replacing the components that have been used up by the division that put the empty box on its pallet. Attached to the boxes are "kanban" (flags) indicating the division from which the box was taken, the division that has the responsibility for manu-facturing the desired component to be placed in the box by the receiving division, the exact specifications for the component and the number that are to placed in the box. After the division has produced the components it places the box back upon its pallet, where the roaming vehicles can pluck it up, returning it to the division that originally dispatched it, the "kanban" providing the requisite information about where the box is to be destined.

Consider a concrete example. A door assembly division requires a certain type of bolt for its work. As its supply of bolts dwindles it empties the box for the bolts, placing it on its pallet with the requisite flag directing the box to the bolt division. The bolt division receives the box and produces the bolts working with the machining specifications stipulated on the flag. Production flow is continuous, seamless: bolts are not produced unless they are actually needed in assembly, little warehousing being required, the entire assembly process being pulled by the demands for final vehicle assembly. Using this system a factory can operate with a relatively short production plan, say a two week plan, adjusting to a new plan after the two weeks because of the flexibility built into the system.

A number of economic benefits emerge from this style of manufacturing. Warehousing cost is virtually, ideally, nil. Defects are economically costly. Suppose the bolt division manufactures bolts for the door assembly division that have the wrong threading. The door division will not be able to use them, immediately returning them to the bolt division. Production of doors is temporarily slowed down, making it difficult to meet its daily quota of doors required by the chassis assembly division in the plant. For this reason there is a strong push to obtain zero defect rates throughout the factory, to build quality into the components.

It should be stressed that the system is more than an engineering system. It is also, perhaps fundamentally, a human resource management system. In effect employees monitor each other, a division learning about poor attention to component manufacturing details in supplying divisions right away, the errors not being buried in boxes stacked in a warehouse. It also requires rapid setup times. The bolt division is not producing the same bolts over and over again. Responding to demand for different types of bolts throughout the factory, it has to adjust its machine settings flexibly, thereby being forced to practice machine resetting during downtimes, putting a premium on learning to work faster and more efficiently through practice.

Note that strikes are a real problem in this environment since manufactures cannot go to inventory when there is a work stoppage. The relatively low strike rates characteristic of Japan's highly internalized labor markets were an important part of the background to Toyota's decision to commit itself to a JIT system.

Specialization according to detailed job classifications that are used as the basis for assigning wages presents a problem for a JIT oriented factory. Suppose the chassis division encounters a bottleneck that it is unable to solve. It is able to hit a button that shuts down the plant, bringing in workers from all of the other divisions to help solve the problem encountered. This kind of problem solving is best serviced by a flexible labor force, by *generalists who move around from division to division, understanding the needs of workers in each and every stage of the assembly and manufacturing process. Thus a small number of job descriptions – say five rather than one hundred – is a sine qua non for smooth operation of a JIT system like the "kanban" system. In effect the principle of specialization and division of labor is being overridden by the supermarket principle that makes a virtue of flexible, continuous flow, production.*

The individual who played the leading role in pushing "kanban" at Toyota Motor was Ōno Taiichi, born the son of a ceramics technician working on the South Manchurian Railway in Dairen, Manchuria. His family moving back to Japan, Ōno eventually graduated from Nagoya Higher Industrial School in the early 1930s, joining Toyoda Spinning and Weaving upon graduation. It was at the Toyoda plant that he learned the importance of reducing defects and the importance of motivating workers through flexibility in job assignment. It was this knowledge won from the shop floor of a textiles factory, not from visits to an American or European automobile factory, not from study of books devoted to car and truck manufacturing, but rather from techniques that he had absorbed at Toyoda Spinning and Weaving during the Pacific war that he brought with him when he moved over to Toyota Motors.

Coming with fresh eyes to automobile production, Ōno was prepared to think outside the box, prepared to jettison the Ford Motor Corporation model – relying on scale economies, and relatively low prices won through mass production of vehicles built without variation – which had become the industry standard. One of Ōno's objections to the Ford model was its reliance on the massive stockpiling of inventories, costly in terms of warehousing, costly to finance when demand dropped below expectations. His second objection was the lack of flexibility built into the Ford assembly line. It could not respond as a supermarket could or should to changing consumer tastes, to a demand for diversity.

With this in mind, Ōno set out to design a system for Toyota Motors that mimicked what he thought were the virtues of Toyoda Spinning and Weaving, rising in the company to general manager of Toyota's Kamigo factory, eventually to executive vice-president of the company. Retiring in 1978, he returned to Toyoda Spinning and Weaving, becoming its chairman.

Redesigning shop floors so that workers throughout a plant could and would flexibly respond to bottlenecks breaking out at any particular part of the assembly process, reducing the stocking of inventories of components for later assembly to bare minimums, encouraging groups of workers to form quality control teams that systematically studied ways to improve product quality constitute a set of interlocking innovations that has transformed automobile manufacture in Japan and abroad. This package of practices constitutes a cumulative breakthrough in human resource management far beyond a simple imitative adaptation of foreign techniques to Japanese conditions. Under the system rank and file production workers changed assignments in a plant on a frequent basis, practicing machine setups during lulls in production, and took over many phases of quality control management and production process design customarily assigned to engineers in the West. It was industrial democracy in the best sense of the word. To boot it seemed to call into question the concepts of specialization and division of labor central to classical economic theory.

In understanding why this breakthrough occurred in Japan during miracle growth several points are worthy of mention. First it was compatible with the push toward the wholesale internalization of labor in larger Japanese firms, workers being given permanent employment guarantees, being paid through a combination of seniority/age and merit principles, encouraging workers to invest heavily in skills specific to their particular firm of employment. The impetus to turn much of the quality control program over to blue-collar workers could not have occurred had the educational qualifications of the general labor force not improved so markedly after World War II. The fact that space is at a premium in Japan – the high population densities driving up the cost of land – may have encouraged employees to save on warehouse space, thereby encouraging just-in-time inventory control programs.

Beyond these supply side factors was the nature of demand. Reorienting its trade away from Asia towards the United States first, Europe second – that is swinging away from the relatively low income per capita markets that it focused on during the 1930s toward high income markets in the West – encouraged major Japanese manufactures throughout the transportation equipment industry to upgrade their products, improve their quality, so that they could establish a niche in the West. Establishing an initial beachhead in the huge high per capita income American market was especially crucial to this kind of marketing strategy.

Honda Soichiro, Fujisawa Takeo and the Honda Motor Company

The noted business historian Alfred Chandler has described the successful modern industrial enterprise as an organization combining investments in manufacturing, in marketing and in management. Adding technology to the mix suggests that companies that generate dynamic growth, like the Honda Motor Company, have to be innovative in many distinct areas, ranging from technical invention to an understanding of what sells and how to sell, and how to hold down the production costs for what sells. Seldom does the ability to be innovative in these four different arenas fall on a single pair of shoulders. As often as not, the dynamic enterprise emerges out of the combined activity of two vision driven individuals complementary to one another in their gifts.

A classical eighteenth-century illustration of the importance of combining the talents of two ambitious and talented individuals is the team of Matthew Boulton and James Watt that developed the steam engine, built a factory in Soho near Birmingham in the British midlands to manufacture the engines, and figured out how to adjust its design so that it could be harnessed to spinning machines in textile factories, expanding the market for the engines beyond its initial confines in pumping out mine shafts. In the Boulton-Watt partnership that was founded in 1775 Watt was the inventor, reluctant to venture beyond the designing of steam engines for mining operations; Boulton was the brilliant market oriented entrepreneur who already ran a factory at Soho before enticing Watt to join him in a partnership, imagining fresh outlets for selling the engines in the new factories springing up in the industrial revolution, cajoling his partner into trying out experimental models that would serve as the templates for factory based steam engines.

The story of the emergence of the Honda Motor Company in post-World War II Japan is a story of how a marvelous inventor, Honda Soichiro, teamed up with an equally gifted market oriented entrepreneur, Fujisawa Takeo. Working in tandem the two dynamos moved the enterprise rapidly up the ladder of the motorized vehicle industry. From its initial base in 1948 producing motorized bicycles, the company moved into full-fledged motorcycles (the Dream and the Cub), capturing a devoted consumer base with the innovative Super Cub (employing an unconventional "step through" design developed by Honda that appealed to female enthusiasts). Eventually they moved into automobile production with the fuel-efficient Civic (introduced in the American market in 1972), the nicely handling and more upscale Accord (1976), and the luxurious Acura created in 1986. Along the way the company became famous for its inventive engine designs, launching the VTEC variable valve timing system in the late 1980s.

Honda was the inventor. Restless and committed to fostering creative thinking among the ranks of his engineers and designers, Honda wanted to create a "paperweight" type structure for the product design side of the business – one in which the title chief engineer or executive engineer could be held by a large number of individuals promoted because of their talents not because they were needed as supervisors for subordinate employees – rather than a "pyramid" structure in which the number of persons given titles like chief engineer was limited by the number of employees employed, a chief engineer assigned to lead a production team of a specified size. To facilitate the realization of Honda's dream, Fujisawa recommended that the corporation spin off a separate research and development entity devoted to product design, Honda R & D. Company Ltd. being established in 1960.

Fujisawa equaled Honda's innovative nature but did so not in technical areas but rather in marketing and factory management. He realized early on that the key to successful sales in the Japanese motorcycle market was to establish separate dealership networks for separate products. Following this logic, introducing a new line would not generate dealer resistance, the dealers already having built up inventories of the earlier line that they were determined to sell off before considering the selling of new products. With this in mind, Fujisawa avoided the wholesalers who were handling the Dream when Honda Motor came out with the Cub. Fujisawa was equally concerned about diversifying the production base of the business, promoting the purchase of old run down small (and hence cheap) factories in a variety of locales, including a number in the Kantō area. Fujisawa was also instrumental in making American Honda successful. It is said that his strategy was to initiate entry into the United States market with the Super Cub, building up a dealership base with the popular model. However controversy surrounds this point. Some argue that the initial success of Honda in the American market was not due to any particular strategy – for instance inundating the United States market with relatively low priced motorbikes – but rather lay in flexibility. For instance the American division decided to back off from selling large 300 cc. motorcycles when employees at its San Francisco based headquarters discovered that the Super Cub scooters they were using to get around in were attracting considerable customer interest, outstripping the interest in their large motorcycles.

In addition, in the domestic markets government regulation played a role in promoting the zero-defect ideal: in the automobile industry the *shaken*, the mandatory vehicle inspection system, was a regulatory device designed by the government to ensure high quality standards for passenger cars. Under the system any car over three years in age is subject to a mandatory maintenance check (*shaken*) every other year. If defects are found by inspecting stations these problems have to be addressed, repairs completed and recorded before the car is certified for use.

The precise impact of *shaken* on domestic demand for automobiles cannot be simply evaluated. That there is a costly burden of inspection attached to owning a passenger car raises the overall cost of car ownership to a prospective buyer. At the same time it encourages current owners of cars to sell off their cars after three years. It discourages manufactures from building obsolescence into their cars, a charge leveled by some critics of the American automotive industry during the 1960s and 1970s. In any event, the existence of the *shaken* system during the miracle growth era did give a strong fillip to improving the average quality of Japanese automobiles.

To generalize from the examples we have briefly surveyed: several factors encouraged reduction in real production costs in Japanese manufacturing. One was accumulation of capital that drove down the mean age of the capital stock, leading to embodiment of newer technologies in plant and equipment. Another was pure innovation, advances in knowledge crystallized in new products and in new production methods like *kanban*. The net effect of these types of changes sweeping across most sub-sectors of manufacturing – especially across the export oriented subsectors – was a general lift in total factor productivity (that is in output per unit of input) throughout manufacturing. In the older industries that had already absorbed and adapted Western technology – in textiles and food products – the gains were minimal, muted at best. This is apparent from Panel C of Table 8.3. In the newer sectors – those expanding aggressively during the 1960s – like transportation equipment, machinery and rubber products – total factor productivity increase was substantial. What is interesting about the figures in Table 8.3 is that wage growth was pretty much the same, both in sectors with low rates of total factor productivity growth and in sectors with high rates of total factor productivity growth. Why this is the case is a topic to which we turn in the next section.

In appreciating the implications of the massive expansion of manufacturing that was the hallmark of miracle growth the continuing pressure on firms due to competition in product markets should not be overlooked. Where gains in labor productivity (output per worker) were rapid competition tended to drive down product prices. This statement assumes that wage growth is fairly uniform across industries, a tendency that we shall discuss in the next section. We have already hinted at this tendency with Panel C of Table 8.3. The figures assembled in Panel D of Table 8.3 support our assertion. For instance the tendency for prices to drop in the electric machinery subsector is attributable to the high rates of growth of labor productivity that prevailed there. The competitiveness of the Japanese marketplace should never be underestimated.

Labor

The institutions of the thoroughgoing internalization of Japanese labor during the miracle growth era are famous. They are often referred to as the "three jewels" of the Japanese employment system: lifetime employment; wages paid according to age and seniority (so called *nenkō* wages); and enterprise unionism.

Referring to these as the "three jewels" is misleading. In practice "lifetime employment" was a guarantee of employment until compulsory retirement to workers (not caught carrying out illegal activities or acts subversive to the company), typically age 55 during the miracle growth era. Even under strict *nenkō* guidelines workers were paid according to two principles: "*nen*" standing for age/seniority; and "*kō*" indicating merit.

It has been argued at least initially, during the 1950s when the standard of living in Japan was low that the age/seniority component reflected the needs of typical workers, family related financial responsibilities rising with age due to marriage, procreation and the rearing of offspring, and the assuming of responsibility for caring for aging parents. The merit or productivity component was reflected biannual bonuses that mirrored fairly accurately contributions to the firm. In addition workers competed for promotion to positions of greater influence and greater financial reward in companies. So even during the heyday of *nenkō* – the 1950s – average wage profiles for workers reflected productivity based factors independent of age.

Additionally the proportion of the labor force working in firms offering the "three jewels" package was limited. Agriculture did not offer the package. Small business did not offer the package. Self-employed individuals paid themselves wages. Government workers were not really covered under the system. Using a cut-off for firm size of one thousand workers or over as the percentage of workers definitely covered by the "three jewels" system, it is apparent from Panel A.1 of Table 8.4 that at least a third of male workers in manufacturing were covered by the rules of the system. To be sure, many employees in medium sized firms – those employing between 100 and 999 workers – were covered by institutional guarantees similar to those applicable in the large firm sector. However many were not.

The Japanese labor market of the miracle growth era was highly dualistic. Some workers gained relatively well paying employment, largely in bigger private sector firms; others worked on their own, managing family enterprises in farming or in manufacturing; some worked in small and medium sized enterprises typically at wage levels lower than those prevailing in larger firms. Evidence on the wage differentials prevailing during the period 1951–85 appears in Panel A.2 of Table 8.4. It is important to keep in mind that dualism was not a feature of the Japanese manufacturing scene in the early twentieth century when most employment in manufacturing was in light industry and was heavily female. Dualism emerged during the second decade of the twentieth century – especially during the World War I boom – associated with male workers in the nascent heavy industries in the main.

Wage levels reflect labor productivity levels that in turn are impacted by the capital/labor ratio. As is apparent from Panel A.3 dualism impacted the workplace in a myriad of dimensions: in terms of capital per worker and in terms of the value added that their labors generated. Not surprisingly, worker mobility was intertwined with the wage levels and the nature of the work environment. In small firms, workers moved around with considerable frequency. Indeed, it is not inaccurate to describe wage determination in that sector as reflecting the forces of supply and demand on the spot market first and foremost. On the other hand in large firms mobility was limited. Worker mobility within the firm may have been high, workers being promoted, being moved from one plant to another, being trained in a wide variety of skills and tasks. But mobility between firms was fairly uncommon.

Given the distinctive dualism of the Japanese labor market during miracle growth, one wonders how prospective entrants to the labor market were sorted out between prospective employers. How did large firms – those implicitly trusting their new hires to bond with the firm, tying their personal career development to the success of their employees – recruit? Matching new workers with new jobs offered in the labor market was mediated through the educational system. Achieving certification by a particular educational school sent a signal out into the labor market, one picked up upon by prospective employers.

Table 8.4 Labor during miracle growth and its aftermath

Panel A.1   *Dualism in Japanese manufacturing, percentage of male employees in firm size groups (classified by number of employees)*

Year	1–29	30–99	100–999	1,000+
1965	23.5	17.1	26.4	32.7
1985	16.9	16.9	27.0	32.5

Panel A.2   *Dualism in Japanese manufacturing, wage differentials by firm size (average wages for firms with 1,000+employees = 100)*[a]

Year	1–29	30–49	50–99	100–199
1909	80.7	90.8	94.5	96.8
1951	41.7	54.4	60.3	68.5
1967	33.2	64.2	65.9	69.6
1985	n.a.	59.8	60.2	63.7

Panel A.3   *Dualism in Japanese manufacturing, value added and capital per worker by firm size (average levels for firms with 1,000+employees = 100)*

Year	20–29	100–199	300–499	500–999
Value added per worker				
1955	37.2	65.0	83.2	95.7
1967	44.1	58.0	71.9	84.1
1985	36.9	45.3	75.2	80.2
Capital per worker				
1985	30.1	38.1	56.6	65.1

Panel B.1   *Age-wage profiles, relative wages (monthly contracted including overtime) of workers aged 55–59 to those aged 20–24 = 100*

Year	Males			Females	
	Total	Old middle school/new high school	College	Total	Old middle school/new high school
1954	190.8	242.3	315.0	96.7	140.3
1965	185.0	223.6	318.0	111.6	158.6
1985	178.7	182.2	268.7	120.0	141.7

Panel B.2   *Model wage tables, relative wages of male workers aged 55 to those aged 22*[a]

Year	Middle school graduates (production workers)	High school graduates (production workers	College graduates (white collar)	Medium sized firms		
				Middle school graduates (production workers)	High school graduates (production workers	College graduates (white collar)
1965	300.4	374.8	508.6	261.7	300.4	350.5
1985	252.7	268.0	396.6	n.a.	n.a.	n.a.

Table 8.4 Continued

Panel C   *Retention rates (10 year), males classified by education, 1970 to 1980*

Accumulated years of seniority in 1970	Old middle school, new high school graduates		College graduates	
	Age in 1970		Age in 1970	
	25–34	*35–44*	*25–34*	*35–44*
0–4 years	51.2	54.9	63.4	58.5
5–9 years	62.0	65.6	74.0	73.8
10 years or more	69.9	68.2	79.3	85.4

Panel D   *The fruits of shuntō collective bargaining*[a]

Period	Large companies		Percentage of small & medium sized companies (3)	Percentage of days lost to strikes and sized lockouts of companies over ½ day duration per 100 employees (4)	Percentage increase rate for consumer price index (5)	Percentage estimated real wage growth for large companies (column 1– column 5 value) (6)
	Mean % (1)	Coefficient of variation (2)				
1956–1960	7.1	0.23	n.a.	25.4	1.6	5.5
1961–1965	11.3	0.14	13.5	17.4	6.0	5.3
1966–1970	14.2	0.08	15.0	9.5	5.5	8.7
1971–1972	16.1	0.08	17.4	16.3	5.3	10.8
1973–1975	22.0	0.09	23.0	20.4	16.0	6.0
1976–1980	7.3	0.13	7.9	4.3	6.5	0.8

Source: Various tables in Mosk (1995).

Note
a n.a. = not available.

In appreciating the way signaling through certification in the educational system operated, in appreciating why the relative earnings of persons with various levels of certification changed over time, one must realize that the educational system was not static during the miracle growth period. On the contrary it was dynamic. It was dynamic because it was heavily – but not exclusively – market driven, responsive to supply and demand shifts. Increase in the demand for education over and above compulsory secondary schooling responded to increments in average levels of per capita household income (which soared during miracle growth). The capacity of households to pay for the higher education of their children improved. Demand shifts stimulated supply shifts, supply shifting as a combination of political pressure on the public sector and market pressure acting on the private sector drove school advancement rates upward at a dizzying pace. The advancement rate to high school leaped upward from about 55 percent in the late 1950s to over 90 percent by the 1970s. Educational institutions – academic high schools, technical vocationally oriented high schools, two and four-year colleges – proliferated over the miracle growth era, many of them privately financed. Of the 247 universities added between 1950 and 1980, 87 percent were private.

Within the graduating classes at each level of the educational system there were gradations marked by the hierarchical ranking of the schools involved. Cut throat competition on grueling entrance examinations that put an emphasis on copious memorization of facts significant and silly differentiated the schools at the top of the pecking order from schools further down in the hierarchy. With the Ministry of Education setting slots for each department in each university on the basis of quantitative criteria – the ratio of students to seats and library books for instance – the higher ranked schools in the hierarchy were those rejecting the greatest proportion of prospective entrants. Other things equal hard working diligent ambitious students preferred to apply to the top national universities – Tokyo, Kyoto, Osaka, Hitotsubashi – because tuition was considerably cheaper at national universities than at private universities. But in the private sector competition for enrollment slots was equally intense, schools like Keio and Waseda that enjoyed premiere reputations sitting at the top of the pecking order. For most students securing admission to a high ranking school – a high ranking vocational school for those terminating at that level; a high ranking university for those advancing to the pinnacle of tertiary schooling – the prospects for securing a position in a profitable and prestigious large firm were excellent. Top firm personnel departments, relying heavily on selecting prospective employees on the basis of educational credentials, ensured that students who successfully navigated through a seemingly endless maze of daunting tests to reach the apex of the educational stream they had selected had at least one, perhaps all three, of the following three characteristics: diligence, dogged perseverance or intelligence. Firms further down the pecking order resigned themselves to picking up graduates from less highly ranked institutions or worse dropouts from the school system.

To recapitulate: on the demand side of the labor market rising income per capita and employment opportunities in successful firms were crucial, especially for males expecting to pursue careers as employees. On the supply side government policy played a role. The Ministry of Education set minimum accreditation standards. In principle student slots for departments in universities, academic high schools, technical high schools were allocated by the bureaucracy on the basis of the number of faculty members, the seating capacity of classrooms and the number of books in academically oriented institutions or the number of machines in vocationally oriented establishments. In practice, the Ministry tolerated some overcrowding, some watering down of standards.

As in the prewar period, the Ministry of Education had available to it short-run indicators – like the number of *rōnin* attending cram schools with the aim of gaining admission to schools that had rejected them at least once – upon which it could base decisions about accrediting more institutions, in which it could permit overcrowding. For long-run planning it relied on projections of future demand based upon combining demographic projections with expectations about advancement rates. As important as market driven demand in the labor market was to shaping the supply of new entrants to that market, supply, therefore policy, mattered as well.Given the importance of the educational system for sorting out entrants into the labor market – who gets into prestigious firms and who does not, what are the expectations for future promotion within the firm doing the hiring – it is not surprising that the steepness of wage profiles for workers reflected their educational attainment. Evidence bearing upon expectations appears in Panel B.2 of Table 8.4. The figures are averages for so-called "standard workers," those expected to stay with their firm from recruitment until compulsory retirement. Therefore the figures are for larger firms, not those small enterprises lacking formal personnel departments. What they suggest is that upon being hired a college graduate recruit in the mid-1960s could expect to advance far faster up the promotional ladder than a high school graduate.

In short, the expected payoff to graduating from a university during the 1950s and 1960s was substantial. It set a signal about diligence and dedication that larger firms valued, thereby increasing the probability of being hired by a larger enterprise and the probability of being promoted along a fast track within the internal labor market. Even taking into account figures on wage profiles for a broader range of employment opportunities in the private sector – in small, medium and giant enterprises – does not reverse the finding that college graduates generally moved up the advancement ladder with greater success than high school graduates. This is the message of Panel B.1 of Table 8.4. The signal sent out by the educational system was crucial in the dualistic economy.

Given the high anticipated returns to getting a university education it is not surprising that the proportion of individuals advancing on through high school to the tertiary sector jumped dramatically during the miracle growth period. If their parents could afford to support them through three years of high school and four years of college, if they were able to garner credible scores on standardized tests, they were likely to try to secure a university or college credential. The net effect of this surge was an increase in the relative supply of college/university graduates relative to those with high school and junior high school credentials. Reflecting the shift in relative labor supply, the opportunity for university graduates to shine in companies large and small diminished. As their promotional chances dimmed – as they crowded up against one another – the wage profiles for higher educational graduates flattened, becoming more and more like those for high school graduates. The figures for the 1980s in Panels B.1 and B.2 reflect these supply shifts, rewards in both internalized and spot labor markets operating as market principles suggest they should.

The lesson of this discussion on education specific wage profiles is that the stylized "three jewels" of the Japanese labor market are part myth, part reality. The same statement applies to permanent employment. As Panel C of Table 8.4 shows, ten-year retention rates measuring the likelihood that a male worker would remain with a firm for another decade are quite high for workers who have already been with the firm for at least ten years, but significantly lower for recent recruits. To some extent this probably reflects promotion, both records of advancement already achieved and expectations for the future. The fact that college graduates are less likely to abandon an employer than a high school graduate seemingly testifies to this fact.

How are we to understand from a theoretical viewpoint the way internalized labor markets operate in Japan? Sociologists like Dore (1973, 1987) who emphasize the operation of Confucian principles in Japan argue that norms of benevolence, loyalty and respect for age and seniority are crucial. Reasoning along these lines one can argue that the labor contract governing large firms involves an implicit gift exchange, younger workers giving effort in exchange for current wages and opportunities for advancement, older workers being rewarded for helping guide their junior colleagues, for mentoring them. Echoing Dore's emphasis on norms and values but not Confucianism Inagami (1988) argues that the lack of specific job assignments stemming from rotation of tasks within work groups and promotional possibilities – the age/seniority component of *nenkō* assuring workers that they will not suffer a loss in earnings by jettisoning tasks they have done in the past in order to master new skills – makes the work place interesting and stimulating for most rank and file workers in larger enterprises. Workers seek a challenge. Large firm employers in Japan give them the opportunity to experience it.

In mainstream non-Marxist economics there are a variety of views, most stressing the importance of firm specific human capital. The argument here is that the combination of age/seniority wage payments and permanent employment encourages workers to invest in human capital that they can utilize in their current employment environment but not necessarily elsewhere. For example an automobile worker in a Toyota plant learns how to operate with the *kanban* (flag) system that is not employed at Nissan or Honda. Retirement is mandatory because at some point the contribution of workers to firm output falls below the wages paid to them. An alternative line argument, advanced by Mosk (1995) is rooted in efficiency wage theory. Workers are paid a premium wage in exchange for the extra effort they expend on behalf of the enterprise.

The third "jewel" in the crown of the Japanese employment system is enterprise unionism, the establishment of unions organized along firm lines rather than along industrial or craft lines encompassing and representing the interests of workers from a variety of employers. Given the dues that must be paid to support a union – to pay wages for full time union organizers and wage negotiators – it is not surprising that most unions in manufacturing are organized in large firms not in small enterprises. For this reason there is a strong overlap of the three phenomena we have been discussing – *nenkō*, permanent employment and enterprise unionism – with one another. In the dualistic economy of miracle growth, the institutions typical of large and those typical of small firms were completely different from one another.

As we have discussed already, theories abound as to why enterprise unionism became the norm in Japan after 1945. Some emphasize the demands of labor, the fact that attempts at unionization prior to the late 1930s went hand in glove with the demand on the part of rank and file production workers to secure the same internalized labor status accorded to white-collar employees. Another view emphasizes the role of government policy. Officials organizing the popular labor front in the total war period along firm lines followed legislation passed in Nazi Germany, laying the groundwork of enterprise based unionism in the late 1940s and early 1950s. Another view is that companies fought for it, management breaking industry wide unionism through bitterly fought lockouts, promoting alternatives to industry wide unions by encouraging the organizing activities of workers sympathetic to enterprise unionism. In any event it is apparent that the union form most compatible with the idea of the personnel department determining promotions and bonuses, and with the concept of continual job rotation within work groups is the enterprise-based form. Wage scales determined for specific job classifications through extensive negotiation between labor and management do not rest easily with the human resource management approach taken by most Japanese companies.

In the wake of the spread of enterprise unionism, the leaders of unions realized that they must band together to coordinate their campaigns for wage increases. If workers in a particular company perceive that going out on strike will first and foremost serve to damage their firm's market share within an industry, rival firms not impacted by strikes picking up contracts for output that their own firm can not honor, they will be reticent to brandish the strike-threat club. The general strike is the solution. Driven into federations by this hard cold reality, unions agreed to coordinate their efforts. The most famous coordinated campaign – not the only one taking place during miracle growth – is the *shuntō*, the Spring Offensive.

A myriad of disparate unions harnessing their efforts under *shuntō* style collective bargaining, hitting upon the simplest formula for bargaining was crucial, in the interests of both union federations and business federations. The solution was the base-up increase: increase the overall wage bill by a specific percentage, letting the personnel departments in individual firms distribute wages and bonuses to individual workers in accordance with age, seniority, education, position in the company hierarchy and productivity over the recent period. Given the desire on the part of the both workers and management in the least profitable companies within an industry to stay afloat (if an enterprise goes under so does the union organized within it), it is not surprising that the base-up formula is set so that most participating enterprises avoid bankruptcy. While the union federation organizing the *shuntō* attempts to pick a "top batter" set of firms that are successful and crucial to manufacturing – for instance iron and steel firms during the 1950s and early 1960s, automobile firms later on – the reality is that the coordinated push to get wage settlements during the spring of each year tends to generate base-up increases permitting most firms in Japan to survive. More profitable firms can settle along lines close to those acceptable to their less fortunate rivals, adding to their profitability, permitting them to make especially generous bonus payments to their employees, rewarding them for their extra effort.

Getting a national consensus for wage increases – one most firms in most industries can live with – became the watchword of the spring offensive for negotiators cutting deals at a highly federated level. The negotiated norm in the world of the large unionized company spilled over into the world of the non-unionized small scale enterprise. Some figures illustrative of the way *shuntō* operates appears in Panel D of Table 8.4. Notable is the sharp decline in the coefficient of variation – a measure of the variability of – base-up wage settlements between the late 1950s when the system was just getting off the ground and the 1970s. Also notable is the sharp decline in the number of strikes carried out. The sharp upward spike in prices in the 1973–75 period associated with the surge in oil prices brought on by a coordinated campaign among petroleum exporting nations to withhold shipments of oil temporarily disturbed the relatively peaceful coexistence of union stalwarts and management federations. But cooperation soon resumed. Strike activity virtually disappeared during the second half of the 1970s.

At first glance it would seem that the key elements of the "three jewels" of the Japanese labor-management system might yield rigidity. Linking wages to age or seniority within the enterprise; the enterprise guaranteeing workers employment regardless of business conditions; negotiating between union and management within the microcosm of the enterprise would seem to be a recipe for a system caught between the rock of inflexibility on the one side and the rock of fragmentation on the other. Remarkably the system seemed to produce its opposite: a relatively flexible management–labor environment that allowed individual companies to innovate in a variety of ways, experimenting with everything from use of digitally controlled machines to worker group managed quality control circles; at the same time relatively consensual wage determination, wage increases in most enterprises moving in tandem with one another. Welding labor flexibility that could and did accommodate much individual company experimentation, generating bold new initiatives for organizing shop floor flow of work, to consensus style across the board coordination in establishing base-up wage increases is one of the great achievements of miracle growth.

Industrial structure

Implicit contracts, unwritten guarantees, cementing trust between employers and employees within enterprises, wedding company fate to employee career, are supposed to lie at the heart of Japan's internalized labor markets according to much expert opinion. Similar arguments are made about the vertical ties that bind the fate of individual firms to their industry federations that bind sub-contractors and sub-sub-contractors to parent and grandparent companies. Similar arguments are made about the horizontal ties that link firms, across industries: those involving the connections between a main bank and the firms dependent on it for funding; those involving cross-sharing of stock and sharing of information in lunch clubs within the *keiretsu* that emerged out of the ashes of the liquidated *zaibatsu* and *shinzaibatsu*; those involving distribution chains, the products of firms being handled by specific wholesalers and retailers.

Legions of sociologists and economists have accepted these arguments, arguing that Japan is a highly networked society, costly information and financial capital flowing between the key nodes. For instance the sociologist Dore (1987) argues that a web of relational contracts both vertical and horizontal help insure enterprises against bankruptcy, spreading both risk and information, placing community interests above narrow corporate interests. Typical of much of the industrial organization literature in economics concerning miracle growth capital markets, Caves and Uekasu (1976) argue that *keiretsu* ties were important in shaping commercial dealings, resulting from Japan being a group oriented society, cooperation being a fundamental virtue. The book edited by Aoki and Patrick (1994) captures the reasoning behind mainstream economist thinking about the importance of main banks for the financing of Japanese investment during miracle growth.

Taking on the whole panoply of these arguments – vertical sub-contracting, horizontal *keiretsu*, horizontal main bank and client firm – Miwa and Ramseyer (2006a) attempt to debunk the entire concept of implicit contracting in Japan, arguing that it has created a picture of the Japanese economy that is wrongheaded, missing the fundamental point that cutthroat competition not cooperation is key to the drive of Japanese industry. Of the horizontal relationships perhaps the greatest controversy has surrounded the relationship between main banks and clients. The idea is simple: during miracle growth capital for investment was hard to come by. The domestic capital market was largely closed off to foreign investors. Due to severe conditions imposed on firms allowed to float equity issue in the stock and bond market most companies large and small were constrained to finance their investment through indirect finance, relying upon banks and their own recycled profits for funding. Financial intermediaries, mainly banks, were heavily regulated by the Ministry of Finance and the Bank of Japan, and were unable to charge rates above a specified cutoff on long run loans. The regulators encouraged them to ration their scarce funds, informally assigning them firms to which they were to be main banks.

The main bank was supposed to serve as a kind of lender of last resort for the firm. It was supposed to step in when and if the firm floundered, pumping liquidity into the firm during periods of distress, guaranteeing it would stay afloat, staving off bankruptcy. In addition the main bank monitored companies dependent on it – doing what auditors, bond rating companies and members of board of directors having an arm's length relationship with the firm do in the United States – often placing key bank officers on the boards of the companies linked to them through the main bank relationship. Those firms not enjoying main bank connections – especially small enterprises without many capital assets that they could offer as collateral – could be and were rationed out of the market particularly during periods when the monetary authorities tightened up on the money supply.

Many economists argue that this system was basically cooperative, basically healthy, directing capital where it was used most efficiently in a miracle growth economy, the huge and surging levels of investment demand always threatening to outstrip supply of savings. Critics of the main bank thesis point out a number of facts inconvenient for the theory.[1] Critics point out that firms did raise equity on the stock and bond markets. They note that banks could easily avoid regulations setting ceilings for the interest rates they charged. One approach was to cut up the loan into smaller slices, each one of which fell below the level at which an interest rate ceiling kicked in. A second approach was to require that the borrower keep a compensating balance – a certain amount of the total borrowed – in an account within the lending institution, thereby raising the effective interest rate charged by the bank. In addition the evidence on placing bank officers on boards of directors of borrowing firms and the evidence on extending loans to firms under siege due to poor business decisions is ambiguous.

A second criticism of the main bank hypothesis is that the relationship between bank and borrower was not especially cooperative, rather largely exploitative. According to Weinstein and Yafeh (1998) main banks acted like local monopolists, charging interest rates to firms higher than would have been the case had capital markets been open and competitive, extracting a share of the profits earned by the companies through their investments in new plant and equipment and their innovations. While not completely rejecting the thesis that main banks may have provided implicit insurance against bankruptcy – a thesis that Miwa and Ramseyer (2006a) do attempt to throw out – the thrust of Weinstein and Yafeh (1998) is that the main banks were more dependent on the firms, on the profits earned by businesses, rather than vice-versa.

Paralleling debate about main banks, controversy has surrounded the horizontal *keiretsu* groups. Many of these emerged during the miracle growth era as the former companies held together under *zaibatsu* holding companies reassembled as groups linked together through lunch clubs in which presidents of the affiliated companies met periodically to hear speakers and chat informally, through use of the group logo, and through cross-shareholding of stock. Operating under the umbrella of a typical miracle growth *keiretsu* was a bank, an insurance company, a group of heavy industries (e.g. iron and steel, shipbuilding, automobile manufacturing), electric machinery, a real estate firm and a general trading company.

Were the destinies of the enterprises in a miracle growth *keiretsu* intertwined with one another? At one extreme is the view that the *keiretsu* pursued a strategy of having "one set". There was competition about opposing *keiretsu* groups. If one introduced a new type of enterprise – say a company making aluminum – the other groups felt compelled to follow suit, all desiring the same "one set". According to this view investment in miracle growth could and did become excessive, fanatical pursuit of the "one settism" principle driving capital formation. How fanatical is adherence to "one-settism"? Invoking the monopolistic competition model may provide an economic rationale for "one settism": to establish credibility in the market as a viable monopolistic differentiating its products with the *keiretsu* label, new start up firms flocked to *keiretsu*.

At the opposite extreme is the view that *keiretsu* ties were weak. Little was discussed in lunch club meetings. Cross-shareholding of stock was very limited.

Most company heads of companies in the group were too heavily immersed in what was going on within their own industries and too focused upon their own personal management challenges to pay much attention to what was going on among other firms within the *keiretsu*. The salience of vertical relations is equally controversial. Consider industrial associations. How important were these for facilitating information flow back and forth between the industries and industrial bureaus in the Ministry of Trade and Industry? Dore (1987) and Teranishi (2005) think they were crucial to the implementation of administrative guidance in industrial policy, helping the industry and the ministry set up recession cartels to protect the industries from spewing out gluts of the market. But there is opposition to this view. Especially hostile are those economists skeptical about the value or effective operation of ministry regulated cartels and those economists who argue that administrative guidance was more myth than substance, the ministries having little power to enforce their policies on particular firms, let alone particular industries.

The other type of vertical relationship frequently cited is the vertical *keiretsu* involving parent company interacting with subcontractors and sub-sub-contractors and sub-sub-sub-contractors in long chains of complexity. A classic example often referred to is the cluster of automotive parts suppliers located in the vicinity of Toyota Motors Corporation in Toyota City near Nagoya. The number of companies involved is over one hundred. How intertwined are the destinies of these companies?

Some experts argue that this cluster is deeply intermeshed. Subcontractors deliver goods to Toyota Motors on a just-in-time basis. Technology flows back and forth between parent and child (Toyota Motors being the parent, a company like Denso the child company manufacturing electronic equipment parts for instance), between child and grandchild, and so forth. When Toyota wishes to upgrade its capital equipment, it is inclined to sell off some of its used machinery to sub-contractors. Workers retiring from Toyota may well take jobs in subcontractors, or even set up sub-sub-contractors on their own. By not vertically integrating these parts suppliers into the Toyota Motor Corporation, Toyota stays lean and mean, avoiding taking on numerous employees to whom it would be obligated under the permanent employment system. Rather than guarantee these workers jobs under all business conditions, Toyota leaves the responsibility to take care of these workers to the other, financially independent, enterprises operating under the umbrella of its *keiretsu*.

To repeat: the idea is that a high level of relational contracting based upon implicit contracts between firms within descending *keiretsu* cascades in Japan creates efficiencies. In other economies vertical integration is more likely to take place, sub-contractors being absorbed into parent companies. In other economies vertical integration is preferred because businesses at the top of a supplier chain are not willing to allow their deliveries to be held hostage to the changing whims of their sub-contractors.

Rather than continually write legally binding contracts on an ongoing basis to cover each and every new contingency that develops as the nature of the subcontracting components changes, companies in North America for instance opt for vertical integration. Trust being limited, transaction costs are considerable. The command and control system prevailing within the boundaries of the typical Western firm – managers and design engineers sending down orders from above to the shop floor – proves to be a more efficient method for carrying out assembly line production using components than a decentralized relational contracting system. In Japan, networking is so widespread, trust is so pervasive, the importance of the hierarchical exchange of benevolence for loyalty and diligence is so strong, that implicit contracts dominate, the supply chain *keiretsu* becoming a dominant form of organization throughout manufacturing, and throughout the distribution system.

Critics of this argument point out that most sub-contractors supply components to a variety of assembly enterprises. For instance Honda and Toyota both buy sparkplugs from the same supplier on occasion. Moreover – as I was informed personally by the manager of a sub-contracting company making ball bearings for truck and automobile assembly companies – higher level companies in a chain rarely intervene to bail out their sub-contractors. Stockholders and other stakeholders having an interest in a particular enterprise expect the enterprise's management to take responsibility for its own bottom line, not someone else's bottom line. This said there are less costly measures that a parent company can take. For instance a major company like Toyota may provide an important service for the owner of a sub-contractor or sub-sub-contractor by introducing him or her to the officers of a bank that Toyota deals with on a regular basis (its main bank if one believes that the main bank system was ubiquitous during the miracle growth period). Clout counts.

In many analyses of the miracle growth economy, implicit contracts take center stage. Coming out of the sociological literature are claims are being made about the so-called homogeneity of preferences and values in Japan or claims regarding the influence of Confucianism interpreting the capacity to arrive at implicit contracts in terms of norms and values. For instance one hears arguments that begin with assertions that the Japanese are group oriented. This may be true. But to extend the argument past the confines of the enterprise one must make assumptions about how and why people in other enterprises matter. If the argument is institutional – certain institutions like the main bank system emerging out of the crucible of the total war and occupation experiences – one is tempted to ask whether the institutions hindered or hampered miracle growth. Given the relatively high and rising rate of domestic savings were there not other potential avenues, just as potent as those that did develop, whereby investment could have been channeled to firms in an efficient manner, whereby more vertical integration might have generated even more rapid growth in output than actually occurred?

Policy

The literature concerning the impact of economic policy upon miracle growth is voluminous. For many scholars this is the real story of miracle growth. Since policy is a many-headed hydra, since policies can conflict from time to time, we need to keep in the background a battery of questions as we examine the issue of how policy making influenced miracle growth. Who makes policy? How is it implemented? What penalties are levied upon enterprises ignoring or consciously rejecting the policies? Do policies conflict or are they consistent?

In regard to these issues it is helpful to remind the reader of the various ways government can and does interact with the economy. These were discussed in Chapter 1 in the section dealing with Table 1.1. With this in mind we can name the key actors responsible for making and implementing policy. In principle, elected politicians – in particular by cabinets formed by the Liberal Democratic Party – laid out the key directions of economic policy during the miracle growth period, the cabinet and especially the prime minister drawing upon the professional expertise of the Economic Planning Agency in drafting specific proposals. In turn the cabinet left it to the various ministries with authority over specific jurisdictions – in fiscal affairs to the Ministry of Finance that set spending levels for itself and all the other ministries and came up with taxation formulas; in monetary affairs to the Bank of Japan largely operating under the aegis of the Ministry of Finance during the miracle growth era that attempted to adjust the money supply and control the volume of business loans; in industrial policy to the Ministry of International Trade and Industry – to actually implement the policies.

The validity of this characterization has been much debated. There is an important school of thought that views bureaucrats in the ministries as the linchpin of economic policy making, especially during the miracle growth period. The Liberal Democratic Party faction ridden, individual politicians committed to the parochial interests of their specific communities – to farmers, to small businesses – turnover of politicians assigned to head up specific ministries was frequent, often occurring every two years. According to the logic of this thesis, politicians reign; bureaucrats rule.[2]

In any event policy is implemented by ministries that compete for resources to fund their staffs, competing for influence over industries, engaging in turf wars. Not surprisingly the ministries break into factions, both internally and as a group. Is it realistic to assume that they coordinate their efforts, mutually supporting one another's actions?

The view that coordination occurs, either explicitly or implicitly, is sometimes crudely characterized by the term "Japan, Inc.". According to this view the miracle growth economic bureaucracies operated mainly through non-legislative means, through informal guidance, through cajoling and threatening banks, industrial firms, construction companies, marginalizing those that do not dance to their tune through pressure tantamount to blackmail. Using the weapon of administrative guidance, the economic bureaucracy created an economy with the following characteristics: a high rate of savings mainly channeled through banks, especially big city banks, to industrial concerns targeted by the bureaucracy. The type of coordination envisioned by the "Japan, Inc." hypothesis has the following key features: rationing of bank credit, interest rates set below the level that would clear in a competitive open capital market; a balanced budget for the governmental sector; and industrial policy sending signals, direct commands upon occasion, to the business sector regarding the structure of the economy desired by the bureaucratic planners. We should differentiate two versions of the "Japan, Inc." thesis: that meant to apply to the miracle growth economy at all times: and that meant to apply to the miracle growth economy during periods of aggregate economic imbalance. By aggregate economic imbalance is meant domestic investment exceeding domestic savings, or the alternative statement that imports exceed exports. Let us call the first view the strong "Japan, Inc." thesis; the second the weak "Japan, Inc." thesis.

We shall review evidence supporting the weak version here; we shall not pretend to defend the strong version in these pages. Arguments that we have already encountered – about banks evading the regulations on interest rates for sizable loans by cutting up loans into smaller components or requiring compensating balances – seem too powerful to ignore. However the weak version of the hypothesis is easier to justify at least partially. In reviewing monetary and fiscal policy we shall encounter it.[3]

We begin with monetary policy. In a typical central banking regime, private banks make deposits in the central bank. These are mandated reserves. The central bank sets the reserve ratio – the ratio of the deposits held in the central bank to the total customer deposits made into the bank – in order to ensure that there is liquidity available to the bank so that it can meet the demands placed on it by its customers for cash. The higher the reserve ratio, the less likely a bank will be imperiled by a bank run, caught between its illiquid loans outstanding and the demands of its depositors for cash. The central bank pays interest on the reserves held in its coffers, the rate of interest called the discount rate. If the central bank wants to contract the money supply, it can raise the reserve ratio, thereby curtailing the loan activity of each bank in the system to a degree, or it can raise the discount rate, thereby discouraging the bank from making marginal loans likely to pay anticipated returns below the discount rate. One policy lever makes use of the price mechanism – the interest rate – the other lever quantity, namely the reserve ratio. Again in a typical central bank system the central bank can carry out a bond for money swap known as an open market operation. When the central bank sells bonds to the banks, the banks have less money available to them to loan out since they have expended funds on the purchase of the bonds. The money supply falls. Bond prices fall as the bonds are sold off, driving interest rates up (bond prices and interest rates move against each other). The contraction in money is associated with a rise in the price of securing it for loans, namely the interest rate. Increasing the money supply involves a bond for money swap in the opposite direction: the central bank buys bonds from the member banks in the system. An open market operation involves manipulating the price at which money is borrowed by investors.

The fourth mechanism available to the central bank is window guidance, the central bank authorities exerting pressure on member banks to cut back on their loans, hence on the volume of new investment projects financed by the banking system as a whole. In most central bank systems, this is not widely utilized, central banks preferring the open market operation or ratcheting up or down the discount rate. In miracle growth Japan, however, window guidance was the weapon of choice.

The reason why the Bank of Japan relied mainly on guidance is well known. The bond market was fairly thin, the government running balanced budgets until the mid-1960s, issuing very little debt, some larger private enterprises raising capital through the equity market. More importantly, the Bank of Japan allowed overloan to occur, big city banks being permitted to have negative reserves with the Bank of Japan, to loan out more than 100 percent of their total deposits plus debentures. Under the overloan system, big city banks staved off bank runs by borrowing from the Bank of Japan against collateral held at the Bank of Japan, and by borrowing from smaller banks in the short-term call money market. How could the Bank of Japan use hikes in the discount rate or in reserve requirements to cut the money supply when big city banks were allowed to run negative reserves? How could it make use of open market operations when the bond market was so underdeveloped? Under the circumstances guidance seemed to be the most viable approach.

Since big city banks were the primary lenders to large corporations, the overloan system favored the interests of larger enterprises, those awash in assets that could be put up for collateral. Small companies, unable to float bonds, relied almost exclusively upon accumulated profits and bank loans, typically paying higher borrowing costs, higher interest rates on loans, due to having less collateral that could be seized by the bank in the event that the borrower could not repay the loan. When the monetary authorities were satisfied that there was no aggregate demand imbalance, most borrowers with credible projects could find financing. When exports fell below imports, when a current account crisis developed, however, the Bank of Japan stepped in, forcing banks to cut down on loans, to ration. Not surprisingly, small companies were rationed out in these tight money phases, many slipping into bankruptcy.

Consistent with this logic, Ackley and Ishi (1976) demonstrate that Japanese recessions occurring during the period 1953–73 followed closely upon tightening up of loan activity stemming from Bank of Japan window guidance. Interestingly, in each of the major contractions – during 1954, during 1957–58, during 1964–65, during 1970–71 – export growth exceeded import growth, the balance of payments correcting. Indeed in all but one case, imports nose-dived while exports surged. In these episodes of tightening the monetary authorities wanted companies with a capacity to export to secure funding, other enterprises being rationed out if need be. To a substantial degree small and medium sized businesses paid the penalty for the Bank of Japan's pursuit of aggregate demand balance. When it was actively applied during miracle growth monetary policy was restrictive, designed to generate sharp and fairly immediate contractions, mainly because it worked through guidance and rationing rather than through slower moving responses to changes in the price of borrowing money.

Was fiscal policy coordinated with monetary policy? Evidence suggests that it was not. Indeed during almost every year of miracle growth, fiscal policy was modestly expansionary because it centered upon cutting taxes. Adhering to the Dodge Line, the government ran balanced budgets until 1965, not borrowing from the Bank of Japan or issuing bonds. In general because the government preferred regulation over direct ownership of companies, it held government expenditure below a quarter of national income, considerably lower than the ratios prevailing in Western Europe during the golden age of convergence.[4] Even when monetary policy geared up to generate a recession driven correction to aggregate demand imbalance, fiscal policy seemed to move along separate tracks, modestly expansionary because of the tax cutting agenda of the Ministry of Finance. On the other hand the fact that the Ministry of Finance was committed to the Dodge Line for many years kept it from raising funds through debt issue, thereby deterring it from crowding out the private sector in capital markets. In this sense the low interest policy of the Bank of Japan was at least consistent with the balanced budget commitment of the Ministry of Finance. Still it is hard to defend the idea that monetary and fiscal policies were entirely coordinated as is suggested by either strong or weak versions of the "Japan, Inc." thesis.

As controversial as rationing in effecting monetary policy during miracle growth is, controversy surrounding it pales in comparison to the discussions about the wisdom and effectiveness of facilitating/coordinating policies, especially the industrial policies carried out by the Ministry of International Trade and Industry's wielding of administrative guidance. The controversy over industrial policy in Japan, at least in academic circles outside of Japan, took off after the publication of Johnson's (1982) volume, *MITI and the Japanese Miracle*. Making a distinction between plan rationality and market rationality, Johnson argued that the kernel of the development state concept promoted especially by the Ministry of International Trade and Industry lay in the early Meiji period, originally trumpeted by the Ministry of Agriculture and Commerce that adhered to a plan rationality model, bureaucratic planning taking precedence over the vagaries of the market.[5] With the establishment of the Ministry of Commerce and Industry in 1925 and the Planning Bureau established in 1937 to wage total war, the planning model loomed larger and larger, only to spread its wings with the Ministry of International Trade and Industry during the Occupation and its miracle growth aftermath. Key to the Ministry's great success – which according to Johnson was realized with stunningly positive results in the massive expansion of the heavy and chemical industries during the 1950s and early 1960s – was administrative guidance, the informal pressure, tantamount to blackmail on occasion, exerted by highly respected and feared ministry bureaucrats committed to nationalistic economic development. The economic bureaucracy ruled during miracle growth. How effective was administrative guidance? Very, says Johnson (1982) citing a number of examples including a case involving a housing contractor in the city of Musashino, a suburb of Tokyo, and the oft-cited case involving the Sumitomo Metals Company. The former story revolved around the resistance of a large contractor being forced to cooperate with city authorities in

Captive bureaucrats?

How insulated are the Japanese bureaucrats in a ministry that regulates an industry from the pressures arising from the very enterprises within the industry that the ministry regulates? To what extent are Japanese bureaucrats captives of their industries, rather than disinterested agents operating in the public interest above the competitive fray of the business world? Do relationships of interdependence between regulator and regulated promote bureaucratic control over industries or do they promote private sector control over the regulating government agency?

While the interactions between regulated and regulators may take place on many levels – through arrangements of marriage of children, through social mixing at parties – there is a well documented type of interaction: "amakudari". "Amakudari" (literally "descent from heaven") refers to the re-employment of officials retiring from government (leaving "heaven") by private companies, the former bureaucrat typically obtaining a senior management position in, or appointment to the board of directors of, the enterprise. "Amakudari" is one of four avenues that bureaucrats can pursue when they leave service in a ministry and look for paid post-retirement opportunities. They can move laterally into a public company ("yokosuberi" indicating "sideslipping"); they can move back and forth between private and public corporations; or they can stand for election as a political candidate.

Recognizing the potential conflict between being a current regulator and becoming a future representative of a regulated enterprise, the National Civil Service Law was put on the books, in principle prohibiting the re-employment of retiring officials into private companies for two years after their retirement. However, after it conducts an investigation of the particulars of a proposed "amakudari" appointment, the National Personnel Authority can waive this requirement.

Students of "amakudari" point to a variety of rationales for "amakudari": transfer of highly knowledgeable individuals from regulator to regulated, increasing the knowledge base of the private sector regarding the rationale for particular ministry policies; networking, improving the flow of information from the industry to the ministry and back from ministry to industry; monitoring the private sector, descending-from-heaven bureaucrats dropping down into troubled enterprises that the ministry believes require advice about how to get their house in order; and creating incentives for hard work in government service, only the most successful and rapidly promoted bureaucrats being invited to take on lucrative positions in the private sector. The last rationale points to an interpretation of "amakudari" as deferred compensation for former highly deserving bureaucrats who were underpaid during their official careers.

While there is no consensus of scholarship on the rationale for "amakudari", the view that companies are calling the shots, dominating ministry policy making through the influence of the former bureaucrats that they have appointed seems fairly farfetched. More commonly held is the view that "amakudari" actually increase the power of ministries over the industries that they regulate, largely by seeing to it that retiring bureaucrats serve as agents of their former employer, advocates or spies if you will. More generally, the "iron triangle" theory of Japanese corporatism – the view that the elites in business, politics and bureaucracy are all cut from the same cloth, that they think along similar lines, that they share ideas and attitudes – suggests that "amakudari" is simply one of the many glues that bind together the three worlds of the elitist iron triangle in Japan.

After the run-up and then bursting of the bubble economy, the Japanese economic bureaucracy – in the Ministry of Finance, in the Ministry of Economy, Trade and Industry (formerly the Ministry of International Trade and Industry) – often became an object of derision in the media and among many voters. Public hostility was fed by a perception that the bureaucracy had failed to come up with wise policies, that the bureaucracy had made claims for its contribution to miracle growth that were over inflated and ungrounded. It was also fed by the reporting of scandals involving the corrupting of prominent officials. The fact that the Japanese government was embarking on campaign of deregulation added to the public perception that the economy had been over-regulated in the past. Reflecting this popular perception the government launched a reform of the system of promotion for government officials in 2003 aimed at restricting the incidence of the "amakudari" practice.

acquiring land on which elementary schools were to be built. "No way" said the contractor, arguing that he was solely in the business of building housing projects. According to Johnson, the story goes on as follows: the contractor found the water and sewage lines that he had laid down for his housing project capped with concrete; enraged, the contractor went to court only to be turned down by the law ruling in favor of the city.

More famous is the example of Sumitomo Metals. Using its power to allocate foreign exchange in closed capital markets as a basis for its claim to sweeping powers over industries, the Ministry of International Trade and Industry cajoled the key firms in the iron and steel industry to form a production cartel to stave off a projected drop in the demand for steel in 1965. When Sumitomo Metals refused to comply with the production target it was assigned, arguing that it wished export volumes excluded from the target it was given, the Ministry announced that it would restrict Sumitomo's right to import coking coal using its legal powers, eventually breaking Sumitomo, forcing its president to abjectly bow to the wishes of the presidents of the other iron and steel companies in the cartel. According to Johnson, victories of the Ministry in cases like that involving Sumitomo Metals established the power of the economic bureaucracy over the rights of businesses to put profits first, over the right of private sector management to make unconstrained judgments about market supply and demand.

Some are not willing to join Johnson in arguing that the Musashino and Sumitomo Metals cases revealed the power of bureaucratic administrative guidance to order businesses around. Most notable in their dissent are Miwa and Ramseyer (2006). They argue that the two stories have not been told correctly, leading to very misleading interpretations about the power of bureaucrats. They point out that the contractor actually triumphed over the city of Musashino: he got the courts to declare that the city had to provide him with water, forcing it to unplug the pipes for his condominiums; he sued both the mayor of the city and the city itself for damages, winning in the High Court, the Supreme Court affirming the High Court's decision. In the Sumitomo Metals case, Sumitomo fought the Ministry of International Trade and Industry with an end run: instead of using coking coal to make steel it started bringing in pig iron that could be freely imported. Facing a confrontation that it did not want to lose, the Ministry backed down, eventually declaring that exports would be excluded from the quotas established for the production cartel. In both cases administrative guidance was on the losing side.

Steering a midcourse between the views of Johnson (cowering business people, arrogant bureaucrats pushing their weight around) and Miwa and Ramseyer (cowering bureaucrats, self-confident entrepreneurs and corporate executives getting their way), Uriu (1996) paints a picture of how administrative guidance works that takes into account the interests of the firms and their workers in the regulated industries, political pressure both foreign and domestic, and the logic of bureaucratic decision making. Focusing on industries facing a decline in demand for their products, many reaching out to the Ministry of International Trade and Industry to assist them in forming production cartels monitored by the government (making it harder for individual firms within the cartel to cheat), Uriu argues that the characteristics of the industries involved influence the courses of action that they take. In concentrated industries in which a few large enterprises compete – shipbuilding, aluminum manufacturing for instance – firms will tend to opt for economic restructuring, perhaps exiting and letting their capital be utilized more fruitfully elsewhere, perhaps diversifying into new fields of endeavor. When the size of the labor force involved in a concentrated industry is large, management may face strong opposition to downsizing, thereby encouraging firms to seek the aid of politicians and bureaucrats in managing their adjustments. In the case of fragmented industries in which many small firms compete – textile manufacturing is a good example – firms are vulnerable to bankruptcy, hence more likely to pursue political solutions.

What did the Ministry of International Trade and Industry actually do – or attempt to do – with its tools of administrative guidance? At least three types of policies are commonly cited in the literature: stabilizing industries facing temporary or permanent declines in demand; coordinating the purchase of foreign technology and promoting its rapid diffusion within industries; and targeting industries that the Ministry viewed as strategically important.

A classic case of Ministry stabilization in the face of long-term decline in demand involves the decision on the part of the Japan Spinners Association to form a cartel in 1952 as American Korean War related military demand for uniforms fell. The Ministry was ambivalent about shoring up an industry that it did not view as strategically important for postwar economic development. After a series of bankruptcies amongst spinning firms made the plight of the industry increasingly apparent, the Ministry began using administrative guidance in an effort to ensure that all spinning firms cut their output by a specified percentage amount (40 percent). From this example it is clear that the Ministry was responding to pressure from key firms in the industry, rather than vice-versa.

In many ways coordinating the purchase of foreign technology was similar. It was in the interests of particular industries – for instance the automobile industry seeking to acquire patent rights for the use of new technologies, better transmissions, more powerful engines – to agree on which firm was to license the technology. In this way they could avoid competition between automobile companies – between Honda, Toyota, Mitsubishi, Nissan, Mazda, Isuzu – all vying to license a particular technology from Mercedes Benz driving up the price of the license. In a number of such cases the Ministry of International Trade and Industry designated one firm to license the technology, guaranteeing to other firms in the industry that the length of time exclusive patent rights on the technology would run within Japan would be short lived. In this way technology was purchased relatively cheaply and technology was diffused relatively quickly.

A third use of administrative guidance involves targeting, overcoming market failures to promote the rapid development of an industry favored by the Ministry. A classic case is the computer industry. During the late 1950s IBM was the dominant computer manufacturer internationally, enjoying a first mover advantage in the industry because of its deep financial resources. Instead of selling mainframe computers that were the industry standard at the time it could afford to rent them to users, charging them user fees, making money from servicing the machines and developing software that met the specifications of individual users. In the late 1950s it introduced its second-generation computers, the IBM 1401. By the early 1950s the Ministry of International Trade and Industry was flooded with requests from companies to import the IBM 1401. To kick start the Japanese computer industry the Ministry decided to do three things: it allowed IBM to set up a subsidiary in Japan, Japan IBM; as a quid pro quo extracted from IBM it required IBM to give up some of its proprietary technology to potential Japanese competitors; and it set up the Japan Electronic Computer Company whose main function was to purchase computers from Japanese computer manufacturers, renting them to individual users. In short it set out to organize a semi-private/semi-public company that could beat IBM at its own game, undercutting its first mover advantage.

Whether the growth of the Japanese computer industry stemmed from the Ministry's policies or from the headlong drive of private companies to harness and develop the latest technologies in the field is a matter for debate. What is clear is that the proportion of the Japanese corporate share within Japan's computer market jumped by leaps and bounds. In 1958 it was a mere 7 percent; by 1972 it had risen to 53 percent; and by 1986 it was over 76 percent. In particular the share of the market enjoyed by Japan IBM plummeted.

How effective was miracle growth industrial policy taken as a whole? Many economists are skeptical about its impact, arguing that it was either positively harmful, hindering the operation of market forces, or completely ineffective. Stories abound: industrial policy temporarily stabilized industries like textiles that should have declined faster than they did; targeted industries like commercial airplane manufacturing that floundered; and largely ignored industries like automobiles that did grow by leaps and bounds. The volume by Beason and Patterson (2004) is scathing in its critique of industrial policy.

Working with four industrial policy tools – Japan Development Bank loans, direct subsidies, tax relief, trade protection (tariffs) – but leaving out administrative guidance that is hard to quantify, Beason and Patterson (2004) argue that industrial policy and economic growth were negatively correlated over the period 1955–73. Industries that were heavy beneficiaries of industrial policy actually did worse than industries that were not favored by industrial policy. The high growth subsectors of Japanese manufacturing – electrical machinery, general machinery, transportation equipment, fabricated metals – were less likely to secure industrial policy aid than low growth subsectors like textiles, processed foods, mining and basic metals. A note of caution: administrative guidance is not taken into account in these calculations. Still the results suggest that healthy briskly growing sectors were less likely to pressure the industrial policy bureaucracy for favors, pointing to an interpretation of industrial policy in which shoring up the fortunes of declining industries, of losers, was more important than targeting and promoting the growth of winners.

From our review of the literature on policy it is clear that there are widely divergent schools of thought concerning the impact of government policy on miracle growth. Reviewing the literature leaves one with the uncomfortable impression that the professional affiliation and/or ideological viewpoint of the analyst trumps analysis itself. Economists committed to free markets – Miwa and Ramseyer (2006a) and Beason and Patterson (2004) are good examples – seem to think policy mattered little, or was detrimental to growth. At the other extreme the development state view of a political scientist like Johnson (1982) finds much to admire in Japanese economic policy making. In any event what is clear is that "Japan, Inc." in the strong sense is a myth. One possible way to reconcile these diverging views is to accept the thesis that facilitating/coordinating is crucial to Japanese policy making. Under this rubric the regulated industry itself proposes many of the practices carried out by the ministry or ministries ostensibly guiding the industry. Naturally this kind of policy making is market conforming. Who is in charge? The industry or the ministries that ostensibly regulate them? The answer is not obvious. That is the point.

Trade

In the field of trade there are both strong continuities and strong discontinuities between the prewar and postwar periods. The strongest continuity involves the product cycle, the flying geese pattern, now stripped of its policy significance for empire building. The old-line industries that dominated exports in the interwar period – fibers and textiles – had a brief resurgence in the early 1950s, followed by precipitous decline. The high growth sectors in manufacturing – iron and steel, automobiles, machinery especially electrical machinery – those enjoying exceptionally high rates of total factor productivity increase, and dramatic declines in price, surged to dominate exports in both volume and value by the 1960s. The strongest discontinuity is the geography of Japanese exports: in 1930, 46 percent of exports went to Asia, the percentage rising to 62 percent in 1940. By 1965, this percentage was down to 33 percent. By contrast the proportion of Japanese exports going to North America surged, rising from 16 percent in 1951 to 35 percent in 1965. The American market became increasingly important to Japanese companies, automobile exports to the United States growing particularly briskly after the mid-1970s.

In understanding the importance and logic of Japanese trade during miracle growth two facts must be kept in mind: the proportion of imports and exports in national income was relatively modest; and intra-industry trade was largely non-existent. Regarding the trade proportion what is striking and perhaps unexpected is that it actually declined after World War II: in the early 1930s the proportion was almost 40 percent; during the 1950s and 1960s it was below 20 percent. On this ground alone it is apparent that export-driven theories of miracle growth are improbable. For most Japanese producers the domestic market – large by European standards due to the relatively large size of the Japanese population relative to those in European countries – is far more important than any foreign market. Equally striking is the fact that the major imports to miracle growth Japan were exclusively raw materials – iron ore, petroleum, copper ore, bauxite, and cotton – while exports were almost exclusively manufactures. Within categories of manufacturing, there was little intra-industry trade. Either Japanese manufactures produced the commodity in which case imports of the commodity were close to zero; or Japanese manufactures did not produce the commodity in which case imports might be substantial.

These two characteristics of Japan's miracle growth trade set it apparent from the Western European countries that also converged. Most European nations engaged in intra-industry trade, importing and exporting automobiles for instance. And in most European countries trade proportions were far higher than they were in Japan, especially in smaller countries like Sweden, Finland, the Netherlands, and Denmark. Economists committed to market driven explanations explain Japan's "peculiar" trade pattern in terms of comparative advantage and geographical distance. Writings like Saxonhouse (1988) point out that a country lacking raw materials but awash in human capital will be best off economically if it pursues its comparative advantage, importing raw materials, exporting manufactures embodying high quality labor input in the value added on to the raw materials within its home economy. Advocates for this approach point out that Japan was geographically isolated from other manufacturing nations. In contrast most Western European countries had highly industrialized neighbors.

One problem with these market driven arguments is that Japan's comparative advantage was changing rapidly during miracle growth. Does comparative advantage mean much when it is in constant frenzied motion? For instance the share of labor intensive industries in exports – textiles and clothing, building materials, food and beverages – fell from 65 percent in 1955 to around 44 percent in 1973. During the same period the share of capital intensive and high wage industries in exports soared, from around 19 percent in 1955 to almost 29 percent in 1973. Moreover the share of research and development and capital intensive industries – chemicals, office machines, photographic equipment – jumped from under 6 percent in 1955 to over 9 percent in 1973. Miracle growth comparative advantage was hardly stable.

Those critical of purely market driven arguments tend to emphasize protectionist policy and the existence of implicit contracts, especially those supposedly holding together vertical *keiretsu* in wholesaling and retailing. Critics like Lincoln (1990) point out that before Japan joined the General Agreement on Tariffs and Trade and the Organization for Economic Cooperation and Development during the 1960s, it set high tariffs on imports of manufactures, low tariffs on raw materials imports. Once committed to trade liberalization in principle drastically cutting tariffs and jettisoning quotas, government policy continued to protect Japanese industry. A combination of quality based regulations – like the *shaken* for automobiles – and industrial policies designed to shore up declining industries with cartels that set shares of the Japanese market to particular firms were powerful barriers to imports. Added to these policy walls was the distribution system in which long-standing relations between manufacturers, wholesalers and retailers made it difficult for importers of products made abroad to establish substantial niches in the domestic market.

Lincoln draws an important implication for Japanese exports from this argument about import barriers. He points out that if Japanese domestic manufactures can charge higher prices in the domestic market for their products due to the lack of foreign competition therein, they can cross-subsidize the products they export abroad, undercutting producers in other markets – like the United States – by effectively "dumping" their exports abroad. Prima-facie evidence supporting this argument exists: during the 1960s, through the lens reflex cameras sold by Japanese companies tended to be cheaper in the United States than they were in Japan. Japanese tourists knew this, traveling to Hawaii or California for a vacation, enjoying the added bonus of being able to buy a Japanese camera sold there at a much lower price than they would pay within their own country.

Miracle growth: markets, norms or policies?

In our discussion of miracle growth the full force of the debate over Japanese capitalism has confronted us in an almost unrelenting fashion. Was Japan's remarkable convergence towards American and Western European standards of living primarily due to the operation of relatively unregulated private markets? Or was it driven by Confucian values, to loyalty, to a reluctance to be too egocentric, subjecting one's personal interests to that of the frame one is located in? Or again was it largely driven by political choices made by Japan's bureaucratic or political elite?

In one sense the market driven thesis is highly appealing. It is parsimonious, relying on the idea that competition in markets – for resources, for foreign technologies – sorted out the economically viable from the incompetent. Because gains in total factor productivity could be realized through rapid structural change (reducing the proportion of the labor force in primary industry for instance), and because expected profits were higher in the sectors of manufacturing in which foreign advances in technology created the greatest gaps between internationally competitive and Japanese best practice techniques, capital was naturally attracted in high growth sectors of manufacturing.

Especially attractive in this reasoning is that Japanese miracle growth can be readily fitted into a story about convergence that can be applied across the board to Western Europe and Japan. The Japan specific story is really empty. The core laws of miracle growth are simply the laws of mainstream neo-classical economics. Using this logic one simply relies on the Swann-Solow model to explain why Japan's miracle growth rates tended to exceed the convergence growth rates hammered out in Europe. In the early 1950s the marginal product of capital was exceptionally high because the Japanese capital/labor ratio was low. The high and rising rate of savings – coupled with the low rate of population growth that kept capital widening demands on accumulation modest – generated a dramatic buildup of the capital/labor ration. To this one can add that the rate of total factor productivity growth – as contained in the parameter indexing the level of technology and organization in the Swann-Solow formulation – was exceptionally high because Japanese companies had a long way to go in "catching-up" with American and European firms in technology.

As appealing as this logic is, it is hard to abandon the notion that some Japan specific factors are important. Would technological innovation have been as rapid as it was had large enterprise labor markets not been highly internalized? Would profit rates for innovative firms have been as high as they were had the Spring Offensive system not developed? Is it reasonable to deny that vertical and horizontal *keiretsu* ties had no influence, for instance in the speed with which new technologies like just-in-time inventory control diffused in Japan? Was not protection – either stemming from deliberate government policies like tariffs, industrial policy and regulation of product quality – or the existence of *keiretsu* in the distribution sector important for infant industries just getting off the ground during the late 1950s and early 1950s?

Finally one wonders about the relevance of invisible hand market-driven theories of Japanese development like those advanced by Miwa and Ramseyer (2006). Sure, businesses did not always follow the rules; some banks evaded restrictive caps on the large loans they made. So what? What's so special about that? On occasion drivers break the traffic rules: they may back up on streets; they may run red lights; they may even drive in the wrong lane on occasion, in the wrong direction as it were. Perhaps a frantic husband is hurrying to get to the hospital so his wife can deliver his first baby in a hospital room and not on the front seat of his car. Rules are broken, indeed they are meant to be broken on occasion. But that does not mean rules do not matter. Most drivers, most of the time, follow the rules otherwise the frequency of accidents and carnage on the road would be far greater than it is. This is true in North America. This is true in Europe. This is true in Japan. And in Japan it is not only true for drivers – it is also true for members of cartels monitored by the Ministry of International Trade and Industry.

In sum, a combination of forces – market, norms and values, and policies – shaped miracle growth. Over-determination occurs. The telling of the story of miracle growth by any one particular author may or may not reflect this fundamental point. As often as not, beauty is in the eye of the beholder.

Key terms and concepts in Chapter 8

Growth accounting estimates for Japan during the miracle growth era

Price and income parity formulas used for government purchase of rice

Substitution of machines for labor in agriculture

Scale economies in Japan and Western Europe during the golden age of convergence compared

Zero-defect and quality control

Shaken

Kanban

"Three jewels" of the Japanese employment system

Nenkō

Base-up wage settlement

Coefficient of variation in wage settlements

Keiretsu

Main bank

"One settism"

Just-in-time

Sub-contracting and sub-sub-contracting

Economic Planning Agency

Ministry of Finance

Ministry of International Trade and Industry

Window guidance by the Bank of Japan

Overloan

"Japan, Inc." thesis

Plan rationality and market rationality

Administrative guidance

Cartels

Targetting

Japan Development Bank loans

"Dumping" exports abroad

9 The social transformation

Consumerism

Even in the face of miracle growth piling up stunning annual increments in output per capita, there was biting criticism of Japan's economic achievement. It was said that the Japanese were "economic animals", sacrificing welfare in a head-long drive to aggrandize manufacturing capacity. It was said that banks were solely focused upon funding investment in business, neglecting the consumer. It was said that Japan's housing was a disgrace, people living in rabbit hutches. It was said that the environment was being sacrificed. The picture of a national population proud of the fact that they could rarely see magnificent Mount Fuji through a haze of industrial pollution – after all this meant that factories were proliferating like mushrooms in a damp darkened forest – disturbed many foreigners simultaneously impressed and revolted by the growth of Asia's new economic giant.

Danchi

With industrialization, Japanese urbanization rates, already substantial during the Tokugawa period, rapidly increased, population crowding into the cities throughout the country but especially in the big six cities – Tokyo and Yokohama in the Kantō plain; Nagoya on the Nobi plain; and Kyoto, Osaka and Kobe in the Kinai district fed by the great Yodo River. As population densities in these massive urban centers rose, land rents and housing prices shot up.

The proliferation of intercity electric railroads addressed the growing problem of congestion in the great metropolitan centers to a degree. During the first three decades of the twentieth century, the big six cities spawned satellite cities, bedroom communities for their burgeoning phalanxes of factory employees and white collar staffs. Soon enough, the satellite cites too became congested.

To accommodate workers, employers and private real estate developers built multi-unit wood frame tenements known as nagaya, individual rooms designed along traditional Japanese lines with tatami mats accessing a common kitchen, typically located on the ground floor. After the great Kantō earthquake of 1923 that left many residents of Tokyo and Yokohama homeless, government and private developers began constructing large Western style apartment buildings, a typical unit having two rooms and a small kitchen. Prior to the 1950s these prototypes for the postwar danchi (large scale apartment dwellings containing up to four hundred units) were constructed of wood.

During the miracle growth years 1955–70, Japan's industrial labor force skyrocketed. Concerned that the demand for affordable housing in metropolitan centers and satellite cities would be unprecedented, putting incredible pressure on the social fabric, the national government established the Japan Housing Corporation in 1955, building rental housing throughout the country, especially in the most congested communities. The archetypical danchi unit was a 2DK, indicating two rooms and a dining-kitchen area, the entire apartment taking up about 86 square feet.

As per capita income rose and the demand for more household living space accelerated, private developers responded by constructing "manshon" (the term derived from the English word "mansion"), renting units and also selling them as condominiums. Over time the Japan Housing Corporation also adjusted to a market in which more and more households could afford to buy or rent units larger than the 2DK, building LDK, (indicating "living room-dining/kitchen area"). Soon 2LDK (a unit having a small balcony and space for a washing machine and clothes drying lines in addition to two "living area" rooms and a dining/kitchen space) became standard both in private and public constructed danchi. With growing affluence, 3LDK units became increasingly popular among families with children, and one-room apartments (wan-rumu manshon) amongst the growing legions of employed singles enjoying an affluent and independent lifestyle prior to marrying and raising a family.

Many residents of danchi struggle with alienation brought on by living in massive complexes remote from their families of origin and their friends, their children playing in complex playgrounds lacking sunlight cut off by the high rise towers. During the 1950s and 1960s, the incidence of "apartment complex sickness", a syndrome characterized by depression, spread amongst housewives cooped up in danchi.

For a North American household – typically used to spreading out and rambling around in the comparative sprawl of a 2,000 or 3,000 square foot residence – living in a Japanese danchi would present a tremendous challenge, working within the narrow confines requiring an ingenuity in temporary storage of objects that get daily use that most North Americans have never exercised. The lack of space is daunting even for Japanese born and raised in relatively cramped quarters. One suspects that one of the factors underlying Japan's relatively low birth rate in the post-1970 era is the high cost of space, either in a public or private danchi or in a manshon.

To many old Japan hands it seemed that the old Japan was being torn apart to accommodate an out of control industrial machine voracious in its demand for resources, spewing out chemicals in the water, carbon dioxide into the atmosphere. This characterization is not completely inaccurate. Still, it is distorted. True, households had little access to consumer credit. Typically, they had to save in order to purchase consumer durables. But purchase they did. Consider the figures in Table 9.1. In the figures assembled in Panel A the striking decline in proportion of household expenditure upon necessities – food, housing, clothing and footwear – is unmistakable. The proportion fell from almost 39 percent of household income in the early 1960s to around 32 percent in the early 1970s, to around 26 percent in the early 1980s. More and more, households were able to sequester away resources from bare bone essentials to luxuries, to refrigerators, to radios and television sets, to washing machines and vacuum cleaners. Panel B of Table 9.1 illustrates this point.

It should be kept in mind that the quality of the consumer durables improved over time as a combination of rising household income and declining costs of manufacturing turned niche elitist markets into mass markets. Particularly instructive in this regard is the fate of monochrome (black/white) televisions: the

Table 9.1 A consumer revolution, 1964–1985

Panel A   *Composition of worker household expenditures (%)*

Period	Necessities (food, housing clothing)				Other			
	Food	Housing	Clothing and footwear	Total	Medical care	Transport & communication	Education	Reading & recreation
1964–1965	27.4	3.7	7.7	38.8	1.9	2.5	2.9	5.8
1966–1970	25.1	3.8	7.1	36.0	1.9	3.6	2.4	6.2
1971–1975	21.8	3.7	6.7	32.2	1.8	4.5	1.9	6.2
1976–1980	19.8	3.3	5.6	28.7	1.7	5.4	2.3	5.7
1981–1985	17.8	3.2	4.7	25.7	1.6	6.3	2.6	5.8

Panel B   *Diffusion of consumer durables (percentage of all families surveyed possessing indicated item)* [a]

Period	Electric vacuum cleaner	Refrigerator	Electric washing machine	Television, black/white [b]	Television, color	Air conditioner	Passenger car
1964–1965	65.0	44.8	65.0	88.9	n.a.	n.a.	n.a.
1966–1970	84.0	76.5	84.0	94.4	9.5	3.9	14.8
1971–1975	96.5	94.1	96.5	65.4	71.1	11.9	34.9
1976–1980	98.5	98.8	98.8	32.0	96.6	30.0	51.2
1981–1985	98.6	99.0	99.0	18.7	98.9	46.9	63.1

Source: Japan Statistical Association (1987), *Historical Statistics of Japan. Volume 4*: various tables.

Notes

a n.a. = not available.

b The figure for 1981–1985 is actually for 1981–1982.

diffusion rate for this type of television grew through the 1960s and early 1970s, only to decline thereafter as a superior substitute – color television – established a growing hold over the market.

Responding to the growing demand for consumer durables, Japanese companies jumped into the fray, designing a bewildering array of products that would fit into cramped quarters. How could you fit an American style refrigerator into a tiny Japanese kitchen? Especially innovative were the consumer electronics enterprises – Sony, Matsushita, Canon, Fujitsu, Hitachi, Sharp – tapping the wellsprings of a population fastidious and faddish in its tastes. Fads – booms – abounded. Bowling alleys proliferated, only to shut their doors as the boom faded, consumers turning elsewhere, to video games, to automobile racing, for entertainment. It was a fickle consumer market, one hard to tap into if one was not on the ground in Japan, tuned to the latest booms building up groundswells in trend setting markets like Tokyo.

As television spread so did the hold of Tokyo over the culture of Japan. The Tokyo style of speaking Japanese gained popularity, gradually diminishing adherence to local dialects, those in complete command of the musical lilt of Kyoto speech steadily vanishing as one generation gave way to the next. In this sense, mass consumerism promoted cultural homogeneity.

Working against the tendency toward homogenization was the domestic tourist industry, promoting hot spring resorts in remote regions "untouched" by factory production. Local craft traditions were revived in rural districts in response to the demand for the different. Ironically, mass consumerism was a double-edged sword: destructive of the old Japan in the burgeoning industrial belt, at the same tine promoting, even spawning new, traditional crafts and foodstuffs in niche markets. In many locales where tourism became the linchpin of the economy – the ancient imperial capital of Nara is a good example – tradition was invented.

One of the consequences of the spread of consumerism was a rise in the savings rate. Consumer credit being hard to come by, households saved in order to build up a nest egg. In the separation of tasks increasingly characteristic of a labor market in which wage and salary employment took over from self-employment, housewives specialized in managing household budgets, figuring out how to save a little bit here and there so the family could afford a color television, an air conditioner, a video game console. Consumerism was one of the factors driving the surge in miracle growth savings apparent in Table A.5 in the Appendix.

Savings

The rise in savings during miracle growth is one of its most distinctive features. Had the savings rate not risen as it did, private sector investment could not have increased as much as it did, at least not in the closed capital market conditions of the 1950s and 1960s. In understanding why savings rose, it is important to decompose it into its three components: private sector savings, that occurring in households and corporations; government savings (the difference between government revenue and government expenditure); and rest-of-world savings (the difference between exports and imports). During miracle growth rest-of-world savings was negligible: during most years the country ran a modest balance of payments deficit. Similarly because the government hewed to the Dodge Line until 1965 (when it countered a recession with expansionary fiscal policy) and was committed to tax cutting, government was not a major source of savings, positive or negative. Profits bolstered corporate savings however. And most important households saved increasingly large proportions of their intake. Why did household savings rise?

There are many models, formal and informal, of savings that have been applied to Japan. In the Appendix to this volume I discuss three functional forms that have been fitted to data for Japan. Here we will take up a broader range of arguments. One class of arguments is related to consumerism. Another group of theories revolves around household demographic structure, household spending priorities, and the cultural rules governing the stem family system. Some are based on institutional features of the labor market. Some are rooted in government policies. And some are based upon taking into account the growth of income per capita itself.

Consider consumerism, the desire of households to build up material assets commensurate with their incomes. Suppose, for instance, that households want to maintain an asset/income ratio of four to one. When their income rises sharply, they step up their savings in order to accumulate assets. If the consumer demonstration effect is operating strongly – the existence of fads and booms in Japan seems to testify to this fact – households with lower incomes than their neighbors may feel under pressure to accumulate assets to a point where their asset to income ratio actually exceeds that of their neighbors. In the United States this is known as "keeping up with the Joneses". Key to this argument is the lack of consumer credit during miracle growth: banks favored businesses; credit cards were not available.

A second line of argument hones in on spending priorities in the Japanese style stem family system. In the standard Confucian model the eldest son is assumed to take responsibility for his aged parents; more generally at least one of the children, maybe all, take on that responsibility. If parents expect to depend on the income of at least one child, they have a strong incentive to invest in the education of their children, especially the eldest son. In doing so they may or may not be altruistic, wrapping up their welfare in the welfare of their offspring. If they are not altruistic but are simply selfish and if they expect the return on the educational attainment of their children to exceed the returns they can secure from other assets, they could be highly motivated to save for the education of their children. The rapid expansion of the private higher educational system during miracle growth is consistent with this thesis. Implicit in this argument is that the social welfare system of miracle growth Japan was poorly developed.

Saving for the wedding(s) of daughter(s) could be rooted in a similar logic. Weddings in Japan are typically expensive affairs: the work colleagues of husband and wife, often the work colleagues of the father and/or mother (if she is employed) attend. Marrying off a daughter to a groom who is expected to advance economically can be a good investment, perhaps paying off for the father of the bride in personal networking connections. Altruism may be at work, to be sure. But it may not be.

The logic of these arguments suggests that savings should rise in households as the couple ages, at least up to the point where all children are educated, perhaps married off. In other words assets – including human capital assets – rise until a target age for the household head. Households headed up by those past this target age may well start drawing down their remaining savings, liquidating financial assets in order to fund their consumption. In the case where the target age is the age at which the head of the household retires from his or her main career employment – perhaps working part time elsewhere after retirement – it is reasonable to suppose that savings should fall. This line of reasoning supports the view that the aggregate level savings rate for a population rises or falls with the changing age structure of the population.

With this in mind consider Panel B of Table A.5 in the Appendix. As can be seen the population of Japan during miracle growth was quite young. A sharp trend toward aging – an increase in the proportion over age 65 – did not set in until the 1970s. Simply basing our analysis on age structure offers an explanation as to why saving rates began to fall off during the 1980s. The population was aging, in fact at accelerating rates.

The nature of the labor market is frequently cited in accounting for the relatively high level of savings. It is pointed out that self-employed households – farming families, small business – have difficulty distinguishing between personal savings and investment in their businesses. For salaried employees in major companies the logic of the argument is different: because the exact level of the bonus may not be perfectly anticipated by a worker, he or she treats it as least in part as windfall, transitory, income. According to the permanent income hypothesis (see the Appendix to this volume) households attune their consumption to their long-run anticipated permanent income, saving much of their transitory positive injections of income. To this it is added that hours of work were long during miracle growth – thereby depressing demand for consumption – and mandatory retirement was relatively young, typically at age 55.

Government policy is also cited in the literature on miracle growth savings. Tax breaks for saving (designed to bolster investment) coupled with a lack of tax deductions for interest paid on mortgages may have stimulated savings in banks and the postal savings system, depressing building up assets in housing. The fact that the income tax burden was relatively light, that it built in generous deductions on items other than housing ownership is also mentioned. That tax rates were consistently reduced during miracle growth may have pushed the savings rate up. The lack of a social security system certainly must have been a factor. Households felt constrained to take care of themselves. Presumably this encouraged them to invest more heavily in the education of their children than they would have otherwise.

That income per capita rose rapidly during miracle growth may have drawn up the savings rate. Habits change slowly. When household income jumps year after year, the gap between planned consumption and income received creates an unintended avenue for savings to expand. This is the argument we encountered in Chapter 6 in discussing the Ohkawa–Rosovsky theory of trend acceleration. Note that the slowdown in income per capita growth after the early 1970s should depress the savings rate. Coupled with an aging of the population, the slowdown in growth probably depressed the household savings rate.

Urbanization

As employment in the industrial belt of Japan soared, the proportion of the population classified as urban expanded by leaps and bounds. This is clear from Table A.2 in the Appendix. To be sure some of the increase in measured urbanization is due to administrative reorganization during the 1950s. In order to deliver water more efficiently, as well as sewage treatment and infrastructure to the rural suburbs surrounding core cities, the government expanded the geographic boundaries of many of Japan's cities, incorporating rural *gun* into urban *shi*. Still, the main reason for growing urbanization is a real transformation in living arrangements, villages declining, cities being increasingly important in the economy and polity.

The hiving off of satellite cities – bedroom communities – was partially driven by improvements in the transportation infrastructure. This is an old theme, going back to the first decade of the twentieth century. Technological innovation after the war accelerated what had been going on for at least a half century. Construction of the high-speed bullet train line (the *shinkansen*) was typical of the postwar era. After *shinkansen* service between Tokyo and Osaka was initiated in 1964, one could travel by rail the 550 kilometers separating the two cities in slightly over three hours. By the early 1970s *shinkansen* were departing Tokyo and Osaka every fifteen minutes during peak demand times. With the giant strides being made in transportation infrastructure, housing projects in the suburbs of the big six cities of Japan – Tokyo, Yokohama, Nagoya, Kyoto, Osaka and Kobe – spread, land being converted from rice paddy and dry fields to residential and industrial purposes at a bewildering pace, giant construction companies and contractors spearheading much of the drive. This tendency is mirrored in the figures on the percentage of the population residing within the administrative boundaries of the big six cities. After the late 1960s the proportion living in these cities falls off. Increasingly families fled the high real estate prices in the central cities for bedroom communities.

As more and more persons took up residence in cities, the connections between village and urban Japan attenuated, presenting the Liberal Democratic Party with a major political challenge. A significant share of their voter base was in rural Japan, in villages, among farming households. To some extent they could stave off the inevitable by resisting reallocation of seats in the Diet, seats assigned to electoral districts on the basis of the size of voting populations in the districts. However as more and more urbanites were second or third generation city dwellers the willingness of the average voter to prop up farmer income through price supports for rice, the willingness of voters to tolerate pollution, was sorely pressed.

The revenge of the environment

One of the consequences of a policy bias in favor of industrial production over improvements in welfare – reflected in the fact social security was given short shrift in contrast to the focus on building up the welfare state typical of Western European countries – was growing pollution, especially in urban Japan. Two types of pollution received particular attention: organic and inorganic pollution in water; and air pollution. Of the two, water pollution posed a greater challenge for the Japanese public than air pollution.

Organic pollution of the water stems from the disposal or discharge of organic materials into the water, materials that decay, removing dissolved oxygen from the water. When enough dissolved oxygen is removed, fish can no longer survive in the water. In a nation in which eating fish is a major part of the cuisine this posed one problem. Another was the strong stench that emanates from the medium. Were these the only adverse side effects of industrial expansion, the water pollution problem in Japan would not have been as grave – and as newspaper headline getting – as it was. Inorganic pollution of the water, due to the discharge of chrome, arsenic, lead, mercury into rivers and oceans, posed a greater danger to the public. Particularly dramatic was the Minamata Bay contamination that first came to the attention of the public when a patient was admitted to a hospital in Minamata city in southern Kyūshū in 1956. The patient exhibited horrific neurological symptoms, numbness, and sensory disturbances leading to a gruesome death. More cases of the incurable Minamata disease soon came to light. Although it was soon established that Minamata disease was caused by mercury poisoning, by mercury discharged into the bay by a chemical plant, the government did not actually impose severe restrictions on industrial discharge of mercury into the water until 1968. In the meantime other outbreaks of the disease were reported, for instance in the Agano River basin of the Japan Sea.

Cadmium poisoning also emerged as a politically potent issue. A company engaged into mining and smelting discharged the mineral into waters that fed into irrigation ditches used by rice farmers. The result of consuming the mineral was itai-itai ("ouch-ouch") disease, symptoms including weakening of the bones to the point where any usual movement on the part of the sufferer breaks them.

Air pollution – the discharge in the atmosphere of carbon monoxide, sulfur oxides, hydrocarbons – also garnered increasing attention during the miracle growth era as the volumes of emissions from factories, the burning of coal in thermal electricity generating plants, and use of transportation grew with explosive force. Working to hold down the level of air pollutants in the air over Japan, however, was the fact that most Japanese commuted by train and subway, not by automobile, population densities being high in the heavily urbanized districts, driving one's own vehicle to work involving delays in time due to congestion on roads and high costs for parking vehicles.

By the mid-1970s it was clear to the Liberal Democratic Party that it faced a political crisis over the pollution issue. For instance, a survey carried out in 1976 reported that while 60 percent of those respondents who did not think that the environment was an issue supported the party, only 22 percent of those who did think it was an issue, supported the party. Because those concerned with the environment tended to live in cities, and because the share of the Diet representatives elected from urbanized areas was growing as a result of urbanization, the party realized it had to oversee thoroughgoing reform aimed at controlling pollution. Beginning in the early 1970s it initiated the process of cleaning up the environment, creating the Environmental Agency, shepherding over ten laws controlling pollution through the Diet during the next decades, pumping public funds in the private sector to alleviate the costs that it was incurring in cutting down on emissions. In carrying this program out politically it was helped by one powerful fact: the business community had no other political party to turn to. Moreover the left-wing parties – the Socialist Party for instance – were ambivalent about the anti-pollution drive. Many of their members were in unions that feared loss of jobs if a stringent anti-pollution regime was imposed on the industrial sector.

That the Liberal Democratic Party was able to realize its politically driven agenda in the environmental field is interesting in and of itself. It bears upon the debate over who rules, bureaucrats or politicians. Winning election after election, dominating the lower house of the Diet year after year, the party moved to increase its power over policy making. It formed the Policy Affairs Research Council, setting up divisions corresponding to the various ministries. When a freshly elected Liberal Democratic Party member enters the Diet, he or she joins one or two of the divisions of the Policy Affairs Research Council, mastering the intricate details of policy formulation and drafting of legislation in the fields of relevance to the parallel ministry. Whether the bureaucracy was dominant or not during the early years of miracle growth is one question; whether it slowly had to surrender its power to the Liberal Democratic Party Policy Affairs Research Council is another. What is clear is that the Policy Affairs Research Council loomed increasingly larger in the affairs of the party itself: chairing the council was an important stepping stone on the road to becoming president of the Liberal Democratic Party, thus to becoming Prime Minister.

The demographic transition continues

As we learned in Chapter 5, Japan's demographic transition was definitely gaining headway during the period between the world wars. Indeed, even during the period of military rule bent upon passing pro-fertility legislation – the National Eugenics Law of 1940 was crafted to encourage couples to bear children, particularly sons who could serve their *kokutai* as soldiers or sailors in the future – the birth rate was falling, especially in central Japan and in the cities of the industrial belt.

In the aftermath of Japan's surrender, mortality and fertility resumed their downward course. Fertility rebounded somewhat as soldiers were repatriated and couples separated by war were reunited. Then it began to fall precipitously. This is apparent in Panel B of Table A.2: the net reproduction rate fell from the above replacement levels – from values above one – characterizing the 1950s to below replacement levels in the 1960s. Life expectancy at birth for males jumped from the mid fifties in the late 1940s to the low seventies by the early 1970s; female life expectancy at birth from the late fifties to the high seventies over the same period. Most remarkably, infant mortality plummeted over the same era, declining for the mid 1960s to around ten per thousand in the early 1970s. While the transition in birth and death rates did not come to a screeching halt during the 1970s, the pace of improvement in life expectancy and the control over reproduction did decelerate. Once infant mortality dropped down to levels below ten per thousand, for instance, there was relatively little room for future gains.

There is little doubt that some of the improvement in life expectancy is attributable to enhanced consumption of food, in turn attributable to rapid increase in income per capita. Even if the income elasticity of demand for food is relatively low at moderate to high levels of income per capita, it is positive. Figures for the elasticity of 0.1 or 0.2 are not unreasonable. What Japanese agriculture did not generate was made up from imports, rice being the prominent exception. Increasingly meat, fish, poultry and grains were imported from abroad.

The dramatic improvements in male standing height apparent in Table A.7 reflect a number of factors – including decline in the incidence and virulence of infectious diseases amongst children and the removal of children from debilitating physical work through the mid-teens due to the expansion in compulsory schooling – but gross intake of calories, proteins and vitamins is definitely one of them. Some of the improvement in life expectancy should be attributed to the rise in income per capita occurring during miracle growth.

This said, there is little doubt that most of the gains in life expectancy were due to technological improvements in the public health and medical fields, especially pharmaceuticals, largely made in Europe and the United States during the 1940s and 1950s. Vaccines and antibiotic drugs came on the market at affordable prices, mass production methods being developed to harness scientific advances, mostly applications of the germ theory of disease. This is apparent from the figures on case rates and deaths per case for selected infectious diseases (cholera, dysentery, typhoid, smallpox and diphtheria) assembled in Panels A.1 and A.2 of Table 9.2.

In overcoming infectious mortality through the mass application of vaccines and antibiotic drugs, densely populated cities have a strong scale advantage in distribution over rural isolates. In terms of cold-blooded economic calculus, major hospitals and state of the art clinics should be built where demand for their services is most intensely felt. Reflecting this reality age standardized death rates – once higher in urban centers than in rural districts (see the figures for 1908 assembled in Panel B of Table 9.2) – fell especially rapidly in the industrial belt during the late 1940s and early 1950s. But convergence soon took place. As can be seen from Panel B of Table 9.2 by 1960 age standardized death rates were low throughout all districts, industrial and rural, densely populated or sparsely inhabited.

Why did the birth rate fall so precipitously during the 1950s and 1960s? To suggest an answer to this question it is useful to decompose the birth rate into

Table 9.2 Aspects of the demographic transition

Panel A.1   *Cases per 100,000 persons, selected infectious diseases*[a]

Period	Cholera	Dysentery	Typhoid	Smallpox	Diphtheria
1920–1929	0.65	31.30	80.15	1.90	25.05
1930–1939	0.01	76.40	57.00	0.25	39.15
1940–1949	0.15	76.45	49.15	3.00	64.20
1950–1959	0.00	98.40	3.00	0.00	15.15
1960–1969	0.00	57.75	0.85	0.00	4.85

Panel A.2   *Deaths per case, selected infectious diseases (percentage)*

Period	Cholera	Dysentery	Typhoid	Smallpox	Diphtheria
1920–1929	64.0	36.9	20.4	18.9	23.9
1930–1939	14.6	33.1	18.2	13.2	17.0
1940–1949	0.0	24.9	15.2	14.4	10.3
1950–1959	0.0	9.7	5.8	5.4	6.6
1960–1969	0.0	1.0	1.6	0.0	1.9

Panel B   *Age standardized death rates and infant mortality rates for the prefectures classified in terms of percentage of male labor force engaged in primary industry (pmlpi) in 1930, 1908–1960*

pmlpi	Age standardized death rate (all causes)				Infant mortality rate		
	1908	1930	1950	1960	1920	1950	1960
Under 30%	2572	1897	1075	712	184	48	24
30% – 49%	2213	1921	1131	848	161	62	32
50% – 54%	2404	1969	1184	765	169	67	35
55% – 59%	2119	1825	1145	755	158	60	34
60% and over	2065	1985	1277	815	163	73	38

Panel C   *Hutterite indices for marital fertility (I_g) and proportion females married (I_m), rural and urban sectors of the prefectures classified by percentage of male labor force engaged in primary industry (pmlpi) in 1930, 1930–1960*

pmlpi	Rural			Urban		
	1930	1950	1960	1930	1950	1960
	Hutterite index of marital fertility (I_g)					
Under 30%	0.52	0.50	0.30	0.43	0.44	0.28
30% – 49%	0.54	0.50	0.29	0.43	0.45	0.28
50% – 54%	0.57	0.50	0.28	0.46	0.44	0.28
55% – 59%	0.58	0.53	0.30	0.48	0.45	0.28
60% and over	0.60	0.56	0.42	0.50	0.49	0.29
Hutterite index of proportion married (I_m)						
Under 30%	0.67	0.57	0.56	0.63	0.58	0.54
30% – 49%	0.71	0.61	0.63	0.64	0.58	0.58
50% – 54%	0.70	0.61	0.63	0.60	0.56	0.58
55% – 59%	0.69	0.59	0.63	0.59	0.57	0.57
60% and over	0.73	0.62	0.66	0.59	0.56	0.59

Sources: Tables 7.3 (p. 206) and 7.16 (p. 225) in Mosk (1983); Table 1 (p. 433) in Mosk and Johansson (1986); Tables 3.7 and 3.8 in Mosk (1991)

Note

a Values less than 0.01 treated as zero.

two components, one bearing on marriage customs (specifically the proportion of females in the reproductive age range between ages 15 and 49), the other reproduction within marriage. Fortunately we can employ the Hutterite indices assembled in Panel C of Table 9.2 to realize this decomposition.

What are the Hutterite indices? They are measures based upon an ingenious procedure of comparing the actual fertility experiences of the populations that a researcher is interested in with the fertility experience of the Hutterites who entered the historical demography literature as a much-utilized standard during the 1950s. Why use Hutterite reproduction as a standard? Hutterite women in the period between the world wars married at very young ages and had as many children as they could. The Hutterite sect took very seriously the Biblical injunction to "be fruitful and multiply". Moreover the Hutterites who settled in the great plains of the United States and the prairies of Canada lived on large farms and had a strong demand for child labor. A typical Hutterite woman had a total fertility rate (the sum of the age specific birth rates, an approximation to the total number of children she would give birth to over her reproductive life) of over twelve. Using the Hutterite standard allows us to estimate the degree to which a population falls short of its maximal reproductive potential.

The Hutterite indices measure the relative level of marital fertility, illegitimate fertility, proportion married and overall fertility for any jurisdiction that has counts of births classified by legitimacy status and counts of population classified by gender and marital status in the five year age groups. The idea is to use figures on women and married women in the five year age groups in a given population of interest to the researcher to compute the level of fertility and marital fertility that would occur if these women reproduced as Hutterite women in the cohorts of the 1920s and 1930s did. The age specific rates (for five year age groups) at which Hutterite wives reproduced are known and these are used in conjunction with the actual data on population and births to compute the Hutterite indices.

In assessing why populations fall below maximal reproductive potential it is important to separate out the impact of low proportions married from the impact of sharply diminished reproduction within marriage. The Hutterite index for marital fertility (I_g) for a given population is the ratio of the legitimate births occurring in that population to the number that would occur if the women reproduced as the Hutterites did. The Hutterite index for proportion married (I_m) is the ratio of married women weighted by the Hutterite fertility schedule – take the number of married women in each age group and multiply this number by the corresponding level of Hutterite fertility for the age group, thereby giving heaviest weight to the most reproductive ages – divided by the total number of women weighted by the Hutterite schedule. The Hutterite index for illegitimate fertility (I_h) is the ratio of the number of illegitimate births to those that would occur had the unmarried women reproduced as the Hutterite women had reproduced. The overall Hutterite index of fertility (I_f) is the ratio of total births occurring in a population to those that would have occurred had the women been as fruitful as the Hutterite women. The last measure offers an overall summary for fertility.

One of the convenient properties of the Hutterite indices is their multiplicative property. If the index of illegitimate fertility is zero (typically it is close to zero), then the Hutterite index for overall fertility is the product of the Hutterite indices for marital fertility and proportion married, namely $I_f = I_g * I_m$. It is this property that we exploit in Panel C of Table 9.2. As can be seen from the figures in the Table 9.2, fertility fell in miracle growth Japan for two reasons: because the proportion of women married fell, albeit modestly in some districts; and because reproduction within marriage declined dramatically everywhere, in rural zones, in urban conglomerations.

The transformation of marriage was inextricably linked to a variety of social changes. Most notable were a reshaping of the demand for female labor and a slow but steady reshaping of processes bringing individuals together as couples. In describing these changes it is difficult to avoid characterizing human relations in absurdly stylized fashion. Still something must be said. Prior to the miracle growth era, most marriages in Japan were arranged. Typically this happened through the offices of a go-between hired by the parents of the prospective groom and bride. The go-between might even employ a private detective agency to look into the background of the bride or groom: was his or her family healthy? Was alcoholism a problem in the family? Was the groom likely to be a good economic bet? Indeed it is not too farfetched to describe marriage as a merger of human and physical capital arranged by households to insure the extended group of relatives against economic adversity. In most low-income societies marriage has this function: in the absence of banks, government social welfare programs and the like, family ties are often crucial to economic survival.

As economic development occurs, however, as income per capita improves, as the density of banks soars, as companies or government take on greater responsibility for the welfare of families, the institution of arranged marriage loses much of its appeal, its luster tarnished. Rather than meet through formalized intermediaries controlled by parents, young adult children were likely to meet their prospective mates through work, through higher education, through social clubs. Thus arranged marriage gives way to love marriage. Couples are more likely to meet and fall in love in colleges, factories, and offices than through parental pressure. Thus marriage ages tend to rise as girls postpone marrying until they have had a chance of making the acquaintance of a wide pool of prospective mates.

Not surprisingly the actual marriage patterns in terms of who married who did not change as dramatically as did the way marriages were arranged. Better educated males tended to marry better-educated females under the arrangement model; this continued to be the case under the love model. Male farmers tended to marry girls who grew up on farms. Marriage as a merger of human and physical capital is an admittedly extreme idea. Still it captures an important slice of the underlying reality.

One of the consequences of this type of mating behavior is that better-educated wives are likely to be better producers of human capital within a household. Girls growing up on farms are better equipped to train their children in the skills needed in farming than city girls. College graduate mothers are better equipped to raise their offspring so that they internalize the social behaviors needed to pass demanding entrance examinations for schools than farm girls. Lurking behind these arguments is the human capital model that emphasizes human resource development as a crucial aspect of economic modernization. Skills learned on and off the job, formal schooling, parental inputs of time and financial resources utilized in raising children, secular trends in the anthropometric measures like those illustrated in Table A.7 are grist for the human capital mill.

The key insight in the human capital model is that "shadow prices" – implicit prices – matter. Children are not a consumer durable purchased by couples (adopted children accounting for a relatively small number of the children raised by households). Babies do not appear in maternity wards of hospitals with a barcode price attached. But cost they do. Parents raising small children sacrifice leisure activities. They spend on clothing, parties and vacations to satisfy their children. Typically they rent or purchase larger homes to accommodate having offspring. The human capital approach is rooted in the notion that the "shadow price" of children mirrors prices for goods, services and wages forgone by those tending to the raising of the children.

In effect the human capital model of the household envisions the typical household engaging in trade with the rest of the economy. It trades labor services (or products it produces on its property for the market) for earned income. This eats up part of the daily allocation of time – 24 hours – not spent sleeping, at least for those household members working for the market. Other members of the household may well specialize in producing goods at home for consumption at home: raising the children, cooking the meals, cleaning the house. As the forgone earnings of those who stay at home to engage in within home production increase the cost of the activities the stay at home person engages in – the cost in terms of market opportunities not seized – goes up. This is the reasoning behind the proposition that the cost of children may go up dramatically as an economy develops. Time is money.

Armed with this logic consider the impact of industrialization upon marriage (I_m) and reproduction within marriage (I_g). As the structure of the labor force changed – salaried employment becoming increasingly important, self-employment and farming less – the demand for marriage partners changed. For salaried males in manufacturing or the service sector, marrying a high school or college graduate became a priority. But a better-educated woman can command a higher wage on the labor market. The opportunity cost of staying at home and raising children rises, at least in terms of forgone hourly earnings. Reflecting this reality, typical couples opt to have fewer children, mirroring in their reproductive behavior within marriage the cost of time. To this argument one can add the point made earlier (in Chapter 5) that the income elasticity for child quality (education) exceeds the income elasticity of demand for child quantity. This is the essence of the human capital theory of fertility: income and price effects dominate in the fertility transition, not changes in norms, not changes in political or social constraints on the capacity to restrict unwanted births. Demand matters. Supply is secondary.

The so-called education mother – *kyōiku mama* – became the symbol of the new low fertility family. Focused intensely upon gearing up her two children for the rigors of the educational competition, she passed on the human capital she had acquired, and the associated social norms, to the next generation. Was this the result of unconstrained choice as the human capital model suggests? Or was it the result of social pressure? Can we ignore supply constraints? Can we ignore norms?

It is possible that the transformation in the supply constraints overshadowed changes in demand for fertility. In 1948 – later on 1948 and 1952 – the National Eugenics Law was amended, ultimately being turned on its head in the process, being revised from a pro-fertility policy to one legalizing abortion. It is said that farm wives pressed to do the work in the fields that their husbands used to perform (their husbands working elsewhere in factories) opted for abortion rather than giving birth during the times of the year when they were busiest, in transplanting, in harvesting. As the costs of preventing births fell, the ability of households to hit their target surviving family sizes improved. What was socially disapproved during the years of military rule was now socially acceptable. One could argue that the political constraints and social norms propping up a regime of high fertility were undercut in the aftermath of the Second World War.

An additional constraint that changed was the length of compulsory schooling. Children could no longer be counted upon to do heavy physical labor on a protracted basis in the family business until they graduated from compulsory middle school, say around age fifteen. This reduced the economic value of children in terms of the cold calculus of labor services expected from the younger generation. The anticipated costs of having large numbers of children on farms and in small businesses rose. And the expected benefits fell.

During miracle growth the social landscape of Japan was reworked. The demographic transition was by and large completed. Mass consumerism took off by leaps and bounds. At the same time the household savings rate soared. The population became increasingly concentrated in densely populated, and polluted, conurbations, as people moved from rural Japan to the industrial belt where employment opportunities were the greatest, wages the highest, the chance to garner a prestigious education the greatest. Miracle growth was not only an economic success story. It involved a drastic reworking of the social fabric, of household life and living arrangements. Having passed through miracle growth, Japan shed many of the vestiges, the garments and garbs, of its prewar past. It could not forget that past. It could not ignore it. But the country would never be the same again.

Key terms and concepts in Chapter 9

"Economic animals"

Consumerism

"Keeping up with the Joneses"

Mandatory retirement

Bedroom communities

Shinkansen

Organic and inorganic pollution of water

Minamata disease

Itai-itai disease

Environmental Agency
Policy Affairs Research Council
National Eugenics Law
Hutterite indices
Arranged and love marriages

Human capital
 model
"Shadow price"
Time is money
Kyōiku mama

Part IV
Deceleration

10 The slowdown

The inevitable reversal in the trend rate of growth

During the early 1970s the golden age of convergence ended. While the empirical symptoms of this watershed are manifold the story is most strikingly expressed in terms of growth rates for the Western European countries and Japan. Between 1950 and 1973 the average growth rate in income per capita for twelve Western European countries – those listed in Panel A of Table 7.1 – was 3.8 percent; for Japan the corresponding growth rate was 8.0 percent. Over the next two decades, 1973–92, the average growth rate in income per capita was 1.8 percent; for Japan, 3.0 percent.

Japan continued to grow faster than the Western European countries during 1973–92. Still, its growth was truly within the Western European range. According to convergence theory countries with the lowest initial levels of per capita income should grow faster than those enjoying higher per person incomes. The three Western European countries with per capita incomes in 1973 close to Japan's level are Finland, Italy and Norway. Both Italy and Norway experienced per capita income growth as close to, or closer to Japan's, than to the average for the twelve countries. Indeed Norway's growth rate – 2.9 percent- was nearly as high as Japan's growth rate. Convergence theory suggests one important reason why the slowdown occurred: as the converging countries approached the levels of the leading country, the United States, in terms of capital/labor ratios, levels of technology and organization, economic structure and scale economies, their growth slowed.

Let us consider each element of this account in a bit more detail, focusing upon Japan's case. From Table A.1 we can see that the Japanese capital/output ratio grew rapidly during miracle growth, reaching American levels by the late 1970s. Indeed after the early 1980s the Japanese ratio soared to dizzying heights far above that of the United States. As more and more capital is accumulated and the marginal productivity of capital falls, the incremental contribution to output flowing from more private and public capital – from more factories, more robots, more trucks and high speed trains, more roads and airports, more hydroelectric lines – declines. The rate of return that investors in companies – banks, owners of stocks and bonds – can reasonably anticipate garnering from the savings they plough into savings account and into equities, drops. This is an inexorable consequence of accumulation. The Swann-Solow model neatly captures this argument. In Figure 1.5 A of Chapter 1 the point is illustrated graphically with the flattening off of the labor productivity curve with rising levels of per worker capital. Indeed it is plausible that Japanese capital accumulation had become excessive by the mid-1980s. While the ratio of investment to national income did drop after the early 1970s – after all the relatively high rate of return on new capital acquisition was a major rationale for high rates of investment during miracle growth so that a falloff in the rate of return should temper investment – it remained high by the standards of the Western European countries and the United States. Japan was steadfastly falling victim to its spectacularly high savings rate.

The second source of slowdown was the exhausting of technological catch-up potential. According to Panel B.2 of Table 8.1, advances in knowledge constituted a major source of growth in miracle growth Japan. As Japanese firms within particular industries closed the gap between themselves and the international leaders in that industry – whether the leader is located the United States, Germany, the United Kingdom, or Sweden – the gains to total factor productivity from ferreting out best practice technique and imitating it dry up. Again this point can be illustrated with the Swann-Solow model. The pace of the upward drift in the labor productivity/capital–labor curve slows down for a nation as its firms switch from being followers to being leaders, developing the technologies of the future within their research laboratories.

Two other sources of the slowdown can be gleaned from the Denison and Chung estimates appearing in Table 8.1. Gains from improved resource allocation were drained away during miracle growth as most of the farming population abandoned agricultural pursuits to take up jobs in the burgeoning industrial and service sectors. By the early 1970s the proportion of the population making a living primarily from agricultural pursuits had fallen to such low levels that further gains from structural change were all but completely exhausted. As the proportion of the self-employed labor force dwindled, less and less gain could be expected from shifts into salaried occupations. As the economy grew to gargantuan size, less and less could be expected from scale economies. Generating growth from improvements in output per unit of input was being steadily eroded as Japan converged toward American levels.

By the same token, improvements in the quality of factor inputs illustrated in Panel B.1 of Table 8.1 were also vanishing. As more and more individuals went on to tertiary schooling – to two-year junior college or four-year university – the returns to schooling dropped, discouraging the marginal applicants to higher education, those lacking the drive to excel in the examination competition, from attempting to gain advanced educations. The rate of growth of the advancement rate to high school and tertiary schooling declined. As for the capital stock it is true that high rates of accumulation kept the average vintage of the stock young, hence more likely to be compatible with the latest technologies. Working against this advantage was the fact that the pace of technological progress was slowing down. In short less and less was to be expected in terms of growth potential from improvements in the quality of capital and labor.

While the slowdown in Western Europe and Japan can be readily analyzed in terms of the Swann-Solow model and the Denison and Chung growth accounting decompositions, it would be misleading to limit our account of the slowdown to the within nation factors pinpointed by those frameworks. After the early 1970s the international economic order began to change in fundamental ways: the Bretton Woods system collapsed; oil prices began to skyrocket; finally the United States, reeling from deficits in its international trade account (imports exceeding imports) began to draw away from the leadership role in promoting tariff reduction and a relatively free and open trade regime through multilateral institutions like the General Agreement on Tariffs and Trade (later becoming the World Trade Organization) it had embraced during the golden age of convergence, moving gradually toward a regime of strategically linking limited protectionism and market opening demands through bilateral as opposed to multilateral negotiation. All of these changes impacted Japan.

The United States, like England before it, was unable to remain the linchpin of the international monetary system as more and more countries caught up with it. By the late 1960s European countries became increasingly restive with a United States dollar based gold standard, refusing to absorb dollars at fixed exchange rates, refusing to buy into the upward drift in American inflation rates attributable in part to the way the Vietnam War was being financed. In 1971, President Richard Nixon bowed to the inevitable, severing the connection between the United States and gold, precipitating devaluation of the dollar. Shortly thereafter, Japan abandoned the Dodge Line, allowing the yen to adjust up somewhat relative to the United States dollar (see Panel B of Table A.4). In theory appreciation of the yen relative to the dollar made Japanese exports to its major markets – especially to the United States – more expensive, hence less attractive to foreign purchasers.

The second shock to the international economic order came from the expansion of demand for petroleum worldwide, from countries converging towards American levels of income per capita in Western Europe, from the nations of Latin America and Eastern Europe that grew rapidly in terms of total income but did not necessarily converge toward American per capita income levels, and of course from Japan itself. Taking advantage of this upward thrust in demand, petroleum exporters – having formed a cartel, the Organization of Petroleum Exporting Countries, well aware of the fact that their reserves would be gradually but inexorably depleted in the future – engaged in strategic management of sales of crude in order to extract higher prices for their precious resource. Since the price of oil affects the price of most goods and services – oil being used as grease for machines, as fuel for trucks used to transport commodities – the oil shocks of the early 1973–74 period set off inflationary tendencies throughout the industrial world, worsening the trade balances in those countries importing more oil than they exported. From Panel A of Table A.4 it is apparent that Japan was no exception. The consumer price index jumped by an annual rate of 11.5 percent during 1971–75.

The reluctance of the administration in the United States to allow the American economy to absorb more goods from abroad than it exported indefinitely took five main forms during the post-1970 period: encouraging devaluation of the dollar relative to other key currencies (Germany's and Japan's in particular); imposing sanctions on countries accused of dumping goods in the American market; negotiating industry specific voluntary export restraints with countries exporting to the United States; putting pressure on countries like Japan that enjoyed massive bilateral trade surpluses with the United States to open up their markets to American goods and to American investment; and promoting an enrichment of the menu of goods tradable on international markets through the twin avenues of multilateral and bilateral negotiations, promoting globalization of services like banking, computer software, and most recently e-commerce.

A dramatic reworking of the aggregate economic balance

Beginning with the early 1970s Japan's aggregate economic balance underwent a decisive structure shift. Private investment rates fell short of private savings rates; the government began to run deficits on its fiscal account, expending in excess of the revenue it took in through taxation, tariffs and user fees; and the economy began to run surpluses on its trade account, exporting more than it imported. Table A.6 in the Appendix illustrates a number of these points.

That investment fell short of savings was due to two factors: a decline in the expected return on capital that depressed somewhat business enthusiasm for acquiring new plant and equipment; and a steady falloff in the proportion of aggregate demand stemming from consumption (see the figures in Table A.6). Much – but not all – of the gap between savings and investment was now accounted for by government negative saving, the government's fiscal balance shifting into the red as the Dodge Line of balanced budgets was effectively jettisoned. Why did government begin running unbalanced budgets, financing its deficits with bonds? As Lincoln (1988) convincingly demonstrates the reason does not lie in an expansion of government spending, for instance on a "cradle-to-grave" style welfare state erected along Scandinavian lines. Rather it lies in the fact that tax intake growth began to lag behind relatively modest expenditure increase (by European standards welfare related spending in Japan remain muted throughout the 1970s). During miracle growth, government had consistently underestimated income growth rates. After the early 1970s it began to consistently overestimate income growth rates, the Ministry of Finance bureaucracy being used to piling up revenue increases year after year.

As Table A.6 shows, government spending jumped significantly from the low and declining levels experienced during the miracle growth decade 1976–85. Then it began to decline somewhat. Why? Alarmed by the growth of government deficits, by a rise in the proportion of government expenditure in total national income, and especially by concerns that welfare state programs were growing rapidly and were projected to explode as the population aged, the business community represented by Keidanren lobbied through the Liberal Democratic Party to establish a Commission for Administrative Reform, *rinchō* in Japanese. Working with an agenda that administrative reform should be achieved without further increasing taxes, the commission issued a series of reports over 1981–83.

Its recommendations included cutting the number of government employees, reining in social security benefits, cutting public works investments, and privatizing three government corporations including Japan National Railways and Nippon Telegraph and Telephone. By the mid-1980s most of these recommendations had actually been implemented.

What was the ideological and analytical basis for the *rinchō* administrative reform movement, for the energy and resources Keidanren put into pushing the reform agenda? The self interest of the business community was obvious. Japanese corporate taxes were and are relatively high in comparison to personal income taxes.This is because personal income taxes enjoy generous deductions from income earned, depressing the marginal income tax rates that households are obligated to use in paying their household taxes. The business community was naturally concerned that future tax increases might come at its expense, raising the costs of producing output, making Japanese products more expensive on international markets. Setting this concern aside there was strong opposition to governmental expansion of the welfare state on ideological grounds. This was long standing. Throughout the period since Japan's industrialization commenced most of its business community opposing government meddling with the paternalistic arrangements arrived at by employers and employers in the welfare field. Vocal corporate objection to passage of the Factory Law of 1911 was rooted in this logic. According to the logic of this theory Japanese style welfare is best left to firms to implement, not placed in the hands of government that is too bureaucratic, too rule driven, too willing to overlook realities on the ground.

A second line of concern motivating Keidanren to act was new, not old. It arose from problems encountered in Western Europe and North America with welfare state policies. We can understand these problems in terms of the efficiency wage and aggregate demand/supply frameworks introduced in Chapter 1 (we can follow the logic of the argument using Figures 1.3 and 1.4 E in the Appendix to Chapter 1). Suppose a combination of government unemployment insurance and welfare program supports generates a standard of living floor higher than that than an individual can expect to generate from employment in a small or medium sized company (but not in a well paying large enterprise). In the diagram illustrating the efficiency wage principle (Figure 1.3) the government's support level "wage" – call it w_g – is less than the efficiency wage w_e but greater than the market wage w_m. If this is the case the incentives are clear. Individuals not successful in the queue for a well paying efficiency wage are likely to opt for the government's support level wage over the small and medium sized firm wage w_m. Unemployment grows at the expense of employment in small and medium sized firms, shifting in the natural rate level of national income (in Figure 1.4 E Y_f shifts in, "full employment" actually now means most but not all members of the labor force are actually working). The work ethic is eroded. Taxes have to be raised to pay for the programs. Big firms – those dominating Keidanren – may lose subcontractors as small firms encounter increasing difficulty recruiting workers.

In short, ideological concerns rooted in attitudes of business leaders going back to Meiji if not before were wedded to a general sense of unease with Keynesian deficit spending cum the welfare state in the Keidanren inspired *rinchō* campaign. How sweeping was the victory of the *rinchō* movement? In terms of its stated goals dimensions the answer is clear. It was a resounding success. But the goals were formulated with political constraints in mind. The electoral base of the Liberal Democratic Party being eroded by structural change – the shift out of agriculture, rapid urbanization – was a hard cold reality that the administrative reform movement had to take into account. Do not cut into the pork barrel projects – the infrastructure construction outlays – dear to the hearts of rural voters. Do not so tie the hands of the Ministry of Welfare that it cannot implement some welfare initiatives like a national pension program, especially when newspapers and television are focusing with growing enthusiasm on the rapid aging of the population, handing over to the opposition to the Liberal Democratic Party a set of issues that they can exploit in elections.

Returning to the aggregate economic balance, government deficits absorbed most of the savings not channeled into domestic investment but not all of the excess. Some of the margin of savings over domestic uses of savings became capital export, flowing out of Japan into foreign lands. Japan gradually emerged as the world's major creditor country, Tokyo joining London and New York as one of the key financial centers.

Unlike American investment abroad that tended to take the form of foreign direct investment, the Japanese outflow of capital mainly involved purchasing foreign securities, government bonds and the like, especially in the United States, the United Kingdom and on the European continent. To be sure Japanese companies began to set up subsidiaries. In countries like the United States companies set up plants in order to get around voluntary export restraints or domestic content regulations or to take advantage of free trade agreements like the North America Free Trade Agreement. In Southeast Asia and later on in China, Japanese companies in labor-intensive industries like textiles began setting up production facilities with the aim of cutting labor costs. As the yen appreciated on international markets, Japanese wages rose relative to wages in the less industrial regions of Asia.

Why was the flow of capital coming out of Japan heavily focused on purchase of securities rather than on foreign direct investment? The most obvious candidate is the rate of return on securities earned at home and abroad. If American securities earn nominal returns of 10 percent (because savings rates are low in the United States) and Japanese securities 3 percent (because savings rates are high) the incentives seem clear. But are they? As we know from Panel B of Table A.4 the yen appreciated against the dollar through most of the 1970s. When the dollar falls relative to the yen – say by 5 percent in a given year – the return on an American dollar dominated asset earned by a Japanese investor falls by that rate. If American securities earn 7 percent in nominal terms and Japanese securities 3 percent and the rate of yen appreciation over the relevant period for the investment is 5 percent, a Japanese investor is better off sticking to Japanese securities.

To be sure, investors operate on expectations, not known outcomes. Perhaps Japanese investors allowed access to foreign markets – insurance companies, exporting corporations, banks, and finance specialists – were simply trying to hedge against movements in the yen up or down (note that the yen did fall against the dollar over the period 1981–85). By keeping their assets in two denominations, calibrated in terms of the crucial dollar (the dollar remaining the key international currency despite the abandonment of the Bretton Woods system) and the yen, investors could protect themselves to some extent against appreciations or depreciations of the yen. Diversifying into European currency denominated assets was a further step along the road to reducing risk by diversifying financial portfolios.

An additional possibility is that Japanese companies did not believe that their system of production was easily exported to foreign lands. True, managers could go to the United States, to England, to Thailand, to the Philippines, to China to supervise workers who were mostly non-Japanese. But could these workers be motivated to work the way Japanese in Japan were motivated to work? Could the production system function smoothly in the absence of the domestic bureaucratic hand of administrative guidance providing arenas for cooperation between competing companies within the manufacturing sector? An alternative theory is that Japanese investors distrusted their own financial system, feeling that the banks were inefficient, or alternatively that administrative guidance in the financial field was woefully misguided, promoting moral hazard through a coordinating/facilitating model in which regulated and regulators mutually interacted, banks encouraging the Ministry of Finance to regulate in a way that appeared to shore up their activities.

From an aggregate economic balance point of view, capital export is the inverse – the negative – of the trade balance. As can be seen from Table A.6, Japan began to consistently run a trade surplus after the late 1960s. In principle, the surplus of savings over the combined sum of government deficit and domestic investment equals the trade balance. The national income not absorbed in the sum of consumption, investment and net government savings (negative when the government runs a deficit on its fiscal account) takes the form of net exports. In this sense Japan emerged as the mirror opposite of the United States during the period 1970–90. True, both countries were running negative balances on their government fiscal accounts. But Japan exported capital, its investment falling short of its savings; the United States imported capital, its investment exceeding its savings. Substantial shares of Japan's trade surplus flowed into the American capital market, snapping up a hefty share of the bonds being issued by the American government to fund its budget deficit, in effect making up for the low level of American savings, staving off the tendency for American government deficits to choke off domestic American investment demand through the crowding out effect (see Figure 1.4 C in Chapter 1). Growing capital market integration increasingly caused the destinies of the two great economic giants to intertwine, forcing their political leaders to find common ground in attempting to manage their economies, keeping the two locomotives of economic expansion running on a common timetable as it were.

Japan's emergence as a net exporter in no way means that export demand was driving its economic growth after the miracle growth. Appearing in Panel B of

Table A.6 are percentage contributions to aggregate demand expansion over successive five-year periods. Over the period 1971–95, net export demand tended to depress growth in gross domestic expenditure, not increase it (1981–85 is the sole exception to this rule).There are negative signs for most terms under the ΔNX column from around 1971/75 until 1991/95. That net exports did not play an important role – either during or after miracle growth – is actually not surprising. In order to export goods, Japanese firms must import raw materials and energy – natural gas, petroleum, and coal – from abroad. Net exports are not a large share of the post-1955 Japanese economy whether they are positive or negative. They cannot be a major shaper of Japan's aggregate demand growth.That said, export demand was very important to Japan's big ten internationally known "name brand" companies, companies like Sony, Toyota, Nissan, Honda, Mitsubishi, Toshiba, all monopolistic competitors. Sales of these particular companies depended heavily upon courting foreign consumers. It is crucial to differentiate between the aggregate situation and individual firm circumstances in regard to exports. Had the big ten companies been unable to export as they did, Japan's aggregate trade balance would have been modestly negative, not modestly positive.

Aging in a changing labor market

When a country's population passes through the demographic transition it becomes older and older. This is an inevitable consequence in a population closed to immigration of shifting from low life expectancy to high life expectancy; from a high gross reproduction rate to a low gross reproduction rate (cf. Panel B of Table A.2). It is a theorem of formal demography that the fall in fertility overshadows the rise in life expectancy in accounting for this tendency. That Japan's gross reproduction rate fell below a value of one during the 1970s meant that aging would be relatively rapid.

That Japan's population was almost completely closed to net immigration is apparent from a comparison of Japan's population growth rate with its natural rate of increase, the two rates shown in Panel A of Table A.2. That the population was relatively young during the miracle growth years and has been aging rapidly since is clear from the figures given in Panel B of Table A.5. A population aging as Japan has been after the 1970s confronts two major economic challenges: at the social, public, level how to support its elderly in retirement; at the corporate level how to cope with a labor force in which the ratio of older, veteran, workers to younger fresh entrant workers is increasing. Not surprisingly given the opposition of the administrative reform movement to the growth of Japan's welfare state and given the preference of the government for facilitating/coordinating approaches, responses by government – the public authority – and the private sector were actually deeply intertwined.

Perhaps the most pressing issue posed by rapid aging of the population was how to handle mandatory retirement in the corporate sector. During the 1950s and early 1960s mandatory retirement was typically set at age 55, a policy introduced for white-collar workers during the interwar period. During the 1920s life expectancy at birth for males was around 55 so the policy made sense for both companies and employees. As life expectancies soared during the 1950s and 1960s it made less sense for workers. Most of them moved to another company – typically to a small or less prestigious enterprise – upon retirement.

From the corporate viewpoint relatively early mandatory retirement made sense. Under *nenkō* rules wages tended to rise with age and seniority. Promotions tended to be automatic. Younger workers tended to contribute more to a firm's bottom line than they took out in wages; older workers tended to cost more than they contributed. By the late 1960s – as miracle growth was winding down and many large firms were experiencing slower and slower growth in their internal labor markets – alarm bells started going off. Declining sectors like iron and steel and shipbuilding were becoming so concerned about the problem that they diversified into wildly different fields like amusement park management, hiving off redundant older workers into these new ventures. Something needed to be done to dampen the headlong increase in wage bills. Hiking mandatory retirement ages would only make matters worse.

From the government's viewpoint not raising mandatory retirement ages posed equally intractable problems. Was the treasury going to be raided and depleted by government funded pension programs that a Liberal Democratic Party concerned about its slipping voter base might be constrained to legislate? Not surprisingly government ministries were pressuring corporations to increase mandatory retirement ages, threatening to promote legislation designed to do precisely that if the companies did not respond "voluntarily". Begging off the immediate introduction of mandatory legislation, the Nikkeiren and Keidanren business federations agreed to implement hikes to mandatory retirement ages as part of a set of reforms designed to restructure internal labor markets. Through a set of protracted negotiations between the Nikkeiren business federation and the union centers, mainly taking place under the *shuntō* umbrella, tradeoffs were worked out. Firms agreed to increase mandatory retirement ages to age 60. In exchange unions agreed to be flexible. They agreed to moderate "base-up" wage increases so that exporting companies could continue to export successfully even as the yen appreciated. They agreed to make the export oriented automobile sector the "top-batter" in wage negotiations. Most important they agreed to let management modify the *nenkō* rules, and they agreed to let management experiment with forced transfers of workers to other companies, especially to sub-contractors.

Under the negotiated agreements, companies began vigorously promoting a functional status system (*shokunō shikaku seidō* in Japanese) as a replacement. Under this system workers are paid according to

1   family and individual needs;
2   age, education and seniority;
3   performance rating determined by the company's personnel office;
4   status (*shikaku*), the rank – like corporal or sergeant in a military organization – attaching to a worker regardless of his or her work assignment; and
5   occupation.

Items (1) – (3) were found in the classical *nenkō* system. The crux of the innovation involved bringing in items (4) and (5), making specific occupational assignments and status key to worker evaluation.

Under the revised system, a freshly inducted "standard worker" enters an internal labor market from the educational sector, experiencing automatic promotions for a number of years. However after a specified number of years, the employee reaches a "break point." To move up further in status the employee enters into competition for promotion, contending with his or her colleagues for further advancement. The personnel department of the company limits the number of slots available at the higher grade in order to slow wage growth attached to promoting junior workers, in order to select the most hard working and productive for fast tracking, sending a signal to the unsuccessful that they are likely to advance fairly slowly in the future. A battery of tests – reminiscent of those used in the educational system – a host of interviews with personnel office representatives, and a comprehensive review of performance to date, served to winnow out the more productive from the less productive, to separate out the wheat from the chaff so to speak.

To further weed out deadwood older employers, the business federations pushed the idea of forced transfers of selected workers in their negotiations with the union centers. Under a typical transfer program (*shukkō* in Japanese), there are two main options. In the more favorable (from the worker's point of view) of the two options, a standard worker's personnel file is kept in the firm that he or she entered upon graduation from an educational institution (his or her home enterprise). If he or she is transferred to a firm paying lower wages than he or she would naturally receive in the home enterprise, the firm sending out the worker agrees to pay the transferred worker the difference between the two wages. However, the home company makes it clear all future promotions are out of the question so that difference between the two wages does not grow appreciably in the future. In the less advantageous form of transfer (again looking at the matter from the worker's point of view), the personnel file of the employee moves together with him or her to the new company. The likely outcome of this transfer is a fall in earnings.

That these innovations staved off wage growth with age, flattening the age–wage profile, is apparent from Panels B.1 and B.2 in Table 8.4. The movement to bring retirement ages more in line with life expectancies than they had been in the past rendered the typical internal labor market a harsher, more competitive, more dog-eat-dog environment. Is it surprising that young Japanese became increasingly cynical about the virtues of the so-called "three jewels" of the labor market contract?

While the governmental sector solved some of its problems by working with the tools of administrative guidance in a facilitating/coordinating manner, brandishing the cudgel of mandatory legislation as a last resort, to encourage companies to raise mandatory ages, it still had to deal with the growing number of workers and their dependents reaching age 60. As the media beat the drums of the aging problem, the Liberal Democratic Party felt compelled to act, the progressive parties to the left emboldened by the growing attention being given to the aging problem. Adding to the drive to introduce and manage a national government sponsored pension program was the logic of bureaucratic "catch-up", rationally shopping among foreign models developed elsewhere. Japanese ministries – especially in the welfare and labor fields – look abroad for models. In welfare, this meant looking to Western Europe in particular. The Western European countries were gradually experimenting with the Third Way, a comprehensive set of welfare programs providing their publics with a "cradle-to-grave" safety net, jacking up income taxes in order to pay for the redistribution programs. By comparison, the United States was far less innovative, far more committed to equality of opportunity but not equality of outcome.

Drawing upon a wide ranging menu of foreign models, working under the umbrella of the National Pension Law of 1959 (passed by the Diet at a time when the Japanese population was relatively youthful) the Ministry of Welfare began overseeing two major programs, the Employee Pension System for employees working in enterprises ranging from the smallest to the largest companies (under the opportunities mandated by the system benefits for employees in larger firms generally exceeded those for employees in smaller firms) and the National Pension System for farmers, shopkeepers, and some self-employed. Under the rules set out under the two systems some of the self-employed were covered under the Employee Pension System that tended to be more generous than the National Pension System.

As Campbell (1992) shows, the resources handled under the two programs grew appreciably throughout the 1970s and early 1980s. Their growth was reined in to an extent in the mid-1980s when concerns over future drains on the fiscal resources of the government – concerns highlighted by the administrative reform movement – increasingly shaped debate over policy making. An example of how these concerns impacted policy is the pension reform of 1985 that was designed to rein in the growth of government outlays directed toward pensions for the retired and elderly. Still, despite its image as a country lacking vigorous government sponsored welfare programs Japan had actually become a welfare state, albeit not one embracing the "cradle-to-grave" model of Western Europe, by the 1970s. The myth about welfare in Japan is that family and company matter more in Japan than government. It is a myth.Through the last half of the twentieth century Japan has managed the transition from a relatively young to a relatively old population. Adjustments have been required. Welfare programs have drained away fiscal resources that once were used for infrastructure or for subsidizing export oriented companies. Corporations have revamped their internal labor markets. Savings rates have fallen.

But what does the future portend? Like most of Western Europe predictions suggest that by 2030 the proportion of Japan's population over age 65 will exceed 25 percent. Aging is an inexorable consequence of low gross reproduction rates and high life expectancies. All countries that have passed through the demographic transition will grow older. In this respect Japan's likely demographic future is similar to that of Italy where the proportion over age 65 is projected to exceed 27 percent by 2030. How will the problems of providing pensions and setting retirement ages be handled in such an environment?

One way to stave off – or rather to mitigate a bit – some of the effects of aging on government managed pension programs is to promote immigration, particularly of young working age adults. Japan has a long history of being relatively closed to immigration. True, during the period when its Empire was growing by leaps and bounds, some immigration did occur. Koreans came into Japan proper after 1910 for instance. But stung by discrimination – in the aftermath of the great Kantō earthquake, Japanese attacked Koreans in Tokyo – their numbers were limited.

Beginning in the late 1980s small and medium sized enterprises facing shortages of recruits for jobs viewed as dirty and onerous by young Japanese brought up in a relatively affluent homes bristling with a growing number of consumer durables lobbied the government for a relaxation of its stringent constraints on immigration. The policy response smacked of *nihonjinron*. It was largely limited to encouraging the immigration of descendants of Japanese emigrants, the *nikkeijin* living in societies with per capita incomes below that of Japan to take up these positions. The biggest target for this program was the *nikkeijin* population living in Brazil. Perhaps it was felt that Brazilian Japanese could be more easily assimilated into Japan than other peoples. Perhaps the logic of the program was rooted in the view that young adults growing up in households where Japanese values and Japanese cultural traditions were practiced could more easily fit into Japan than Taiwanese, Filipinos, and Indonesians. If this was the view it proved to be a myth. As Tsuda (2003) were truly strangers in their ethnic homeland. They spoke Portuguese, they danced the samba, and they rooted for Brazilian soccer teams.

Over its long history since 1600 Japan has been relatively closed. Opening up – economically, demographically, and politically – has been a process fraught with difficulties for a country that existed in a virtual state of autarky between the 1650s and the 1850s. Miracle growth largely took place in closed capital markets. Import and export ratios were relatively low. Entire sectors – banking and insurance, agriculture, wholesaling and retailing – were almost completely insulated from the outside world through the golden age of convergence. But as Japan entered the 1970s, its exports eating up a growing share of the American consumer market, this state of affairs was about to change.

Key terms and concepts in Chapter 10

Capital/output ratio
Devaluation of the U.S. dollar and the collapse of the Bretton Woods system
Aggregate economic balance and the gap between savings and investment
Rinchō
Keidanren
Shokunō shikaku seidō
Shukkō
Third Way
National Pension Law
Brazilian *nikkeijin*

11 The bubble economy

A Japanese system?

During the 1970s and early 1980s the nature of Japan's economic success loomed larger and larger on the international stage. In one sense this simply reflected the fact that Japan's national income had reached gigantic size. Japanese goods showed up everywhere. Even with a low ratio of imports and exports to GDP, the sheer volume of Japanese goods sold abroad, and the sheer volume of Japanese purchases of raw materials – of coal, iron ore, nickel, zinc, petroleum, potash, timber, and rubber – grew by leaps and bounds during miracle growth, reaching massive levels by the early 1970s.

Consider automobiles. New Japanese cars made huge inroads in North American and European markets, in part because they were fuel efficient and small, in part because they embodied quality in their components, their excellent repair records garnering praise in consumer magazines. Used Japanese cars – sold by Japanese drivers wishing to avoid the *shaken* – appeared all over Southeast Asia, even in New Zealand. Taxi cab drivers in Bangkok were churning the streets with Toyotas and Hondas.

There was a second reason why the subject of Japan's economy became a matter of burgeoning interest to Americans and Europeans: trade deficits. In the United States in particular the bilateral trade imbalance between itself and Japan became an increasingly potent political topic. Since the 1960s the American government establishment responsible for trade negotiations (the office of the United States Trade Representative office, Congressional committees appointed to look into trade related matters) tends to focus on that country enjoying the largest bilateral trade surplus with the United States. Spurred on by political demands on the part of industries that felt besieged by imports from Japan – the American iron and steel industry pressed for a trigger-price mechanism designed to drive up prices of imports of Japanese steel on the American market, the American automobile industry lobbied for the negotiation of voluntary export restrictions that would restrict the volume of cars brought in from Japan – Congress appointed a committee of American economists with expertise on Japan to better learn about Japanese exporting companies, to better understand how American companies could make inroads into the Japanese consumer market.

In the case of the United States some of the concern was about global leadership, both technological and economic. In the late 19th century the

United States supplanted England as the global technological leader. After World War II it emerged as the political leader committed to promoting international trade through its support for multilateral organizations like the General Agreement on Tariffs and Trade, the World Bank, the United Nations. In addition it underwrote international currency markets with the Bretton Woods system. Some of the concern in the United States about Japan's rapid growth and its gargantuan economic size reflected anxiety that Japan was now taking over global leadership from the United States. Linear projections suggesting that Japan's economy would soon become the biggest in the world bolstered the view that Japan was rapidly becoming an economic "superstate", a cornucopia for commercial and industrial innovations, the world's largest capital market to boot.

Interest in Japan's successful development also blossomed in the developing world. In many ways South Korea and Taiwan, two of Japan's former colonial possessions, seemed to imitate Japanese economic policy making and Japanese economic performance. Industrial policy and *zaibatsu*-style combines (called *chaebol* in Korean) were especially important in South Korea's remarkable economic growth between the mid-1960s and the late 1980s. To policy makers in the nations of Southeast Asia, to Latin American regimes struggling with the problem of moving from import substitution to export promotion – along the lines of the flying geese model of trade – it seemed that Japan offered a better model of development than did the more market driven model associated with United States economic advance. Of course drawing this conclusion required that one buy into a particular theory of Japanese economic development, one in which political constraints and/or norms and values played an important role along with invisible hand market forces.

In short, Japan's remarkable success forced intellectuals and policy makers in both the advanced industrial world and in the developing world to ask a set of probing questions. What can be learned from the Japanese experience? Are there aspects of the Japanese economy that are transferable to other economies? How do foreign leaders cope with, negotiate with, Japan? Can they, should they, shape and change Japanese practices? How did Japan get to where it was in the early 1980s? How is it likely to change in the not so distant future?

To many foreign students of the Japanese the problem of Japan's global leadership posed disturbing thoughts itself. One concern was political corruption as exemplified in the political rise of Tanaka Kakuei, prime minister of Japan and author of a prominent treatise, a vision statement, about how Japan should revamp itself in the future. Tanaka's volume – published in English 1972 – entitled *Remodeling of the Japanese Archipelago* seemed to be a direct extension of the pork barrel logic he had used in rising to national power. A second concern was Japan's closed nature. The growing popularity of *nihonjinron* books in Japan exemplified an attitude of Japan as different – unique – impossible to imitate or really learn from.

A third concern was that Japan's economy was part of a system in which politics and policies, economic behavior, and social norms and values interacted.

Tanaka Kakuei, master of pork, and the "Remodeling of the Japanese Archipelago"

There is no better illustration of the importance of the three adages of politics in a democracy – "money is the mother's milk of politics", "all politics are local", and "power corrupts; absolute power corrupts absolutely" – than the career of Tanaka Kakuei, prime minister of Japan between 1971 and 1974.

Perfecting the art of pork barrel politics that had permitted him to consolidate his hold over the politics of rural Niigata prefecture, Tanaka Kakuei mastered the art of the shady real estate deal, adroitly using his money and his personal connections to build a powerful faction in the Liberal Democratic Party. Eventually grasping the reins of power with the prime minister's post, Tanaka accepted bribes amounting to $1.8 million from the Lockheed Corporation in exchange for his directing Japan's national airlines to purchase the Lockheed L-1011 aircraft. Arrested in 1976 for accepting the bribes, Tanaka was convicted in 1983 and sentenced to four years in prison. He died in 1993 with his appeal of the conviction lingering on the docket of Japan's Supreme Court.

Tanaka built his power base through the sponsorship of a group known as the Etsuzankai (the "Niigata Mountain Association"). The function of the group was to review local applications for government funded pork barrel projects, choosing a select group to promote in the Diet – like the Tadami River hydroelectric power project, the New Shimizu Tunnel, and a bullet train Shinkansen line that snaked its way out to Niigata – in exchange for contributions to the Etsuzankai. During the 1950s Tanaka would bring Etsuzankai members to Tokyo, sponsoring tours of the Diet and the Imperial Palace, wooing most on an individual basis in one-on-one meetings.

Through these dealings Tanaka became known as the godfather of Japanese politics, earning a shady gangster like reputation that his dabbling in shady land deals did nothing to dispel. Slated to become secretary general of the Liberal Democratic Party when Satō Eisaku became prime minister in 1965, Tanaka was forced to surrender his bid for the powerful position when the Black Mist scandal that centered upon Tanaka's dealings in the Tokyo land market broke.

Despite his compromised image for corruption, Tanaka's base in the Etsuzankai made him a formidable rival to Fukuda Takeo, who was Tanaka's chief rival for becoming the heir to Sato's faction in the Liberal Democratic Party. Testimony to Tanaka's staying power in the "Kaku-Fuku war" within the party, prime minister Satō appointed Tanaka minister of international trade and industry in 1967, turning the most powerful economic ministry during the miracle growth era over to the Niigata politician, signaling his appreciation for Tanaka's political skills by rewarding him with one of the chief posts in the cabinet.

Flaunting his influence over Japanese industrial policy Tanaka gained considerable leverage over American negotiators attempting to secure quotas, limits, on Japanese exports of certain products, meeting with many of them on an ongoing basis. Exploiting these connections with the American diplomatic corps posted to Tokyo, Tanaka played a major role in negotiating the reversion of Okinawa from American to Japanese rule, enhancing his image as a no-nonsense politician capable of dealing with American political pressure.

Assuming the position of prime minister in 1971, Tanaka sought to enunciate a vision for Japan, one that would provide direction for his government, one that would constitute his political legacy. In 1972 he published "Rettō kaizō ron" subsequently translated into English as "Building a New Japan: A Plan for Remodeling the Japanese Archipelago." In the volume Tanaka advocated setting up a central administrative body to handle land development, including the building of new Shinkansen bullet train lines designed to knit the nation's land markets closer together. He proposed construction of new high-rise danchi apartment buildings housing higher-quality units than those commonly built during the 1950s and 1960s. He also pushed for the promotion of key nodal cities that would serve as growth poles for regional economic expansion, thereby raising the income per capita levels in rural regions to those characteristic of the great metropolitan centers. He envisioned a new zoning approach, facilitating the conversion of the agricultural land that continued to pockmark urban landscapes to non-agricultural purposes, freeing up real estate for infrastructure construction. Finally Tanaka's fifth proposal was to tap the high level of national savings so that this thoroughgoing, radical, remodeling of Japan could be achieved.

Sadly for his legacy, Tanaka was unable to muster the political muscle or governmental access to the financial resources needed to realize his grand scheme. Instead of leaving a legacy graced by credit for the redirecting of regional Japanese economic development, Tanaka's legacy was dominated by scandal, influence trading and pork barrel politicking, his restless striving for power and money overcoming his patriotic love for Japan and for the welfare of the common Japanese citizen.

Note: Tanaka's volume was translated into English, published as Tanaka (1972).

There was a System, the Japanese System. The chief advocate for this view was von Wolferen (1989). He argued that holding and achieving power was paramount in Japan. For this very reason it was widely diffused: bureaucrats, political elites, corporate managers, and union federation leaders, all having some power. With power came responsibility. To blunt the efforts of those enjoying less power to make claims on the powerful, to keep at bay attacks on one's power from other power seeking quarters, those with power attempted to hide, disguise, their prowess. The result was a System without a core. No one was in charge. No one holder of power could easily impact the behavior of other power centers. The Japanese state was doughnut-like, lacking a true center, power diffused around the ring.

This view suggested three disturbing conclusions. It would be difficult to negotiate with Japan because it would be impossible to find someone who was truly in charge. It would be difficult to learn from Japan since behavior in any one sector of the society was connected to behavior in every other sector, the System being in some kind of equilibrium. How could you pluck out one practice, one lesson, when everything was intertwined? It would be difficult to change the economic and political behavior of the System since it was in some kind of long-standing equilibrium. Indeed von Wolferen (1989) went as far as to argue that Japan had been this way since the 8th or 9th century. He did not rule out change. But he thought it would be difficult.

An equally provocative account of Japan's disturbing place in the world was Schmiegelow and Schmiegelow (1989). The focus of their volume was on how Japan's performance challenged the very conceptual bases of Western social science. No Western models were up to the task of understanding how and why Japan performed as well as it did. Japan fit into every theoretical competing category in at least some ways, hence in none. It could not be pigeonholed. The key to their interpretation was that Japan was Schumpeterian in a novel way: policy making was innovative, emphasizing strategic pragmatism. Key Japanese innovations were administrative guidance, the promotion of implicit contracts linking public actors and corporations, negotiating potential conflicts between policy outcomes by establishing clear hierarchical ranking of policies, and the managing of markets in danger of being disrupted for instance by gluts of production or excessive growth.

Most social scientists were not willing to go this far. For instance Vogel (1979) argued that there were very specific aspects of Japan's society, polity and economy that could and should be emulated or at least learned from. From the

"Japan as Number One"

During its heyday in the 1950s and 1960s, there was a decided tendency in the literature on modernization, especially in that penned by American scholars, to assume that societies successfully achieving economic development were increasingly likely to mimic the society that was considered to be economically most advanced, namely the United States.

There is a target for modernization. The target is the United States. Modernization is basically a linear process, less developed nations all moving towards the same target.

Analogous is the interpretation of income per capita convergence in terms of sigma convergence: countries with income per capita levels falling short of the United States (assumed to be the technological and market leader) are assumed to grow until they catch up with the leader. By contrast beta convergence involves a shrinking of variance between nations. Some might converge downward, actually experiencing a fall off in income per capita; some might converge upward, their income per head expanding. Unlike sigma convergence, beta convergence does not assume that there is a leader, a target, toward which other nations are moving.

By the early 1970s, the emergence of Japan as a world beating economic dynamo was calling into question the simple linear development hypothesis implicit in much of the modernization doctrine. Particularly impressive was the growth rate of the Japanese economy, linear extrapolation suggesting that Japan's per capita income would surpass that of the United States within a matter of decades. For instance, during the period 1956–60 the relative level of Japanese income per capita compared to the United States set at a value of 100 was 29.9; by 1971–75 it was 66.1; and during the late 1970s it was 68.5. That Japanese politics and society seemed so radically different from that of the United States and yet Japan seemed to be on a growth trajectory to pass by the United States in economic affairs, called into question the very foundations of modernization theory.

This is the background for the publication of "Japan as Number One: Lessons for America" by Harvard University sociologist Ezra Vogel in 1979. In this volume Vogel turned his back on modernization theory, arguing that there are different flavors of democracy, different flavors for the welfare state, different flavors for industrial competitiveness, different flavors for learning, different flavors for governing. Even between two countries where the level of per capita income is similar, where the technologies applied in manufacturing are relatively identical there can be profound differences in social customs and political practices.

Vogel pinpointed seven features of Japanese society and polity that he believed made Japan radically different from the United States: group-oriented, as opposed to individual-oriented learning, reaching consensus being a salient feature of the Japanese landscape; meritocracy in a bureaucracy that exercises far greater leverage over policy than it does in the United States; multi-purposed group democracy, villages, firms and professional organizations in Japan being strongly held together by group solidarity and a commitment to everyone getting a "fair share" of the economic pie; "bottom up", as opposed to "top down", decision making in

Japanese enterprises; the use of competitive examinations coupled with uniform national standards in shaping basic education in Japan; enterprise as opposed to state based welfare; and a high level of professionalism amongst Japanese police officers and public cooperation in identifying potential criminal behavior resulting in low crime rates per capita.

Taken as a whole, Vogel believed that these seven features of the Japanese environment made the Japanese formidable competitors to the United States, not only in economic matters, but also in developing technology and in providing global leadership to market oriented economies. Thus his title "Japan as Number One." He chose a deliberately provocative title as a wake up call to Americans.

In making his case for Japan as number one, Vogel was not only intent on wakening up Americans to the Japanese challenge to American leadership. He was also using his argument to encourage change within the United States, to force Americans to borrow from Japan, to become more like the Japanese. In effect he was saying that beta type convergence rather than sigma type convergence should be the rule of the day. Japan might become more like the United States and at the same time the United States might become/should become more like Japan.

While the audience Vogel seemed to address was American, the irony is that the book became a best seller in Japan. For a country obsessed with ranking, the fact that a Harvard professor – Harvard commonly considered the top ranked university in the world in the Japanese media – had proclaimed Japan to be number one was an event to be much celebrated. But this was in the late 1970s, when many Japanese were feeling immense confidence, even arrogance, over the performance of their economy. In the aftermath of the bursting of the bubble economy, in the wake of scandal after scandal among bureaucrats and politicians, in the aftermath of growth in antisocial behavior among teenagers, matters look quite different than they once did. Indeed, returning to income per capita as an admittedly imperfect indicator of performance, we see that Japan's relative level compared to the United States, 88.1 in 1991–95, had dropped to a level of 81.6 in 1996–2000. That Japan is no longer perceived as number one in the United States or in Japan seems to be widely accepted at the end of the twentieth century. More important is the possibility that there are no targets toward which societies are or perhaps should move. To put the matter somewhat differently: is conceptualizing national economic and social development in terms of a ranking scheme for nations desirable? Can we not argue that no society is number one, that particular societies enjoy impressive strengths in some areas and at the same time glaring weaknesses in other dimensions?

Note: Vogel's book was published in hardback by Harvard University Press and in a paperback edition as Vogel (1979).

economist's viewpoint, however, the most concerted attempt to argue that Japanese economic behavior was explicable in terms of Western social science concepts and transferable abroad was due to Aoki (1988). Aoki's key points concern the different ways hierarchies and information flows are managed in typical Japanese and in typical American companies (he calls the former the J-firm, the latter the A-firm). Armed with these arguments, Aoki concludes that a hybrid form is emerging, one that combines features of the two extreme opposite models of market oriented enterprises.

Aoki (1988) rests his analysis on theoretical arguments made about why firms exist anywhere and on empirical studies of job rotation in Japanese work groups notably the observation field work of Koike (1984). The basic argument is that when transactions costs are sufficiently expensive, firms – by definition organizations in which hierarchical command and control modes of behavior are normal – dominate over invisible hand market solutions. For instance, we have seen how putting-out gave way to factory production with the introduction of steam power and the orientation of manufacturers toward wide ranging mass markets. Specifically organizing production in firms provides the following benefits: by centralizing information about material requirements to meet production objectives, a hierarchy can economize on inventories stockpiled, on how materials are most efficiently utilized on the shop floor; by encouraging specialization and division of labor and repetition of tasks, firms drive down labor input costs per unit of output; by centralizing information, hierarchies can respond to changing demand for the output that they generate.

As Aoki (1988) notes, these arguments are typically used to justify the existence of the A-firm. In the typical A-firm, a small group of managers and engineers establish plans for production, laying out tasks to be performed on the shop floor, giving orders about how many components of a product are to be manufactured in a given period, how many are stockpiled. Production decisions are highly centralized. By contrast in a typical A-firm evaluation of workers and assignment of wages is done in a decentralized manner. Shop stewards and union representatives work with detailed scales set through collective bargaining or at least posted by management for all to see.

The J-firm is the mirror opposite. Personnel decisions – wage determination – are highly centralized. They are made in the company personnel division that enjoys a wealth of information about each and every worker. But the production plan is implemented in a decentralized, non-hierarchical manner. Job rotation is common, workers changing work assignments on an ongoing basis, flexibly adjusting to changing market demand conditions, filling in for one another when someone is ill or disabled due to accident or injury.

In short, a duality principle applies. In the A-firm, personnel decisions are decentralized, production decisions centralized and hierarchically applied. In the J-firm, personnel decisions are centralized and hierarchically applied, production decisions decentralized. There are two distinct models of how information flows and hierarchies are established in capitalist firms.

Aoki (1988) argues that the J-firm type model is transferable. Indeed, steps taken in some American firms during the 1980s to reduce the number of distinct occupational codes – from hundreds to five or six – seemed to bear out his prediction. In advancing this line of analysis he criticizes the view of social theorists like Nakane who believe Japanese are prone to form small groups, frames into which they fit. He notes that keeping the small work group from spiraling off on its own, losing its connection to the rest of the factory, would be a real problem in the J-firm if Japanese workers were simply committed to working in small work teams.

What about negotiating with Japan? There is ample evidence that the political leaderships of the two nations could and did work together in an effort to correct the trade imbalance between the two countries that was generating waves of concern in Washington. Getting agreement between the central banks of the two nations was key to negotiating the Plaza accord that led to dramatic appreciation of the yen relative to the United States dollar. When this policy of manipulating

The Plaza Accord

The political friction over Japan's continuing ability to rack up bilateral trade surpluses with the United States became an ongoing drone, a rhythmic drumbeat, for American diplomacy with its great Pacific economic rival. It played a role in the negotiations over Okinawa's repatriation, in Nixon's decision to impose quotas on selected Japanese products, and it threatened to stabilize the mutual security treaty binding the militaries of the two countries together.

At the same time it roiled multilateral trade negotiations and the stability of the international exchange rate system. It would not be correct to attribute the decision of the executive branch in the United States to end the Bretton Woods system in 1971 by severing the connection between the United States dollar and gold solely to Japan's current account surpluses with its most important export market. Problems with the Bretton Woods system had developed earlier with the Western European countries, especially with Germany and France. Still, the decision to let the American dollar devalue in 1971 did have the effect of pushing the yen up from its Dodge Line value of 360 yen to a dollar.

The theory that adjustment in exchange rates will lead to adjustments in trade surpluses and trade deficits has been discussed earlier in this volume. If one's products become cheaper on international markets one expects to export more; if one's products become more expensive one exports to export less. Complicating this simple story are some important details that bear rehashing here.

First, inflation rates in countries trading with one another may be different. In this case the real exchange rate may not mimic movements in the

nominal exchange rate. Second, the J-curve holds, at least in the short run. When the currency of an exporting nation is pushed upward, the financial aspects of all import/export agreements already entered into change, but the quantities do not necessarily change. Suppose a Toyota dealer in San Francisco has already placed an order for one hundred Toyota trucks. If the yen appreciates before the vehicles are shipped the order still goes through but the dollar cost of completing the order actually goes up, making the bilateral trade deficit between the United States and Japan temporarily worse when it is denominated in dollars (in yen terms there is no change as long as the dealer sticks to its commitment to take the one hundred trucks). In the long run the dealership is likely to cut back on the volume of Toyota trucks that it brings in, thereby making the adjustment envisioned by the exchange rate theory of trade.

There is a third problem, peculiar to the country whose currency serves as the main linchpin of the global monetary system, most goods shipped internationally – crude oil, wheat, coal, zinc, and coffee beans – being priced out in units of its money supply (the United Kingdom in the period 1870 to 1914; the United States after 1945). In the post-1945 period, when the currency of a country appreciates relative to the United States dollar, the cost of importing raw materials falls in terms of its own currency. This was the situation that Japan found itself in as the yen began to appreciate upward relative to the dollar: the price of raw materials fell, counteracting to some extent the rise in its export prices attributable to yen appreciation. The price of a Japanese automobile reflects both production costs in Japan (labor, land, capital) and the costs of the imported raw materials used in its production. Thus yen appreciation was a two-edged sword.

A fourth factor involves restrictions on imports from other countries, either in the form of tariffs, or quotas, or other non-tariff barriers like those established by a regulatory agency in a country that sets product standards that apply to both domestic production and to imported items.

This was the background for the Plaza Accord of September 1985 – signed onto the central banks of France, West Germany, Japan, the United States and the United Kingdom – in New York. The goal of the accord was to devalue the dollar against the yen (then trading at 235 yen to the dollar) and the German Deutsche Mark by intervening in currency markets, selling dollars, buying yen and marks. The intervention was deemed successful in the sense that it did not produce panic in world financial markets, although speculation against the dollar did drive it below the level planned by the central banks. It was also deemed successful in reducing the United States trade deficit with Western Europe. However it did not appreciably impact Japan's bilateral trade surplus, at least as denominated in United States dollars, for the four reasons suggested above.

In part because the Plaza intervention did not correct the bilateral trade imbalance between the United States and Japan, and in part because the American position was based on a two-pronged theory of why the imbalance existed – the yen was undervalued; and domestic aggregate demand growth in Japan was too lackluster – American and Japanese negotiators continued to meet, trying to work out solutions to the bilateral problem. In 1986, the Baker–Miyazawa agreement was hammered out, Japan committing itself to stimulating its economy through a variety of means, thereby presumably increasing its demand for American goods and services. Again, in 1987, in the Louvre accord, negotiators for Japan agreed to "follow monetary and fiscal policies which will help it to expand domestic demand and thereby contribute to reducing the external surplus".

If the response of the trade imbalance between the two countries to the Plaza Accord seemed to be paradoxical, even more unexpected was the response to the Baker–Miyazawa and Louvre accords. By agreeing to expand its money supply (see Table A.4, concentrating on the figures for 1986–90), the Bank of Japan intervened in its domestic financial market, driving interest rates down in order to stimulate investment. In increasing the volume of yen outstanding it cheapened the value of the yen on international markets, thereby counteracting the impact of the Plaza Accord to some extent. In increasing the domestic money supply it also gave an additional upward kick to asset prices that were moving upward with the changing terms of trade, and hence with the United States dollar/yen exchange rate, for reasons discussed in the text of this chapter.

relative prices failed to correct the trade imbalance, the two governments worked together to hammer out agreements on structural issues that they believed would help address not only the trade imbalance but also other sources of political friction in the two countries associated with the trade imbalance. In the Strategic Impediment Initiative negotiations and talks that took place in the late 1980s, both countries demanded more open access to one another's markets. The United States was keen to break up the hold that the vertical *keiretsu* in the distribution system seemed to have, relaxing of the restrictions on department store square footage specified in the Large-Scale Retail Store Law, and speeding up of import clearance procedures. Japan was equally keen to see the United States clarify its anti-dumping measures, making them more transparent; end language based discrimination in the way the United States adhered to international patent agreements (involving a requirement that the patent be expressed in the English language); and encourage reform of product liability laws. In short, recognizing that their combined national incomes were almost 40 percent of world GDP, recognizing the growing capital market integration of the two economies, encouraged the governments of both Japan and the United States to reach cooperative agreements in the economic field.

Interestingly enough, as Alexander (2002) shows, negotiations designed to mitigate trade friction between the two economies went on a completely separate track from negotiations over other bilateral issues, military security for instance. Both countries avoided linking their economic negotiations to geopolitical issues. As important as correcting the bilateral trade imbalance was to the United States, it was not important enough to endanger strategic military arrangements that mutually benefited both nations, perhaps East Asia more generally.

The yen/dollar exchange rate

The upward drift in the yen turned into a gallop after the Plaza Accord. This is apparent from Table A.4 and from Figure 11.1. More important, the Plaza Accord marked a fundamental change in the terms of trade (the price of exports relative to import prices). As Figure 11.1 shows there is a tendency for movements in the yen/dollar exchange rate to be associated with, to be mirrored by, parallel movements in the terms of trade. When the yen goes up, the relative price of exports improves. However, prior to the mid-1980s, export prices tended to fall faster than import prices, regardless of whether the yen was appreciating or depreciating relative to the dollar. Prior to the mid-1980s import prices tended to go up even though each yen was buying more raw materials, more natural gas, more petroleum, more iron ore, most of these commodities denominated in

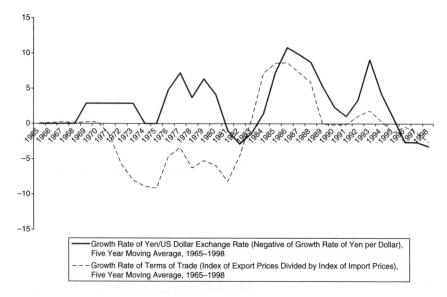

Figure 11.1 Growth rate of yen/US dollar exchange rate (negative of growth in number of yen per US dollar) and growth rate of terms of trade (index of export prices divided by index of import prices), five year moving averages, Japan, 1965–1998.

United States dollars. To some extent this was the result of the price hikes for petroleum that roiled the global economy during the 1970s.

From the mid-1980s Plaza Accord until the mid-1990s, appreciation in the yen went hand in hand with positive movements in the terms of trade. Import prices fell more than export prices. Japanese firms were paying less and less for the raw materials that they were bringing in. The tendency of import prices to fall – because the international purchasing power of the yen was going up – kept export prices from rising as much as they would have risen in the absence of yen appreciation. This was one reason why the dramatic appreciation in the yen (known as *endaka* in Japanese) after 1985 did not correct the bilateral United States/Japan trade imbalance, at least as it was calibrated in United States dollars. A number of other factors operating in the medium run kept the bilateral balance computed in dollars from closing. First under the agreements reached in the *shuntō* that mainly dealt with extending the retirement age, the union federations agreed to modify their wage demands so that exporting firms could continue to export even under *endaka*. This kept a lid on inflationary pressures in the Japanese economy. As can be seen from Panel A of Table A.4, the consumer price index hardly increased during the late 1980s or 1990s. Cost-push due to upward movement in nominal wages was muted under the collective bargaining umbrella. Because inflationary pressures were less in Japan than in the United States, the real exchange between the yen and the dollar did not increase as much as the nominal exchange rate. This worked to keep Japanese goods competitive in the American marketplace.

Alexander (2002) shows the yen/dollar nominal exchange rate did tend to diverge from the real exchange rate after 1985, the yen growing stronger than would be expected taking into account inflation rates in the two economies. Why? The answer lies in the discrepancy between movements in prices for goods and services only produced and consumed in Japan – wholesale and retail, rent on land, infrastructure – the so-called non-tradable sector, and movements in prices of tradable exports and imports. As you can see from Table A.4 tradable goods and services fell in price (export prices continued to decline throughout the period 1980–2000) while overall goods and services, tradable and non-tradable, rose somewhat in price over the same period. The export oriented sector was far more efficient – enjoyed more rapid productivity growth – than did the non-export oriented sector. The result is that the nominal yen/dollar exchange that mainly reflects the flow of traded goods and capital movements moved up more vigorously than the real exchange rate.

Second, the total cost of consumer durables includes the discounted costs of maintenance and repair. Once a Japanese automobile is purchased in the United States and used there, maintenance costs are expressed in United States dollars and are unaffected by any further changes in the yen/dollar exchange rate. The reputation for building quality into cars that Japanese manufacturers enjoyed allowed them to hold onto market share in the United States despite *endaka*.

In the short term there are two factors that always help explain why the bilateral trade balance at least measured from the American side, in United States dollars, did not vanish. The J-curve is one factor. Once orders are placed by wholesalers and retailers in the United States for Japanese goods, the dealer must absorb any depreciation in the dollar relative to the yen occurring between the date the order is placed and the date shipment takes place, paying out more dollars than the dealer originally expected to spend. This J-curve effect weakens the bilateral trade imbalance calibrated in United States dollars. Adding to these concerns is currency speculation. Acting on expectations about future movements in the yen/dollar exchange rate, speculators can drive the exchange rate at least in the very short run. In the medium term, fundamentals shape exchange rates. But in the short run speculation can drive it.

In one sense, in terms of actual volumes of goods traded, the bilateral trade imbalance between the two countries did shrink as the yen appreciated relative to the dollar. Indeed, calibrated in yen the bilateral imbalance actually shrunk. Negotiators for Japan could and did point this out to their American counterparts. Unfortunately for the American side what counted was the bilateral trade imbalance computed in American dollars. It was cold comfort that the Japanese side was observing shrinkage when it carried out its computations in yen.

The bubble

From the mid-1980s until it began bursting in December 1989, Japan was caught up in talk of twin bubbles in land prices and in stock prices. Is this description an accurate reflection of the facts on the ground?

The figures in Table A.4 and the graphical evidence presented in Figure 11.2 suggest that talk of a bubble was exaggerated. The inflation in land and stock

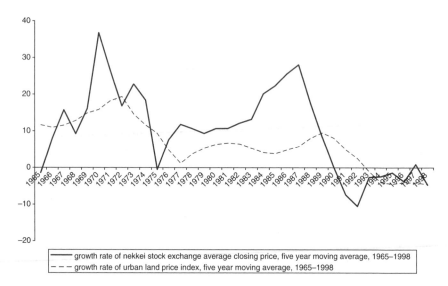

growth rate of nekkei stock exchange average closing price, five year moving average, 1965–1998
- - - growth rate of urban land price index, five year moving average, 1965–1998

Figure 11.2 Growth rate of Nikkei stock exchange average closing price and growth rate of urban land price index, five year moving averages, Japan, 1965–1998.

market prices was greater during the 1970s than it was during the late 1980s. Indeed in the first two decades of the twentieth century, when the intercity railroad lines were being built and bedroom suburbs were proliferating, the upward thrust in land prices was probably equal to that of the 1970s. Is this surprising? When rapid urbanization is occurring, dabbling in land speculation is a natural thing to do. Buy cultivated fields and unused land when it is still cheap; sell it when it becomes dear. Moreover, investing in housing that appreciates in value is a good way to make more money on asset holding than by putting your funds into a bank account, particularly with a shaky financial institution that might go under.

The only way to make sense of the talk of a bubble economy is to relate the upward thrust in land and stock prices to *endaka*. Once one does this talk of a bubble makes sense. Calibrated in American dollars land and stock in Japan became incredibly expensive. It is the linkage between the yen/dollar exchange rate and domestic land prices that makes the idea of a bubble occurring during the late 1980s reasonable.

A price tag for the Imperial Palace and its immediate environs

The upward surge in asset prices – for real estate prices and for stocks and bonds bought and sold on the Nikkei exchange – characterizing Japan's so-called bubble economy is evident in the cold hard growth rate estimates for the period 1986–90 appearing in Table A.4. But grasping the sheer dramatic extent of the inflation in Japanese assets is difficult to do through a simple perusal of these figures. A better vehicle for communicating the extremity of Japan's asset inflation is to consider the price of the Imperial Palace and its immediate surroundings, namely the price tag for several hundred acres of downtown Tokyo. At the height of the bubble in 1989 the value of this small piece of real estate had the same value as all of the land in Canada, the same value as all of the land in California!

There is no doubt that the upward spike in Japanese real estate values was especially pronounced in Tokyo, especially in the commercial properties of downtown Tokyo for which prices more than doubled between 1986 and 1990. But residential prices in Tokyo also soared, roaring up by almost 70 percent during 1988 alone, a year that saw Tokyo commercial real estate values jump by almost 80 percent. And what was true in Tokyo was true elsewhere in urban Japan, in great metropolitan centers like Osaka and Nagoya, and in relatively remote cities like Sendai in northeastern Honshū and Sapporo in Hokkaidō.

If we are using the value of the Tokyo real estate as a barometer for Japan's bubble, it is fair to use its value as a barometer for the bursting of that very same bubble. By 2001 the highest priced real estate in Tokyo was trading at about a quarter of its value at the peak of the bubble. What went up like a rocket came down like sledgehammer, reminiscent of the crash in tulip prices in early 1637 in Amsterdam and the sharp fall off in closing stock prices on the New York exchange in 1929 as the American economy lurched its way into the Great Depression of the 1930s. In Japan the bursting of the bubble seemed to mimic the dismal American experience, ushering in the lost decade of the 1990s.

Why did land and stock prices escalate during the late 1980s? In the literature on the subject we can distinguish three major lines of argument: those that mainly focus on domestic circumstances; those that take into account globalization, Japanese companies increasingly financing their activities abroad, foreign financial institutions moving into the Japanese market, the range of tradable services being extended to finance and banking; and those that directly link movements in the yen/dollar exchange rate and the terms of trade to the inflation in land and stock prices.

We begin with arguments centering upon domestic circumstances. Consider expectations. What counts in a stock or bond market is what other people do. One forms expectations based on what you think other people expect. In this way, expectations can drive expectations. This may explain some of the most famous bubbles in history. Underlining these arguments is deregulation of the stock and

The tulip mania and the South Sea bubble

Asset price bubbles are not necessarily typical of market economies, but they do occur with some frequency. Two of the earliest well documented bubbles occurred in seventeenth and eighteenth-century Europe. In both cases expectations about future asset prices seemed to drive the run-up and then collapse of the markets. In both cases the specific institutional rules underlying the operation of the financial markets played a role in generating expectation driven buying of the assets.

The tulip mania was largely confined to Holland in the 1630s. The tulip bulb, considered an especially exotic and attractive flower, cannot be rapidly multiplied, thus opening up the possibility of demand outstripping supply, generating a rise in tulip prices relative to other prices. Complicating matters was the fact that a tiny fraction of the tulips in seventeenth-century Holland were infected. Attacked by a mosaic virus, the infected tulip generated petals of contrasting colors, flamed as it were. These were especially rare and hence commanding of exceptionally inflated prices.

Further contributing to the bubble in tulips was the existence of a futures market in Holland. Purchasers could pay for the flowers well in advance, obtaining delivery of them during the ensuing spring. During 1636–37, the market for tulips spread rapidly in taverns, the prices for all bulbs – but especially for the flamed bulbs – rising dramatically. The market broke in February 1637, prices dropping drastically thereafter. Future contracts were not enforceable, leading to the bankruptcy of many speculators in the market.

The term South Sea bubble actually refers to two bubbles, both taking place in 1720, one occurring in England and the other in France. At the heart of the bubbles was the fact that the state governments in both countries had allowed for the establishment of joint-stock companies that issued shares on the stock market in exchange for taking on the public debt of the governments. The particular joint-stock companies involved invested in other activities, but at their financial heart was management of the public debt.

As a result of the government support for, and dependence on, joint-stock activity for handling debt, speculation in the shares of the companies spread from London and Paris to Amsterdam and Hamburg. Expectations for further increases in share prices tended to bid up share prices. Benefiting from the surge of interest in joint-stock issue, shares in the South Seas Company surged upward in the summer of 1720. When confidence in the company collapsed, financial panic ensued, exacerbated by rumors of insider trading, directors of the company issuing new stock to the public while selling off their own shares at the same time. As a result of the fiasco the British government decided to prevent any new joint-stock companies from being formed, issuing the Bubble Act that stayed on the books until the 1850s.

Other famous bubble collapses include the panic of 1837 in the United States involving speculation in land, the panic of 1847 in Europe that centered around investments in mining and railroads, and the panic of 1873 in the United States that followed upon the foundering of the banking firm of Jay Cooke that had lavished funds on the building of the Northern Pacific Railroad. The most famous of the collapses occurred in the twentieth century however: the stock market collapse of 1929 in the United States. Fueled by the growth of investment trusts that used funds that they acquired from the public to purchase stocks and bonds, operating under the claim that the experts in the investment trusts were wiser than the public in the ways of the market, the stock market mania of the 1920s was driven by investment trusts buying shares in investment trusts, and by margin buying, a purchaser of a stock or bond only putting down a portion of the purchase price at the time the purchaser acquired the asset. Once the industrial conditions underlying the stock mania of the 1920s turned sour, once the

> *threat of trade wars in retaliation for American protectionism as the high
> tariff Smoot-Hawley bill made its way through the halls of Congress
> became a real possibility, the mania broke, the stock market diving during
> the fall of 1929. From the United States the ensuing downturn in investment
> and production spread to a broad range of countries worldwide.*
>
> *Note:* This discussion draws heavily upon O'Donnell (2003).

bond market. Had the volume of securities traded on the Nikkei exchange not
exploded as fast as it did the bubble would not have gathered the force it did. As
Lincoln (1988) points out the Japanese government had no choice but to deregulate
the equity market during the early 1970s since it was increasingly engaging in
deficit financing – bond issue – in order to raise funds to cover its outlays.

An alternative view, also domestic in its orientation, has to do with the rate of
return on capital in the industrial sector. As we have seen the capital/output ratio
in Japan surpassed the American level during the late 1980s. Other things equal
this should drive down the marginal product of capital. Investing in corporations
became increasingly unattractive. Seeking higher returns on alternatives to industrial loans, banks turned to funding real estate developers who put up land as collateral. As the value of the collateral held by real estate developers escalated so
did the attractiveness of continuing to lend to them. Compounding the bubble like
potential of this type of market activity was the linkage of stock market prices to
land prices (cf. Figure 11.2). Banks lent to individuals wishing to speculate in
stocks on the basis of collateral, in particular on the assessed value of the land
assets that they held. As land prices jumped so did stock and bond prices. The
headlong upward drive of the market became self-fulfilling, expectations feeding
on expectations.

Moral hazard is usually invoked in stories that emphasize bad banking practices. As long as banks think that they will be bailed out – under the convoy system by other banks, the scenario played out under Ministry of Finance
administrative guidance or by the Bank of Japan or by the taxpayer – they have
little incentive to be cautious in their decisions. As long as a market is on an
upward spiral, as long as the downside risk of failure is negligible, why not jump
in, riding upward with the rest of the market? This is a basic theorem of financial
economics. Allen (2001) provides a good treatment of the logic underlying this
theorem.

Financial globalization may help account for the bubble. In 1980 the Japanese
government revised the Foreign Exchange Control Law, allowing Japanese firms
to freely issue unsecured foreign bonds. Attracted by the less regulated atmosphere in overseas markets, major Japanese firms entered the Euromarket, floating
bonds and stocks, raising funds that they could use to liquidate their obligations
to Japanese banks. In effect globalization encouraged Japanese companies to

switch from indirect financing of their debt using banks to direct equity issue, issuing stocks, bonds and debentures on both domestic and foreign markets. Banks had no choice but to switch away from loaning to export oriented prestigious companies to loaning to real estate developers, construction companies and more risky domestic manufacturing ventures. In this version of the story the emphasis is on deregulation rather than on the declining marginal productivity of capital. But the two arguments are not inconsistent with one another.

Foreign pressure to open up the Japanese capital market to non-Japanese banks and investment houses increased competition in the financial market, applying further pressure on Japanese banks. Many bankers felt that Japanese banks had to consolidate through wholesale mergers before Western banks were allowed relatively free entry into the Japanese market. Foreign banks were far more knowledgeable about financial opportunities than Japanese banks that had relied almost exclusively on industrial loans to make returns on their capital. Not coincidentally Western banks tended to crowd into the heart of the Tokyo financial district, adding fuel to the flames of land inflation in the center of Japan's capital.

A third line of analysis links movements in terms of trade to the movements in the stock market, hence to the land market. Consider Figure 11.3. As you can see the terms of trade and the Nikkei stock exchange index tend to move together from the mid-1970s until the bubble had fully burst in the early 1990s (the terms of trade did not start moving as long as Japan was adhering to the Dodge Line with a fixed exchange rate of 360 yen to a dollar). The key to a possible linkage between the two variables lies in expectations about the fortunes of the major

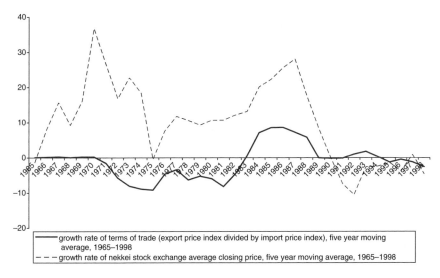

Figure 11.3 Growth rate of terms of trade (index of export prices divided by index of import prices) and growth rate of Nikkei stock exchange average closing price, five year moving averages, Japan, 1965–1998.

exporters, of the top ten "name brand" companies in particular. As the terms of trade improved so did the expectations about future profits in the exporting sector. This drove up stock prices in the tradable goods sector. Stock – like land – could be used as collateral. In this version of the story trade becomes crucial to the bubble.

Regardless of which story one finds the most convincing one thing is certain. Any convincing story about the bubble economy must include a discussion of *endaka*. In that sense the bubble economy was an outgrowth of the process by which a once tightly shut system was being integrated into the international economic order, an international economic order in which the menu of tradable goods was being steadfastly enriched. Globalization and the bubble economy went hand in hand.

Key terms and concepts in Chapter 11

Chaebol
Remodeling of the Japanese Archipelago
Japanese System
Strategic pragmatism
Duality principle
Strategic Impediment Initiative

Large-Scale Retail Law
Plaza Accord
Endaka
J-curve
Foreign Exchange Control Law
Terms of trade
Nikkei stock exchange index

12 Stagnation and reform

Deceleration with a vengeance

In the wake of the initial bursting of the bubble in late 1989 Japan's growth rate slowed to a crawl. This is apparent from Figure 1.1 in Chapter 1 and from the figures in Table A.1 in the Appendix. During the bubble phase and even during the first five years after the bubble began to burst Japan's per capita income continued to converge towards American levels. However during the next five-year period – between 1996 and 2000 – it diverged.

Whether this divergence will persist is unclear. Projections for Japan's growth of income have a high level of variance. There are a number of reasons why the variability of the estimates is considerable: as you know from the discussion in Chapter 1 national income is estimated imperfectly at best; and as you know from the discussion in the Appendix to this volume nailing down statistical models of an economy that can be usefully employed in forecasting is treacherous, highly controversial at best. Compounding difficulties are ongoing technical disputes about whether the national income accounting schemes employed by the governmental agencies in charge of national income estimation are used to confuse and mislead rather than inform the citizen about the underlying reality. After all, politicians do not like figures showing anemic growth in national income. Why not cook the books?

This said, most estimates suggest that the Japanese per capita income has grown over the post-1990 period and will continue to grow in a range between 1 percent and 2 percent per year (extreme optimists put the figure higher at 3 percent but this is less likely). While the difference between the two rates appears to be small, the difference does matter significantly in the long run: if the economy grows at 2 percent per annum in per capita terms, real income per capita doubles in 35 years; if it grows at 1 percent per annum income per capita doubles in 70 years.

Growing from 1–2 percent per annum is respectable. Indeed in a Swann-Solow model in which the capital/labor ratio is high, the marginal product of capital low, and there is relatively slow growth in technological progress achieving growth in this range is completely expected. Growing at rates in the 1–2 percent range puts Japan's growth squarely within the economic territory occupied by other advanced industrial countries. However, in terms of Japan's historical record – growing faster than the other advanced industrial economies over the last half century – the possibility that Japan has once and for all entered a new era of dramatic deceleration is a very sobering thought indeed. To bureaucrats and politicians accustomed to growing far faster than other advanced industrial economies the slowdown to so-called normal growth seemed to be a chastening experience.

Does the bursting of the bubble represent a fundamental watershed in Japan's economic development, a sharp structural break with the past? In a provocative book Teranishi (2005) argues that it has. Reasoning that a capitalist economy has three major subsystems – the division of labor between private sector and government, the institutions of the private sector, and the interface of government and private sector – Teranishi argues that fundamental system change takes place when three conditions characterizing a political economic system occur. The economic costs of maintaining it are too costly; the political costs of keeping it going are too high; and the rules governing the operation of the system become incompatible with social norms and values. When these conditions are met, the prevailing system becomes dysfunctional. Evolution takes place. A new system emerges out of the ashes of the old structure being discarded.

Using this framework, Teranishi argues that post-1870 Japan has passed through two systems: the Meiji-Taishō system and the high (miracle) growth era system. In the Meiji-Taishō system the private sector dominated the economy, government playing a relatively minor role. The main interface between government and the private sector was local, the *meibōka* elite lobbying for infrastructure in their districts in return for drumming up votes for the two major political parties. Local pork barrel politics dictated what the bureaucrats in the national ministries could and did accomplish. Eventually, during the 1920s and 1930s this system became dysfunctional. Extension of the franchise empowered tenant farmers; agriculture's share in national product fell, weakening a fiscal system mainly dependent upon the land tax; small rural banks became increasingly fragile; and many companies that had carved out niches during the World War I boom when imports were largely cut off became shaky, bringing down banks with them in some cases.

Out of this system emerged – during the late 1930s, World War II and the American Occupation – the institutions of the high-speed growth era. These included internalization of labor, extensive intervention of national government ministries in the private economy, industrial policy emerging as the key interface between the private and public sectors. This was the system that generated miracle growth.

Eventually it too became dysfunctional. Rising political costs of carrying out industrial policy were one problem. Increasingly, ministries were at cross purposes in implementing industrial policy, declining sectors competing for attention, each demanding intervention, cutting into the interests of other sectors when they managed to get protection from imports or subsidies that propped them up at least temporarily. The economic costs of maintaining the system soared as the yen appreciated. Consumers clamored for the benefits of a strong yen, becoming increasingly restive over high prices that they attributed to excessive regulation. In addition consumerism affected social values. The younger generation became oriented towards consumption of material goods, less inclined to derive satisfaction from being a member of a prestigious "name brand" corporation. The bubble economy marked the last gasp of the high-speed growth system. A new system began emerging during the 1990s.

Is there evidence bearing out the notion of a system change? There are at least four quantitative indicators that suggest that a new era has dawned: a substantial drop in the investment and savings rates; a rise in unemployment rates, especially for young individuals, from the extremely low unemployment levels of the miracle growth period; a worsening of the income distribution; and consolidation and restructuring of the financial sector.

Consider investment and savings. As Table A.6 demonstrates investment demand has been falling off: particularly striking is the sharp drop in the contribution that investment demand growth makes to aggregate demand growth during 1991–2000 (see Panel B of the table). Even more striking is the decline in measured household savings rates. Estimates suggest that the rates have steadily declined over the 1990s – from around 10.8 percent in 1990 to 6.4 percent in 2000, tumbling further to around 2.4 percent in 2004. Moreover, credit card usage has spiraled upward during the same period. Estimates for 1980 showed Japan with a ratio of consumer credit to disposable income of around 10 percent (about half of the level in the United States). During the 1990s Japan's rate was actually greater than the American rate, dropping back to around 20 percent during the early years of the twenty-first century. During miracle growth most households in Japan had to save in order to purchase consumer durables. No more.

Showing that a structural break has occurred in savings behavior can be justified by considering the impact of factors that probably shaped savings in the past: income per capita growth, the level of assets relative to income, and aging. True, the Japanese population continues to age, thereby depressing savings. But the drop in savings in the 1990s and early 2000s is far too dramatic to be explained away in terms of aging. True assets have fallen relative to income in the aftermath of the bursting of the bubble. But savings rates were dropping even as asset prices were being driven up during the 1980s. Finally income per capita growth – embarrassingly low by miracle growth standards perhaps – has tended to be positive, albeit low, beginning in the early 1990s.

The labor market has also been transformed. From Table A.3 it is apparent that the rate began to creep up after the era of miracle growth had largely come to a close, accelerating in the late 1990s. Particularly striking is the growth of unemployment amongst the young aged 15–19. The growth of young adult unemployment has gone hand in hand with the proliferation of "freeters". The term "freeter" is an amalgamation of the German word "frei" (or the English word "free") with the German word "Arbeiter" (worker). It describes a person who is either unemployed or underemployed (moving in and out of employment) or working as a freelance worker, perhaps for a company that dispatches temporary workers to employers seeking an employee who works on a short-term basis.

Examples of "freeter" employment are convenience store workers, supermarket checkout employees, fast food employees and waiters in restaurants. Estimates of the number "freeters" in Japan varies depends on which ministry is doing the counting. The Japanese Ministry of Labor began publishing estimates of the number of NEET (not in education, employment or training), a definition that approximates the freeter definition, in 2000. A White Paper on National Life in 2003 estimated the number of freeters at over 4.1 million (an alternative official estimate was about half that number).

What motivates an individual to choose a freeter work style? The Japan Institute of Labor classifies freeters into two categories. One describes those who reject the values that the adult generation of the miracle growth era held regarding working for a large prestigious company. To some degree these individuals may be reacting to the way the implicit contracts of internalized market were revamped in the aftermath of miracle growth: the struggle for promotions was intensified, the possibility of forced transfer becoming a disquieting reality. A second type is the individual who has no alternative, who has no chance of securing employment in a good salaried position.

The social consequences of the freeter life style are important. Earnings being low most freeters cannot afford to marry and start a family. Female freeters tend to marry late or not marry at all. Often they end up living with their parents, joining the ranks of the so-called "parasite singles". As more Japanese embrace the freeter life-style, it is likely the gross reproduction rate will continue to fall.

Does low fertility encourage even further drops of fertility in post-1990 Japan? One can argue that parents are willing to tolerate housing freeters precisely because the number of children that they raised is small.

Another sign of changing labor market institutions is the growth of demand for mid-career hires. Rather than relying on fresh school graduates more and more companies are recruiting workers who have experience working elsewhere. Is this due to the increasing presence of foreign managed companies and subsidiaries in the Japanese market? Or is it the result of an increasing disintegration of the internal labor market model? Is Japan's labor market converging toward an American style market in which ten-year job retention rates are relatively low, especially for adults in their twenties and thirties?

Has the natural rate property of the Japanese economy changed? Has the Japanese economy shifted from one where the non-inflationary rate of unemployment, the so-called natural rate of unemployment, is over 4 percent, as opposed to the rates ranging between 1 and 1.5 percent characteristic of miracle growth?

One of the miracles in miracle growth was the fact that high-speed growth was achieved with equity. This surprised many economists. One of the assumptions made by most mainstream economists is that there is a tradeoff between growth and equity. At a low level of income per capita when agriculture predominates income is assumed to be distributed fairly equally. With industrialization and rapid accumulation of capital this changes. For instance when dualism emerged in Japan during the early twentieth century, income inequality did worsen. But during miracle growth income inequality seems to have been muted, partly because agriculture was subsidized with the government's rice procurement program, partly because of the way the *shuntō* operated. Using estimates of the Gini coefficient (the lower the level of the Gini coefficient the more equal is income distribution) for Japan in 1968 (0.350) and in 1979 (0.336), we see that income distribution in miracle growth Japan and its immediate aftermath was relatively equal. However during the 1990s this changed: the Gini coefficient seems appears to have shot upward, from around 0.4 to around 0.433 (estimates of the Gini coefficient vary a bit depending on the nature of the households surveyed). There is little doubt that this trend mirrors the increasing presence of freeters and unemployed in the labor force.

Another quantitative indicator of structural change is the shakeup in the banking sector. Some banks were allowed to fail. As van Rixtel (2002: 250) shows, between 1990 and 1998 three city banks disappeared, eight second-tier regional banks vanished, 109 credit cooperatives closed their doors, and most dramatically over 2,000 agricultural and forestry cooperatives folded. Has Japan entered an era when unconditional moral hazard – every bank is bailed out no matter how badly managed it is, no matter how bad its loan program is – has given way to conditional moral hazard? Under conditional moral hazard government stands prepared to salvage responsible banks, not those managed irresponsibly. True, fear of foreign takeovers of Japanese banks limits the willingness of the Ministry of Finance and the political leadership to carry out a consistent conditional moral hazard approach. But the existence of bank failures suggests that the days of unconditional moral hazard are over.

Hyogo Bank goes under

From the theory of moral hazard, we have learned that an insuring agent – a central bank, a private insurance broker selling automobile premiums – can provide too much insurance, encouraging profligate and irresponsible behavior. For this reason there are limits to a central bank's willingness to bail out private banks whose managers may have made badly conceived non-performing loans, to fledging startup companies in industries going nowhere, to real estate speculators building structures that no one is likely to purchase, let alone occupy.

As we have seen there are two practices, peculiar to but not unique to Japan, that created an atmosphere of moral hazard in Japanese financial circles: the over loan policy of the Bank of Japan and the convoy system managed by the Ministry of Finance. Under the logic of the convoy system, groups of banks insured each other against the possibility of bankruptcy. In the event of a commercial bank failure government regulators would move in, arranging a merger of the embattled financial institution facing insolvency with a solvent bank. What was the incentive for the healthy bank to acquire a bad business? Dangled in its face by the regulators was the acquisition of the acquired bank's branching rights (allocated by the regulators), potentially very valuable for future growth in depositors, especially in the big six cities. In addition, an acquiring bank might expect to be especially well treated by the Ministry of Finance, perhaps securing preferential treatment.

In August 1995 Hyogo Bank announced that it was failing. The regulators had finally decided to draw a line in the sand. Giving up on their effort to arrange assistance for beleaguered Hyogo with a package involving a group of strong banks, regulators let a very big bank – the Hyogo Bank was the thirty-eighth largest bank in Japan – that had made too many non-performing loans, had lost too much money in the Nikkei and land market rundowns of the early 1990s as the bubble economy came crashing to a dismal close – go under.

To some degree the willingness of the regulators to allow a major bank to fail was the result of the "big bang" reforms of the 1980s, substituting ex post *inspection of banking practices for advance guidance by the regulators. But it was also a signal that the Ministry of Finance was only willing to go so far in cleaning up messes attributable to poor commercial calculation, bad luck, or a combination thereof.*

This said it is clear that the regulators were not willing to jettison bailouts as a general rule. For instance in March 1998 the government pumped around 1.8 trillion yen into twenty-one banks perched on the edge of ruin, and another 7.46 trillion yen into fifteen large banks in March of the following year. When deemed necessary, the regulators were prepared to use funds taxed away from the public to shore up a shaky profit oriented banking system.

The willingness of the government to abandon its blanket bailout policy impacted international financial markets. Letting a major commercial bank like the Hyogo Bank fail triggered the emergence of the "Japan premium", a term describing the extra interest charged to Japanese banks by foreign lenders based in other countries. Unlike a Japanese bank's domestic depositors whose accounts are almost certain to be partially guaranteed in the event of a bank's failure, offshore lending to the bank is unlikely to be guaranteed. Hence foreign investors expect to receive a higher rate of interest than a domestic investor would, the premium for a specific bank reflecting perceptions of its stability and the expected returns to creditors following an unexpected failure.

Studies show that the Japan premium emerged in the wake of the Hyogo Bank's collapse, declined in 1996, remaining low through until late 1997 when a fresh rash of bank failures occurred, including the collapse of a "city bank", Hokkaidō Takushoku. Since late 1997 the amount of the premium has fluctuated, the market responding to informed opinion and rumors about the stability of particular banks and the willingness of the regulators to carry out thoroughgoing bailouts in the aftermath of the bubble economy collapse.

In addition to quantitative indicators of system change there are a number of qualitative indicators suggesting that Japan was undergoing substantial and wrenching change in the aftermath of the bursting of the bubble. International surveys of happiness carried out in the early twenty-first century ranks Japan very low; suicide rates for middle aged men terminated from their jobs appear to have been increasing during the 1990s and early 2000s; a Japanese television series about "Project X" highlights quality defects in Japanese manufacturing. Egregious examples cited in the television series include Sony's recall of over 300,000 batteries and a upward surge in the number of recalls carried out by Toyota, that latter committing itself to hiring thousands of engineers in an effort to reverse criticism of its deteriorating quality. To a growing number of Japanese consumers it appeared that South Korea, Taiwan and China were producing higher-quality goods than Japanese manufacturers were.

Teranishi's theory of sweeping structural transformation aside, economists and political scientists have weighed in with an abundance of theories about why growth in Japan has slowed down as much as it has. One argument that you should be familiar with from Chapter 1 is the liquidity trap theory (see Figure 1.4 D). The idea here is that interest rates had been driven to such a low level during the 1990s by Bank of Japan policy that further use of expansionary monetary policy was impossible. In one variant of this hypothesis emphasis is put on expectations about the yen/dollar exchange rate. To encourage investors to purchase American securities in the face of a possible depreciation of the dollar relative to the yen, Japanese interest rates dropped to a low level. True, nominal interest rates in Japan declined to extremely low levels during the 1990s. But as we can see from Table A.4 inflation rates were also very low during the late 1990s and the dollar actually appreciated against the yen during this period. Still, if Japan was in a liquidity trap during the 1990s, monetary policy became useless, sharply limiting the number of stabilization policy options.

A second line of argument focuses on facilitating/coordinating policy, especially industrial policy in manufacturing and Ministry of Finance administrative guidance in the case of banking. Anchordoguy (2000) argues that Japan's system of "catch-up" capitalism in which the Ministry of International Trade and Industry promoted models for acquiring foreign technology from international industry leaders began to sour during the post-miracle growth era. Using the software industry as an example, Anchordoguy argues that the Japanese computer companies became obsessed with using IBM style methods under administrative guidance from the Ministry of International Trade and Industry, employing reverse engineering wherever possible. In 1982, Mitsubishi and Hitachi were caught stealing IBM technology, ultimately being forced to fork over massive annual fees to IBM for the use of the technology. Reacting to the "IBM industrial spy incident" the Japanese government sponsored a series of research and development projects designed to lead the industry away from the IBM standard, the most ambitious being the TRON project aimed at creating a Japan-specific operating system. While this project had some limited success within Japan itself, outside of the country it had little appeal. Internationally, IBM mainframe and personal computer software had a dominant position that TRON could not assail. Japan had locked itself out of international markets in the mainstream software sector.

Japan's computer game sector offers an interesting contrast according to Anchordoguy (2000). Largely left alone by the Ministry of International Trade and Industry it has flourished, enjoying strong demand in both domestic and international markets. The lesson is clear: industrial policy may be a good way to speed the process of "catch-up" growth. But it is a bad strategy for creating industries that flourish on their own innovative drive in a post-"catch-up" environment.

The critique by Van Rixtel (2002) of Ministry of Finance administrative guidance in the financial sector emphasizes other problems in the facilitating/coordinating model of policy-making, policy arising partly out of the regulated industry itself. Van Rixtel argues that Ministry of Finance accommodation of the wishes of the banks helped fuel the bubble itself, whose bursting undercut the viability of many of the banks. In effect he argues that administrative guidance in the financial field spawned moral hazard problems that would not have occurred had a different type of regulatory regime been in place. The problem was not regulation *per se*. The problem was the type of regulation.

The plight of the banks is often cited in explaining Japan's slow growth during the 1990s and early 2000s. It is said that they did not lend enough – or rather that they were not willing to lend to potentially innovative entrepreneurs – that they became overly cautious, that they refused to terminate non-performing loans. The fact that land prices continued to fall throughout the 1990s (see Table A.4) certainly made their fiscal lives difficult. As long as the value of their collateral kept following they were reluctant to terminate non-performing loans, continuing to extend credit to bad borrowers.

As is pointed out in the introduction to Blomström, Gangnes and La Croix (2001) the fact that Japanese banks were viewed as increasingly shaky and ill advised in their lending policies created growing distrust of Tokyo as a world-class financial center. Stung by this evaluation – maintaining the prestige Japan had garnered during the late 1970s and 1980s cannot be discounted as a motivation – the government further deregulated the industry with the Big Bang reforms of 2003. Despite these reforms many foreign financial institutions remain skeptical of the Japanese government's commitment to a responsible regulatory regime, in large part because of Ministry of Finance use of administrative guidance as opposed to clear and transparent rules.

For many students of the Japanese economy, however, it is not the banks, not aggregate stabilization policy, not administrative guidance and industrial policy, which is at the roots of Japan's current economic woes. Rather according to Katz (2003) the problem is total factor productivity. As long as sectors are protected from imports and thus shielded from the sting of global price reduction stemming from technological change in leading countries (whether the leader in a particular sector be the United States as in information technology and general purpose software, or Germany in the case of automobiles) productivity growth in Japan is likely to lag behind that of other countries. Exacerbating this problem is the fact that the most successful exporting companies, Toyota and Honda for instance, are increasingly carrying on their manufacturing outside of Japan. Another factor cited in discussing Japan's productivity problem: a decline in the skills acquired by youthful engineers, perhaps fueled by a failure of the Japanese educational system to keep up with trends in schooling initiated elsewhere. Is the long-standing emphasis on rote memorization in examinations catching up with the Japanese educational system? Or is the shop floor – once stimulating, indeed exciting to work in – becoming boring as workers are replaced with robots and digitally controlled machines?

True productivity can grow from sources other than total factor productivity. Accumulation – an increase in the capital/labor ratio – can fuel it. But as we know from Table A.1, Japan's capital/output ratio is already extremely high. So this is not a likely source for growth, at least for quite a while. Again, productivity growth can come from shifting resources like labor out of low productivity areas of a sector into higher productivity areas of the same sector. Moving workers from "mom and pop" retail outlets to convenience stores is one example of a possible productivity spur. How much productivity gain can be squeezed out of this type of change is questionable however. Unlike the sweeping gains during miracle growth in which agricultural employment gave way to manufacturing employment (one sector giving way to another), the type of structural change envisioned here involves change within a sector, less likely to boost the productivity figures at the aggregate level.

The political response

The fact that the bubble economy and the retardation afterward coincided with a growing number of scandals involving high level bureaucrats and politicians did not go unnoticed by the Japanese voter. Not surprisingly the Liberal Democratic Party's political support continued to erode. Still a fragmented opposition was having difficulty capitalizing on the disenchantment with the party that had ruled the country for so long. Growing dissatisfaction with this state of affairs was the political backdrop for the jettisoning of the system of voting for lower house representatives that had been put into place during the American Occupation, the multi-member medium sized district system being abandoned in favor of a system that mixed proportional representation with a single member district scheme.

As Reed (2003) points out there has been ongoing debate among students of democracy over the merits of single member "winner takes all" versus proportional representation systems. Those who think that it is important to have a majority in government – one that can actually pass legislation, one that can be held accountable in a future election for its deeds – favor "winner take all" systems in which one candidate from an electoral district emerges triumphant. This approach is known as majoritarian. The alternative view is that obtaining discussion, dialogue and consensus is the proper goal of democracy. Each voice should be heard. Parties should be represented in the legislature in proportion to their relative vote getting power in elections.

Between 1993 and 1996 Japan changed its system, moving away from the multi-member district system in which a voter cast one non-transferable vote, to a mixed system in which a voter cast one vote for a single candidate in a single member district and a second vote for the party of his or her choice, the proportional representation component of the election system. That Japan took this radical step – relatively few democracies have tinkered with their electoral systems in the post-World War II period (New Zealand has taken similar steps) – suggests that the Diet was concerned about growing discontent with the political status quo. Less convincing as a theory of the why the political system was willing to gamble on a radical change in the electoral system is the much vaunted theory that the Japanese people seek consensus. If this were true, why was proportional representation not adopted earlier?

Indeed, in the 1993 election the Liberal Democratic Party did not actually garner a majority of seats in the Diet. Thirty-nine members of the party precipitated the 1993 election by voting to support a no-confidence motion aimed at bringing down the party's cabinet. In bolting from the ranks of the Liberal Democratic Party they formed several new parties, including the Renewal Party and the Japan New Party. A combination of Liberal Democratic Party defections and the possibility of voting for fresh new parties ended almost four decades of Liberal Democratic Party rule. Ironically introducing the new voting system actually helped the Liberal Democratic Party. No longer were its candidates pitted against one another in districts. Now individual Liberal Democratic Party candidates could draw upon party funds, rather than upon individually managed local fundraising bases, in standing for election. Rather than minority/coalition governments emerging from the new voting system, the Liberal Democratic Party's fortunes were revitalized.

While Liberal Democratic Party hegemony over the national political scene soon resumed it occurred in an environment in which the demand for economic and political reform continued. As a result the party itself split into reformist and non-reformist wings, in effect one wing of the party engaging in all out political warfare with the other wing. The result was the dramatic election of 2005 in which Prime Minister Koizumi Junichiro triumphed over the opposition of his own Liberal Democratic Party colleagues. At the heart of his campaign was a drive to weaken the faction within the party committed to the Tanaka Kakuei pork barrel approach to policy making.

Postal reform as political theater

In a parliamentary democracy the astute prime minister must master the art of strategically picking clearly etched battles. Focusing on one or two symbolic issues designed to rally political allies and flesh out political enemies is one key. Another is timing. Knowing when to dissolve parliament and call an election; knowing how to frame the dissolution decision; knowing how to carry the battle to the electorate. In Japan post-bubble economy Koizumi Junichiro has proven to be a master of the art.

Making reform of Japan Post symbolic of his drive to transform Japan's political economy, Koizumi turned the lower house elections on 11 September 2005, into political theater of the highest order. Returned to power in 2003 with a diminished majority for his Liberal Democratic Party, facing an apparently increasingly popular Democratic Party of Japan, Koizumi had watched the fortunes of his party falter, mired as it was in a reputation for corruption, tarnished as it was for creating the regulatory politics of the 1960s and 1970s whose apparent legacy was the bubble economy.

Securing lower house passage of the postal reform in July, 2005, by a vote of 233–228, dividing his own party in the process, Koizumi's commitment to postal reform ran into concerted opposition in the upper house which voted down the measure by a 125–108 vote. Unable to muster enough votes in the lower house to override the upper house vote, Koizumi dissolved the lower house, calling for a September election to decide the fate of his proposed reform package. In the September election, Koizumi was triumphant, securing a landside, winning a commanding 296 seats in the 480-seat lower house, forcing the twenty-two members of the Liberal Democratic Party in the upper house who had voted against the reform to reconsider their positions.

To understand why the September 2005 election represents one of the most important examples of post-1950 political theater in Japan, an understanding of what Japan Post is and what privatization of the system (specifically splitting the banking and insurance services of the system off from mail delivery in 2007 and selling the banking and insurance services a decade later) may accomplish, is essential. In doing so, it is important to consider economic aspects of the privatization scheme separately from political aspects although they are both ultimately intertwined.

The economic reform drive centers upon reducing the role of government in the Japanese economy, increasing the returns on pensions (which will be a growing political issue as Japan ages), and making the financial sector more competitive. Japan Post is one of the most powerful financial institutions in the country, managing around a quarter of Japan's personal assets, around 85 percent of Japanese having savings accounts or other deposit accounts in the system. In 2006 it employed over 250,000 workers in about

25,000 post offices around the nation, far exceeding the 2,600 branches of the seven major banks.

Privatizing the financial wing of the system creates a major player in the private financial sector, one that can muster clout in going head to head with commercial banks. In theory privatizing the system, making it more competitive and market oriented, should increase the returns that investors in the system earn, bolstering pensions built up within it. From an economic viewpoint, postal reform is tantamount to making the Japanese economy more market oriented.

As important as the symbolic breakup of Japan Post is for the economy, as crucial as it may be to making a break with an overly regulated economic past, it is in the political arena that Koizumi's postal reform victory of September 2005 seems to be especially path breaking. In rural areas the post office has been intertwined with politics, used as a vote-generating machine by powerful politicians bent on keeping their Diet seats, used as a funding vehicle for pork barrel projects dear to the local rural district. Liberal Democratic Party politicians based in rural areas naturally wanted to keep this system functioning, protecting the jobs of postal workers who had assisted them in past campaigns, therefore breaking with their own party leader over the reform proposal.

Having gone to the polls with a clear intent of defeating this rural based old guard of the Liberal Democratic Party, Koizumi has effectively transformed the image of the party, making it more urban in its orientation, making it less dependent on the rural political machine wing that tended to prioritize the interests of farmers and rural pork masquerading as infrastructure needed for assisting remote villagers.

One can argue that Koizumi was completing a process initiated by the administrative reform movement of the late 1970s and early 1980s. In that movement the bureaucracy was under attack, but not the Tanaka style model of dispensing pork for votes. Koizumi carried the logic of the attack one step further. After all, Koizumi had progressed through his political career during the heyday of the administrative reform movement. His thinking was shaped by the debates going on about the spectrum of reforms that should be packaged into the *rinchō* program.

One of the main tenets of the administrative reform movement, however, was reining in government spending. Koizumi adhered to the logic of this position, thereby discouraging the use of expansionary fiscal policy as a tool for stimulating growth and reducing unemployment. In this sense, his commitment to political reform may have hampered his willingness to counteract Japan's economic doldrums through bold stabilization measures. Concerns about ineffi-cient uses of public funds in pork barrel projects, concerns about controlling the bureaucracy, concerns about the impact of aging on the viability – in short structural concerns – dominated the Koizumi agenda.

The question whether this approach to reform will continue to dominate Japan's politics remains to be answered. What is clear is that Liberal Democratic Party rule in the early twentieth century (if it continues) is likely to look very different than it did in the miracle growth period and its immediate aftermath.

Paths walked, paths taken

Path dependence is a strong concept. Whatever happens in the future depends at least partly on what has gone before.

Many social scientists think the idea is absurd. Consider Japan's economic transformation over the period 1886–2000 as captured in the snapshots that are Tables A.1–A.7 in the Appendix. By all accounts Japan is so different in the early twenty-first century from how it was in the late nineteenth century – in terms of per capita income, in terms of life expectancy and fertility, in terms of structure of output and labor force, in terms of the structure of aggregate demand, in terms of the anthropometric measures of height and weight – that talk of continuity over time is seemingly ridiculous.

Still continuity abounds. Indeed one can argue that the greatest continuity is in the very drive to innovate what became apparent when entrepreneurs built the first steam driven integrated spinning and weaving mills in Osaka in the 1880s. Even during the bubble and its problematic aftermath Japanese companies continue to be innovative, continue to take risks, continue to push into new ventures. In so innovating, they embody a past that they project into the future.

Sharp gambles on liquid crystal display technology

In the Schumpeterian model of invention, innovation, imitation and creative destruction corporate survival depends upon taking risks, gambling on new products, jettisoning old product lines. In the course of an industry's evolution, companies come and go, those wedded to the ways of the past disappearing, new startups taking their place.

The company that manages to remain in the marketplace for a long time – for a half century or more – goes through a parallel evolution, its product line and its target base continually changing as the industry it is associated with twists and turns through the forces of innovation and creative destruction. In this process of transformation, an externally imposed crisis can play a positive role, forcing management to think anew about the company's focus, necessity being the mother of invention as it were.

Sharp is an old company. Originally established in 1912, the company was founded by Hayakawa Tokuji to manufacture mechanical pencils, "ever sharp" pencils, hence taking on the name Sharp. From pencils Sharp shifted its manufacturing focus to vacuum tube radios, exporting them throughout Asia during the 1930s. After the American occupation ended, Sharp moved into television set production, following other Japanese consumer electronics companies into making air conditioners and appliances for the rapidly growing domestic market of the miracle growth era.

In the early 1970s Sharp began to shift out of labor intensive manufacturing of consumer durables into the new technology intensive sector developing around the manufacture of semiconductors and especially electronic calculators. Through the 1960s and the 1970s Sharp research laboratories churned out impressive inventions in the calculator field – the world's first all transistor-diode electronic calculator in 1964, the first electronic calculator with solar cells in 1976, the world's first 1.6 millimeter thin electronic calculator in 1979 – putting Sharp in the forefront of the industry, focusing on the younger generation of consumers in Japan and abroad with "life products" exemplified by clever designs and aesthetics attuned to persons in their twenties. In pursuing this strategy, Sharp's management put strong emphasis on selling abroad, exports accounting for almost 60 percent of sales in the early 1980s. Then came the violent upward movement of the yen, rapid appreciation following the 1985 Plaza Accord.

In the wake of yen appreciation, sales of calculators dropped precipitously. Avoiding layoffs at all costs, Sharp focused on introducing emergency measures, cutting costs on all fronts and establishing new lower prices for exported products. More important, Sharp decided to initiate a shift away from labor-intensive consumer electronics exemplified by its calculators and semiconductors to knowledge intensive products, exemplified by its research and development in the liquid crystal business. Continuing to manufacture calculators while it built up its liquid crystal technological base, Sharp gambled on a technologically oriented strategy, risky because research and development takes time, often proceeding down blind alleys.

That Sharp was willing to enthusiastically embrace the new and risky and downplay the old and well worn was partly due to the relatively youthful structure of its management and its rank and file employee base. Of course the association between the youthfulness of a company and its innovation capacity is tricky. Innovative companies tend to grow fast, taking on young recruits at a higher rate than less innovative competitors, ending up younger.

Despite its attempts at restructuring initiated in 1986 in the wake of the Plaza Accord, Sharp continued to struggle through the late 1980s and early 1990s as weak sales of its calculators resulting from growing competition from manufacturers elsewhere in Asia imitating Sharp's products cut into its profits. By 1998 when Machida Katsuhiko took over the reins of the enterprise, the company was mired in a serious financial crisis.

Once again, Sharp's management responded to crisis by playing the card of technology, of innovation. Machida decided that Sharp needed to give up completely on semiconductors, computer monitors and tube televisions, products that had become increasingly cheap as global production and global imitation drove down profit margins for already established producers. Instead, Machida argued that the company needed to focus completely on its knowledge intensive product lines, especially those exploiting its own research advances in liquid crystal display that Sharp management had invested in aggressively on the heels of the rapid yen appreciation of the mid-1980s.

Focusing on flat-panel televisions that took advantage of the liquid crystal display technology that it originally developed in the 1970s for calculators and had improved upon in its laboratories during the 1980s and 1990s, Sharp's management turned the fortunes of the enterprise around, bolstering its formerly embattled profit margins in the early 2000s. Root and branch restructuring paid off. Still the restructuring of the late 1990s and early 2000s would have been far harder to carry out, perhaps impossible to achieve, had an earlier management team not committed itself to intense research and development in liquid crystal display technology during the crisis of the 1980s brought on by rapid yen appreciation. In this sense necessity, pounding on the door of Sharp several times, was the mother of Sharp's newest revival as it pushed into its ninth decade of continuous operation.

True, much of the innovation in Japan involves hybridization, the adapting of foreign technology to the Japanese economic, social and political environment. But this is true everywhere. Indeed the same charge was leveled against the American innovating entrepreneurs during the 19th century. One of the greatest examples of Japanese innovation is in facilitating/coordinating policy making, an area that may be proving to be as much a barrier as a fillip to future economic advance in Japan. But as we have seen administrative guidance is itself undergoing change, unconditional moral hazard giving way to conditional moral hazard in the financial field.

It is easy to dismiss Japan's long-run growth potential in light of the struggle its economy has been enduring in the wake of the bursting of the bubble economy. That would be a mistake. When the Western powers broke Japan open in the 1850s they set in motion one of the greatest locomotives of economic growth the world has ever witnessed. Once unbound from its shackles, this locomotive of growth – powered by innovation – has continued on its dramatic journey for over a century.

It will continue on that journey, perhaps gaining speed at times, perhaps slowing down at times, for centuries to come. The strongest continuity in Japan's modern history is change itself. Whether we view Japan through the lens of markets, or norms and values, or political constraints, the continuity of change is the one overriding reality, the one bedrock proposition that we should never ignore. Emerging out of Japan's long and tumultuous history, wedding traditional norms and values to Western institutions and technology, the Japanese company is a formidable innovator, a formidable competitor, adapting to changing market conditions, to changing political realities, to changing social norms. That is the most important implication to draw from this account of Japan's remarkable long-run economic development.

Key terms and concepts in Chapter 12

Forecasting national income
Freeter
Gini coefficient
Moral hazard and conditional moral hazard
Changes in the voting system introduced during the early/mid-1990s

Appendix

Japanese economic development, 1886–2000 – a statistical portrait

A rich statistical record

One of the great attractions of becoming a student of Japan's economic development is access to statistical documentation covering Japan's economy prior to, during and after, its extensive industrialization and transformation from low to high levels of per capita income. Indeed, it is difficult to deny the statement that the statistics documenting Japan's economic development are more wide ranging and detailed than are the statistics of any other country undergoing development in the nineteenth, twentieth and twenty-first centuries.

Ultimately, Japanese government ministries deserve our gratitude for collecting, processing and publishing tabulations from the censuses and surveys they have carried out since the 1870s. While corporations and individuals have left useful statistical records of their activities, it is the Japanese government agency that has done the lion's share of documenting Japan's economic transformation. It should be kept in mind that while some of the numerical information available is generated from administrative functions carried out by officials – for instance collecting taxes and duties on imports, administrating employment exchanges, managing welfare offices, counting persons who clear customs at airports – much of the data was secured through special surveys. Some surveys, like the population census, attempt to count everyone residing in Japan. Other surveys attempt to sample from the population in order to make reasonably reliable inferences about the population or sub-populations as a whole.

For those interested in working with the original publications of Japanese ministries, a word of warning is in order. The names of the publishing agencies change due to administrative revamping and reform in Japan's national, prefecture and local bureaucracies. For instance consider the agency that publishes the statistical yearbook for Japan. Between 1881 and 1939, the Cabinet Bureau of Statistics (Naikaku tōkeikyoku) was responsible for issuing the *Statistical Annual of the Japanese Empire*; in the early 2000s it is the Statistics Bureau of the Ministry of Internal Affairs and Communications that publishes the yearbook and maintains the website (www.stat.go.jp/english/data/chouki) containing long-term historical statistics for Japan. Or consider the census. Between 1920 and 1940, it was administered and processed, by the Cabinet Bureau of Statistics. Beginning in 1947, the Prime Minister's Statistical Office (Sōrifu tōkeikyoku) took over this responsibility. By the time the 1985 census was issued the Statistics Bureau of the Management and Coordination Agency was in charge of the census.

In moving toward a system of national income accounts, Japan was doing what many other countries were doing. It was responding to a growing international interest in national income accounting, exemplified by the United Nations adopting a system of national income accounting in 1953. As a result of the growing interest in national income accounting within Japan one of the great projects in Japanese quantitative economic history emerged under the auspices of the Institute of Economic Research of Hitotsubashi University. This project is known as the Long Team Economic Statistics (LTES) project and it operated under the stewardship of Ohkawa Kazushi, Shinohara Miyohei, and Umemura Mataji. Research at Hitotsubashi University under the stewardship of Ohkawa Kazushi, Shinohara Miyohei, and Umemura Mataji.

Operating with grants from the Ministry of Education and the Rockefeller Foundation, the LTES project coordinators assembled a large team of researchers who ultimately published 13 volumes in the LTES series. A number of these volumes (volume 1 dealing with national product, volume 3 estimating capital formation, volume 5 focusing on savings, and volume 6 with personal consumption expenditures) came up with estimates for a wide range of national income accounting variables by working from the original publications of various agencies of the Japanese government. The volumes were issued over an eighteen-year period, beginning with 1965 and ending with 1983 (the last volume dealt with regional economic statistics). While the LTES estimates have been rejected as unreliable by some scholars – after all estimates are estimates and the degree of belief in the reliability of official statistics varies from scholar to scholar – they earned sufficient credibility to be republished in the massive 5-volume *Historical Statistics of Japan* issued by the Japan Statistical Association in 1987. Created as an affiliate of the Cabinet Bureau of Statistics in 1878, the Japan Statistical Association is responsible for disseminating knowledge about Japan's rich statistical heritage. It maintains a website at www.jstat.or.jp.

In creating the set of basic statistical tables that appear in this Appendix, I have relied mainly on figures issued by the Japan Statistical Association and by Statistics Bureau and Statistical Research and Training Institute of the Ministry of Internal Affairs and Communications.

Basic statistical tables

I have created seven basic statistical tables for this volume, most of them giving averages for successive five year periods between 1886 and 2000: Table A.1 provides estimates of real income per capita for Japan and the United States in international dollars; Table A.2 estimates of population dynamics; Table A.3 measures of labor force structure; Table A.4 figures on price change (inflation or deflation) and money supply growth; Table A.5 figures on savings and age structure of populace; Table A.6 estimates of the composition of gross domestic expenditure; and Table A.7 indicators of health and human development. For each table I have listed the specific sources that I used in generating the estimates.

How is the student to approach these tables? My advice is to read the tables through after reading Chapter 1, returning to them as the student's attention is drawn to specific tables in the remainder of the text. How does someone "read" a table? In reading a table the student should try to tell a story about the numbers in the table. For each variable in the table is there a trend or fluctuating pattern that is evident? If so, do the variables move together or do they seem to be unrelated? What interpretations of the movements seem plausible? What does comparison of the tables tell us? For instance how can we use figures in Table A.2 to shed light on trends apparent in Panel B in Table A.5?

To assist the student with this process, I discuss briefly each of the tables, beginning with Table A.1.

Table A.1 Income per capital and the capital/output ratio: Japan and the United States (Maddison's estimates)

Years	Income per capita for Japan[a]			Capital/output ratios[b]	
	y	*G(y)*	*R(y)*	*Japan*	*U. S.*
1886–1890	907	0.97%	27.1%		
1891–1895	1,004	2.08	28.5		
1896–1900	1,094	3.13	28.5		
1901–1905	1,130	1.66	25.1		
1906–1910	1,259	0.90	25.5		
1911–1915	1,324	3.95	26.3		
1916–1920	1,633	2.87	29.6		
1921–1925	1,775	0.15	30.1		
1926–1930	1,849	−0.25	28.1		
1931–1935	1,951	4.14	37.8		
1936–1940	2,443	5.19	37.7		
1941–1945	2,408	−9.93	23.4		
1946–1950	1,627	8.36	17.8		
1951–1955	2,393	6.74	22.5	1.44	2.28
1956–1960	3,291	8.51	29.9	1.23	2.35
1961–1965	5,046	8.01	41.1	1.28	2.23
1966–1970	7,822	9.03	53.5	1.44	2.09
1971–1975	10,579	3.11	66.1	1.81	2.20
1976–1980	12,218	3.58	68.5	2.23	2.25
1981–1985	14,247	2.89	75.2	2.55	2.36
1986–1990	16,995	4.36	79.9	2.72	2.32
1991–1995	19,451	1.15	88.1		
1996–2000	20,554	0.66	81.6		

Sources: Various tables in Maddison (1995, 2000).

Notes
A blank cell indicates that there is no estimate available.
a *y* stands for income per capita for Japan; *G(y)* for the growth rate of income per capita for Japan; and *R(y)* stands for the income per capita of Japan relative to that of the USA 5 100.
b Both national income (GDP) and capital (non-residential structures plus machinery and equipment) are measured in 1990 Geary-Khamis dollars.

Table A.1 gives estimates of income per capita in Japan and the United States in international (Geary-Khamis) dollars. Working with a wide range of national accounting statistics and carrying on the tradition of quantitative economic history pioneered by Simon Kuznets, Angus Maddison has attempted to adjust for the purchasing power of different currencies in order to put long-term statistics for a variety of economies in a common currency. Maddison has also generated capital stock figures for Japan and for the United States over the post-1950 period.

Ask yourselves the following questions: keeping in mind that the Maddison estimates are for annual income per capita and assuming that a figure of about $2 a day indicates extensive national poverty how poor was Japan in the late 1880s? During the late 1940s? During what periods was growth in per capita income unusually rapid? Why is comparison with the United States relevant?

Working with the approximation

$$G(x * y) = G(x) + G(y) \tag{A.1}$$

where "x" and "y" are any two variables, use the figures on growth in, and levels of, population given in Table A.2 to estimate the growth of total income (GDP) for five year periods and the level of income for Japan for the five year period 1936–40 (you will have to divide the "gp" figures in Table A.2 by the number 10 in making these calculations). In 1940 the Japanese population was about 73 million and the American population about 133 million. How large was Japan's economy relative to that of the United States? What does this tell you about the wisdom of Japan's attacking the United States in 1941? Compare the growth rates of real per capita income with the growth rates of total real income for five year periods. Do the rates seem to move together? If so, why?

Table A.2 gives figures on Japan's population. In Panel A, there are estimates of the crude vital rates (births and deaths per 1,000 persons) and of the difference between the birth rate and the death rate, the natural rate of increase. The virtue of working with the crude vital rates is obvious: they are easy to compute. However, their value depends strongly on the age structure of the population under examination. For instance populations with a substantial proportion of women in the reproductive age groups (e.g. in the age range 20 to 35) tend to have a relatively elevated crude birth rate. By the same token, in populations skewed towards the aged (having a heavy proportion of individuals age 65 and over, for instance), the crude death rate will be relatively pronounced.

To avoid analyzing population dynamics in terms of rates whose values are capturing age structure at the expense of vital processes, demographers have worked up measures based upon age specific hazards, probabilities of giving birth, becoming ill, dying and so forth. Panel B provides estimates of several summary measures reflecting age dependent probabilities: life expectancy and the gross and net reproduction rates (the gross reproduction rate is the sum of the age specific female birth rates for women between the ages of 15 and 49, the reproductive age range; the net reproduction is this sum discounted for the

Table A.2 Population

Panel A *Population (P, in 1,000s), crude birth rate (b), crude death rate (d), natural rate of increase (nri), population growth rate per 1,000 persons (gp), population density (pd, – persons per square kilometer), urbanization (u% – percentage of population in cities) and percentage of persons in six big cities (b6c% – Tokyo, Yokohama, Nagoya, Kyoto, Osaka and Kobe): 1886–2000*

	Rates per 1,000 persons				P	pd	Urbanization	
	b	d	nri	gp			u%	b6c%
1886–1890	28.8	20.8	8.0	8.2	39,130	103		
1891–1895	29.0	21.4	7.6	8.2	40,864	107		
1896–1900	31.7	21.1	10.5	10.8	42,906	112	12.4	
1901–1905	32.5	21.0	11.5	12.3	45,525	119	15.0	
1906–1910	33.6	21.5	12.1	10.8	48,031	126	17.3	
1911–1915	34.5	20.7	13.9	14.1	51,305	134	17.5	
1916–1920	33.7	24.1	9.6	11.9	54,673	143	18.9	9.8
1921–1925	34.7	21.9	12.8	13.1	58,158	152	21.6	11.1
1926–1930	33.4	19.3	14.1	15.3	62,581	164	24.0	11.8
1931–1935	31.6	17.9	13.7	14.5	67,377	176	33.0	18.3
1936–1940	28.8	17.3	11.5	7.6	71,014	186	38.3	20.0
1941–1945	31.2	16.3	14.9	0.7	73,116	193		
1946–1950	32.2	12.3	20.0	29.0	79,765	217	35.3	11.9
1951–1955	21.9	8.7	13.2	14.2	86,969	236	56.3	15.9
1956–1960	17.7	7.7	9.9	9.1	91,785	248	63.5	16.5
1961–1965	17.5	7.2	10.3	10.2	96,216	260	68.1	17.3
1966–1970	17.8	6.8	11.0	10.9	101,364	274	72.2	18.1
1971–1975	18.7	6.5	12.2	15.4	108,871	293	75.9	16.9
1976–1980	14.9	6.1	8.7	9.0	115,133	309	76.2	16.0
1981–1985	12.6	6.2	6.4	6.7	119,469	321	76.7	15.7
1986–1990	10.7	6.4	4.3	4.2	122,692	329	77.4	15.5
1991–1995	9.8	7.0	2.7	4.7	125,501	337	77.4	15.0
1996–2000	9.5	7.5	2.0	0.6	126,416	339	78.7	15.2

Panel B *Infant mortality rate (imr), life expectancy at age 0 for males (lem) and for females (lef), gross reproduction rate (grr) and net reproduction rate (nrr): 1891–2000*

Years	imr	Life expectancy at age 0		Reproduction rates	
		lem	lef	grr	nrr
1891–1895		42.8	44.3		
1896–1900					
1901–1905	152.0	43.9	44.9		
1906–1910	158.3				
1911–1915	156.7	44.3	44.7		
1916–1920	173.7				
1921–1925	159.3	42.3	43.2		
1926–1930	136.6	44.8	46.5		
1931–1935	120.4	46.9	49.9		
1936–1940	106.6				
1941–1945	85.4				

(*Table A.2 continued*)

Table A.2 Continued

Years	imr	Life expectancy at age 0		Reproduction rates	
		lem	lef	grr	nrr
1946–1950	65.3	54.8	58.4	2.06	1.69
1951–1955	48.0	63.6	67.8	1.34	1.20
1956–1960	35.9	65.3	70.2	1.01	0.95
1961–1965	23.4	67.7	72.9	0.98	0.95
1966–1970	15.4	69.3	74.7	0.99	0.96
1971–1975	11.2	71.7	76.9	1.01	0.98
1976–1980	8.4	73.4	78.7	0.87	0.86
1981–1985	6.3	74.8	80.5	0.87	0.85
1986–1990	4.8	75.9	81.9	0.80	0.79
1991–1995	4.3	76.4	82.9	0.72	0.71
1996–2000	3.5	77.7	84.6	0.67	0.67

Sources: Japan Statistical Association (1987), *Historical Statistics of Japan. Volume 1*: various tables; and various tables at the www.stat.go.jp/english/data/chouki website (downloaded in April, 2006).

Notes

A blank cell indicates that there is no estimate available; some of the figures, especially those in Panel B, are point estimates, namely for one (or perhaps two) year(s) during the interval indicated. In a few cases, the averages are for three or four years rather than for five years.

loss of females to mortality prior to entering the reproductive ages and during reproduction).

Think of the net reproduction rate "nrr" as the average number of daughters a woman born into a population would expect to have over her life. Note that a "nrr" equal to one implies zero population growth in the long-run, a "nrr" greater than one implies population increase, and a "nrr" less than one population decline. What is the relationship between the "nri" and the growth of population "gp"? What does this tell you about the rate of Japan's net immigration or net emigration? What is the relationship between the infant mortality (the "imr") and life expectancy? In what period did the long-run growth potential of Japan's population switch from positive to negative? What is the relationship between movements in the "nri" and movements in the "nrr"?

Table A.3 gives figures on the labor force. Panel A documents unemployment and the degree of self-employment and family work in three highly aggregated sectors of the Japanese economy; Panel B the relative labor productivity of the three sectors. Relative labor productivity (rlp) is computed by dividing the percentage of national income (GDP) in a sector by the percentage of the labor force in the sector

$$rlp = (\% \text{ of GDP})/(\% \text{ of labor force}) \tag{A.2}$$

Why is the unemployment rate higher for young persons (aged 15 to 19) than the remainder of the labor force? Why is the rate of self-employment and family

Table A.3 Labor force

Panel A *Labor force participation rate (lfpr – percentage of the population aged 15 and over in the labor force), unemployment rate (ur) ,unemployment rate for persons aged 15–19 (yur%), monthly hours worked by regular workers in the non-service sector in firms of 30 workers or over (mhw), and percentages of primary, secondary and tertiary sectors who are self-employed or family workers (sefw%)*[a]: *1920–2000*

Year(s)	Unemployment rates				Self-employed or family workers		
	lfpr	ur	Yur	mhr	Primary	Secondary	Tertiary
1920	72.8						
1930	69.8						
1940	71.1						
1947	55.9	1.9					
1950	65.4	2.0		195			
1951–1955	67.3	1.9		193	93.3	24.5	40.8
1956–1960	67.4	0.8		200	92.3	18.9	36.8
1961–1965	66.0	1.4		197	92.6	14.9	30.4
1966–1970	67.1	1.1	2.0	191	94.0	16.8	26.9
1971–1975	64.2	1.4	2.8	180	93.6	17.4	24.3
1976–1980	64.0	2.1	4.3	176	92.5	17.9	22.9
1981–1985	63.5	2.5	6.2	177	91.5	17.7	21.2
1986–1990	63.1	2.5	7.2		90.7	16.4	19.4
1991–1995	63.6	2.6	7.2		88.8	13.4	16.0
1996–2000	61.1	4.1	10.6		87.8	11.8	14.2

Panel B *Relative labor productivity of the three major sectors of the labor force*[a]: *1951–2000 (P = Primary; S = Secondary; T = Tertiary)*

Years	Percentage of labor force in sector:			Percentage of GDP in sector:			Relative labor productivity in sector:		
	P	S	T	P	S	T	P	S	T
1951–1955	38.5	24.5	37.0	18.4	34.6	46.9	47.9	141.3	126.8
1956–1960	32.9	26.7	40.4	14.9	37.9	47.3	45.2	142.0	117.0
1961–1965	26.2	30.9	42.9	10.6	41.0	48.4	40.5	132.6	112.9
1966–1970	19.8	33.8	46.3	7.8	41.1	51.1	39.1	121.4	110.5
1971–1975	13.9	35.9	50.0	5.4	41.5	53.2	38.9	115.6	106.4
1976–1980	11.5	34.7	53.6	4.5	38.0	57.6	38.7	109.5	107.4
1981–1985	9.3	34.3	56.1	3.2	36.8	60.0	34.8	107.1	107.0
1986–1990	7.9	33.6	58.0	2.6	35.9	61.5	33.2	106.6	106.0
1991–1995	6.1	33.6	59.9	2.0	32.6	65.3	32.8	97.1	109.1
1996–2000	5.3	31.7	62.5	1.5	29.1	69.3	28.4	91.7	111.0

Sources: Japan Statistical Association (1987), *Historical Statistics of Japan. Volume 1:* various tables; and various tables at the www.stat.go.jp/english/data/chouki website (downloaded in April, 2006).

Notes
A blank cell indicates that there is no estimate available. In a few cases, the averages are for three or four years rather than for five years.

a The primary sector consists of agriculture, forestry and fishing; and the secondary sector of mining, construction and manufacturing. The tertiary sector consists of electricity, gas, heat supply and water; transport and communication; wholesale and retail trade; eating and drinking places; financing and insurance; real estate; services; and government (including not elsewhere classified).

worker input in primary (agriculture, fishing and forestry) high in Japan? Do you think this is true in other countries? Why do you think the rate of self-employment/family work has declined in the tertiary sector? Why do you think the relative labor productivity of primary industry in Japan has fallen over the period 1951–2000? If one moves a person from a low labor productivity sector to a sector with high labor productivity what happens to overall labor productivity for the economy as a whole? What does this tell you about productivity gain due to industrialization (i.e. to the shifting of labor force from primary to secondary industry)?

Table A.4 provides estimates of inflation/deflation in overall prices, land prices, import and export prices, the yen/dollar exchange rate, the Nikkei stock exchange closing price, and the terms of trade (export prices divided by import prices). These are highly aggregated indicators of price levels for the economy as a whole. They are relevant in discussing the quantity linkage (aggregate demand/aggregate supply) model summarized in the Appendix to Chapter 1. In particular in examining the logic of the quantity linkage model with variable prices, we introduced the equation

$$\pi = \text{gm} - \text{gY} \tag{A.3}$$

where "π" is the inflation rate, "gm" is the growth of the money supply, and "gY" is the growth of real output (the idea being that money supply growth that is not required to grease the wheels of – facilitate the transactions required by – additions to economic activity tends to fuel price increases, money supply increases not needed for transactions increasing the supply of money relative to goods and services and assets, pushing up the prices of those goods and services and assets in nominal terms). When was money supply growth the most rapid? During what periods did high rates of money supply growth translate into rates of high inflation? During the 1980s growth in the consumer price index was modest but growth in land prices and the security prices on the stock market was explosive. What is the relationship between movements in land prices and the Nikkei stock exchange closing price? Do you think a mixed inflation rate – an index based upon goods and services combined with assets – mimics growth in the money supply adjusted for real income expansion?

Now consider trade related prices. Keeping in mind that Japan imports most of its energy and raw materials used to manufacture goods – in 1971 99.7 percent of its crude petroleum, 99.3 percent of its iron order, 100 percent of its lead ore, bauxite and wool were imported – consider the potential impact of a growth in the prices that Japanese exports command relative to the prices of its exports. Why might improvement in the terms of trade counteract the impact of money supply growth on the consumer price index? In formulating an answer to this question, ask why rises or declines in energy prices influence most goods and services prices.

Table A.5 gives figures on household savings (savings as a percentage of disposable post-tax household income, where the household sector includes

Table A.4 Prices and money supply

Panel A *Percentage growth in domestic prices (overall prewar price index, pwi; consumer price index, cpi; land price index for all cities, ulpi; land price index for six big cities, b6clpi) and money supply (Bank of Japan notes, BOJ; currency, cur; and money stock, ms): 1901–2000*

Years	Overall prices		Land prices[a]		Money[b]		
	pwi	cpi	ulpi	b6clpi	BOJ	cur	ms
1901–1905	5.0				8.7		
1906–1910	0.8				5.3		
1911–1915	1.3				1.5		
1916–1920	22.0				28.8		
1921–1925	−4.4				2.7		
1926–1930	−7.2				−2.3		
1931–1935	2.9				4.4		
1936–1940	10.7				22.4		
1941–1945	17.5				74.7	71.4	
1946–1950	161.5				56.8	56.2	
1951–1955	7.8				10.0	10.5	
1956–1960	0.6		23.0	24.2	13.0	13.4	
1961–1965	0.4		22.8	31.4	15.8	15.8	
1966–1970	2.2		12.8	9.5	16.8	17.0	17.1
1971–1975	10.0	11.5	14.6	14.1	18.0	17.9	18.9
1976–1980	5.9	6.7	3.8	5.4	9.0	8.9	11.9
1981–1985	−0.1	2.8	5.3	6.5	5.7	5.9	8.3
1986–1990		1.4	8.0	24.5	9.4	9.8	10.4
1991–1995		1.4	−1.0	−11.1	3.1	3.1	2.1
1996–2000		0.3	−4.5	−7.9	6.7	6.4	3.3

Panel B *Percentage growth in price indices for trade and the Nikkei stock exchange closing price*

Years	Trade			Yen/US dollar exchange rate[d]	Closing average price for the Nikkei stock exchange
	Export price index	Import price Index	Index for Terms of Trade[c]		
1961–1965	−0.8	−0.1	0.3	0.0	0.7
1966–1970	1.4	1.4	0.1	0.0	9.2
1971–1975	7.1	18.4	−8.0	2.9	22.8
1976–1980	1.5	11.3	−6.3	3.7	10.6
1981–1985	−0.4	−0.8	0.6	−1.4	13.2
1986–1990	−3.2	−6.5	5.9	8.7	17.6
1991–1995	−4.4	−6.1	1.9	9.1	−2.6
1996–2000	−1.4	1.5	−2.6	−3.2	−4.7

Sources: Various tables at the www.stat.go.jp/english/data/chouki website (downloaded in April, 2006) and *Japan. Statistical Yearbook 2006* published by Japan. Ministry of Internal Affairs and Communications. Statistics Bureau (2005: p. 7).

Notes
A blank cell indicates that there is no estimate available. In a few cases, the averages are for three or four years rather than for five years.
a The six big cities are Tokyo, Yokohama, Nagoya, Kyoto, Osaka and Kobe.
b Money stock (ms) includes "near-money" (e.g. certificates of deposits).
c The terms of trade are the ratio of export prices to import prices. Growth rates in the terms of trade in this table were computed by computing the growth rate for the ratio of the index of export prices divided by the index of import prices (both indices based at the year 2000 with an index value of 100).
d Growth rate in the yen/US dollar exchange rate was defined as the negative of the growth rate in the number of yen equaling one US dollar at the official exchange rate.

Table A.5 Savings and age structure

Panel A *Household savings rate (hsr) and characteristics of households surveyed about accumulation of financial assets (total household members, hm; earners in household (earn); ratio of household members to earners (hmpe); average age of household head (ahh); and ratio of financial assets accumulated to household income (rfay)*[a]*: 1906–2000*

Years	hsr[b] %	Financial asset accumulation survey variables				
		Hm	earn	hmpe	ahh	rfay
1906–1910	3.2					
1911–1915	0.8					
1916–1920	13.2					
1921–1925	−1.9					
1926–1930	2.2					
1931–1935	12.5					
1936–1940	22.8					
1941–1945	36.2					
1946–1950	2.0					
1951–1955	10.8					
1956–1960	13.4					
1961–1965	15.4	4.3	1.6	2.7	44.2	0.91
1966–1970	15.9	4.1	1.6	2.5	44.5	1.08
1971–1975	20.5	3.9	1.6	2.5	44.7	1.11
1976–1980	20.5	3.8	1.5	2.5	44.8	1.17
1981–1985	16.6	3.8	1.5	2.5	47.0	1.41
1986–1990	15.3	3.7	1.6	2.4	48.8	1.85
1991–1995		3.5	1.6	2.2	50.8	2.06
1996–2000		3.3	1.5	2.2	52.5	2.26

Panel B *Population aged 65 and over as a percentage of population aged 15 and over*

Year	Males	Females	Both sexes combined
1920	7.3	9.2	8.3
1930	6.4	8.6	7.5
1940	6.4	8.6	7.5
1950	6.7	8.5	7.6
1960	7.4	9.0	8.2
1970	8.4	10.1	9.3
1980	10.4	13.3	11.9
1990	12.2	17.2	14.8
2000	17.6	22.9	20.3

Sources: Horioka (1993: 282–4) and various tables at the www.stat.go.jp/english/data/chouki website (downloaded in April, 2006).

Notes
A blank cell indicates that there is no estimate available. In a few cases, the averages are for 3 or 4 years rather than for 5 years.

a The assets documented in the survey are financial assets, including debts to institutions and individuals, and holdings of stocks, bonds and deposits in mutual loan and savings associations. Excluded are houses, automobiles and other consumer durables, artwork and other physical tangible illiquid assets accumulated by households.

b These estimates are from three separate series reported by Horioka (1993). The estimation techniques underlying the figures vary from series to series, and therefore in the years when at least two surveys report figures the estimates differ somewhat.

households, private unincorporated non-financial institutions, and private non-profit institutions at the service of households). What does this data suggest about the impact of (per capita) income growth rates on savings? What does it suggest about the impact of aging upon the household savings rate?

Table A.6 provides a breakdown of the structure of aggregate demand (levels of gross domestic expenditure) relevant to the discussion of the quantity linkage aggregate demand/supply model. The figures in Panel B provide estimates of the impact of changes in the level of consumption, investment, government consumption expenditure, and net exports on changes in the level of gross domestic expenditure. What do you observe about trends in consumption demand as a percentage of total aggregate demand? During what periods is investment demand relatively high and relatively low? Why do you think it has fluctuated? Why do you think it has declined after the early 1970s?

Compare the figures on investment demand to those on the capital/output ratio given in Table A.1. Do you observe a relationship between the capital/output ratio and the contribution that investment demand makes to aggregate demand increase in Panel B of Table A.6? Why do you think this relationship exists? Focus on absolute increases in gross domestic expenditure. When were the increases the greatest? Are these periods the same periods when real income growth was the most buoyant? If not, how do you explain the disparity between the two phenomena?

Now consider the trade sector. Why do the figures assembled in the two panels call into question the validity of the "export-led" hypothesis, according to which the source of Japanese growth lies in foreign demand, the so called export engine for expanding aggregate demand?

Table A.7 displays information on health and human development. In accordance with the discussion of efficiency wage feedback, the anthropometric measures (height, weight, the body mass index, chest girth, etc.), especially for young persons, are employed as proxies for the real standard of living and for the capacity to engage in physical and intellectual activity. More generally, the human development index – an index of health, educational attainment, and per capita income – attempts to capture the real standard of living of populations calibrated in terms of the social capacity to generate economically productive output. What trends are apparent for the anthropometric measures and for the human development index? When was growth in the two types of measures the most rapid? What does this tell us about the dynamics of the convergence (1955–70) period? To what extent did the improvements in human development and physical abilities spillover into periods subsequent to the convergence era?

Uses and misuses of the statistical record

An economy rich in statistics is an economy that commands the attention of the quantitative economist passionate about testing theories of economic behavior. Not surprisingly, economists from around the world have been drawn to the data on Japan. Can statistical probing reveal an accurate explanation of economic

Table A.6 Gross domestic expenditure

Panel A *Composition of gross domestic expenditure (GDE) in terms of percentages. Percentage attributable to consumer demand (C%), gross domestic fixed-capital formation (I%), government consumption expenditure (G%), exports of goods and services (EX%), imports of goods and services (IM%) and net imports (NX% = EX%-IM%): 1886–2000*

Years	Percentage of gross domestic expenditure [a]					
	C	I	G	EX	IM	NX
1886–1890	85.2	9.0	6.9	3.2	4.2	−0.9
1890–1895	84.0	9.4	7.9	3.7	5.1	−1.4
1896–1900	85.4	12.1	7.5	4.9	9.9	−5.0
1901–1905	80.2	10.6	14.3	6.5	11.7	−5.2
1906–1910	79.6	13.5	11.3	8.0	12.4	−4.4
1911–1915	79.0	15.6	9.1	10.7	14.4	−3.7
1916–1920	74.9	17.9	8.1	13.8	14.6	−0.8
1921–1925	82.3	18.8	9.0	10.4	20.4	−10.1
1926–1930	79.8	17.8	10.3	14.5	22.3	−7.8
1931–1935	74.0	16.5	12.7	19.3	22.5	−3.2
1936–1940	63.8	25.7	12.9	21.2	23.4	−2.3
1941–1945						
1946–1950	62.2	21.1	9.9	4.1	6.8	−2.6
1951–1955	61.9	17.8	14.8	8.3	6.9	1.4
1956–1960	61.6	22.8	11.9	8.8	8.0	0.8
1961–1965	56.8	30.5	9.6	9.5	9.7	−0.2
1966–1970	55.5	34.3	7.8	12.1	11.1	1.0
1971–1975	53.8	36.3	8.6			0.9
1976–1980	57.3	31.7	10.5			0.5
1981–1985	55.1	29.3	13.8			1.9
1986–1990	53.8	30.6	13.3			2.3
1991–1995	54.5	29.8	13.8			1.9
1996–2000	55.9	27.4	15.5			1.3

Panel B *Growth in real gross domestic expenditure. Absolute magnitude of changes in GDE over 5 year periods (ΔGDE), and percentage contributions that absolute increments to consumption (ΔC), absolute increments to gross domestic fixed capital formation (ΔI), absolute increments to government consumption expenditure (ΔG), and absolute increments to net exports (ΔNX) make to the changes in GDE: 1886/90–1996/2000*

Five year period	ΔGDE	Percentage contribution to ΔGDE [b]			
		ΔC	ΔI	ΔG	ΔNX
1886/1890	525	100.2	18.3	−2.3	−21.9
1891/1895	792	56.7	12.6	45.3	−14.7
1896/1900	389	75.6	9.8	20.3	−5.7
1901/1905	363	−40.5	40.2	267.5	−167.2
1906/1910	1,147	99.0	24.4	−37.0	13.5
1911/1915	564	103.4	−37.8	−12.4	47.9
1916/1920	2,118	64.8	57.6	13.9	−36.3
1921/1925	729	156.2	−58.2	−5.4	7.3
1926/1930	1,521	38.7	6.1	26.1	29.2
1931/1935	4,118	31.8	27.7	6.2	33.5
1936/1940	4,303	11.1	81.6	28.9	−21.6

Table A.6 Continued

Five year period	ΔGDE	Percentage contribution to ΔGDE^b			
		ΔC	ΔI	ΔG	ΔNX
1941/1945					
1946/1950	7,556	55.8	5.1	11.9	11.4
1951/1955	2,353	73.8	20.2	2.6	−2.3
1956/1960	5,811	52.9	41.8	4.5	−0.6
1961/1965	9,125	58.7	33.6	7.9	7.0
1966/1970	21,259	39.3	47.3	4.1	0.5
1971/1975	11,528	94.0	7.6	25.0	−14.7
1976/1980	20,377	44.9	35.3	27.0	−7.2
1981/1985	13,920	57.4	7.8	12.8	22.1
1986/1990	25,804	48.5	53.4	10.4	−12.3
1991/1995	1,204	397.8	−486.8	213.1	−24.1
1996/2000	4,666	65.3	−66.0	69.0	31.6

Sources: Ohkawa and Shinohara with Meissner (1979: pp. 256–60) and *Japan. Statistical Yearbook 2006* published by Japan. Ministry of Internal Affairs and Communications. Statistics Bureau (2005: 2).

Notes

A blank cell indicates that there is no estimate available. In a few cases, the averages are for three or four years rather than for five years.

a The estimates for components of gross domestic expenditure in both Panels A and B are based on estimates in constant prices (in 1934–6 prices for the pre-1941 period and in 1965 prices for the post-1945 period).

b Due to the method of calculation and to rounding error, the percentages do not necessarily add to 100.

behavior, one that is convincing to everyone? That it cannot do so is the message I want to deliver here. Statistical analysis is helpful. But when all is said and done, when the dust has settled, there is yet room for vigorous debate and argument.

To give a concrete example: what explains the level of the household savings in Japan? Why did it rise to levels that seemed to dwarf savings rates in other economies? Why have the rates been in decline since the early 1990s?

There are three main problems in formulating "tests" of the determinants of the Japanese savings rate that might usefully shed light on the nature of savings behavior: (1) deciding how to measure savings; (2) setting up a sequence of tests that pit opposing theories against each other, sorting out strong from weak theories; and (3) reliance on quantitative data.

On the first point, it should be noted that different systems of national accounts generate different household savings rates for Japan. Moreover, household surveys – like the financial assets survey relied on for measures of saving in Panel A of Table A.5 – restrict their surveying to financial assets (e.g. bank and postal system deposits, stocks and bonds, and the like), excluding an important source of savings, namely the accumulation of assets in real estate and consumer durables. If scholars cannot agree on how to measure the dependent variable of interest to them, how can they agree on the analysis of savings determinants?

Table A.7 Health and human development

Panel A   *The anthropometric record. Male standing height (msh) at ages 6, 12 and 18 (in centimeters); male weight (mw) at ages 6, 12, and 18 (in kilograms); and male body mass index (bmi) at ages 6, 12 and 18: 1901–2000*

Years	msh			mw			bmi		
	6	12	18	6	12	18	6	12	18
1901–1910	106.7	133.6	159.9	17.5	29.8	52.3	15.4	16.7	20.5
1911–1920	106.9	134.4	160.8	17.6	30.2	53.1	15.4	16.7	20.6
1921–1930	107.7	136.2	161.6	17.7	31.4	53.8	15.3	16.9	20.6
1931–1940	108.8	138.2	162.9	18.2	32.7	55.0	15.4	17.1	20.7
1941–1950	108.5	138.4	162.9	18.3	32.6	55.0	15.5	17.0	20.7
1951–1960	110.3	139.3	165.0	18.7	33.3	55.7	15.4	17.2	20.7
1961–1970	113.4	144.9	167.7	19.6	36.7	57.9	15.3	17.5	20.6
1971–1980	115.3	148.6	169.0	20.5	40.2	60.0	15.5	18.2	21.0
1981–1990	116.4	150.4	170.6	21.2	42.2	62.1	15.7	18.7	21.3
1991–2000	116.8	152.2	171.1	21.7	44.5	63.0	15.9	19.2	21.5

Panel B   *The Human development index (HDI) and various* measures of educational attainment

Year	Educational attainment variables[a]			HDI[b]
	centr	eadv	E	
1900	0.82	0.07	0.57	0.57
1910	0.98	0.09	0.69	0.61
1920	0.99	0.16	0.71	0.64
1930	1.00	0.21	0.73	0.65
1940	1.00	0.37	0.79	0.70
1950	1.00	0.44	0.81	0.69
1960	1.00	0.61	0.87	0.75
1970	1.00	0.86	0.95	0.83
1980	1.00	0.99	1.00	0.89
1990				0.90
2000				0.92

Sources: Mosk (1996) pp. 20–4 (2005) pp. 142–3; United Nations Development Programme (various years: various tables); and various tables at the www.stat.go.jp/english/data/chouki.website (downloaded in April, 2006).

Notes

A blank cell indicates that there is no estimate available.

a The educational variable E is estimated by adding the value of the "centr" variable weighted by 2/3 to the value of the "eadv" variable weighted by 1/3 for each year in Panel B of the table. The "centr" variable measures the enrollment rate for compulsory schooling (between 1900–44 this refers to schooling between ages 6 and 12, that is to compulsory elementary school; after 1945 this refers to schooling between ages 6 and 15, that is to compulsory elementary and middle school). The "eadv" variable measures the advancement rate for students leaving compulsory schooling, including vocational schools and middle schools before 1945, and high schools and vocational schools after 1945.

b To compute the "HDI" variable for all years prior to 1990 (the values for 1990 and 2000 are based on the estimates prepared by the United Nations Development Programme), I added together estimates for a per capita income variable (I), the educational variable E described in note a to this table, and an anthropometric proxy for health (H) reported in Panel A of this table, dividing the resulting sum by 3. That is

$$HDI = (I + E + H)/3$$

Where $I = [\ln(y) - \ln 100] / [\ln(40,000) - \ln(100)]$

"y" being the Maddison estimate for per capita income in international dollars in each year and "ln(x)" the natural logarithm function; and

Where $H = [(0.5)*(msh / 172)] + [(0.5)*\{(1000 - imr) / (1000 - 6)\}]$

"msh" being the measure for male standing height in year in "imr" being the estimate for the infant mortality rate reported on in Panel B of Table A.2 for each year.

On the second point, consider three hypothesized models of savings behavior, one derived from the Keynes' original formulation of a theory of aggregate demand; one taking into account asset accumulation over the life cycle of the household; and one based upon habits. All three models are plausible on a priori grounds. Consider the first model that is derived from the logic of Keynes that consumption rises with income but at a declining rate, not being strictly proportional with income:

$$S = Y_d - C = Y_d - (C_0 + c \, Y_d) = (1 - c)* Y_d - C_0 \qquad (A.4)$$

that is the standard Keynesian saving function, "c" being the marginal propensity to consume out of disposable income. In this model the savings rate "s" rises as disposable income rises because the ratio of the fixed level of consumption "C_0" to disposable income falls as disposable income rises:

$$s = [(1 - c) * Y_d - C_0] / Y_d] = [(1 - c) + (C_0 / Y_d)] \qquad (A.4')$$

In the second model (usually associated with the names Modigliani and Ando and based on the idea that households build up assets until retirement after which they run down their assets in order to consume after their labor income vanishes), consumption depends upon accumulated assets and income, namely:

$$C = a_0 * Y_d + a_1 A \qquad (A.5)$$

"A" being total assets accumulated. Assuming that households have a target level of assets relative to income, so that $A = \lambda * Y_d$ (for instance, in some empirical versions of this model, λ is set equal to 4.75), equation (2) becomes

$$C = a_0 * Y_d + a_1 * (\lambda * Y_d) = (a_0 + a_1 \lambda) Y_d \qquad (A.5')$$

and savings S is the difference between this C and disposable income,

$$s = (1 - [a_0 + a_1 \lambda]) \qquad (A.5'')$$

where "s" is the savings rate. Note that the aggregate household savings falls as the population ages (i.e. the proportion of the population over age 15 who are over age 65 rises) in this model because increasingly percentages of the adult population become "disavers", consuming their accumulated assets in retirement.

In the third model, households are assumed to change their consumption tastes slowly. Therefore there is a lag between rises in per capita income and increases in consumption, namely

$$s = b_0 Y_d + b_1 (gY_d) \qquad (A.6)$$

where "gY_d" is the growth of disposable household income.

In the classical theory of statistical testing, one generates estimates of the parameters in a model from some data set using ordinary least squares regression analysis (OLS) or maximum likelihood estimation. A researcher using the OLS methodology specifies a liner relationship – the independent variables may be squared or cubed values or logarithms of an original set of fixed independent variables – fitting a line that minimizes the sum of the squares of the residuals (the difference between the actual values of the dependent variable and the values predicted from the linear relationships). For instance letting "y" stand for a dependent variable and "$x_1, \ldots, x_n$" a list of independent variables. A simple regression equation takes the form:

$$y = c_0 + c_1 * x_1 + \cdots\cdots + c_n * x_n + \varepsilon \qquad (A.7)$$

where the "c_i's" are parameters to be estimated and "ε" is the error term. The OLS technique minimizes the sum of the squared values of the difference between the value of "y_P" predicted by the regression for a specific set of values for the dependent variables and the actual value of "y" in the data.

To use OLS without adjustment a number of conditions must be met: the error term has an average value of zero; the covariance between any two different observations is zero; the variance of the error term is constant for all values of the error term; there is no correlation between the independent variables and the error term. Kennedy (1985) provides a useful treatment of the problems arising when these conditions are not met. He also provides an overview of problems encountered when the independent variables are correlated with one another. In accomplishing these tasks he provides a readable summary of the general approaches employed by econometricians – statisticians who specialize in analyzing economic data – that avoids the cookbook recipe style that plagues most of the textbooks written to teach students econometrics.

The maximum likelihood technique is typically used for non-linear relationships. A likelihood function is generated with the method, one maximizing the probability of generating the observed data for the entire set of variables, dependent and independent. In practice the maximization is carried out by numerical methods. Using these methods amounts to determining whether the estimated parameters are statistically significant and different from zero at some predetermined cutoff level of significance. Note that one is not "running a horse-race", testing one of the models against another. One tests the model against a single alternative: that its parameters are not significantly different from zero.

Recognizing the limitations of an approach to formulating, testing and modifying models some econometricians embraced the Bayesian methodology. In the Bayesian framework, one adjusts one's assumptions about reality by conducting a sequence of tests. For instance one can imagine comparing the results of probing each of the three models laid out above in a sequence, starting with the first model and proceeding to the third, revising one's assumptions about the relevance of the models as one proceeds. An example is readily at hand. Scrutiny of the (five year averages) for post-1950 household saving given in Panel A of

Table 4 savings would seem to rule out the simple Keynesian model for Japan (the savings rate declining after the early 1980s in the face of increases in income per capita seems to contradict this model).

Still, while the Bayesian approach would seem to be superior to the classical testing method because it allows us to pit alternative hypotheses against each other, using it does not allow us to escape the measurement conundrum. If scholars cannot agree about how to quantify savings for instance (do we include equity in housing as accumulated savings?), it is difficult to see how they can resolve the issue of what determines savings. Moreover, how does one know whether one has considered all possible options with any one set of competing mathematical formulations (the Bayesian methodology is limited to setting up mathematical forms for testing)?

This brings us squarely to the third problem, the one that is most fundamental in the opinion of this author: the possibility that quantitative measures cannot completely capture the matter at hand (so that even proceeding through a Bayesian testing sequence is inherently incomplete, failing to resolve the issue). For instance suppose expectations about consumption are formed in childhood. Growing up in poverty encourages one to be conservative in consumption, to pinch every penny, to prize highly every material purchase. Being reared showered with digital readout toys, crystal display television rivaling rugs in area, automobiles with built in sound systems far superior to those installed in the homes of the less fortunate, spoils a person for life, often rendering the individual profoundly indifferent about consumer purchases no matter how well crafted, no matter how attractive they are to those less fortunate.

The generation of Japanese that was born in the 1920s and 1930s had modest expectations about consumption, naturally saving aggressively as their incomes soared during the 1955–70 period. By contrast the generation growing up in the affluent 1980s was far less inclined to be impressed and excited about acquiring radios, television sets, and refrigerators, despite the quality improvements made in these products between the 1960s and the 1990s. Simply incorporating a dummy variable for the generation that one was born into does not really nail down concretely the impact of changing expectations. Has the "generational dummy" variable captured expectations or something else (for instance, educational attainment)?

Similar comments can be made about the possible ways that religious orientation or exposure to foreign cultures through travel may shape consumption tastes and hence the rate of savings out of disposable income.

To reiterate: statistics provide us with important information. But they are imperfect. They are measured with error. They are derived from samples and different samples may yield sharply contrasting statistical stories. Typically they do not come to us in a pure form: rather they are massaged and reworked through algebraic filters. Like qualitative data they must be interpreted. Scholars can and do differ in interpreting numerical information just as they differ in interpreting literary evidence. The student should be cautious and not be seduced by the false claims of statisticians.

This said, it is important to not throw out the baby with the bath water. Empirical analysis is a useful complement to logical argument and qualitative description. However it never has delivered results impervious to criticism. It never will. Properly used, it sheds light. Improperly used, it can spread confusion and error or, far worse, distrust of statistics and the uses to which they are put.

Notes

1 Markets, norms, constraints

1 Basing his screenplay on Akutagawa's famous short stories ("Rashomon" and "In the Grove"), the great Japanese film director, Kurosawa Akira created one of the greatest motion pictures of the 1950s, released in the West under the title Rashomon.
2 A list of mainstream economist interpretations of Japanese economic development would be very long (a list of writings in Japanese would be far longer). Later on in this text we will deal with the specific economic principles elaborated here as they crop up in explaining particular developments. Many of these references are to journal articles. For books giving general accounts of Japanese economic development with a strong focus on the role of markets, see Beason and Patterson (2004); Bloomström, Ganges and La Croix (2001); Flath (2000); Ito (1992); and Patrick and Rosovsky (1976). It should be noted that some of these authors favor invisible hand type principles, looking at how particular product markets evolve in Japan, and some give greater emphasis to aggregate level change, especially Ito (1992) and some of the chapters in Patrick and Rosovsky (1976).
3 For discussions of Japanese economic development highlighting the importance of Confucianism see Bellah (1957), Dore (1973) and Morishima (1982). To refute those who think arguments of this sort are limited to sociologists, it is worth noting that Morishima is a famous economist.
4 McVeigh (2004) gives a good account of the various forms of nationalism that shaped Japanese thinking and policy making before and after World War II.
5 Johnson (1982) is the most noted advocate of the view that the economic bureaucracy in Japan largely shaped the contours of Japan's post-World War II economic policy making. He argues that the main role of the politicians was to provide cover for the bureaucrats. Beason and Patterson (2004) and Ramseyer and Rosenbluth (1995) disagree with this view, arguing that most economic policies in Japan since the establishment of the Diet reflect local grassroots political interests.

2 Before industrialization

1 This table draws heavily from the analysis put forward by Diamond (1997). I draw upon Diamond (2005) for my discussion of the management of forests during the later Tokugawa period.
2 On the Gokaidō road network see Vaporis (1994).
3 This discussion follows that given in Yamamura (1973).

3 Meeting the Western challenge

1 Since the Meiji Restoration, Japanese historical periods are delineated by a name associated with the particular individual holding the position. The Meiji period ended

with the death of the Emperor whose period was called Meiji. It was followed by the Taishō period, then the Showa period.

2 For a thorough discussion of the *fukoku kyōhei* ideology and its relationship to the advancement of technology in Japan see Samuels (1994). Samuels characterizes the ideology as "technonationalism".

3 For background on the debates and discussions leading up to passage of the Land Tax Reform of 1873, see Yamamura (1986).

4 Figures taken from Mosk (2005: p. 143, Table 6.1).

5 Mosk (1995: pp. 58–76) offers evidence that supports this interpretation of surplus labor.

6 For accounts of Shibusawa and other Meiji era entrepreneurs, see Hirschmeier and Yui (1975), Nakamura (1971) and Yamamura (1974).

7 On the growth of general trading companies in Meiji Japan, see Yamamura (1976).

4 Infrastructure and heavy industry

1 Under the terms of the negotiations between Japan and those Western powers that enjoyed extraterritorial rights in the country, constraints on the capacity of the Japanese government to set its own tariffs were completely abolished in the early twentieth century.

6 Under the shadow of militarism

1 The account of Nissan's pre-World War II activities is based upon the discussion in Cusumano (1985).

7 Japan in the new international economic order

1 For instance both Noguchi (1998) and Teranishi (2005) argue that the bureaucrats of the total war period basically set up the government policies and practices prevailing during the Occupation period and the miracle growth era (1955–75). Kosai (1986) gives greater weight to the role of the occupiers. Mosk (1995) argues that a number of the Occupation period policies were the brainchildren of liberal bureaucrats whose views had been squelched during the period of military rule.

2 For the discussion of the new Japanese constitution I rely heavily upon the accounts in Dower (1999) and Nishi (1982).

3 I rely on Ward (1990) for most of the details concerning both prewar and postwar land reforms. In the discussion of the postwar land reform the rules on landlord average maximum retained area exclude Hokkaidō where farm sizes far exceeded those in the remainder of the country.

4 For a good discussion of the Dodge Line see Kosai (1986: 39 ff.).

5 See Curtis (1988) on the politics of the Occupation and miracle growth periods.

8 Miracle growth

1 I rely heavily upon Miwa and Ramseyer (2006) for these criticisms.

2 This is the view expressed in Johnson (1982).

3 For the treatment of monetary and fiscal policy, I rely heavily upon the discussion in Ackley and Ishi (1976).

4 On the penchant of the Japanese government for regulation over direct ownership see Samuels (1987). In this context it is noteworthy that the Japanese government sold back to the private sector the electric power companies it took over during the total war period in the aftermath of World War II.

5 The name of the Ministry of International Trade and Industry has been changed to the Ministry for Economy, Trade and Industry.

Bibliography

Ackley, E. and Ishi, H. (1976) "Fiscal, Monetary and Related Policies," in H. Patrick and H. Rosovsky (eds.) *Asia's New Giant: How the Japanese Economy Works*, Washington, D.C.: The Brookings Institution.

Akutagawa, R. (1952) (trans. T. Kojima) *Rashomon and Other Stories*, New York: Liveright Publishing Corporation.

Alexander, A. (2002) *In the Shadow of the Miracle: The Japanese Economy Since the End of High-Speed Growth*, New York: Lexington Books.

Allen, F. (2001) "Do Financial Institutions Matter?," *The Journal of Finance*, LVI: 1165–74.

Anchordoguy, M. (2000) "Japan's Software Industry: A Failure of Institutions?," *Research Policy*, 219: 391–408.

Aoki, M. (1988) *Information, Incentives, and Bargaining in the Japanese Economy*, New York: Cambridge University Press.

Aoki, M. and Patrick, H. (eds) (1994) *The Japanese Main Bank System: Its Relevance for Developing and Transforming Economies*, Oxford: Oxford University Press.

Beason, D. and Patterson, D. (2004) *The Japan That Never Was: Explaining the Rise and Decline of a Misunderstood Country*, Albany, NY: State University of New York Press.

Bellah, R. (1957) *Tokugawa Religion: The Values of Pre-industrial Japan*, Boston: Beacon Press.

Bloomström, M., Gangnes, B. and La Croix, S. (2001) *Japan's New Economy: Continuity and Change in the Twenty-First Century*, New York: Oxford University Press.

Bowen, R. (980) *Rebellion and Democracy in Meiji Japan: A Study of Commoners in the Popular Rights Movement*, Berkeley: University of California Press.

Callen, T. and Ostry, J. (eds) (2003) *Japan's Lost Decade: Policies for Economic Revival*, Washington, DC: International Monetary Fund.

Campbell, J. (1977) *Contemporary Japanese Budget Politics*, Berkeley and Los Angeles: University of California Press.

—— (1992) *How Policies Change: The Japanese Government and the Aging Society*, Princeton: Princeton University Press.

Caves, R. and Uekasu, M. (1976) "Industrial Organization," in H. Patrick and H. Rosovsky (eds) *Asia's New Giant: How the Japanese Economy Works*, Washington, DC: The Brookings Institution.

Chie, N. (1970) *Japanese Society*, Berkeley and Los Angeles: University of California Press.

Clark, G. and Feenstra, R. (2003) "Technology in the Great Divergence," in M. Bordo, A. Taylor, and J. Williamson (eds) *Globalization in Historical Perspective*, Chicago: The University of Chicago Press.

Curtis, G. (1988) *The Japanese Way of Politics*, New York: Columbia University Press.

—— (1992) *Policymaking in Japan: Defining the Role of Politicians*, New York: Japan Center for International Exchange.

Cusumano, M. (1985) *The Japanese Automobile Industry: Technology and Management at Nissan and Toyota*, Cambridge, MA: Harvard University Press.

Deckle, R. and Hamada, K. (2000) "On the Development of Rotating Credit Associations in Japan," *Economic Development and Cultural Change*, 49: 77–90.

Denison, E. and Chung, W. (1976) "Economic Growth and Its Sources," in H. Patrick and H. Rosovsky (eds) *Asia's New Giant: How the Japanese Economy Works*, Washington, D.C.: The Brookings Institution.

De Vos, G. (1973) *Socialization for Achievement: Essays on the Cultural Psychology of the Japanese*, Berkeley and Los Angeles: University of California Press.

Diamond, J. (1997) *Guns, Germs and Steel: The Fates of Human Societies*, New York: W.W. Norton.

—— (2005) *Collapse: How Societies Choose to Fail or Succeed*, New York: Viking.

Dore, R. (1973) *British Factory Japanese Factory: The Origins of National Diversity in Industrial Relations*, Berkeley and Los Angeles: University of California Press.

—— (1987) *Taking Japan Seriously: A Confucian Perspective on Leading Economic Issues*, London: The Athlone Press.

Dower, J. (1999) *Embracing Defeat: Japan in the Wake of World War II*, New York: W.W. Norton & Company.

Duus, P. (1968) *Party Rivalry and Political Change in Taishō Japan*, Cambridge, MA: Harvard University Press.

Feenstra, R. (2004) *Advanced International Trade: Theory and Evidence*, Princeton: Princeton University Press.

Feenstra, R., Huang, D.-S. and Hamilton, G. (2003) "A Market-Power Based Model of Business Groups," *Journal of Economic Behavior and Organization*, 51: 459–85.

Fei, J. and Ranis, G. (1964) *Development of the Labor Surplus Economy*, Homewood, IL: Richard D. Irwin, Inc.

Flath, D. (2000) *The Japanese Economy*, New York: Oxford University Press.

Garon, S. (1987) *The State and Labor in Modern Japan*, Berkeley and Los Angeles: University of California Press.

Hayami, A. (1997) *The Historical Demography of Pre-modern Japan*, Tokyo: Iwanami Shoten.

Hayami, A., Saitō, O. and Toby, R. (eds) (1999) *The Economic History of Japan: 1600–1990*, New York: Oxford University Press.

Hayami, Y., Akino, M., Shintani, M. and Yamada, S. (1975) *A Century of Agricultural Growth in Japan: Its Relevance to Asian Development*, Minneapolis: University of Minnesota Press.

Hirschmeier, J. and Yui, T. (1975) *The Development of Japanese Business 1600–1973*, Cambridge, MA: Harvard University Press.

Horioka, C. (1993) "Consuming and Saving," in A. Gordon (ed.) *Postwar Japan as History*, Berkeley and Los Angeles: University of California Press.

Inagami, T. (1988) "The Japanese Will to Work," in D. Okimoto and T. Rohlen (eds) *Inside the Japanese System: Readings on Contemporary Society and Political Economy*, Stanford: Stanford University Press.

Ito, T. (1992) *The Japanese Economy*, Cambridge, MA: The MIT Press.

Jansen, M. and Rozman, G. (1986) *Japan in Transition: From Tokugawa to Meiji*, Princeton: Princeton University Press.

Japan Ministry of Internal Affairs and Communications. Statistical Research and Training Institute (various dates) *Historical Statistics of Japan*, Tokyo: online at www.stat.go.jp/english/data/chouki.

—— (2005) *Japan Statistical Yearbook 2006*, Tokyo: Japan Statistical Association.

Japan Statistical Association (1987) *Historical Statistics of Japan, Volumes 1–5*, Tokyo: Japan Statistical Association.

Johnson, C. (1982) *MITI and the Japanese Miracle: The Growth of Industrial Policy, 1925–1975*, Stanford: Stanford University Press.

Katz, R. (2003) *Japanese Phoenix: The Long Road to Economic Revival*, Armonk: M.E. Sharpe.

Kawabe, N. and Daitō, E. (eds) (1993) *Education and Training in the Development of the Modern Corporation*, Tokyo: University of Tokyo Press.

Kennedy, P. (1985) *A Guide to Econometrics, Second Edition*, Oxford: Basil Blackwell.

Koike, K. (1984) "Skill Formation System in the U.S. and Japan," in M. Aoki (ed.), *The Economic Analysis of the Japanese Firm*, Amsterdam: North-Holland.

Kosai, Y. (1986) *The Era of High-Speed Growth: Notes on the Postwar Japanese Economy*, Tokyo: University of Tokyo Press.

Kuznets, S. (1971) *Economic Growth of Nations: Total Output and Production Structure*, Cambridge, MA: Harvard University Press.

Lincoln, E. (1988) *Japan: Facing Economic Maturity*, Washington, DC: The Brookings Institution.

—— (1990) *Japan's Unequal Trade*, Washington, DC: The Brookings Institution.

Maddison, A. (1995) *Explaining the Economic Performance of Nations: Essays in Time and Space*, Aldershot, Hants, UK: Edward Elgar.

—— (2000) *Monitoring the World Economy, 1820–1992*, Paris: Development Centre of the Organisation for Economic Co-operation and Development.

McVeigh, B. (2004) *Nationalisms of Japan: Managing and Mystifying Identity*, New York: Rowman and Littlefield Publishers, Inc.

Minami, R. (1994) *The Economic Development of Japan: A Quantitative Study*, Houndmills, Basingstoke, UK: Macmillan Press Ltd.

Miwa, Y. and Ramseyer, M. (2006a) *The Fable of the Keiretsu: Urban Legends of the Japanese Economy*, Chicago: University of Chicago Press.

—— (2006b) "Japanese Industrial Finance at the Close of the 19th Century: Trade Credit and Financial Intermediation," *Explorations in Economic History*, 43: 94–118.

Mokyr, J. (2003) "Industrial Revolution," in J. Mokyr (ed) *The Oxford Encyclopedia of Economic History. Volume 3*, New York: Oxford University Press.

Morishima, M. (1982), *Why Has Japan 'Succeeded'?: Western Technology and the Japanese Ethos*, New York: Cambridge University Press.

Morley, J. (ed.) (1971) *Dilemmas of Growth in Prewar Japan*, Princeton: Princeton University Press.

Mosk, C. (1983) *Patriarchy and Fertility: Japan and Sweden, 1880–1960*, New York: Academic Press.

—— (1991) *"Paternalism and Health: Income, Technology and Institutions in the Japanese Mortality Decline"*, Victoria, British Columbia: unpublished manuscript.

—— (1995) *Competition and Cooperation in Japanese Labour Markets*, Houndmills, Basingstoke, UK: Macmillan Press.

—— (1996) *Making Health Work: Human Growth in Modern Japan*, Berkeley and Los Angeles: University of California Press.

Mosk, C. (2001) *Japanese Industrial History: Technology, Urbanization, and Economic Growth*, Armonk, NY: M.E. Sharpe.

—— (2005) *Trade and Migration in the Modern World*, London and New York: Routledge.

Mosk, C. and Johansson, S. (1986) " Income and Mortality: Evidence from Modern Japan," *Population and Development Review*, 12: 415–40.

Nakamura, T. (1971) *Economic Growth in Prewar Japan*, New Haven: Yale University Press.

Nishi, T. (1982) *Unconditional Democracy: Education and Politics in Occupied Japan 1945–1952*, Stanford: Hoover Institution Press.

Noguchi, Y. (1998) "The 1940 System: Japan Under the Wartime Economy," *The American Economic Review*, 88: 404–407.

Norman, E. (2000) *Japan's Emergence as a Modern State: Political and Economic Problems of the Meiji Period*, Vancouver: UBC Press (60th Anniversary Edition, reprinting 1940 original).

Obstfeld, M. and Taylor, A. (2004) *Global Capital Markets: Integration, Crisis and Growth*, New York: Cambridge University Press.

O'Donnell, J. (2003) "Financial Panics and Crashes," in J. Mokyr (ed.) *The Oxford Encyclopedia of Economic History. Volume 2*, New York: Oxford University Press.

Ogura, T. (1967) *Agricultural Development in Modern Japan*, Tokyo: Fuji Publishing Co. Ltd.

Ohkawa, K. and Rosovsky, H. (1973) *Japanese Economic Growth: Trend Acceleration in the Twentieth Century*, Stanford, CA: Stanford University Press.

Ohkawa, K., Shinohara, M., and Umemura, M. (eds) (various dates) *Estimates of Long-Term Economic Statistics of Japan Since 1868, Volumes 1–13*, Tokyo: Toyo Keizai Shinposha.

Ohkawa, K., Shinohara, M. with Meissner, L. (1979) *Patterns of Japanese Economic Development: A Quantitative Appraisal*, New Haven and London: Yale University Press.

Ott, D. (1961) "The Financial Development of Japan," *The Journal of Political Economy*, 69: 122–41.

Patrick, H. (1960) "The Bank of Japan: A Case Study in the Effectiveness of Central Bank Techniques of Monetary Control," *The Journal of Finance*, 15: 573–4.

—— (1965) "External Equilibrium and Internal Convertibility: Financial Policy in Meiji Japan," *The Journal of Economic History*, 25: 187–213.

—— (1966) "Financial Development and Economic Growth in Underdeveloped Countries," *Economic Development and Cultural Change*, 14: 174–89.

Patrick, H. and Rosovsky, H. (eds.) (1976) *Asia's New Giant: How the Japanese Economy Works*, Washington, D.C.: The Brookings Institution.

Ramseyer, M. (1996) *Odd Markets in Japanese History: Law and Economic Growth*, New York: Cambridge University Press.

Ramseyer, M. and Rosenbluth, F. (1995) *The Politics of Oligarchy: Institutional Choice in Imperial Japan*, New York: Cambridge University Press.

Reed, H. (1980) "The Ascent of Tokyo as an International Financial Center," *Journal of International Business Studies*, 11: 19–35.

Reed, S. (ed.) (2003) *Japanese Electoral Politics: Creating a New Party System*, New York: RoutledgeCurzon.

Samuels, R. (1987) *The Business of the Japanese State: Energy Markets in Comparative and Historical Perspective*, Ithaca: Cornell University Press.

—— (1994) *"Rich Nation, Strong Army": National Security and the Technological Transformation of Japan*, Ithaca: Cornell University Press.

Saxonhouse, G. (1988) "Comparative Advantage, Structural Adaptation, and Japanese Performance," in T. Inoguchi and D. Okimoto (eds) *The Political Economy of Japan. Volume 2. The Changing International Context*, Stanford: Stanford University Press.

Schmiegelow, M. and Schmiegelow, H. (1989) *Strategic Pragmatism: Japanese Lessons in the Use of Economic Theory*, New York: Praeger.

Schoppa, L. (1991) *Education Reform in Japan: A Case of Immobilist Politics*, New York: Routledge.

Sims, R. (2001) *Japanese Political History since the Meiji Renovation 1868–2000*, London: Hurst & Company.

Smith, T. (1966) *The Agrarian Origins of Modern Japan*, New York: Atheneum (reprint of 1959 original edition).

—— (1988) *Native Sources of Japanese Industrialization 1750–1920*, Berkeley and Los Angeles: University of California Press.

Tanaka, K. (1972) *Building a New Japan: A Plan for Remodeling the Japanese Archipelago*, Tokyo: The Simul Press.

Tanimoto, M. (ed.) (2006) *The Role of Tradition in Japan's Industrialization: Another Path to Industrialization*, New York: Oxford University Press.

Teranishi, J. (2005) *Evolution of the Economic System in Japan*, Northampton, MA: Edward Elgar.

Totten, G. (1965) *Democracy in Prewar Japan: Groundwork or Façade?*, Boston: DC: Heath and Company.

Tsuda, T. (2003) *Strangers in the Homeland: Japanese Brazilian Return Migration in Transnational Perspective*, New York: Columbia University Press.

Unger, J. (1996) *Literacy and Script Reform in Occupation Japan: Reading Between the Lines*, New York: Oxford University Press.

United Nations Development Programme (various dates) *Human Development Report*, New York: Oxford University Press.

Uriu, R. (1996) *Troubled Industries: Confronting Economic Change in Japan*, Ithaca: Cornell University Press.

Van Rixtel, A. (2002) *Informality and Monetary Policy in Japan: The Political Economy of Bank Performance*, New York: Cambridge University Press.

Van Wolferen, K. (1989) *The Enigma of Japanese Power: People and Politics in a Stateless Nation*, New York: Alfred A. Knopf.

Vaporis, C. (1994) *Breaking Barriers: Travel and the State in Early Modern Japan*, Cambridge, MA: Harvard University Press.

Vlastos, S. (1986) *Peasant Protests and Uprisings in Tokugawa Japan*, Berkeley and Los Angeles: University of California Press.

Vogel, E. (1979) *Japan as Number One: Lessons for America*, New York: Harper & Row.

Wada, K. (undated) "Kiichiro Toyoda and the Birth of the Japanese Automobile Industry: Reconsideration of Toyoda-Platt Agreement," University of Tokyo manuscript: download from internet in May, 2006.

Wallich, H. and Wallich, M. (1976) "Banking and Finance," in H. Patrick and H. Rosovsky (eds) *Asia's New Giant: How the Japanese Economy Works*, Washington, DC: The Brookings Institution.

Ward, E. (1990) *Land Reform in Japan, 1946–1950, the Allied Role*, Tokyo: Nobunkyo (Noson Gyosan Bunka Kyokai).

Waswo, A. (1977) *Japanese Landlords: The Decline of a Rural Elite*, Berkeley and Los Angeles: University of California Press.

Weinstein, D. and Yafeh, Y. (1998) "On the Costs of a Bank-Centered Financial System: Evidence from the Changing Main Bank Relations in Japan," *The Journal of Finance*, 53: 635–72.

Wray, W. (1984) *Mitsubishi and the N.Y.K., 1870–1914: Business Strategy in the Japanese Shipping Industry*, Cambridge, MA: Harvard University Press.

Yamamura, K. (1967) "The Role of the Samurai in the Development of Modern Banking in Japan," *The Journal of Economic History*, 27: 198–220.

—— (1973) "Toward a Reexamination of the Economic History of Tokugawa Japan, 1600–1867," *The Journal of Economic History*, 33: 509–46.

—— (1974) *A Study of Samurai Income and Entrepreneurship: Quantitative Analyses of Economic and Social Aspects of the Samurai in Tokugawa and Meiji Japan*, Cambridge, MA: Harvard University Press.

—— (1976) "General Trading Companies in Japan – Their Origins and Growth," in H. Patrick (ed.) *Japanese Industrialization and its Social Consequences*, Berkeley and Los Angeles: University of California Press.

—— (1986) "The Meiji Land Tax Reform and Its Effects," in M. Jansen and G. Rozman (eds) *Japan in Transition: From Tokugawa to Meiji*, Princeton: Princeton University Press.

Index